FRONTISPIECE

WHALING SCENE IN THE CALIFORNIA LAGOONS.

THE MARINE MAMMALS

of the North-western Coast of North America

Described and illustrated

———

Together with an account of

THE AMERICAN WHALE-FISHERY

by Charles M. Scammon

with a new Introduction by

VICTOR B. SCHEFFER

Bureau of Commercial Fisheries
U. S. Fish and Wildlife Service
Seattle, Washington

DOVER PUBLICATIONS, INC.
NEW YORK

Published in Canada by General Publishing Company, Ltd.,
30 Lesmill Road, Don Mills, Toronto, Ontario.
Published in the United Kingdom by
Constable and Company, Ltd., 10 Orange Street, London WC 2.

This Dover edition, first published in 1968, is an unabridged re-publication of the work originally published by John H. Carmany and Company, San Francisco, and G. P. Putnam's Sons, New York, in 1874.

Additional material in this edition consists of a portrait of the author and a new Introduction by Victor B. Scheffer.

The publisher gratefully acknowledges the cooperation of the director of the Hopkins Marine Station Library of Stanford University, Pacific Grove, California, who supplied a copy of the work for the purpose of reproduction.

Standard Book Number: 486-21976-3
Library of Congress Catalog Card Number: 68-54705

Manufactured in the United States of America

DOVER PUBLICATIONS, INC.
180 Varick Street
New York, N. Y. 10014

INTRODUCTION
TO THE DOVER EDITION

CHARLES MELVILLE SCAMMON (1825–1911) wrote one book, and it has fascinated seafaring men, historians, and naturalists for 94 years. I am told by Joel W. Hedgpeth[1] that the book was a financial failure, and that Scammon used to buy copies from the San Francisco printer at cost of the paper to give to his friends. The unsold copies were lost in the earthquake and fire of 1906. Today the book is very rare; it seldom appears on the book market, where it commands a price of $100 or more.

Who was this man, Scammon? Very little biographical information is available.[2,3] Born in Pittston, Maine, on 28 May 1825, he was younger brother of Jonathan Young Scammon, lawyer, legislator, financier, and civic leader in Chicago. He sailed for California in 1850. In his book we first see him at age twenty-seven, watching the "banded seals" on the California coast at Point Reyes. In another essay[4] he may hint at an earlier life as a disenchanted gold-digger in the following words:

> Among the multitude of adventurers who came hither were a class of industrious, energetic, and hardy men, who, from childhood, had passed their time on board the pigmy fishing-vessels, amid the gales, fogs, and rough seas of the Atlantic, varied only by brief respites at home among friends and companions, who shared their precarious earnings. The change from the life of a mariner to that of a miner was not always congenial to these men, whose hereditary avocations were of the sea. Some restless spirits, unsuccessful in gold-hunting, longed to be again afloat. For this reason, there was no lack of experienced hands ready to embark in any marine venture, even in those gold-digging days.

In 1852 Scammon took "command of a brig, bound on a sealing, sea-elephant, and whaling voyage" (this book, p. 11). Starbuck's history[5] shows that the brig *Mary Helen*, 160 tons, left San Francisco on 1 April 1852 under Captain Scammon, bound for "elephanting." She returned on 26 August with 350 barrels of "elephant," which would have been oil rendered from the elephant seals of southern California and northern Mexico. Scammon's travels during the next two decades, capped by the writing of his book, are imperfectly known. I have pieced together a rough account, largely from remarks in *Marine Mammals*, and in his articles in the *Overland Monthly* from 1869 to 1872.

He may have gone on to the Galapagos Islands and Peru in 1853; certainly he was whaling off Panama in March of that year. He whaled in or near the lagoons on the west side of Baja California, where the gray whales still breed, from 1853 to 1860. In 1855 he discovered the shallow, hidden Laguna Ojo de Liebre which is shown today on most English-language maps as Scammon's Lagoon.[6] His ship at the time of the famous discovery was evidently the *Leonore*, 370 tons, which sailed from San Francisco on 3 December 1855 and returned on 25 July 1856 with 60 barrels of "sperm-oil" and 500 barrels of "whale-oil."[5]

Shortly after the outbreak of the Civil War in 1861 Scammon took command, on the first of May, of a revenue cutter in San Francisco. He attained the rank of captain on 11 July 1864, "when the U.S. Coast Guard was known as the Revenue Service, but before he retired [from disability] in 1895 it was known as the U.S. Revenue Cutter Service and retained that identity until 1915 when it received its present name."[7] As "Captain, U.S.R.M., Chief of Marine Western Union Telegraph Expedition, 1865 and 1866," he traveled to Plover Bay (Siberia), to Norton Sound (Alaska), and to other points in the Bering Sea. Shortly thereafter he published "Notes on the Russian American Company's Trading Posts, etc."[8] William Healey Dall (1845–1927) of the Smithsonian Institution was on this expedition, and in 1870 he named Scammon Bay, Alaska, in honor of his captain.

At times from 1868 to 1870 Scammon visited the Strait of Juan de Fuca, between Washington and Vancouver Island. Here in October 1870 he collected the type specimen of the Davidson piked whale, *Balaenoptera davidsoni* Scammon, 1872.[10] He did not try his hand again at systematic zoology.

Later he must have returned to California, for his entries from 1871 to 1873 refer to ports between Santa Barbara and San Francisco. Louis Agassiz (1807–1873) spent some weeks in San Francisco in 1872;[1] since *Marine Mammals* was subsequently dedicated to his memory, Scammon probably met the famous zoologist in that year. He dated the preface of the book May 1874.

I will not follow his career beyond this point, except to point out that he was stationed in Florida in 1880 in command of the *John A. Dix*, a side-wheel steamer. He wrote about the manatee there, though his notes were not published until 1954.[11]

CHARLES M. SCAMMON 1825–1911
Official U. S. Coast Guard Photograph

To a historian I leave the task of writing a full biography of Scammon, and I turn now to his book. "The chief object in this work," he wrote, "is to give as correct figures of the different species of marine mammals . . . as could be obtained from a careful study of them from life, and numerous measurements after death . . ." (this book, p. 11). He lived in an era of *descriptive* zoology.

The concept of a book on seals, sea otters and whales was slowly taking shape in his active mind during his first decade on the west coast. Not until 1862, I think, did he start to measure and to sketch the objects of his interest. Off Baja California that year his men captured three blackfish, and Scammon described the largest one (this book, p. 86). He obtained some measurements of marine mammals (e.g., those of a bowhead and a humpback) from friendly sea captains. I suppose he alerted his cronies to the need for scientific information on the animals they were clubbing, shooting, and harpooning.

In writing his first scientific article he called upon Edward Drinker Cope (1840–1897), who had been named a curator of the Philadelphia Academy of Natural Sciences in 1865. Cope not only edited but also contributed substantially to the report on the cetaceans of the western coast of North America.[12] It is a curious report by modern zoological standards, though typical of its day. Cope, the museum man, was concerned with dry bones and teeth; Scammon the field man, with behavior of the animals, ways of hunting them, and the glamor surrounding the hunt. In this report we see the essential framework of the whale chapters of *Marine Mammals*. When, later, the book itself was being composed, Scammon turned to another expert for help on the systematics of marine mammals, Dall of the Smithsonian.

Also, Scammon began in 1869 to publish a series of short articles in the *Overland Monthly* in the distinguished company of Mark Twain and Bret Harte. His first contribution contained information on the Pribilof Islands of Alaska, which Scammon may have visited in 1868.[13] It was followed by seventeen articles in this journal through July of 1872, at which time he turned his full attention to this book. Eight of the articles dealt with marine mammals—the others with travel scenes, descriptions of lumbering and cod-fishing, the story of Chief Seattle, and so on. The *Overland Monthly* was a magazine of considerable artistic merit. It was published from 1870 to 1875 by John H. Carmany, of San Francisco, who also published Scammon's book.

The main value of *Marine Mammals* lies in its historical, rather than zoological, content. It is a unique segment of Americana. It was published in the year when we Americans tried to save the wild bison. (A bill to "impose a penalty on every man, red, white or black, who might wantonly kill buffaloes" was passed by both houses of Congress but was pocket-vetoed by President Grant.)[14]

Where else can one find a picture like the frontispiece "Whaling Scene in the California Lagoons" or (Plate V) "California Grays among the Ice"?[15] Where else can one find such wealth of detail on methods of the whale fishery from open boats in the North Pacific? I suggest that you read, for example, the dramatic story of Scammon's first attempt to capture gray whales (this book, p. 263). When the first boat returned to the ship "with her freight of crippled passengers, it could only be compared to a floating ambulance crowded with men—the uninjured supporting the helpless." Scammon had been whaling for sixteen years when Svend Foyn, in the North Atlantic, perfected the big harpoon with an explosive head which was to revolutionize whale fishery and finally, in our time, to bring commercial extinction to the blue whale, the greatest animal that has ever lived.

With respect to the zoological content of the book, information far more accurate and more comprehensive has been obtained since 1874. Nonetheless, Scammon wrote of populations, like the sea otters of Washington and Oregon, which were later exterminated. We can see them now through his eyes. When he hunted the gray whales in their breeding waters, they numbered perhaps 25,000; a century later they were nearly gone. Though they are now recovering under strict protection, the shores of Scammon's Lagoon will never again resound to the cries of the whalemen as he heard them in the 1850's.

Victor B. Scheffer
Bureau of Commercial Fisheries
U.S. Fish and Wildlife Service
Seattle, Washington

NOTES

1. Resident Director, Marine Science Laboratory, Oregon State University, and a keen student of the history of science. Some years ago he interviewed the late L. N. Scammon, son of Charles Melville Scammon. I thank Dr. Hedgpeth for help with this introduction.

2. D. Appleton and Co. 1888. *Appleton's Cyclopaedia of American Biography*, vol. 5, p. 413.

3. White, James T. and Co. 1897. *National Cyclopaedia of American Biography*, vol. 7, p. 528.

4. Scammon, Charles M. 1870. "The Pacific coast cod-fishery." *Overland Monthly*, 4(5), p. 436.

5. Starbuck, Alexander. 1964. *History of the American whale fishery* . . . First published 1878; reprinted 1964 by Argosy-Antiquarian, New York, in 2 vols.; see pp. 498–499 and 532–533.

6. Scammon, Charles M. 1870. "On the lower California coast." *Overland Monthly*, 4(3), p. 231.

7. J. W. Duenzl, Public Information Division, U.S. Coast Guard, in a letter dated 15 January 1968.

8. U.S. Congress, House. 1868. St. Paul's Island, Alaska . . . 40th Congr., 2d Sess., House Misc. Doc. 131, p. 12.

9. Orth, Donald J. 1967. *Dictionary of Alaska place names*. U.S. Geol. Surv. Prof. Pap. 567, p. 843.

10. Scammon, Charles M. 1872. "On a new species of *Balaenoptera*." *Proc. Calif.*

Acad. Sci., vol. 4, pp. 269–270. (Printed in advance, 4 October, 1872.)

11. Gunter, Gordon. 1954. "Mammals of the Gulf of Mexico." U.S. Fish Wildl. Serv., Fish. Bull. 55, pp. 543-551.

12. Scammon, Charles M. 1869. "On the cetaceans of the western coast of North America." *Proc. Acad. Nat. Sciences, Phila.*, pp. 13–63.

13. Scammon, Charles M. 1869. "Fur seals." *Overland Monthly*, 3(5), pp. 393–399.

14. Hornaday, William T. 1931. *Thirty Years War for Wild Life*. Chas. Scribner's Sons, New York, p. 247.

15. Despite the signature "C. M. Scammon, del.," I suspect that he had but a minor part in preparing the figures, for his earlier sketches are crude by comparison. He admits as much (this book, p. 12) by crediting Mr. Steinegger for the "excellent sea and landscape backgrounds."

THE MARINE MAMMALS

of the North-western Coast of North America

THE

MARINE MAMMALS

OF THE

NORTH-WESTERN COAST OF NORTH AMERICA,

DESCRIBED AND ILLUSTRATED:

TOGETHER WITH AN ACCOUNT OF

THE AMERICAN WHALE-FISHERY.

BY

CHARLES M. SCAMMON,

CAPTAIN U. S. REVENUE MARINE.

SAN FRANCISCO:

JOHN H. CARMANY AND COMPANY.

NEW YORK: G P. PUTNAM'S SONS.

1874.

THIS VOLUME IS DEDICATED TO THE MEMORY OF

LOUIS AGASSIZ.

AS A HUMBLE TRIBUTE FROM THE AUTHOR.

CONTENTS.

PART III.—THE AMERICAN WHALE-FISHERY.

APPENDIX.

ILLUSTRATIONS.

PREFACE.

BEING on the coast of California in 1852, when the "gold-fever" raged, the force of circumstances compelled me to take command of a brig, bound on a sealing, sea-elephant, and whaling voyage, or abandon sea-life, at least temporarily. The objects of our pursuit were found in great numbers, and the opportunities for studying their habits were so good, that I became greatly interested in collecting facts bearing upon the natural history of these animals. Reference to the few books devoted to the subject soon convinced me that I was at work in a department in which but little definite knowledge existed. This was true even of the whales, the best known of this class; and I was soon led to believe that, by diligent observation, I should be able to add materially to the scanty stock of information existing in regard to the marine mammals of the Pacific Coast. I was the more encouraged to pursue these investigations, because, among the great number of intelligent men in command of whaling-ships, there was no one who had contributed anything of importance to the natural history of the Cetaceans; while it was obvious that the opportunities offered for the study of their habits, to those practically engaged in the business of whaling, were greater than could possibly be enjoyed by persons not thus employed.

The chief object in this work is to give as correct figures of the different species of marine mammals, found on the Pacific Coast of North America, as could be obtained from a careful study of them from life, and numerous measurements after death, made whenever practicable. It is also my aim to give as full an account of the habits of these animals as practicable, together with such facts in reference to their geographical distribution as have come to my knowledge.

It is hardly necessary to say, that any person taking up the study of marine mammals, and especially the Cetaceans, enters a difficult field of research, since the opportunities for observing the habits of these animals under favorable conditions are but rare and brief. My own experience has proved that close observation for months, and even years, may be required before a single new fact in regard to their habits can be obtained. This has been particularly the case with the dolphins, while many of the characteristic actions of whales are so secretly performed that years of ordinary observation may be insufficient for their discovery.

There is little difficulty in making satisfactory drawings of such smaller species of marine mammals as can be taken upon the deck of a vessel, but it is extremely difficult to delineate accurately the forms of the larger Cetaceans. When one of these animals is first captured, but a small part of its colossal form can be seen, as, usually, only a small portion of the middle section of the body is above the water; and when the process of decomposition has caused the animal to rise, so that the whole form is visible, it is swollen and quite distorted in shape. Again: these animals change their appearance in the most remarkable manner with every change of position, so that it is only from repeated measurements and sketches, and as the result of many comparisons, that I have been able to produce satisfactory illustrations of these monsters of the deep.

I take occasion here to acknowledge my indebtedness to Mr. Rey, of the firm of Britton & Rey, lithographers, who laid aside his own business, as far as possible, in order that he might give his personal attention to the execution of nearly all the plates representing whales and seals. The remaining work of that description was put into the hands of Mr. Steinegger, the junior partner of the firm; his excellent sea and landscape backgrounds speak for themselves.

Plain and simple language has been used in description. Where whaling terms have been employed, their definitions are indicated by reference marks, or may be found in the glossary contained in the Appendix.

I desire to tender my sincere thanks to many personal friends and others, not only for literary, but also for financial aid; for, without the generous contributions of gentlemen of the Pacific Coast, and San Francisco especially, this work could not have made its appearance in its present form.

To Professor J. D. Whitney, State Geologist of California, I wish particularly to acknowledge my indebtedness for his encouragement and untiring assistance in preparing this volume for the press. My thanks are also due to Professor S. F.

Baird, of the Smithsonian Institution; Professor George Davidson, of the United States Coast Survey; Doctor W. O. Ayres, of San Francisco; Doctor Theodore Gill, of Washington; Mr. J. A. Allen, of Cambridge; Mr. R. E. C. Stearns, of San Francisco; Mr. Albert Bierstadt, of Irvington, N. Y.; Mr. W. H. Dall, of the Smithsonian Institution; and to Doctor George Hewston, of San Francisco, for special assistance. Also, to Mr. F. C. Sanford, of Nantucket, Mass.; Messrs. Williams and Chapel, of the firm of Williams, Havens & Co., New London, Conn.; and Dennis Wood, Esq., of New Bedford, for valuable statistics relative to the whale-fishery.

It is with pleasure that I also mention the assistance I have received from officers of the United States Revenue Marine, in making scientific collections for the study of whales and seals, and in furnishing specimens for the National Museum at Washington. I would particularly mention Lieutenants George W. Bailey, W. C. Coulson, G. E. McConnell, and Engineers J. A. Doyle and H. Hassel.

The account of the American Whale-fishery has been compiled from the most reliable sources within reach, and from the experience of many whalemen with whom I was associated for several years, while in active service on the principal whaling-grounds then frequented. I have also attempted to give a chronological account of the rise, progress, and decline of our great national maritime enterprise, the whale-fishery; and to make the picture complete, a few pages have been devoted to a description of the every-day life of a whaleman, his characteristic traits, and the incidents that make up the routine of a whaling-voyage.

The "Catalogue of the Cetacea" appended to this work has been drawn up with great care by Mr. W. H. Dall, who has taken pains to do the work as thoroughly as circumstances would permit; and as I have assisted him with my personal knowledge of those species which are of rare occurrence on this coast, and placed in his hands all my notes and collections, I trust that his paper will be found of great assistance to the professional naturalist. As Mr. Dall remarks, however, "Completeness is not claimed for this list. In fact, it can hardly be attained for a considerable period, when the difficulties and expense connected with these researches are appreciated." Only two species of Cetaceans have been added to the list of those mentioned as not being represented by "material sufficient to indicate their zoölogical position;" and these were not known to Mr. Dall at the time he was preparing his list.

The volume now presented to the public has been put together from materials which have accumulated during many years. At sea, when not occupied with official duties, amid calms and storms, I have devoted myself to its preparation; and it is hoped that the public may find in these results of prolonged labor something of the profit and pleasure with which the author has been rewarded while occupied in their collection and elaboration.

CHARLES M. SCAMMON.

SAN FRANCISCO, May, 1874.

PART I.

—————

CETACEA.

PART I.—CETACEA.

INTRODUCTION.

THE order of Cetacea, as established by naturalists, includes all species of mammalia which have been created for inhabiting the water only; and although their forms bear a strong resemblance to those of the ordinary piscatory tribe, still they are animals having warm blood, breathing by means of lungs, and frequently coming to the surface of the water to respire. In nearly all Cetaceans, the nostrils —termed spiracles or spout-holes—are situated on the top of the head. Through these the thick vaporous breath is ejected into the atmosphere to various altitudes, according to the nature of the animal in this particular respect; and through the same orifices a fresh supply of air is received into its breathing system. Although the Cetaceans are strictly regarded as mammals, they have no true feet; their pectorals being in the form of heavy, bony, and sinewy fins, while the posterior extremity of the body terminates in a broad cartilaginous limb of semi-lunar shape, frequently termed the caudal fin or tail, but known among whalemen as the "flukes," the lobes of which extend horizontally.

The different species of Cetaceans are numerous; hence they have been divided into groups, the most prominent of which are the Whalebone Whales, the Cachalots or Sperm Whales, and the Dolphins. The group of *Balænidæ*, or Whalebone Whales, embraces all those which are destitute of teeth when adult, and whose palate is lined on each side with rows of horny plates, called whalebone or baleen, which are fringed on their inner edges. This part of the animal's organization is peculiarly adapted to the nature of its food, which consists of zoöphytes, mollusks, crustaceans, and small fish. The group of Sperm Whales comprises those with inordinately massive heads, whose upper jaw has only rudimentary teeth, or none at all; whose lower jaw is narrow, rounded toward its anterior extremity, elongated and filling the furrow in the upper one, and furnished on each side with a row of heavy conical teeth, with which to procure and devour the enormous cuttle-fish or squid upon which they prey.   The group of Dolphins is made up of those comprised in the Linnæan genus *Delphinus*, and others, whose heads preserve the usual proportion to the body, and whose upper and lower jaws are set with sharp and usually conical teeth.   They are the most active and rapacious of the whole order of Cetaceans.

All Cetaceans produce their young in nearly the same manner as other mammals.   The male is commonly called a bull; the female a cow.   The attitude of the two sexes when having intercourse with each other has been differently represented by numerous observers.   Some maintain that the male covers the female; while others are positive of their lying on their sides breast to breast, or assuming a perpendicular position.   From personal observation, however, we are justified in stating that all are correct.   In fact, it may readily be seen that, with their united efforts, it is easy for the animals to sustain any desired position in their native element, during the period of coition.   The time of gestation is not known; but from our observations we believe it is never less than nine months, and that in some species it extends to one year.   The offspring of the female is called her calf; she nourishes it with rich milk drawn from two teats which lie on each side of her abdomen.

All Cetaceans are destitute of the hair or fur which protects the surface of other marine mammals, and instead thereof the dermis is covered by a smooth and transparent scarf-skin.   Under the dermis is the thick layer of fat, or "blubber," which infolds the whole creature, whose flesh is dark and sinewy, resembling coarse beef.   The natural term of life in Cetaceans can only be approximately determined; it is probably from thirty to a hundred years.   The new-born young are clothed in fatless blubber with a thick dermis, and over all is a delicate cuticle.   The calf, or "cub," follows the dam for several months—perhaps a year with some species— and during that time draws its chief sustenance from the mother.   As her charge matures, its blubber thickens and becomes fat, the dermis becomes thinner but more compact, and the cuticle strengthens and presents a lively glossiness.

Among the *Balænidæ*, the baleen with its fringes grows rapidly, and hardens as it matures.   As old age comes on, the fringes to these horny plates become decayed and broken, and in some instances the baleen falls out.   The thick blubber, once filled with oil, becomes thin and watery, and, for want of proper sustenance, the animal yields to the course of Nature and dies.   Among the *Physeteridæ*, the teeth of the young are sharp and perfect when first developed; but they become more or less broken and worn with age: as years advance, they either fall out or are reduced to a level with the gums, and, like the *Balænidæ*, being deprived of the natural means of obtaining food, the animals become emaciated, and at last expire. The same may be said of the *Delphinidæ* or Dolphins.

All the Cetaceans propel themselves through the water by the action of their pectorals and caudal fin, and the individual motions of the various species are similar. Usually a small portion of the animal is seen rippling along as it makes its respiration, then, after a few moments, settling below the surface, it again appears in the same manner. When descending to the depths below, it rises a little, as in

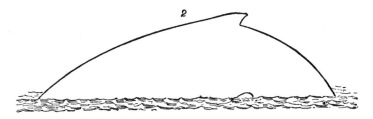

figure 1; then pitching headlong, "rounds out," as in figure 2; then "turning

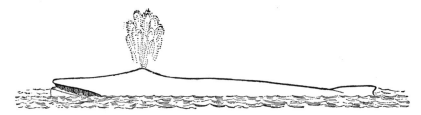

flukes," as in figure 3, disappears. Thus these animals wander through the track-

less waters in their migrations; or, when roving about at leisure on their feeding or breeding grounds, they are sometimes seen in various attitudes, which will be mentioned hereafter.

CHAPTER I.

THE CALIFORNIA GRAY WHALE.

RHACHIANECTES GLAUCUS. *Cope.*   (Plate ii, fig. 1.)

The California Gray is unlike other species of baleen whales in color, being of a mottled gray, very light in some individuals, while others, both male and female, are nearly black.   The head and jaws are curved downward from near the spiracles to the "nib-end," or extremity of the snout, and the lateral form tapers to a ponderous beak.   Under the throat are two longitudinal folds, which are about fifteen inches apart and six feet in length.   The eye, the ball of which is at least four inches in diameter, is situated about five inches above and six inches behind the angle of the mouth.   The ear, which appears externally like a mere slit in the skin, two and one-half inches in length, is about eighteen inches behind the eye, and a little above it.   The length of the female is from forty to forty-four feet,* the fully grown varying but little in size; its greatest circumference, twenty-eight to thirty feet; its flukes, thirty inches in depth, and ten to twelve feet broad.   It has no dorsal fin.   Its pectorals are about six and one-half feet in length, and three feet in width, tapering from near the middle toward the ends, which are quite pointed.   Usually the limbs of the animal vary but little in proportion to its size.

The following measurements give the correct proportions of several males taken in the Bay of Monterey, California, since 1865:

SEX, MALE.	Ft.	In.
Length	42	00
Circumference at point of pectoral	21	00
Length of pectorals	6	06
Width of pectorals	2	10
Nib-end to pectorals	11	00
Pectorals to top of back	4	06
Nib-end to corner of mouth	7	00

* Forty-four feet, however, would be regard- taken that were much larger, and yielding sixty ed as large, although some individuals have been or seventy barrels of oil.

Plate III.

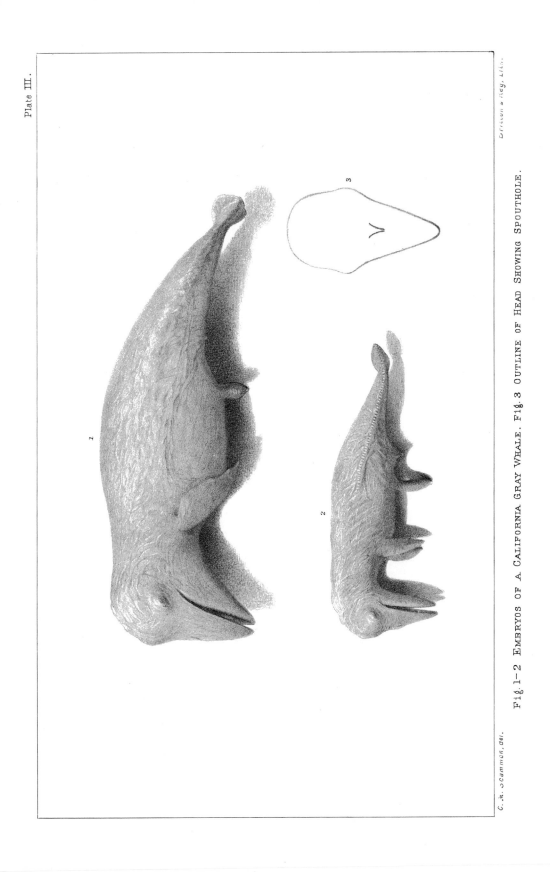

C. M. Scammon, del.

Britton & Rey, Lith.

Fig. 1-2 EMBRYOS OF A CALIFORNIA GRAY WHALE. Fig. 3 OUTLINE OF HEAD SHOWING SPOUTHOLE.

	Ft. In.
... ᴊᵢ mouth to top of head	2 06
Nib-end to eye	7 06
Spout-holes to nib-end	6 00
Length of opening of spout-holes	08
Length of flukes or tail	10 00
Breadth of flukes or tail	3 05
Thickness of each lobe of flukes	09
From fork of flukes to vent	12 00
From fork of flukes to genital slit	16 08
Length of longest baleen	18
Width of longest baleen	09
(Number of layers of baleen on each side of the mouth, 182.)	
Longest fibres to fringe of baleen	05
Average thickness of blubber	07
Depth of small at junction of flukes	18
Length of the fissure between the eyelids	04

Four other individuals, ranging from thirty-five to forty feet, were measured, the result of which showed corresponding proportions, or nearly so.

The animal has a succession of ridges, crosswise along the back, from opposite the vent to the flukes. The coating of fat, or blubber, which possesses great solidity and is exceedingly sinewy and tough, varies from six to ten inches in thickness, and is of a reddish cast. The average yield of oil is twenty barrels. The baleen, of which the longest portion is fourteen to sixteen inches, is of a light brown or nearly white, the grain very coarse, and the hair or fringe on the bone is much heavier and not so even as that of the Right Whale or Humpback. The male may average thirty-five feet in length, but varies more in size than the female, and the usual quantity of oil it produces may be reckoned at twenty-five barrels. Both sexes are infested with parasitical crustaceans (*Cyamus Scammoni*), and a species of barnacle (*Cryptolepas rhachianecti*), which collect chiefly upon the head and fins.*

* Following is W. H. Dall's description of the *Cyamus Scammoni*, and of the *Cryptolepas rhachianecti* (Proceedings Cal. Acad. Sci., Nov. 9th, 1872). Illustrations, figs. 1, 5, plate x.

Genus CYAMUS, Lam.

Cyamus, Lam. Syst. An. s. Vert., p. 166. Bate & Westwood, ii, p. 80.

Larunda and *Panope*. Leach.

Cyamus Scammoni, n. sp. ♂ Body moderately depressed, of an egg-ovate form; segments slightly separated. Third and fourth segments furnished with a branchia at each side. This, near its base, divides into two cylindrical filaments, spirally coiled from right to left. At the base of each branchia are two slender accessory filaments, not coiled, quite short, and situated, one before and the other behind the base of the main branchia. Second pair of hands, with the carpal articulation half-way between the distal and proximal ends, and having two pointed tubercles on the inferior edge, before the carpal joint. Third and fourth segments somewhat punctate above; all the oth-

The California Gray Whale is only found in north latitudes, and its migrations have never been known to extend lower than 20° north. It frequents the coast of California from November to May. During these months the cows enter the lagoons on the lower coast to bring forth their young,* while the males remain outside

ers smooth; the sixth and seventh slightly serrate on the upper anterior edge, and without ventral spines. Color, yellowish white. Lon. 0.70, lat. 0.39 in., of largest specimen.

♀ Similar to the ♂ in all respects, excepting in being a little more slender, and in wanting the accessory appendages to the branchiæ; the ovigerous sacs are four in number, overlapping each other.

Habitat, on the California Gray Whale (*Rhachianectes glaucus* of Cope), upon the Coast of California; very numerous. I may remark here that these species are all so distinct from those figured by Milne-Edwards, Gosse, and Bate & Westwood, that a comparative description has seemed unnecessary; also, that the species obtained on different species of Cetaceans have so far been found invariably distinct. The inference is, of course, that each Cetacean has its peculiar parasites—a supposition which agrees with our knowledge of the facts in many groups of terrestrial animals.

Cryptolepas rhachianecti, Dall, n. s. Valves subequal, rostrum radiate, not alate. Lateral valves anteriorly alate, posteriorly radiate; carina alate, not radiate. Each valve internally transversely deeply grooved, and furnished externally with six radiating laminæ, vertically sharply grooved; the adjacent terminal laminæ of each two valves coalescing to form one lamina of extra thickness; all the laminæ bifurcated and thickened toward the outer edges, with two or more short spurs on each side, irregularly placed between the shell-wall and the bifurcation. Superior terminations of the valves (bluntly pointed?) usually abraded, transversely striate. Scuta subquadrate, adjacent anteriorly, and very slightly beaked in the middle of the occludent margin; terga subquadrate, small, separated from the scuta by intervening membrane; both very small in proportion to the orifice. Membranes very thin and delicate, raised into small lamellæ between the opercular valves. All the calcareous matter pulverulent, and showing a strong tendency to split up into laminæ. Antero-posterior

diameter of large specimen, 1.62 inch; ditto of orifice, 0.63 inch; transverse diameter of orifice, 0.58 inch; lon. scuta, 0.17 inch; lat. ditto, 0.08 inch; lon. terga, 0.07 inch; lat. ditto, 0.07 inch. Color of membranes, when living, sulphur yellow; hood, extremely protrusile.

This species is found sessile on the California Gray Whale (*Rhachianectes glaucus*, Cope). I have observed them on specimens of that species hauled up on the beach at Monterey for cutting off the blubber, in the bay-whaling of that locality. The superior surface of the lateral laminæ, being covered by the black skin of the whale, is not visible; and the animal, removed from its native element—protruding its bright yellow hood in every direction, to a surprising distance, as if gasping for breath—presented a truly singular appearance.

* The question is often raised, as to whether the cetaceous animals have more than one young one at a birth? but it seems evident to us that they never have more than two, for Nature has made no provision whereby more than that number could draw sustenance at the same time from the parent animal; and even where provision is made for two among the marine mammalia, particularly in the case of the seal tribe, it is rarely if ever that the female produces twins. It is true that instances have occurred where two, three, or more cubs have been seen with one California Gray Whale; but this has only happened in the lagoons where there had been great slaughter among the cows, leaving their young ones motherless, so that these straggle about, sometimes following other whales, sometimes clustering by themselves a half-dozen together. We know of one instance where a whale which had a calf perhaps a month old was killed close to a ship. When the mother was taken to the ship to be cut in, the young one followed, and remained playing about for two weeks; but

along the sea-shore. The time of gestation is about one year.* Occasionally a male is seen in the lagoons with the cows at the last of the season, and soon after both male and female, with their young, will be seen working their way northward, following the shore so near that they often pass through the kelp near the beach. It is seldom they are seen far out at sea. This habit of resorting to shoal bays is one in which they differ strikingly from other whales. In summer they congregate in the Arctic Ocean and Okhotsk Sea. It has been said that this species of whale has been found on the coast of China and about the shores of the island of Formosa, but the report needs confirmation.

In October and November the California Grays appear off the coast of Oregon and Upper California, on their way back to their tropical haunts, making a quick, low spout at long intervals; showing themselves but very little until they reach the smooth lagoons of the lower coast, where, if not disturbed, they gather in large numbers,† passing and repassing into and out of the estuaries, or slowly raising their colossal forms midway above the surface, falling over on their sides as if by

whether it lived to come to maturity is a matter of conjecture.

* This statement is maintained upon the following observations: We have known of five embryos being taken from females between the latitudes of 31° and 37° north, on the California coast, when the animals were returning from their warm winter haunts to their cool summer resorts, and in every instance they were exceedingly fat, which is quite opposite to the cows which have produced and nurtured a calf while in the lagoons; hence we conclude that the animals propagate only once in two years.

† It has been estimated, approximately, by observing men among the shore-whaling parties, that a thousand whales passed southward daily, from the 15th of December to the 1st of February, for several successive seasons after shore-whaling was established, which occurred in 1851. Captain Packard, who has been engaged in the business for over twenty years, thinks this a low estimate. Accepting this number without allowing for those which passed off shore out of sight from the land, or for those which passed before the 15th of December and

after the 1st of February, the aggregate would be increased to 47,000. Captain Packard also states, that at the present time the average number seen from the stations passing daily would not exceed forty. From our own observation upon the coast, we are inclined to believe that the numbers resorting annually to the coast of California, from 1853 to 1856, did not exceed 40,000—probably not over 30,000; and at the present time there are many which pass off shore at so great a distance as to be invisible from the lookout stations: there are probably between 100 and 200 whales going southward daily, from the beginning to the end of the "down season" (from December 15th to February 1st).

This estimate of the annual herd visiting the coast is probably not large, as there is no allowance made for those that migrate earlier and later in the season. From what data we have been able to obtain, the whole number of California Gray Whales which have been captured or destroyed since the bay-whaling commenced, in 1846, would not exceed 10,800, and the number which now periodically visit the coast does not exceed 8,000 or 10,000.

accident, and dashing the water into foam and spray about them. At times, in calm weather, they are seen lying on the water quite motionless, keeping one position for an hour or more. At such times the sea-gulls and cormorants frequently alight upon the huge beasts. The first season in Scammon's Lagoon, coast of Lower California, the boats were lowered several times for them, we thinking that the animals when in that position were dead or sleeping, but before the boats arrived within even shooting distance they were on the move again.

About the shoals at the mouth of one of the lagoons, in 1860, we saw large numbers of the monsters. It was at the low stage of the tide, and the shoal places were plainly marked by the constantly foaming breakers. To our surprise we saw many of the whales going through the surf where the depth of water was barely sufficient to float them. We could discern in many places, by the white sand that came to the surface, that they must be near or touching the bottom. One in particular, lay for a half-hour in the breakers, playing, as seals often do in a heavy surf; turning from side to side with half-extended fins, and moved apparently by the heavy ground-swell which was breaking; at times making a playful spring with its bending flukes, throwing its body clear of the water, coming down with a heavy splash, then making two or three spouts, and again settling under water; perhaps the next moment its head would appear, and with the heavy swell the animal would roll over in a listless manner, to all appearance enjoying the sport intensely. We passed close to this sportive animal, and had only thirteen feet of water.

The habits of the Gray have brought upon it many significant names, among which the most prominent are, "Hard-head," "Mussel-digger," "Devil-fish," "Gray-back," and "Rip-sack." The first-mentioned misnomer arose from the fact of the animals having a great propensity to root the boats when coming in contact with them, in the same manner that hogs upset their empty troughs. Moreover, they are known to descend to soft bottoms in search of food, or for other purposes; and, when returning to the surface, they have been seen with head and lips besmeared with the dark ooze from the depths below;* hence the name of

---

* To our personal knowledge, but little or no food has been found in the animal's stomach. We have examined several taken in the lagoons, and in them we found what the whalers called "sedge" or "sea-moss" (a sort of sea-cabbage), which at certain seasons darkens the waters in extensive patches both in and about the mouths of the estuaries. Whether this was taken into the stomach as food some naturalists doubt, giving as a reason that the whale, passing through the water mixed with this vegetable matter, on opening its mouth would of necessity receive more or less of it, which would be swallowed, there being no other way in which it could be

1

2

C. M. Scammon, del.

FIG.1. THE CALIFORNIA GRAY WHALE. (RHACHIANECTES (

"Mussel - digger." "Devil - fish" is significant of the danger incurred in the pursuit of the animal. "Gray - back" is indicative of its color, and "Rip - sack" originated with the manner of flensing.

As the season approaches for the whales to bring forth their young, which is from December to March, they formerly collected at the most remote extremities of the lagoons, and huddled together so thickly that it was difficult for a boat to cross the waters without coming in contact with them. Repeated instances have been known of their getting aground and lying for several hours in but two or three feet of water, without apparent injury from resting heavily on the sandy bottom, until the rising tide floated them. In the Bay of Monterey they have been seen rolling, with apparent delight, in the breakers along the beach.

In February, 1856, we found two whales aground in Magdalena Bay. Each had a calf playing about, there being sufficient depth for the young ones, while the mothers were lying hard on the bottom. When attacked, the smaller of the two old whales lay motionless, and the boat approached near enough to "set" the hand - lance into her "life," dispatching the animal at a single dart. The other, when approached, would raise her head and flukes above the water, supporting herself on a small portion of the belly, turning easily, and heading toward the boat, which made it very difficult to capture her. It appears to be their habit to get into the shallowest inland waters when their cubs are young. For this reason the whaling - ships anchor at a considerable distance from where the crews go to hunt the animals, and several vessels are often in the same lagoon.

The first streak of dawn is the signal for lowering the boats, all pulling for the head - waters, where the whales are expected to be found. As soon as one is seen, the officer who first discovers it sets a "waif" (a small flag) in his boat, and gives chase. Boats belonging to other vessels do not interfere, but go in search of other whales. When pursuing, great care is taken to keep behind, and a short distance from the animal, until it is driven to the extremity of the lagoon, or into shoal water; then the men in the nearest boats spring to their oars in the exciting race, and the animal, swimming so near the bottom, has its progress impeded, thereby giving its pursuers a decided advantage: although occasionally it will suddenly change its course, or "dodge," which frequently prolongs the chase for hours,

disposed of. The quantity found in any one individual would not exceed a barrelful.

From the testimony of several whaling - men whom we regard as interested and careful observers, together with our own investigations, we are convinced that mussels have been found in the maws of the California Grays; but as yet, from our own observations, we have not been able to establish the fact of what their principal sustenance consists.

the boats cutting through the water at their utmost speed. At other times, when the cub is young and weak, the movements of the mother are sympathetically suited to the necessities of her dependent offspring. It is rare that the dam will forsake her young one, when molested. When within "darting distance" (sixteen or eighteen feet), the boat-steerer darts the harpoons, and if the whale is struck it dashes about, lashing the water into foam, oftentimes staving the boats. As soon as the boat is fast, the officer goes into the head,* and watches a favorable opportunity to shoot a bomb-lance. Should this enter a vital part and explode, it kills instantly, but it is not often this good luck occurs; more frequently two or three bombs are shot, which paralyze the animal to some extent, when the boat is hauled near enough to use the hand-lance. After repeated thrusts, the whale becomes sluggish in its motions; then, going "close to," the hand-lance is set into its "life," which completes the capture. The animal rolls over on its side, with fins extended, and dies without a struggle. Sometimes it will circle around within a small compass, or take a zigzag course, heaving its head and flukes above the water, and will either roll over, "fin out," or die under water and sink to the bottom.

Thus far we have spoken principally of the females, as they are found in the lagoons. Mention has been made, however, of that general habit, common to both male and female, of keeping near the shore in making the passage between their northern and southern feeding-grounds. This fact becoming known, and the bomb-gun† coming into use, the mode of capture along the outer coast was changed. The whaling parties first stationed themselves in their boats at the most favorable points, where the thickest beds of kelp were found, and there lay in wait watching for a good chance to shoot the whales as they passed. This was called "kelp whaling."

The first year or two that this pursuit was practiced, many of the animals

---

* Whalemen call the forward part of a whale-boat the head, differing from merchantmen, who term it the bow; still, the oar next to the forward one in a whale-boat is named the bow-oar. And, likewise, when the boat is hauled close up to the whale by heaving the line out of the "bow-chocks," and taking it to one side against a cleat which is placed a few feet aft of the extreme bow, it is called "bowing-on."

† The bomb-gun is made of iron, stock and all. It is three feet long, the barrel of which is twenty-three inches in length; diameter of bore, one and one-eighth of an inch; weight, twenty-four pounds. It shoots a bomb-lance twenty-one and a half inches long, and of a size to fit the bore. It is pointed at the end, with sharpened edges, in order to cut its way through the fibrous fat and flesh, and is guided by three elastic feathers, which are attached along the fuse tube, folding around it when in the barrel. The gun is fired from the shoulder, in the same way as a musket. For illustration, see plate xxiii.

passed through or along the edge of the kelp, where the gunners chose their own distance for a shot. This method, however, soon excited the suspicions of these sagacious creatures. At first, the ordinary whale-boat was used, but the keen-eyed "Devil-fish" soon found what would be the consequence of getting too near the long, dark-looking object, as it lay nearly motionless, only rising and falling with the rolling swell. A very small boat—with one man to scull and another to shoot—was then used, instead of the whale-boat. This proved successful for a time, but, after a few successive seasons, the animals passed farther seaward, and at the present time the boats usually anchor outside the kelp. The mottled fish being seen approaching far enough off for the experienced gunner to judge nearly where the animal will "break water," the boat is sculled to that place, to await the "rising." If the whale "shows a good chance," it is frequently killed instantly, and sinks to the bottom, or receives its death-wound by the bursting of the bomb-lance. Consequently, the stationary position or slow movement of the animal enables the whaler to get a harpoon into it before sinking. To the harpoon a line is attached, with a buoy, which indicates the place where the dead creature lies, should it go to the bottom. Then, in the course of twenty-four hours, or in less time, it rises to the surface, and is towed to the shore, the blubber taken off and tried out in pots set for that purpose upon the beach.

Another mode of capture is by ships cruising off the land and sending their boats inshore toward the line of kelp; and, as the whales work to the southward, the boats, being provided with extra large sails, the whalemen take advantage of the strong northerly winds, and, running before the breeze, sail near enough to be able to dart the hand-harpoon into the fish. "Getting fast" in this way, it is killed in deep water, and, if inclined to sink, it can be held up by the boats till the ship comes up, when a large "fluke-rope" is made fast, or the "fin-chain" is secured to one fin, the "cutting-tackle" hooked, and the whale "cut in" immediately. This mode is called "sailing them down." Still another way of catching them is with "Greener's Harpoon Gun," which is similar to a small swivel-gun. It is of one and a half inch bore, three feet long in the barrel, and, when stocked, weighs seventy-five pounds. The harpoon, four feet and a half long, is projected with considerable accuracy to any distance under eighty-four yards. The gun is mounted on the bow of the boat. A variety of manoeuvres are practiced when using the weapon: at times the boat lying at anchor, and, again, drifting about for a chance-shot. When the animal is judged to be ten fathoms off, the gun is pointed eighteen inches below the back; if fifteen fathoms, eight or ten inches below; if eighteen or twenty fathoms distant, the gun is sighted at the top of its back.

Still another strategic plan has been practiced with successful results, called "whaling along the breakers." Mention has been already made of the habit which these whales have of playing about the breakers at the mouths of the lagoons. This, the watchful eye of the whaler was quick to see, could be turned to his advantage.

After years of pursuit by waylaying them around the beds of kelp, the wary animals learned to shun these fatal regions, making a wide deviation in their course to enjoy their sports among the rollers at the lagoons' mouths, as they passed them either way. But the civilized whaler anchors his boats as near the roaring surf as safety will permit, and the unwary "Mussel-digger" that comes in reach of the deadly harpoon, or bomb-lance, is sure to pay the penalty with its life. If it come within darting distance, it is harpooned; and, as the stricken animal makes for the open sea, it is soon in deep water, where the pursuer makes his capture with comparative ease; or if passing within range of the bomb-gun, one of the explosive missiles is planted in its side, which so paralyzes the whale that the fresh boat's-crew, who have been resting at anchor, taking to their oars, soon overtake and dispatch it.

The casualties from coast and kelp whaling are nothing to be compared with the accidents that have been experienced by those engaged in taking the females in the lagoons. Hardly a day passes but there is upsetting or staving of boats, the crews receiving bruises, cuts, and, in many instances, having limbs broken; and repeated accidents have happened in which men have been instantly killed, or received mortal injury. The reasons of the increased dangers are these: the quick and deviating movements of the animal, its unusual sagacity, and the fact of the sandy bottom being continually stirred by the strong currents, making it difficult to see an object at any considerable depth. When a whale is "struck" at sea, there is generally but little difficulty in keeping clear. When first irritated by the harpoon, it attempts to escape by "running," or descending to the depths below, taking out more or less line, the direction of which, and the movements of the boat, indicate the animal's whereabouts. But in a lagoon, the object of pursuit is in narrow passages, where frequently there is a swift tide, and the turbid water prevents the whaler from seeing far beneath the boat. Should the chase be made with the current, the fugitive sometimes stops suddenly, and the speed of the boat, together with the influence of the running water, shoots it upon the worried animal when it is dashing its flukes in every direction. The whales that are chased have with them their young cubs, and the mother, in her efforts to avoid the pursuit of herself and offspring, may momentarily lose sight of her little one. Instantly she

Plate IV

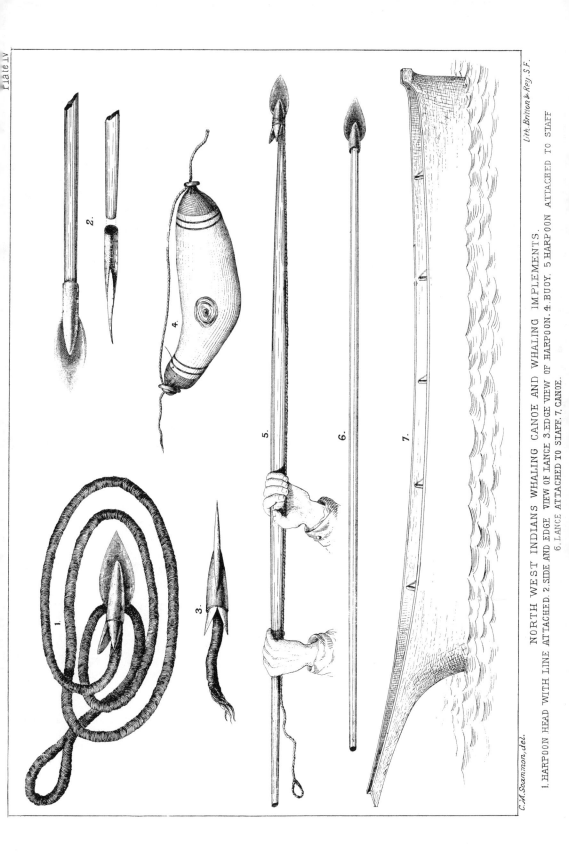

C.M. Seammon, del.

Lith. Britton & Rey. S.F.

NORTH WEST INDIANS WHALING CANOE AND WHALING IMPLEMENTS.

1. HARPOON HEAD WITH LINE ATTACHED. 2. SIDE AND EDGE VIEW OF LANCE 3. EDGE VIEW OF HARPOON. 4. BUOY. 5 HARPOON ATTACHED TO STAFF

6. LANCE ATTACHED TO STAFF. 7. CANOE.

will stop and "sweep" around in search, and if the boat comes in contact with her, it is quite sure to be staved. Another danger is, that in darting the lance at the mother, the young one, in its gambols, will get in the way of the weapon, and receive the wound, instead of the intended victim. In such instances, the parent animal, in her frenzy, will chase the boats, and, overtaking them, will overturn them with her head, or dash them in pieces with a stroke of her ponderous flukes.

Sometimes the calf is fastened to instead of the cow. In such instances the mother may have been an old frequenter of the ground, and been before chased, and perhaps have suffered from a previous attack, so that she is far more difficult to capture, staving the boats and escaping after receiving repeated wounds. One instance occurred in Magdalena Lagoon, in 1857, where, after several boats had been staved, they being near the beach, the men in those remaining afloat managed to pick up their swimming comrades, and, in the meantime, to run the line to the shore, hauling the calf into as shallow water as would float the dam, she keeping near her troubled young one, giving the gunner a good chance for a shot with his bomb-gun from the beach. A similar instance occurred in Scammon's Lagoon, in 1859.

The testimony of many whaling-masters furnishes abundant proof that these whales are possessed of unusual sagacity. Numerous contests with them have proved that, after the loss of their cherished offspring, the enraged animals have given chase to the boats, which only found security by escaping to shoal water or to shore.

After evading the civilized whaler and his instruments of destruction, and perhaps while they are suffering from wounds received in their southern haunts, these migratory animals begin their northern journey. The mother, with her young grown to half the size of maturity, but wanting in strength, makes the best of her way along the shores, avoiding the rough sea by passing between or near the rocks and islets that stud the points and capes. But scarcely have the poor creatures quitted their southern homes before they are surprised by the Indians about the Strait of Juan de Fuca, Vancouver and Queen Charlotte's Islands. Like enemies in ambush, these glide in canoes from island, bluff, or bay, rushing upon their prey with whoop and yell, launching their instruments of torture, and like hounds worrying the last life-blood from their vitals. The capture having been effected, trains of canoes tow the prize to shore in triumph. The whalemen among the Indians of the North-west Coast are those who delight in the height of adventure, and who are ambitious of acquiring the greatest reputation among their fellows. Those among them who could boast of killing a whale, formerly had the most exalted mark of honor conferred upon them by a cut across the nose; but this custom is no longer observed.

The Indian whaling-canoe is thirty-five feet in length. Eight men make the crew, each wielding a paddle five and a half feet long. The whaling-gear consists of harpoons, lines, lances, and seal-skin buoys, all of their own workmanship. The cutting material of both lance and spear was formerly the thick part of a mussel-shell, or of the "abelone;" the line made from cedar withes, twisted into a three-strand rope. The buoys are fancifully painted, but those belonging to each boat have a distinguishing mark. The lance-pole, or harpoon-staff, made of the heavy wood of the yew-tree, is eighteen feet long, weighing as many pounds, and with the lance attached is truly a formidable weapon.

Their whaling-grounds are limited, as the Indians rarely venture seaward far out of sight of the smoke from their cabins by day, or beyond view of their bon-fires at night. The number of canoes engaged in one of these expeditions is from two to five, the crews being taken from among the chosen men of the tribe, who, with silent stroke, can paddle the symmetrical *canim* close to the rippling water beside the animal; the bowman then, with sure aim, thrusts the harpoon into it, and heaves the line and buoys clear of the canoe. The worried creature may dive deeply, but very little time elapses before the inflated seal-skins are visible again. The instant these are seen, a buoy is elevated on a pole from the nearest canoe, by way of signal; then all dash, with shout and grunt, toward the object of pursuit. Now the chase attains the highest pitch of excitement, for each boat being provided with implements alike, in order to entitle it to a full share of the prize its crew must lodge their harpoon in the animal, with buoys attached; so that, after the first attack is made, the strife that ensues to be next to throw the spear creates a scene of brawl and agility peculiar to these savage adventurers. At length the victim, becoming weakened by loss of blood, yields to a system of torture characteristic of its eager pursuers, and eventually, spouting its last blood from a lacerated heart, it writhes in convulsions and expires. Then the whole fleet of canoes assists in towing it to the shore, where a division is made, and all the inhabitants of the village greedily feed upon the fat and flesh till their appetites are satisfied. After the feast, what oil may be extracted from the remains is put into skins or bladders, and is an article of traffic with neighboring tribes or the white traders who occasionally visit them.

These "whales of passage," when arrived in the Arctic Ocean and Okhotsk Sea, are seen emerging between the scattered floes, and even forcing themselves through the field of ice, rising midway above the surface, and blowing in the same attitude in which they are frequently seen in the southern lagoons; at such times the combined sound of their respirations can be heard, in a calm day, for miles across the ice and water. But in those far northern regions, the animals are rarely pursued by the whale-ship's boats: hence they rest in some degree of security; yet even there, the watchful Esquimaux steal upon them, and to their primitive weapons and rude processes the whale at last succumbs, and supplies food and substance for its captors.

The Esquimaux whaling-boat, although to all appearance simple in its construction, will be found, after careful investigation, to be admirably adapted to the purpose, as well as for all other uses necessity demands. It is not only used to accomplish the more important undertaking, but in it they hunt the walrus, shoot game, and make their long summer-voyages about the coast, up the deep bays and long rivers, where they traffic with the interior tribes. When prepared for whaling, the boat is cleared of all passengers and useless incumbrances, nothing being allowed but the whaling-gear. Eight picked men make the crew.* Their boats are twenty-five to thirty feet long, and are flat on the bottom, with flaring sides and tapering ends. The framework is of wood, lashed together with the fibres of baleen and thongs of walrus-hide, the latter article being the covering, or planking, to the boat. The implements are one or more harpoons, made of ivory, with a point of slate-stone or iron; a boat-mast, that serves the triple purpose of spreading the sail and furnishing the staff for the harpoon and lance; a large knife, and eight paddles. The knife lashed to the mast constitutes the lance.

The boat being in readiness, the chase begins. As soon as the whale is seen and its course ascertained, all get behind it: not a word is spoken, nor will they take notice of a passing ship or boat, when once excited in the chase. All is silent and motionless until the spout is seen, when they instantly paddle toward it. The spouting over, every paddle is raised; again the spout is seen or *heard* through the fog, and again they spring to their paddles. In this manner the animal is approached near enough to throw the harpoon, when all shout at the top of their voices. This is said to have the effect of checking the animal's way through the water, thus giving an opportunity to plant the spear in its body, with line and buoys attached. The chase continues in this wise until a number of weapons are firmly fixed, causing the animal much effort to get under water, and still more to remain down; so it soon rises again, and is attacked with renewed vigor. It is the

---

*It is said by Captain Norton, who commanded the ship *Citizen*, wrecked in the Arctic several years ago, that the women engage in the chase.

established custom with these simple natives, that the man who first effectually throws his harpoon, takes command of the whole party: accordingly, as soon as the animal becomes much exhausted, his *baidarra* is paddled near, and with surprising quickness he cuts a hole in its side sufficiently large to admit the knife and mast to which it is attached; then follows a course of cutting and piercing till death ensues, after which the treasure is towed to the beach in front of their huts, where it is divided, each member of the party receiving two "slabs of bone," and a like proportion of the blubber and entrails; the owners of the canoes claiming what remains.

The choice pieces for a dainty repast, with them, are the flukes, lips, and fins. The oil is a great article of trade with the interior tribes of "reindeer-men:" it is sold in skins of fifteen gallons each, a skin of oil being the price of a reindeer. The entrails are made into a kind of souse, by pickling them in a liquid extracted from a root that imparts an acrid taste: this preparation is a savory dish, as well as a preventive of the scurvy. The lean flesh supplies food for their dogs, the whole troop of the village gathering about the carcass, fighting, feasting, and howling, as only sledge-dogs can.

Many of the marked habits of the California Gray are widely different from those of any other species of *balæna*. It makes regular migrations from the hot southern latitudes to beyond the Arctic Circle; and in its passages between the extremes of climate it follows the general trend of an irregular coast so near that it is exposed to attack from the savage tribes inhabiting the sea-shores, who pass much of their time in the canoe, and consider the capture of this singular wanderer a feat worthy of the highest distinction. As it approaches the waters of the torrid zone, it presents an opportunity to the civilized whalemen—at sea, along the shore, and in the lagoons—to practice their different modes of strategy, thus hastening the time of its entire annihilation. This species of whale manifests the greatest affection for its young, and seeks the sheltered estuaries lying under a tropical sun, as if to warm its offspring into activity and promote comfort, until grown to the size Nature demands for its first northern visit. When the parent animals are attacked, they show a power of resistance and tenacity of life that distinguish them from all other Cetaceans. Many an expert whaleman has suffered in his encounters with them, and many a one has paid the penalty with his life. Once captured, however, this whale yields the coveted reward to its enemies, furnishing sustenance for the Esquimaux whaler, from such parts as are of little value to others. The oil extracted from its fatty covering is exchanged with remote tribes for their fur-clad animals, of which the flesh affords the venders a feast of the choicest food,

Plate V.

C.M.Scammon. del.

lith.Britton & Rey. S.F.

CALIFORNIA GRAYS AMONG THE ICE

and the skins form an indispensable article of clothing. The North-west Indians realize the same comparative benefit from the captured animals as do the Esquimaux, and look forward to its periodical passage through their circumscribed fishing-grounds as a season of exploits and profit.

The civilized whaler seeks the hunted animal farther seaward, as from year to year it learns to shun the fatal shore. None of the species are so constantly and variously pursued as the one we have endeavored to describe; and the large bays and lagoons, where these animals once congregated, brought forth and nurtured their young, are already nearly deserted. The mammoth bones of the California Gray lie bleaching on the shores of those silvery waters, and are scattered along the broken coasts, from Siberia to the Gulf of California; and ere long it may be questioned whether this mammal will not be numbered among the extinct species of the Pacific.

CHAPTER II.

THE FINBACK WHALE.

BALÆNOPTERA VELIFERA, *Cope.* (Plate ii, fig. 2.)

Another species of the whale tribe is known as the Finback, or Finner, whose geographical distribution is as extended as that of the Sulphurbottom, and which ranks next to it in point of swiftness.

One picked up by Captain Poole, of the bark *Sarah Warren,* of San Francisco, affords us the following memoranda: Length, sixty-five feet; thickness of blubber, seven to nine inches; yield of oil, seventy-five barrels; color of blubber, a clear white. Top of head quite as flat and straight as that of the Humpback. Baleen, the longest, two feet four inches; greatest width, thirteen inches; its color, a light lead, streaked with black, and its surface presents a ridgy appearance crosswise; length of fringe to bone, two to four inches, and in size this may be compared to a cambric needle.

A *Balænoptera,* which came on shore near the outer heads of the Golden Gate, gave us the opportunity of obtaining the following rough measurements:

	Ft.	In.
Length	60	00
From nib-end to pectorals	15	00
From nib-end to corner of mouth	12	00
From nib-end to eye	12	06
From notch of caudal fin to genital slit	21	00
From notch of caudal fin to vent	19	06
Expansion of caudal fin	14	00

Its side fins and flukes are in like proportion to the body as in the California Gray. Its throat and breast are marked with deep creases, or folds, similar to the Humpback. Color of back and sides, black or blackish-brown (in some individuals a curved band of lighter shade marks its upper sides, between the spiracles and pectorals); belly, a milky white. Its back fin is placed nearer to the caudal than the hump on the Humpback, and in shape approaches to a right-angled triangle, but rounded on the forward edge, curved on the opposite one; the longest side joins the back in some examples, and in others the anterior edge is the longest. The gular folds spread on each side to the pectorals, and extended half the length of the body.

The habitual movements of the Finback in several points are peculiar. When it respires, the vaporous breath passes quickly through its spiracles, and when a fresh supply of air is drawn into the breathing system, a sharp and somewhat musical sound may be heard at a considerable distance, which is quite distinguishable from that of other whales of the same genus. (We have observed the interval between the respirations of a large Finback to be about seven seconds.) It frequently gambols about vessels at sea, in mid-ocean as well as close in with the coast, darting under them, or shooting swiftly through the water on either side; at one moment upon the surface, belching forth its quick, ringing spout, and the next instant submerging itself beneath the waves, as if enjoying a spirited race with the ship dashing along under a press of sail. In beginning the descent, it assumes a variety of positions: sometimes rolling over nearly on its side, at other times rounding, or perhaps heaving, its flukes out, and assuming nearly a perpendicular attitude. Frequently it remains on the surface, making a regular course and several uniform "blows." Occasionally they congregate in schools of fifteen to twenty, or less. In this situation we have usually observed them going quickly through the water, several spouting at the same instant. Their uncertain movements, however —often showing themselves twice or thrice, then disappearing—and their swiftness, make them very difficult to capture. The results of several attempts to catch them were as follows: from the ship one was shot with a bomb-gun, which did its work so effectually, that although the boat was in readiness for instant lowering, before it got within darting distance the animal, in its dying contortions, ran foul of the ship, giving her a shock that was very sensibly felt by all on board, and likewise a momentary heel of about two streaks. We had a good view of the under-side of the whale as it made several successive rolls before disappearing, and our observations agreed with those noted on board the *Sarah Warren* in relation to color and the creases on throat and breast. The under-side of the fins was white also. At another time the whale died about ten fathoms under water, and after carefully hauling it up in sight, the "iron drawed, and away the dead animal went to the depths beneath." Frequently we have "lowered" for single ones that were playing about the ship, but by the time the boats were in the water nothing more would be seen of them, or, if seen, they would be a long way off, and then disappear.

An instance occurred in Monterey Bay, in 1865, of five being captured under the following circumstances: A "pod" of whales was seen in the offing, by the whalemen, from their shore station, who immediately embarked in their boats and gave chase. On coming up to them they were found to be Finbacks. One was harpooned, and, although it received a mortal wound, they all "run together" as before. One of the gunners, being an expert, managed to shoot the whole five, and they were all ultimately secured, yielding to the captors a merited prize. We have noticed large numbers of these whales along the coast during the summer months, and they seem to be more together at that particular season; but, as the opportunities for observing their habits have been much greater at that time of the year, we may have been led into error upon this particular point. Their food is of the same nature as that of the other rorquals, and the quantity of codfish which has been found in them is truly enormous. On the northern coast, the Finbacks, in many instances, have a much larger fin than those in warmer latitudes, and we are fully satisfied that these are a distinct species, confined to the northern waters.

We have had but little opportunity to observe the Finbacks that frequently rove about the Gulf of Georgia and Fuca Strait. Several have been seen, however, in May and June, on the coasts of California and Oregon, and in Fuca Strait in June and July of the year 1864; these observations satisfy us that the dorsal fin of this—the northern species referred to—is strikingly larger than in the more southern Finbacks.

Appended are the outlines of one individual of several seen in Queen Charlotte Sound, in February, 1865, which is a fair representation of them all. Those we have noticed about Fuca Strait seem to have the back fin modified in size between the extremely small one found on the coast of Lower California and the one here represented.

Plate VI.

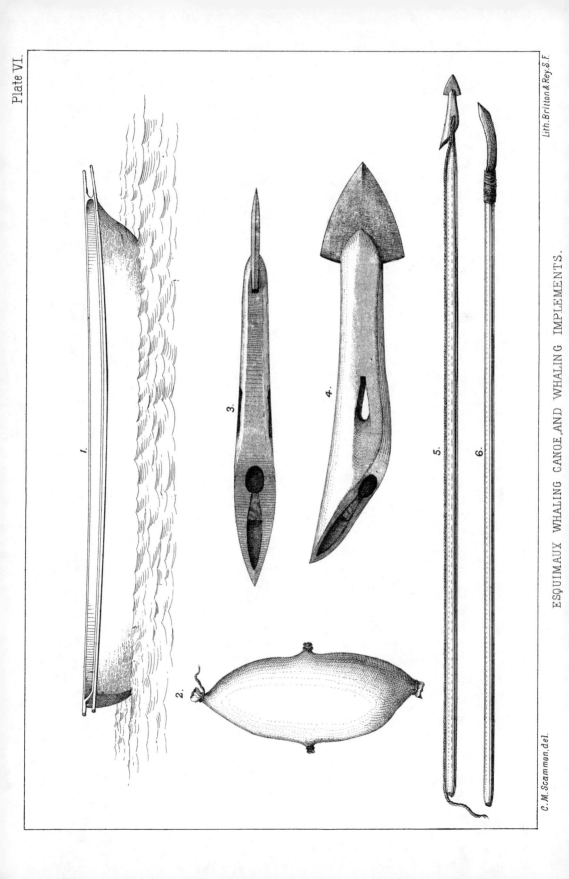

Lith.Britton&Rey.S.F.

C.M.Scammon,del.

ESQUIMAUX WHALING CANOE AND WHALING IMPLEMENTS.

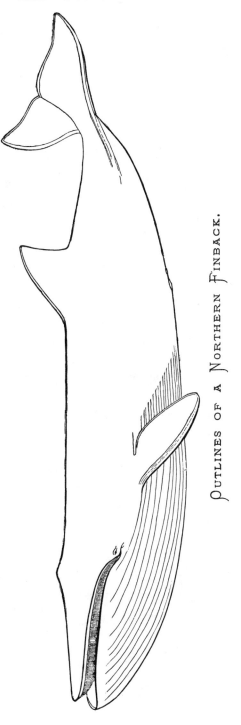

OUTLINES OF A NORTHERN FINBACK.

CHAPTER III.

THE HUMPBACK WHALE.

Megaptera versabilis, *Cope.* (Plate vii, fig. 1.)

The Humpback is one of the species of rorquals that roam through every ocean, generally preferring to feed and perform its uncouth gambols near extensive coasts, or about the shores of islands, in all latitudes between the equator and the frozen oceans, both north and south. It is irregular in its movements, seldom going a straight course for any considerable distance; at one time moving about in large numbers, scattered over the sea as far as the eye can discern from the mast-head; at other times *singly,* seeming as much at home as if it were surrounded by hundreds of its kind; performing at will the varied actions of "breaching," "rolling," "finning," "lobtailing," or "scooping;" or, on a calm, sunny day, perhaps lying motionless on the molten-looking surface, as though life were extinct.

Its shape, compared with the symmetrical forms of the Finback, California Gray, and Sulphurbottom, is decidedly ugly, as it has a short, thick body, and frequently a diminutive "small," with inordinately large pectorals and flukes. A protuberance, of variable shape and size in different individuals, placed on the back, about one-fourth the length from the caudal fin, is called the hump. Another cartilaginous boss projects from a centre fold immediately beneath the anterior point of the under jaw, which, with the flukes, pectorals, and throat of the creature, are oftentimes hung with pendent parasites* (*Otion Stimpsoni*), and on

*We print here Dall's description of the *Cyamus suffusus;* also his remarks on the *Otion Stimpsoni* (Proc. Cal. Acad. Sci., Dec. 18th, 1872). Illustrations, figures 3 and 5, plate x.

Cyamus suffusus, n. sp. Body flattened, elongate; segments, sub-equal, outer edges widely separated. Branchiæ single, cylindrical slender, with a very short papilliform appendage before and behind each branchia. Superior antennæ unusually long and stout. First pair of hands quadrant-shaped; second pair slightly punctate, arcuate, emarginate on the inferior edge, with a pointed tubercle on each side of the emargination. Third joint of the posterior legs keeled above, with a prong below. Pleon extremely minute. Segments smooth. No ventral spines on posterior segments. Color, yellowish white, suffused with rose-purple, strongest upon the antennæ and branchiæ. Length, 0.41 inches;

the males it is frequently studded with tubercles, as upon the head. A bulge also rounds down on the lower part of the "small," nearly midway between the hump and caudal. Its under jaw extends forward considerably beyond the upper one. All these combined characteristics impress the observer with the idea of an animal of abnormal proportions. The top of its head is dotted with irregular, rounded bunches, which rise about one inch above the surface, each covering nearly four square inches of space.

The following measurements and memoranda of a male Humpback were taken by Captain F. S. Redfield, of the whaling and trading brig *Manuella*, while cruising in Behring Sea, September 17th, 1866:

	Ft.	In.
Extreme length	49	7
Length of pectorals	13	7
Breadth of pectorals	3	2
Distance from snout to pectorals	12	0
Distance from corner of mouth to snout	9	6
Distance from eye to snout	10	2
Distance from spout-holes to snout	9	4
Expansion of flukes	15	7
Breadth of flukes	3	4
Distance from anus to flukes	11	6

breadth (of body), 0.25 inches. All the specimens which have passed under my observation, some eight or ten in number, were males.

Habitat, on the Humpback Whale (*Megaptera versabilis*, Cope) Monterey, California.

OTION, Leach.

Otion, Leach. Ency. Britannica, suppl. vol. iii, p. 170.

Otion Stimpsoni, Dall, n. sp.

Scuta only present, beaked, with the umbones on the occludent margins; anterior prolongation the longer, pointed, rather slender; posterior prolongation, rounded, wider; external margin concave; color (in spirits), light orange, with a dark purple streak on the rostral surface and on each side of the peduncle; while the lateral surfaces of the body-case and lobes are mottled with dark purple. The lower lip of the orifice is transversely striated and translucent; the upper margins slightly reflexed internally, white; in some specimens with two prolongations or small lobes above, which are wanting in other specimens. The tubular prolongations very irregular and variable in size and form, usually unsymmetrical; one sometimes nearly abortive. Length of peduncle, 2.08 inches; of body, 2.16 inches; of lobes, 2.00 inches; of orifice, 1.18 inch; of scuta, 0.55 inch; width of scuta, 0.16 inch.

Habitat, on the Humpback (*M. versabilis*); sessile on the *Coronulæ* which infest that species, but never, so far as I have observed, on the surface of the whale itself.

Dr. Leach describes five calcareous species, having the scuta, terga, and rostrum of the typical species (*O. Cuvieri*, Leach) and they are figured by Reeve; but this species has certainly only the scuta. Whether this difference is of more than specific value I am not able to decide, owing to the great paucity of works of reference here. I should be unwilling to describe the species, were it not that it was submitted to the late lamented Dr. Stimpson for examination, and was pronounced by him to be new.

	Ft.	In.
Distance from genital slit to flukes	17	0
Length of folds on belly	16	0
Whole breadth of folds on belly	10	0
Distance from flukes to hump	12	3
Length of hump along the back	3	0
Height of hump	1	0
Depth of small close to flukes	2	6
Thickness of small close to flukes	1	6

Thickness of blubber, five to ten inches; color of blubber, yellowish white; yield of oil, forty barrels; number of folds on belly, twenty-six, averaging from four to six inches in width. These folds, which extend from the anterior portion of the throat over the belly, terminating a little behind the pectorals, are capable of great expansion and contraction, which enables the Humpbacks, as well as all other rorquals, to swell their maws when their food is in abundance about them.

The following additional measurements, etc., were taken from Humpbacks captured on the coast of Upper California, in 1872.

1. Sex, female. Color of body, black above, but more or less marbled with white below. Fins, black above, and dotted with white beneath. Color of blubber, white. Number of folds on throat and breast, twenty-one, the widest of which were six inches. Yield of oil, thirty-five barrels. The yield of bone, which is of inferior quality, is about four hundred pounds to a hundred barrels of oil.

	Ft.	In.		Ft.	In.
Length of animal	48	0	Anus to notch of caudal fin	12	6
Length of each pectoral	13	0	Genital slit to notch of caudal fin	12	11
Thickness of each pectoral	0	8	Length of genital slit	3	6
Breadth of each pectoral	3	5	Size around the body behind pectorals	25	0
Expansion of caudal fin, or flukes	18	0	Average thickness of blubber	0	5
Breadth of each lobe	3	6	Depth of small at junction with caudal fin,	1	9
Thickness of each lobe	0	9	Thickness of small at junction with caud-		
From nib-end to pectorals	16	0	al fin	1	6
Pectorals to top of back	4	6	From nib-end to hump	28	0
Corner of mouth to nib-end	10	0	Height of hump	0	10
Corner of mouth to top of head	5	4	Length of hump	4	0
Eye* to nib-end	10	10	Thickness of black skin	0	0¼
Eye to top of head	4	6	Eye to ear	2	0
Spiracles to nib-end	8	0	Length of ear slit	0	1¼
Length of exterior opening of spiracles	1	6	Navel to genital slit	5	0

The nib-end, or point of the upper jaw, fell short of the extremity of the

*We refer the reader to fig. 4, plate x, for illustration of an eye taken from a Humpback forty-six feet in length. The figure is drawn to natural size.

C. M. Scammon del.

1. HUMPBACK (MEGAPTERA VERSABILIS COPE.) 2. SHA

Plate VII.

ED FINNER (BALÆNOPTERA DAVIDSONI, Scammon.)

Britton & Rey, Lith.

lower one about fifteen inches. The tongue and throat were of a leaden color. The orbit of the eye was four inches in diameter. The longest plate of bone, or baleen, was two feet; its color, black, with a fringe of lighter shade.

2. Sex, female. Color of body, black, with slight marks of white beneath. Color of pectorals, black above, white below. Color of flukes, black above and below. Color of blubber, white; average thickness of same, six inches. Yield of oil, thirty barrels. Gular folds, eighteen. Tubercles on lips, nine.

	Ft.	In.		Ft.	In.
Length of animal	48	0	From nib-end to pectorals	16	6
Length of pectorals	13	0	Notch of flukes to anus	11	6
Breadth of pectorals	3	0	Notch of flukes to genital slit	12	0
Thickness of pectorals	0	8	Length of longest baleen	2	9
Expansion of flukes	14	0	Breadth of longest baleen	0	10
Breadth of flukes	4	3			

3. Sex, female. Color of body, black above, slightly mottled with white and gray below. Fins and flukes, black above, white beneath. Color of blubber, white; thickness of same, six to nine inches. Yield of oil, forty barrels. Number of laminæ, five hundred and forty; black, streaked with white, or light lead color.

	Ft.	In.		Ft.	In.
Length of animal	52	0	End of lower jaw to eye	12	5
Length of pectoral	12	0	Length of longest baleen	2	8
Width of pectoral	3	6	Breadth of longest baleen	0	9
End of lower jaw to spiracles	10	0	Length of fringe to baleen	0	5
End of lower jaw to corner of mouth	11	9			

It is proper to state, that the dimensions of the skull, or upper jaw-bone, of any ordinary sized animal would be about fifteen feet long by six broad. The lower jaw-bones, which are joined by a slight symphysis, are each about the same length in their curves, and are about one foot wide and eight inches thick midway between the extremities. The thickness of the lumbar vertebræ is about eight inches; the distance between the points of the spurs, two feet eight inches; and the weight, twenty-four or more pounds. The largest ribs are from nine to twelve feet long, measured on the curve, and ten to fifteen inches in circumference. The aggregate weight of two well-dried specimens (measuring respectively nine and ten feet) was eighty pounds. The first joint of the pectoral bones may be set down at two and a half feet in length, and the same in circumference at its union with the shoulder-blade. This section of the fin bones exceeds fifty pounds in weight.

The usual color of the Humpback is black above, a little lighter below, slightly marbled with white or gray; but sometimes the animal is of spotless white under the fins and about the abdomen. The posterior edge of the hump, in many examples, is tipped with pure white. The megaptera varies more in the production of oil than all others of the rorquals. We have frequently seen individuals which yielded but eight or ten barrels of oil, and others as much as seventy-five; the length of the animal varying from twenty-five to seventy-five feet. Most of these variations may be attributed to age and sex, as the female with a large cub becomes quite destitute of fat in her covering. These animals, more especially the smaller or younger ones, are infested with parasitic crustaceans (*Cyamus suffusus*), which collect in great numbers about the head and pectorals; or, in case there are any wounds upon the body, these troublesome vermin are sure to find them. On the coast of California, in 1856, we captured a whale of ordinary size, which had many patches of these parasites united almost in one mass upon that portion of the body which was exposed when the animal came to the surface, and when "cut in" it proved to have what is termed a "dry skin," the blubber being destitute of oil; this was attributed to the abundance of these troublesome parasites. The Humpback has also the largest barnacles adhering to, or imbedded in, the epidermis, about the throat or fins. The habits of this whale—particularly in its undulating movements, frequent "roundings," "turning of flukes," and irregular course—are characteristic indications, which the quick and practiced eye of the whaleman distinguishes at a long distance. Even when beneath the surface of the sea, we have observed them just "under the rim of the water" (as whalemen used to say), alternately turning from side to side, or deviating in their course with as little apparent effort, and as gracefully, as a swallow on the wing. Like all other rorquals, it has two spiracles, and when it respires, the breath and vapor ejected through these apertures form the "spout," and rises in two separate columns, which, however, unite in one as they ascend and expand. When the enormous lungs of the animal are brought into full play, the spout ascends twenty feet or more. When the whale is going to windward, the influence of the breeze upon the vapor is such, that a low, bushy spout is all that can be seen. The number of respirations to a "rising" is exceedingly variable: sometimes the animal blows only once, at another time six, eight, or ten, and from that up to fifteen or twenty times.

Although the Humpbacks are found in every sea and ocean, our observations indicate that they resort periodically, and with some degree of regularity, to particular localities, where the females bring forth their young. It seems, moreover, that large numbers of both sexes make a sort of general migration from the warmer to the colder latitudes, as the seasons change. They go north in the northern hemisphere, as summer approaches, and return south when winter sets in.

The following observations were made along the coasts of North and South America, and in Oceanica. In the years 1852 and 1853, large numbers of Humpbacks resorted to the Gulf of Guayaquil, coast of Peru, to calve, and the height of the season was during the months of July and August. The same may be said of the gulfs and bays situated near the corresponding latitudes north of the equator; still, instances are not unfrequent where cows and their calves have been seen at all other seasons of the year about the same coast. In the Bay of Valle de Banderas, coast of Mexico (latitude 20° 30'), in the month of December, we saw numbers of Humpbacks, with calves but a few days old. In May, 1855, at Magdalena Bay, coast of Lower California (about latitude 24° 30'), we found them in like numbers; some with very large calves, while others were very small. The season at Tongataboo (one of the Friendly Islands, latitude 21° south, longitude 174° west), according to Captain Beckerman, includes August and September. Here the females were usually large, yielding an average of forty barrels of oil, including the entrail fat, which amounted to about six barrels. The largest whale taken at this point, during the season of 1871, produced seventy-three barrels, and she was adjudged to be seventy-five feet in length. It is worthy of remark, that a large majority of the whales resorting thither were white on the under side of the body and fins.*

---

* Eminent zoölogists have divided the Humpbacks into several species. Gray, in his *Catalogue of the British Museum*, 1850, makes mention of the following names and outward descriptions:

1. MEGAPTERA LONGIMANA (*Johnston's Humpback Whale*).—Black, pectoral fins and beneath white, black varied; lower lip with two series of tubercles; pectorals nearly one-third the entire length; dorsal elongate, the front edge over end of pectoral; throat and belly grooved. Female: upper and lower lip with a series of tubercles; dorsal an obscure protuberance.
2. MEGAPTERA AMERICANA (*Bermuda Humpback*).—Black, belly white; head with round tubercles.
3. MEGAPTERA POESKOP (*Poeskop or Cape Humpback*).—Dorsal nearly over the end of pectorals.
4. MEGAPTERA KUZIRA (*The Kuzira*).—Dorsal small, and behind the middle of the back; the pectoral fins rather short, and less than one-fourth the entire length of the body; nose and sides of throat have round warts; belly plaited.

We have frequently recognized, upon the California coast, every species here described, and even in the same school or "gam." Moreover, we have experienced the greatest difficulty in finding any two of these strange animals externally alike, or possessing any marked generic or specific differences. If the differences pointed out as constituting different species are maintained, we conclude there must be a great number. We have observed, both in the dead and living animals, the following different external marks: 1st. Body black above, white beneath. 2d. Body black above and below, with more or less white mottling under the throat and about the abdomen; pectoral and caudal fins white beneath, or slightly spotted with black. 3d. Body black above, white beneath,

In the Bay of Monterey, Upper California, the best season for Humpbacks is in the months of October and November; but some whales are taken during the period from April to December, including a part of both of those months. The great body of these whales, however, are observed working their way northward until September, when they begin to return southward; and the bay being open to the north, many of the returning band follow along its shores or visit its southern extremity, in search of food, which consists principally of small fish and the lower orders of crustaceans. When the animals are feeding, the whalers have a very favorable opportunity for their pursuit and capture. The observations of the whaling parties, which have been established at this bay for over seventeen years, furnish reliable data in reference to the periodical movements of whales along the Pacific Coast. Of the Humpbacks, individuals of every variety, size, and age have been taken, including one of the most gigantic specimens of the genus. This animal, which yielded one hundred and forty-five barrels of oil, was taken in 1858, when the usual school of large megapteras was making its annual passage southward. One of the largest of these whales having an unusual mark—a white spot on the hump—was recognized for several years in succession in its periodical mi-

with under side of pectoral and caudal fins of a dark ash-color. 4th. Body black above, with gray mottling beneath. In all these varieties, both the caudal and pectoral fins differ in shape and size; the latter in some individuals being exceedingly long, narrow, and pointed, as represented in figure 1 of plate vii; while others are comparatively short and broad, as shown in the outline (page 47), which also shows the parasites, commonly called barnacles, adhering to the throat, pectorals, and caudal fin. There are still others whose pectorals are of intermediate proportions, but terminate abruptly, as seen on page 48, which also represents the scalloped flukes present in some individuals. (In this figure, the mark "A" shows the outlines of spiracles, which form nearly a right angle). Again, in other examples, the caudal fin is narrow, pointed, and lunate; in others, still, it is broad, and nearly straight on the posterior edge. All these varieties feed and associate together on the same ground, and in every particular their habits are the same, so far as we have been able to ascer-

tain from careful observation; all, likewise, are infested by the same parasites. As to the dorsal protuberance called the hump, it is, as has been previously stated, of no regular shape or size, but is nearly of a uniform height; the posterior edge is sometimes tipped with white. As to the tubercles on the head and lips, they were present on all we have examined, twenty or more specimens; those about the head are always well-developed, while those upon the lips, in many individuals, are scarcely perceptible. In some instances, however, they equal or exceed those which crown the skull. There is no regularity in the number of gular folds, which, as far as observed, vary in number from eighteen to twenty-six. In some cases they run parallel to each other; but usually there are several that either cross or terminate near the pectorals. The animals are all described as being black above; but in the examples which have been examined, there was not one, when closely scrutinized, which did not reveal some slight marks of white.

Plate VIII.

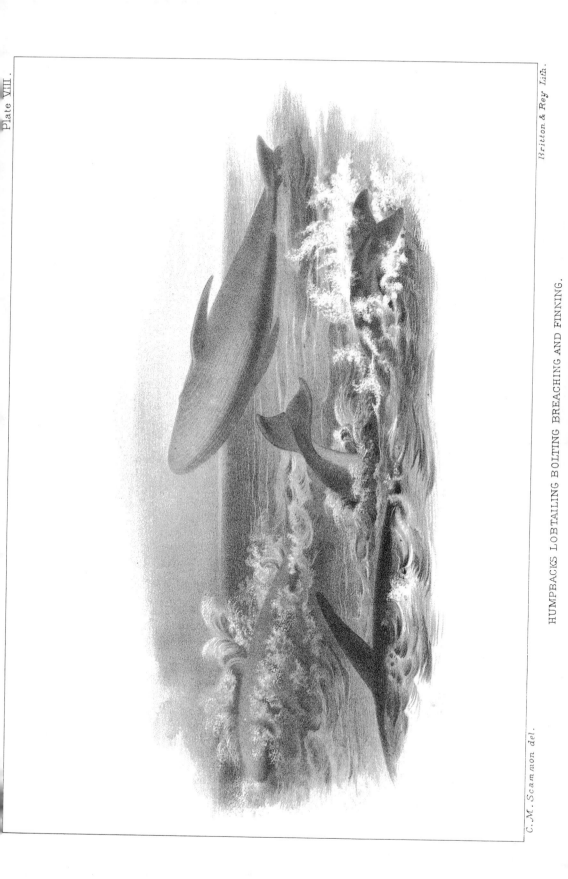

C. M. Scammon del.

Britton & Rey Lith.

HUMPBACKS LOBTAILING BOLTING BREACHING AND FINNING.

grations with the rest of its wandering companions, and the time of passing Point Pinos (the outer headland of the bay), was ascertained to be during or near the month of September. Repeated efforts were made, from year to year, to capture the member of the "gam" thus distinguished by a white hump; but it was only when the bomb-gun and bomb-lance had come into use that its destruction was effected. The animal proved to be of enormous size, but its product of oil was comparatively small, amounting only to about eighty-five barrels.

After many years' study of the characteristic habits of the Humpback, we believe that the females of this species resort in large numbers to favorite inland waters, connected with the ocean, to bring forth their young; but there are many exceptions to this rule, incident to their roving disposition. They are found on different coasts in all accessible latitudes, from the new-born calf to the extremely aged. In their wanderings, they are addicted, more than any other rorqual, to "breaching," "bolting," and "finning." In the mating season they are noted for their amorous antics. At such times their caresses are of the most amusing and novel character, and these performances have doubtless given rise to the fabulous tales of the sword-fish and thrasher attacking whales. When lying by the side of each other, the megapteras frequently administer alternate blows with their long fins, which love-pats may, on a still day, be heard at a distance of miles. They also rub each other with these same huge and flexible arms, rolling occasionally from side to side, and indulging in other gambols which can easier be imagined than described. The time of gestation is not known; but in all probability it is the same as that of other large Cetaceans, not exceeding ten or twelve months. The calf, when brought forth, is about one-fourth the length of the dam; and it suckles by holding the teat between the extremity of the jaws or lips, while the mother reclines a little on one side; raising the posterior portion of her form nearly out of water, and lying in a relaxed condition. This peculiar manner of suckling the young appears to be common to all the whalebone whales. In this way two calves would be enabled to obtain their nourishment at the same time.

The Humpbacks are captured with a common hand-harpoon and lance, or "Greener's Harpoon Gun," and the bomb-lance, by the whaleship's crew; and as they are very liable to sink when dead, every exertion is made to get the harpoon in, with line attached, before the bomb-gun is discharged. Then, if the creature goes to the bottom, a buoy is attached to the end of the line, or a boat lies by it, until the decomposition of its flesh has generated sufficient gas to allow the animal to be drawn up. The length of time that elapses before this takes place of

course depends much on the depth of water and the solidity of the animal's formation; some individuals remaining but a few hours on the bottom, while others will
remain down for two or three days at the same depth. We have known many
whales to be recovered when sunk in from forty to sixty fathoms of water. The
modus operandi in hauling these decomposing subjects to the surface is this: If the
water is rough, the line is taken into the bow-chocks* of the boat; then uniting
two crews in the after part of one boat, they either haul on the line by hand, or
with a tackle, until the boat's bow is nearly submerged, or the whale is lifted; or,
if in a smooth bay, two boats are sometimes used, by laying a spar across both,
and taking the line between them over the spar, which serves as a sort of windlass
purchase. If the dead animal has been long down, in a considerable depth, care is
taken to avoid its coming up under the boat; for as the carcass nears the surface,
its velocity is so much accelerated, that in some instances the animal rises with a
bound which equals its sprightliest actions before life became extinct.

The megapteras are captured by the Indians of the North-western Coast, and
the Esquimaux about the shores of the Arctic Ocean, in the same manner as the
California Grays, as has been described in the opening chapter of this work; and
the natives of the Aleutian Islands pursue them, as well as other rorquals. When
a whale is seen, the *baidarka* (skin-boat) is launched and manned by two or three
men, and a spirited chase ensues. When close to the object of pursuit, their toy-
like harpoons are hurled into the animal. This, however, does not insure an immediate capture; but their weapons, which are pointed with glass or flint-stone,
and barbed with bone, are so fashioned, that, as the wounded creature writhes in
its agony, every motion tends to work the tortuous instrument farther in; and at
last the fatal work is accomplished. Each whaler's spear has his own private
mark, and should the prize be found by others, they seek to ascertain by this
means the rightful owners, who by their laws or customs are entitled to the booty
wherever it may be found.

The best points for Humpback whaling on the coast have been Magdalena,
Balenas, and Monterey bays; but, since the acquisition of Alaska, numerous places
have been found in the bays and about the islands of that Territory, which doubtless in the future will become profitable whaling stations. Several bays around the
Aleutian Archipelago, bordering on Behring Sea, may be indicated as likely to be
valuable for this business.

---

* The bow-chocks are two pieces of wood   boat; between these chocks is a metallic roller,
fastened upon each side of the stem of the   over which the whale-line runs.

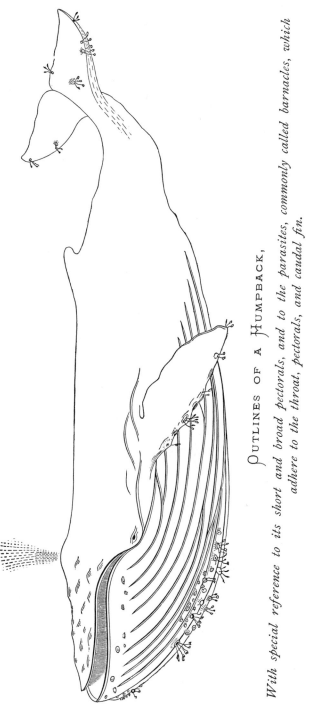

OUTLINES OF A HUMPBACK,

With special reference to its short and broad pectorals, and to the parasites, commonly called barnacles, which adhere to the throat, pectorals, and caudal fin.

ALEUTIAN ISLANDERS WHALE HARPOON.

OUTLINES OF A HUMPBACK, FROM ABOVE.

Plate IX.

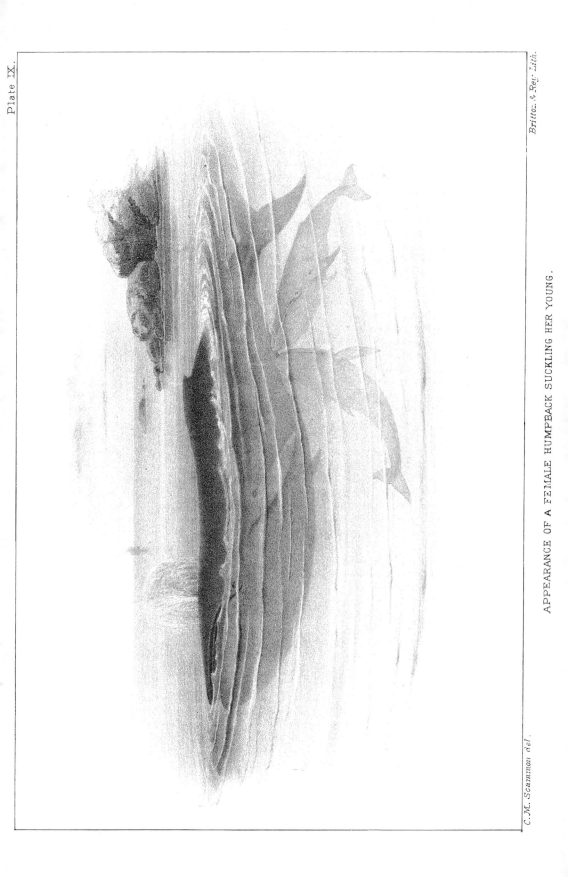

C. M. Scammon del.

Britton & Rey, Lith.

APPEARANCE OF A FEMALE HUMPBACK SUCKLING HER YOUNG.

CHAPTER IV.

THE SHARP-HEADED FINNER WHALE.

BALÆNOPTERA DAVIDSONI, *Scammon*. (Plate vii, fig. 2.)

The name "Sharp-headed Finner" is applied to this, the smallest species of *Balænoptera* known on the coast. The only one we have examined was found dead on the northern shore of Admiralty Inlet, Washington Territory, by some Italian fishermen, in October, 1870; transported by them to the opposite shore, and towed into Port Townsend Bay, where it was flensed on the beach. This opportunity of seeing the animal out of the water became unusually interesting to us, for there was a mystery about its history which we had not been able to solve in the course of twelve years' observations, during which time we had traced it from the coast of Mexico to Behring Sea. In the Strait of Juan de Fuca opportunities were afforded for observing its habits more closely than elsewhere.

The animal in question is generally called by whalers a "young Finback," or a "Finback's calf," and for several years we were under the impression that this inference was correct. In the Strait of Juan de Fuca, these whales were met with in numbers together, or singly, throughout the year; but, though they frequently played around the vessel, we could never get near enough to decide whether they were toothed whales or allied to the whalebone species. The length of the individual captured in Admiralty Inlet was twenty-seven feet. When compared with other *Balænidæ*, it appeared so small, that we were skeptical whether it was an adult or not; but, upon making an examination, a well-developed fœtus* was found

---

* This fœtus was remarkably well formed, and in point of color-marks, corresponded with those upon the parent animal, with the exception of being somewhat dimmer. The following are its dimensions:

	Ft.	In.
Total length	5	6
Caudal fin between extremities	1	2
Width of each lobe of caudal fin	0	4½

	Ft.	In
From fork of caudal to dorsal fin	1	7
Dorsal junction along the back	0	5
Height of dorsal	0	2½
Point of snout to corner of mouth	1	2
Point of snout to eyes	1	2½
Point of snout to pectorals	1	10
From top of back to pectorals	0	9
From top of head to corner of mouth	0	4

in it, five and a half feet long, which dispelled all doubts in regard to its maturity. The principal distinguishing features of this whale are, its dwarfish size; its pointed head, which in form resembles a beak; its low, falcated dorsal fin, which is placed about two-thirds of the length of the animal from the anterior extremity of its lower jaw, which is the longest; and its inordinately small, pointed pectorals, which are marked with a white band above and near their bases, and are placed about one-third of the animal's length from its anterior extremity. The bone, or baleen, in its natural state is of a pure white, with a short, thin fringe of the same color. The number of laminæ on each side of the mouth was two hundred and seventy, and the longest of these measured ten inches. The surface of the animal was a dull black above, white below. The under side of both pectoral and caudal fins was white also. Seventy longitudinal folds extended along the throat and the lower portion of the body, between and a little behind the fins; and, while the outer surface of the folds was of a milky whiteness, the creases between them were of a pinkish cast, imparting the same shade to the throat as far back as the pectorals. The following table gives the proportions of this specimen:

	Ft.	In.
Length of animal	27	0
Length of pectorals	4	0
Breadth of pectorals	1	1
End of snout to spiracles	3	8
End of snout to pectorals	8	6
End of snout to corner of mouth	4	8
Dorsal to fork of caudal fin	9	0
Dorsal junction along the back	2	4
Dorsal's height	0	10
Caudal fin from point to point	7	6
Breadth of lobes of caudal fin	2	1
Fork of caudal fin to anus	8	4
Fork of caudal fin to genital slit	9	6
Depth of animal at pectorals	5	4

The foregoing measurements were hurriedly taken while the whale was being cut up, which was quickly accomplished; for as fast as the Italians stripped off the blubber, the Indians came from a village near, and slashed away at the half-putrid flesh, which they packed off to their camps, declaring loudly that the meat was excellent food. The coating of yellowish fat that incased the body averaged three inches in thickness, and the yield of oil was about three hundred gallons.

The habits of this whale are in many respects like those of the Finback. It frequently gambols about vessels when under way, darting from one side to the other beneath their bottoms. When coming to the surface it makes a quick, faint spout, such as would be made by a suckling of one of the larger Cetaceans; which plainly accounts for whalemen taking it to be the young of more bulky species. At sea the Sharp-headed Finners are seldom seen in pairs, but wander solitarily along, frequently changing their course in the depths below, and meandering along the whole continental coast of the North Pacific; occasionally visiting the large estuaries about the shores. They pass through Behring Sea and Strait into the Arctic Ocean, where they appear to be as much at home as their superiors in size, the Bowheads and the California Grays. Like the latter they thread the icy floes, and frequently emerge through the narrow fissures bolt upright, with their heads above the broken ice, to blow. When roaming about the inland waters of lower latitudes, they often shoot along the shallow borders of the bays in search of the myriads of small fry on which they mainly sustain themselves. They can not be considered as objects of pursuit by whaling vessels, and are but rarely taken by the natives of Cape Flattery—they being the only whalers in that region who attempt the capture of these animals.

CHAPTER V.

THE BOWHEAD, OR GREAT POLAR WHALE.

BALÆNA MYSTICETUS, *Linn.* (Plate xi.)

The Bowhead, or Great Polar Whale, is by far the most valuable, in a commercial point of view, of all the *Balænidæ*, and is the chief object of pursuit by the whalemen in the northern seas. From its great yield of oil, which in some individuals has exceeded two hundred and seventy-five barrels, with a production of bone or baleen equal to over three thousand five hundred pounds,* one might suppose it to be the largest of all the Cetaceans. Such, however, is not the fact, for it seldom attains the length of sixty-five feet, and it is a stout whale which measures fifty feet between its extremities. The striking feature of the animal is its ponderous head, forming, as far as our observations go, more than one-third of the whole creature, which is short, bulky, and bloated in its appearance. Its upper jaw, or the top of the head, is curved downward more than that of the Right Whale (*Balæna Sieboldii?*), to which it bears the nearest resemblance. To the edge of this jaw, the long, finely fringed, transverse layers of baleen are attached, projecting downward and outward, and hedging in, as it were, the animal's tongue, and all is inclosed by the under lip when the mouth is shut. The tongue is incapable of protrusion, being fixed from near its point to the root. It is a mass of spongy fat, intermixed with sinewy flesh, and yields one-tenth as much oil as the "body-blubber." The two extended rows of baleen which line the sides of the upper jaw provide the means by which the animal secures its insect food, which is the chief sustenance of the colossal mysticetus. Its eyes, which in size quadruple those of an ox, are placed, one on each side, about a foot above and behind the angle of the mouth. The spiracles are at the apex of the high protuberance on the head, which is forward of the eyes. Its short but heavy pectorals are placed about two feet from the eyes and nearly in a horizontal line with them. Its ears are a little above and behind the eyes; they are simply openings, not over one-fourth of an

---

* *Vide* Roys' first voyage in the Arctic.

C.M.Scammon,del.

THE BOWHEAD
BALÆ

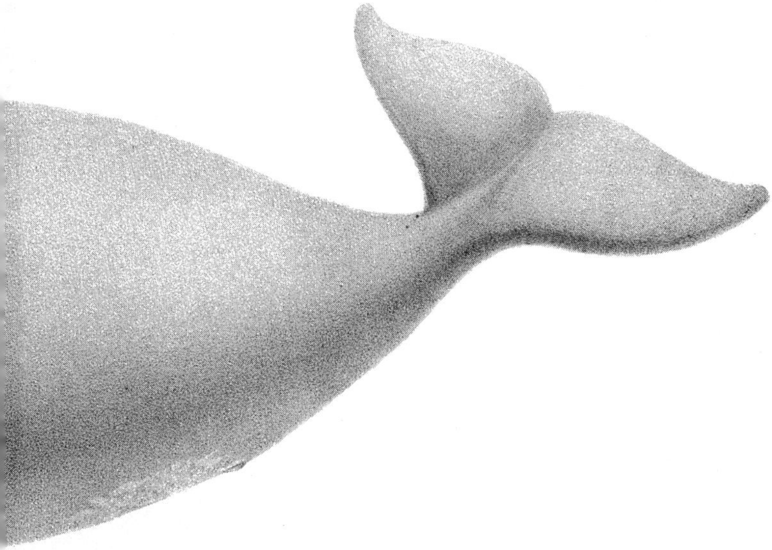

Plate XI.

EAT POLAR WHALE.
TICETUS . LINN

Britton & Rey, Lith.

inch in extent, and in some individuals they are so minute that it is with the greatest difficulty they can be discovered. An immense caudal fin, which forms the posterior limb and extremity of the body, is from sixteen to twenty feet in extension, and in shape thick, broad, lunate, and notched in the centre of the posterior edge, while the extremities are somewhat rounded.

I am indebted to Captain J. F. Poole, formerly of the American bark *N. S. Perkins*, for the measurements and memoranda of a mysticetus, forty-seven feet in length, which was taken in the Arctic Ocean, August, 1867; and to Captain G. L. Smith, of the American bark *Vineyard*, for similar statements of one forty-five feet long, taken in the same ocean during the season of 1870, as follows:*

CAPTAIN POOLE'S WHALE.

Sex, female. Color, black on back and sides; throat white; also, occasional white spots on under side of body. Yield of oil, eighty barrels (the whale was judged large enough ordinarily to have yielded one hundred and fifty barrels of oil).

	Ft.	In.
Length of animal	47	0
Length of pectorals	8	0
Breadth of pectorals	4	0
Distance from nib-end to spout-holes	16	0
Length of spout-holes	1	0
Distance from corner of mouth to nib-end	17	10
Extension of flukes	19	0
Thickest blubber	1	4
Average thickness of blubber	0	11
Thickness of black skin on back	0	1
Length of genital slit	1	10
Distance from genital slit to vent	0	4
Distance from genital slit to flukes	9	0
Length of longest bone or baleen	10	6
Length of fringe or hair on bone	†2	0
Breadth of longest bone	1	01

The bone was imbedded in the gum of the jaw ten inches. Number of layers of bone on each side of jaw, three hundred and thirty;‡ weight of largest slab of

* We regret that our measurements of Bowheads, taken in Tchantar Bay, 1862, were lost in changing from one vessel to another the following year.

† Two feet may be regarded as nearly twice the usual length.

‡ This may be a fair average, and 370 is the highest number we have counted.

bone, seven pounds. The bone extends back of spout-holes in the throat three feet, and falls short of nib-end one foot.

CAPTAIN SMITH'S WHALE.

Sex, male ; color above and below, black.

	Ft.	In.
Length	45	0
Girth in largest place (behind pectorals)	28	0
Length of pectorals	7	3
Breadth of pectorals	3	9
Nib-end or nose to pectorals	18	8
Corner of mouth to nib-end	16	0
Eye to nib-end	16	0
Spout-holes to nib-end	14	0
Length of opening to spout-holes (longitudinally)	1	2
Flukes from tip to tip	16	0
Width of flukes from notch to junction with the body	4	2
Vent to flukes	8	10
Genital slit to flukes	12	0
Size around the "small" at genital slit	19	0
Length of longest bone or baleen	9	6
Width of longest bone or baleen	1	0
Average thickness of blubber	0	9

Color of blubber, slightly reddish. The number of layers of bone on each side of the jaw was three hundred and eight. The yield of oil was sixty barrels; yield of bone, one thousand and fifty pounds.

When the Bowhead feeds, it moves through its native element, either below or near the surface, with considerable velocity, its jaws being open, whereby a body of water enters its capacious mouth, and along with it the animalculæ (termed by the whalemen "Right Whale feed," or "brit"). The water escapes through the layers of baleen,* but the insect food is retained by the fine fringes on its inner edges, and is afterward swallowed. When not disturbed, the animal remains up, generally, to respire, from one and a half to two and a half minutes, during which time it spouts from six to nine times, and then disappears for the space of ten to twenty minutes. The volume of vapor ejected is similar to that of the Right Whale. Sometimes, when engaged in feeding, it remains down for twenty-five minutes or

---

*For illustrations of layers of baleen, or "slabs of bone," as named by whalers, see page 55, which shows the relative proportions of the baleen of the Bowhead, (*Balæna mystice-* *tus*); Right Whale of the North-western Coast, (*Balæna Sieboldii?*); Sulphurbottom, (*Sibbaldius sulfureus*); Humpback (*Megaptera versabilis*); and the California Gray (*Rhachianectes glaucus*).

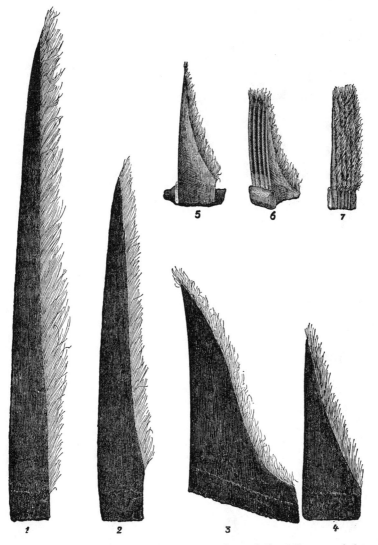

The above illustration represents the relative proportions of the full-grown baleen of different species of whalebone whales, as follows :

1. Baleen of the Bowhead, or Great Polar Whale.
2. Baleen of the Right Whale of the North-western Coast.
3. Baleen of the Sulphurbottom Whale.
4. Baleen of the Humpback Whale.
5. Baleen of the California Gray Whale.
6. Baleen of the California Gray Whale, in a section, showing the manner of its being imbedded in the gum of the jaw.
7. Baleen of the California Gray Whale, in a section, showing how the fringes lie across.

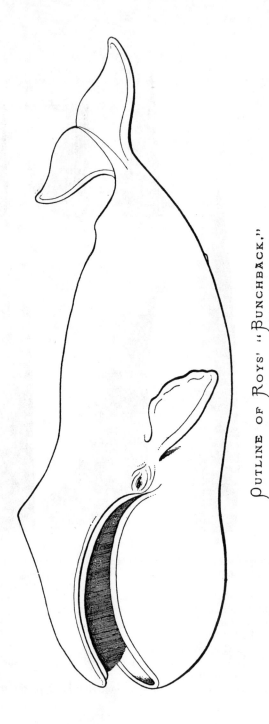

OUTLINE OF ROYS' "BUNCHBACK."

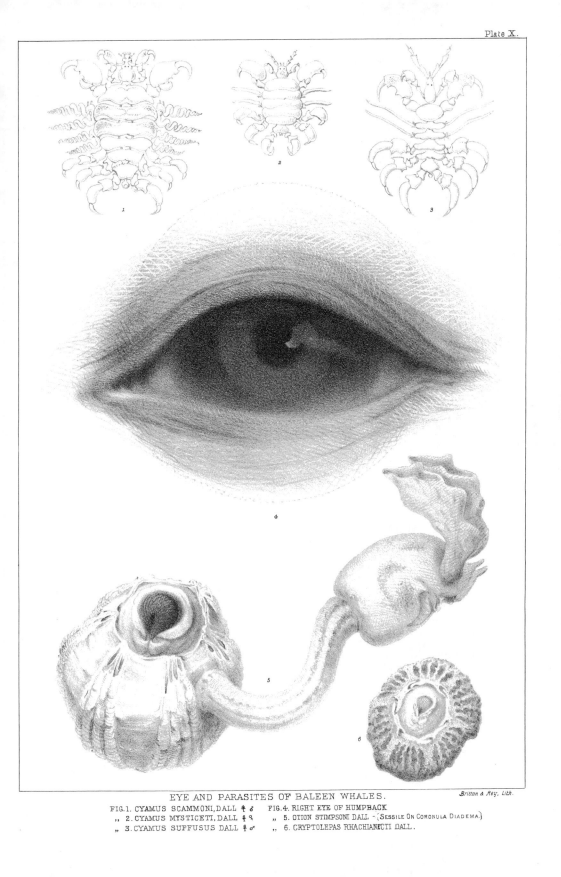

Plate X.

Britton & Rey, Lith.

EYE AND PARASITES OF BALEEN WHALES.

FIG. 1. CYAMUS SCAMMONI, DALL ♣ ♂   FIG. 4. RIGHT EYE OF HUMPBACK.
 ,, 2. CYAMUS MYSTICETI, DALL ♣ ♀   ,, 5. OTION STIMPSONI DALL - (SESSILE ON CORONULA DIADEMA.)
 ,, 3. CYAMUS SUFFUSUS DALL ♣ ♂   ,, 6. CRYPTOLEPAS RHACHIANECTI DALL.

more. The depth to which the animal descends when pursued is not accurately known, for as a general rule, it has been captured "on soundings" in the Arctic Ocean and Behring Sea, as well as in the Sea of Okhotsk, where the depths, in places, do not exceed a hundred fathoms, and from that to less than fifty. Sometimes they have been taken in very shallow water; yet this animal, when in deep water, has been known to "sound out" a line, in its descent and return, equal to a mile in length. But it must not be inferred that this was done by the perpendicular course of the whale, for it is found that the line runs out with great swiftness, when the creature begins its return to the surface. Repeated instances have occurred, where the animal, after being fastened to, would "sound;" and, if the bottom was soft, would there remain motionless for quite an incredible length of time for this species of Cetacea. In several cases, individuals have held their pursuers in momentary expectation of their rising, for an hour or more. One instance occurred with Captain Comstock, (a well-known whaling-master), in the Arctic Ocean, when, after fastening to a huge Bowhead, the creature descended to the muddy bottom, and there remained for an hour and twenty minutes. The day was unusually cold, and the men in the boats became much chilled during this period of inactivity; and to use the captain's own words, when giving an account of the incident, "The old sogger nearly played us a game of freeze-out." When the whale returned to the top of the water, it was literally covered with mud, and appeared much exhausted. A thrust of the lance prevented the animal from again "sounding," and after throwing up heavy volumes of thick blood, in its spoutings, it rolled over, "fin out," with but slight struggling.

The Arctic Bowhead is comparatively free from parasitic crustaceans, as well as barnacles. Occasionally, however, a species of *Cyamus*† is present about the head or fins. The range of this animal extends east and west from Nova Zembla to the coast of Eastern Siberia. Its northern limits remain undefined; and it is sel-

---

† We quote the following from Dall's paper on the *Cyamus mysticeti*. See illustration, plate x, fig. 2:

Cyamus mysticeti, n. sp. Body flattened, and subovate, segments adjacent. Branchiæ single, short, stout, pedunculated, a single papilliform appendage behind each. Head short and wide. First pair of legs very small. Hands all simple and smooth, fingers greatly recurved. Carpal articulation in the second pair of hands, half way between the proximal and distal ends of the hand. Pleon very minute. Color dark brownish yellow. Length 33 inches; breadth (of body) 16 inches. Two female specimens.

Habitat, on the northern Bowhead Whale, probably *Balæna mysticetus*, Linn., near Behring Strait.

This is the most compact of the three species, as well as the smallest. I find, in comparing large series of *C. Scammoni*, that a considerable variation in form obtains so far as regards comparative length and breadth, even in adult specimens, and these differences are greater than those observed, in the same characters, between the sexes.

dom seen in Behring Sea south of the fifty-fifth parallel, which is about the far-thest southern extent of the winter ice; while in the Sea of Okhotsk the southern limit of this species is about the latitude of 54°. In tracing the history of its capture, we can revert to the Dutch and Russian fishery about Spitzbergen anterior to 1615, and we find that, as years passed on, it was extended westward, on the Atlantic side, as far as the icy barriers in Davis Strait, and the adjacent waters connecting with the Frozen Ocean. Everything tends to prove that the *Balæna mysticetus* is truly an "ice-whale," for among the scattered floes, or about the borders of the ice-fields or barriers, is its home and feeding-ground. It is true that these animals are pursued in the open water during the summer months, but in no instance have we learned of their being captured south of where winter ice-fields are occasionally met with. In the Okhotsk Sea and its bays, these whales are found throughout the season, after the ice disappears; nevertheless, they remain around the floes until dispelled by the summer sun; and they are found in the same localities even after the surface of the water has again become congealed by the rigors of returning winter.

Right whales were pursued for several years on the North-western Coast, on the coast of Kamschatka, about the Kurile Islands, and in the Japan Sea, before Bowheads were known to exist in that part of the Arctic Ocean adjoining Behring Strait, or in the Okhotsk Sea. In the year 1848, Captain Roys, in the American bark *Superior*, was the first whaling-master to work his vessel through Behring Strait into the Arctic Ocean, and there found whales innumerable, some of which yielded two hundred and eighty barrels of oil.

The habits of the Bowhead are, in many respects, like those of the Humpback, being irregular in its movements, in its respirations, and in the periods of time either above or below the surface of the water. When going gently along, or lying quietly, it shows two portions of the body: the spout-holes, and a part of the back, on account of the high conical shape of the former, and the swell of the latter, which is about midway between the spout-holes and flukes.

The Bowheads of the Arctic may be classed as follows: 1st class—the largest whales, of a brown color; average yield of oil two hundred barrels. 2d class—smaller, color black; yield of oil one hundred barrels. 3d class—the smallest, color black; yield of oil seventy-five barrels.* Those belonging to the last named class are generally found among the broken floes the first of the season, and they have been known to break through ice, three inches in thickness, that had been

* We do not mean to convey the idea of *species* when mentioning classes, as all observers of our acquaintance agree that the difference in size and shade of color arises from difference in age.

formed over water between the floes. They do this by coming up under and striking it with the arched portion of their heads. Hence they have been called "ice-
breakers." In point of color, nearly all are found with more or less white on the
under side, especially about the throat and fins.

Whalers bound to the Arctic are generally at the "edge of the ice," which is
met with near lat. 60°, about the 1st of May. They then work their way northward as fast as the broken floes will permit, keeping as near shore as practicable,
in order to be on the best "whale-ground," and to avoid the ice. Many whales were
formerly taken off Karaginski Island, lat. 59°, on the coast of Kamschatka. Behring Strait is sufficiently clear of ice from the 1st to the 20th of July, for ships to
navigate with comparative safety. A large fleet collect, and grope their way through
ice and fog into the Arctic (as termed), and frequently reach the high latitude of
72° north. Occasionally an open season occurs, when whalemen hazard their ships
around Point Barrow. Captain Roys entered the ocean in the middle of July, and
left on the 28th of August, but at the present time ships remain until October.

The principal herding-places of the Bowheads in the Okhotsk were at the extremities of this great sheet of water, the most northern being the North-east Gulf
(Gulf of Ghijigha), the most southern, Tchantar Bay. The whales did not make
their appearance in North-east Gulf so soon as in the bay. Whalers endeavored,
as soon as possible, to get to the head of Tchantar Bay, where they found the
objects of pursuit in the intermediate water, between the ice and the shore, long
before the main body of the congealed mass was broken up, and before the
ships could get between the ice and the shore, even at high tide—the boats being
sent forward weeks previous to the ships. Soon after the ships' arrival, the whales
avoided their pursuers by going under the main body of ice, situated in the middle
of the bay, where they found breathing-holes among the floes. The boats cruised
about the edge of this barrier, watching for them to emerge from their covert,
which occasionally they did, when chase was instantly given. Frequently, in sailing
along this ice-field, you could hear distinctly the sound of whales blowing among
it, when no water was visible at the point whence the sound came. The first of
the season, before the ice broke up and disappeared, when there were "no whales
about," the question was frequently asked, "Where are the whales?" and as often
answered, "They are in the ice;" and, "When do you think they will come out?"
was answered by, "When the ice leaves." It has been established, beyond question,
that this species pass from the Atlantic to the Pacific, or rather, if we may be allowed the expression, from the Atlantic Arctic to the Pacific Arctic, by the north;
and, too, it is equally certain that numerous air-holes always exist in the ice that

covers the Arctic waters, even in the coldest latitudes. These fissures are caused by the rise and fall of the tides, and contraction and expansion of the ice. Storms acting upon the water hundreds of miles distant also have their influence in rending asunder the icy fetters of those frozen seas. It appears to us not improbable that the Bowhead, has a feeding and breeding ground in a polar sea. And as they have never been seen during the winter months in any other quarter of the globe, except as before mentioned, it would appear that they must either remain among the rough water and broken ice, at the southern edge of the winter barrier, or migrate to some remote sea unknown to man.

OKHOTSK SEA BOWHEADS.

The preceding remarks have been confined chiefly to the Bowheads of the Arctic, in the vicinity of Behring Strait, north and south. The Okhotsk Sea at one time equaled if not surpassed the Arctic as a productive whaling-ground. Our memorandum does not state with certainty what year Bowheads were first taken in the Okhotsk. It, however, was not earlier than 1847, nor later than 1849.* They were found to be easy of capture, and yielded a large amount of oil and bone. On making further explorations, the whales appeared in great numbers, and, from the peculiar shape of the head, the spout-holes terminating in a sort of cone, they were at that time called "steeple-tops." But a few years elapsed before a large fleet of ships was pursuing the animals throughout the whole extent of this vast inland water. Tchantar Bay, Taousk and Penjinsk gulfs soon became noted whaling-grounds, as well as several other points about the coasts. The whales of this sea, as far as known, are the same species as those of the Arctic; although in the bays is found, in addition, a very small whale called the "Poggy," which yields but little oil (twenty to twenty-five barrels).† Many whalemen are of the

* Captain J. H. Swift, who was cruising in Behring Sea about the year 1847, is quite positive that the French ship *Asia* was the first to take Bowheads in the Okhotsk (in 1847). Captain Roys, of Arctic notoriety (before spoken of), in a recent interview, seemed equally certain that the *Asia* was not the first to take Bowheads in that sea. He thinks none were taken till 1848 or 1849, and that the American ship *Huntsville*, Captain Freeman Smith, was about the first, if not the *first*, to take Bowheads in that region. In justice to both of these experienced and very intelligent whaling-masters, it is desired to make mention, that we are under much obligation to them for valuable data in relation to several species of Cetacea, more especially as they are regarded as very correct and close observers of the *habits of whales*.

† We are convinced that there are two varieties of Bowheads, which are found on the same ground. The variation from the animal above described is a bunch, or sort of hump, present on the top of the "small," which is situated about six feet forward of the flukes, extending

opinion that this is a different species. There is little doubt, however, of this being a young whale of the same species, as its blubber is close and fine, producing but little oil in proportion to size of body, as is the case with all calves or young whales of every description.*

BOWHEAD WHALING.

In the Arctic and about Behring Sea, the whaling is "done from the ship," as it is termed: *i. e.*, the vessels cruise, and the look-outs are kept aloft as usual, and when whales are seen, the boats are lowered and the pursuit is carried on in sight from the ships, unless obscured by fog. In the Okhotsk, much of the whaling is about the bays, particularly Tchantar Bay, and contiguous waters. The nature of the pursuit is such, in these localities, that the *modus operandi* is quite different. Vessels bound to Tchantar Bay endeavor to approach the land off Aian, if the

along the top of the back two to three feet, and in some individuals rises in the highest place about six inches. The sketch on page 56 will perhaps better represent the difference in shape, than a written description. Captain Roys says he has repeatedly taken them in the Arctic, as well as in the Okhotsk. They have been frequently taken in the North-east Gulf (Okhotsk Sea). Our personal observation was only on a dead one (in Tchantar Bay, 1862), and on that individual the protuberance was so slight, that it would not have been noticed unless our particular attention had been called to it. Captain Randolph, of the American whale-ship *South Boston* (1862), informed us at the time that nearly all the whales he had taken that season in the North-east Gulf were "Bunchbacks," and yielded a very large amount of bone in proportion to yield of oil. Captain Roys also mentioned that one season he took numbers of them, and to distinguish them from others they were then called "Bunchbacks." Several whaling-masters who have taken them observed that the spiracles are usually situated higher than upon those not having the bunch or hump on the "small."

* Captain Roys is of the opinion that the

Bowheads breed but slowly. Moreover, his observations of many years in northern whaling, goes to show that the young of this species suck but a short time compared with other cetaceous animals. This opinion seems quite conclusive when we compare the immense head and baleen of even the smallest individuals with those of other species, as though nature had provided them with immensely capacious mouths to gather insect food, instead of drawing sustenance from the dam. As to the linear proportions of the young of the Bowhead, in comparison with the dam, there is a diversity of opinion among those whalers who may be relied upon as men of excellent judgment, but a large majority maintain that the calf is not over one-fourth the length of the cow, and usually the proportions would be nearer one-fifth. From our own observations on the young of other whales, we have arrived at the conclusion that there is considerable diversity of size in the young of all whales when first born; and their rapid growth, until weaned, may doubtless be ascribed to the constant attention of the mother, in affordihg her offspring a bountiful supply of nutritious milk from her capacious and prolific udder.

ice will permit, which is generally sufficiently broken and scattered by the 20th of June; then, working along between the ice and the Siberian coast, to the southward, as far as practicable with the ships, they dispatch boats to follow along the shore and if possible to reach the head of Tchantar Bay, where whales in former years were to be found in very large numbers. These expeditions were always attended with excessive labor, and much exposure as well as risk to the crews. Frequent instances have been known of boats leaving the ships off Aian, then threading their way along the coast, between the masses of ice, or between the ice and shore, as the ebb or flood tides would permit, until they reached the head of Tchantar Bay. On reaching their destination, and finding whales plenty they immediately commenced whaling, and by the time the ships arrived, in several instances, whales enough had been taken to yield a thousand barrels of oil. The elapsed time from leaving the ship till again joining the vessel in the bay would vary from one to three weeks. Meanwhile, the crews lived in or around their boats, being afloat when making the passage or engaged in whaling; and when driven to the shore by the ice ·or by stormy weather, or resorting thither to cook their food, or sleep, the boats were hauled up and turned partially over for shelter, and tents were pitched with the sails. Fallen trees or drift-wood furnished abundance of fuel, and by a rousing fire all slept soundly when an opportunity offered; but the more abundant the whales, the less the chance of sleep for the whalemen in those high latitudes, where daylight lasts nearly through the twenty-four hours during summer.

TCHANTAR BAY WHALING.

Arrived on the ground, with the boats, all surplus provisions and outfits are quickly landed, and the chase begins. Frequent spouts in the air tell that the animals are all around. One of the number breaks the smooth surface of the water, between the land and ice, and is at once pursued; but perhaps, before the boat can reach within darting or shooting distance, the animal goes down. Then comes an impatient waiting for it to rise again. As the Bowhead is irregular in its course, when next seen it may be in another direction. Quickly the boat is headed for it, and before approaching near enough the whale goes down again. In this way the chase is frequently prolonged, sometimes abandoned, and other whales pursued; or, it may be that, when nearly within reach, the animal glides under a floe and thus evades its pursuers; or, if harpooned, it may run for the ice, and before being killed reaches it, and escapes with harpoons, lines, etc. If the pursuit proves successful, the captured whale is towed to the beach at high tide, and a scarf is cut along the body and through the blubber, to which one end of a tackle is hooked, the other end being made fast on shore; then as the tide falls the animal is literally skinned, the carcass rolling down the bank as the process goes on. The bone is extracted from the mouth as the animal is rolled over and presents the best opportunity. As soon as the blubber is taken off it is "rafted,"* and lies in the water until taken on board ship. The water being very cold, the blubber remains in its natural state for a long time, retaining the oil with but small loss. While the whaling is going on in this wise, the captain and the "ship-keepers" improve every opportunity to work the vessel near the whales. If there is an opening between the ice and the shore, she is at once worked through, either by towing, kedging, or sailing. On meeting an adverse wind or tide, the vessel is anchored with a very light anchor, so that if beset by ice unexpectedly, in the night or during the dense fogs which prevail, the vessel will drift with the floe, thereby avoiding the danger of being cut through. Heavy fogs prevail until the ice disappears, and the circumscribed clear water being crowded with vessels and boats, much care and maneuvring is exercised to prevent accident. These fogs frequently are so dense that no object can be seen much farther off than a ship's length; consequently, at such times cruising and whaling in the bays is full of excitement and anxiety. A ship may be lying quietly at anchor one moment, and the next be surrounded by a field of ice, or the close proximity of another vessel may be revealed by the splashing of the water under her bow. Then comes the blowing of horns, the ringing of bells, the firing of guns, or pounding on empty casks, to indicate the ship's position, in order to avoid collision.

Neither fog nor drifting ice, however, prevents the whalers from vigorously prosecuting their work. In thick weather, when neither the spout of the whale nor the animal itself can be seen, its hollow-sounding respiration may be heard a long distance. In such instances the boats approach as near as can be judged where the sound was heard, and if the animal is found and captured, it is at the risk of the boats coming in contact with passing ships, ice, or what not—and, too, not knowing with any degree of certainty what part of the bay they may be in, the first and main object being to capture the whale at all hazards. This being done, it is taken in tow by the boats, or is anchored. Then, if the crew can not discover their own ship, but meet with another, the custom is to go on board to eat or sleep, if necessary, and when recruited, or the fog lifts so as to give them a chance of finding their own vessel, they are supplied with provisions, if needed, until they

* Tied together with ropes in a sort of raft.

can reach her. If anchored, one boat always remains with the whale while the others go in search of the ship. As soon as found, the master, learning of the capture, makes every effort to work his vessel to the dead animal; or, if that can not be done, every favorable tide is improved to tow the whale to the ship, where it is cut in and tried out in the usual manner. As the season advances the ice disappears, leaving more room for cruising with the vessels, when the fleet becomes scattered, and the features of the whaling change. The boats are then kept more of the time on board, look-outs are stationed at the mast-heads, and the whaling is principally "done from the ship." Sometimes two boats are sent to look for whales in an adjoining bay. Meanwhile the nights have become longer. Then comes the "night-whaling." The phosphorescent light caused by the whale's movements in the water shows quite distinctly his whereabout, and, the Bowhead whales being easy of capture compared with other kinds, "night-whaling" is often successfully pursued.

We have spoken of the Bowheads as being comparatively easy of capture, but it must not be inferred that the pursuit is not often tedious or unsuccessful, nor is the attack made without risk of life or limb, as well as in other kinds of whaling. The Bowheads, compared with other species of whales that are pursued, are considered very shy and timid. After the ice leaves the bays, until the fall winds begin, much calm weather is experienced; and, although we have frequently seen large numbers of whales spouting among many boats scattered over the water, not a single animal could be approached near enough to "dart at" with the hand-harpoon, or to present a fair chance to shoot a bomb-lance into it, notwithstanding the boats were rigged with extra large sails, in order to take advantage of the light airs or winds that may prevail in midsummer. The use of oars or paddles would be quite sure to frighten the whales, and when there is not sufficient wind "to sail on to them" there is but little or no chance of "getting fast." After the "irons" are firmly planted in the animal, or, as we frequently hear whalemen say, "after the whale has been fastened to, good and solid," down the creature may go to the bottom, and there roll until either the "irons" are torn from its body or the line is wound about it, and the valuable prize may be lost. Cases have occurred where the animal, after being "fastened to," has darted to the depths beneath in such a state of trepidation as to unheedingly strike the rocks or sand, with so much force as to dislocate its head-bones, and cause instant death.

The breeding-places of the Bowheads seem to be a matter of conjecture among the most observing and experienced whaling-masters. The only place known has already been mentioned, in the vicinity of Tchantar Bay; and a difference of opinion exists as to whether the "Poggies" before mentioned are calves, or whether they are not a "scrag" species, which have a corresponding relation to the full-grown Bowheads that the "scrag" Right Whale has to the larger grades of that species. Admitting, however, that they are the young ones, their numbers are comparatively few to the numerous progeny that are supposed to be brought forth by the cows during each season. Another singular fact is, that no Bowheads of the Okhotsk Sea have ever been seen passing in or out the passages of the Kurile Islands, or from the Okhotsk to Behring Sea, or Arctic whales passing to the Okhotsk. It has been a mystery among the most experienced whalemen, as to where the Bowheads resorted to bring forth their young, or where the young remained until grown to a considerable degree of maturity; but within a few years, whales have been seen around Point Barrow with young calves, and that remote line of open water, inaccessible to ships, between the summer ice-border and the northern shores of the American continent, from Point Barrow to Banks' Land, doubtless affords ample herding and breeding places for the mysticetes and rorquals which are indigenous to those icy regions.

CHAPTER VI.

RIGHT WHALE OF THE NORTH-WESTERN COAST.

BALÆNA SIEBOLDII? *Gray.* (Plate xii.)

This great northern baleen whale, in its principal proportions, resembles the *Balæna mysticetus*. The latter, however, is destitute of the protuberance called the "bonnet," upon the anterior extremity of its beak - like upper jaw, which is a peculiarly prominent feature of the *Balæna Sieboldii*. The color of the Right Whale is generally black, yet there are many individuals with more or less white about the throat and pectorals, and sometimes they are pied all over. Its average adult length may be calculated at sixty feet—it rarely attains to seventy feet—and the two sexes vary but little in size. Its head is very nearly one-third the length of the whole animal, and the upper intermediate portion, or the part between the spiracles and "bonnet," has not that even spherical form, or the smooth and glossy surface present with the Bowhead, but is more or less ridgy crosswise. Both lips and head have wart-like bunches moderately developed, and in some cases the upper surface of the head and fins is infested with parasitical crustaceans. Its tongue yields oil like the mysticetus, but its baleen is shorter and of a coarser and less flexible nature. The average product of oil of the *Balæna Sieboldii* may be set down at one hundred and thirty barrels; yet there have been many individuals of this species, captured in early times, that yielded from two hundred to two hundred and eighty barrels. The amount of bone ranges from one thousand to fifteen hundred pounds. In former years, the Right Whales were found on the coast of Oregon, and occasionally in large numbers; but their chief resort was upon what is termed the "Kodiak Ground," the limits of which extended from Vancouver's Island north-westward to the Aleutian Chain, and from the coast westward to longitude 150°. In the southern portion of Behring Sea, also upon the coast of Kamschatka, and in the Okhotsk Sea, they congregated in large numbers. The few frequenting the coast of California are supposed to have been merely stragglers from their northern haunts. Some, indeed, have been taken (from February to April) as far south as the Bay of San Sebastian Viscaino, and about Cedros or Cerros Island, both places being near the parallel of 29° north latitude; while on the North-western Coast they are captured by the whalers from April to September, inclusive. The *Balæna Sieboldii* is regarded as being a distinct species from the southern Right Whale, and is universally known, by American whalemen, as the "North-west Whale." This distinguished baleen animal of the north, in its geographical distribution, ranges to the Japan Sea and Gulf of Tartary; but how many species or varieties are included under this name is not within our province to decide. Our observations, however, make it certain that there is a "scrag" Right Whale in the North Pacific which corresponds very nearly to that of the southern ocean, known under the technical name of *Balæna gibbosa?* and which yields a paltry amount of oil.

The time of gestation with the *Balæna Sieboldii* is not known, but is supposed to be nearly one year; the dam usually producing but one young at a birth, although, in some instances, twins have been observed. The new-born "sucker" is about one-fourth the length of the parent animal, which relative proportions are approximately uniform in all the whalebone whales which we have had the opportunity of examining. It has ever been a matter of mysterious conjecture with the most philosophical whalemen, where the northern Right Whales go to bring forth their young, and whither they migrate during the winter months. That they do not go into the southern hemisphere is well known, and it is equally certain that but a few stragglers, even, reach within a number of degrees of the northern tropic in their wanderings. The Esquimaux about the north-western shores of Behring Sea speak about the *Balæna mysticetus* resorting to the bays when the "small ice comes," and they look forward to that season as a time of plenty, and reap a kind of marine harvest by catching numbers of them, thus securing an abundant supply of food for winter store. It seems, therefore, beyond question, that the mysticetus is quite at home in that region at the beginning of the Arctic winter, and the immense numbers of Bowheads and Right Whales that would necessarily appear in the temperate latitudes, if they migrated southward, would be sure to arrest the attention of passing navigators, who frequently go far north, even in the winter season, to make their passages from China and Japan. Some have asserted that these animals probably congregate around the borders of the drifting or field ice, which joins the open water of the Pacific about the Kurile and Aleutian Islands. All agree that they do not pass the tropics and reach the southern ocean. The southern Right Whales resort to the bays in that region to bring forth their young, and formerly were sought for in the inland waters of those high southern latitudes, where many a ship quickly completed her cargo by bay-whaling. But no bay has yet been discovered north of the equator, in the Pacific, where the north-western Right Whales go to calve; and, as before mentioned, nothing is definitely known of their winter resort. The last seen of them in high latitudes, by whalemen, is on their return from the Arctic Ocean, when they are found in the vicinity of St. Paul's Island, Behring Sea, in the month of October, and these are usually very large. In view of all the facts we have been able to gather, there is little doubt that these gigantic animals, although of another group, have the same constitutional habits as the Sperm Whales, of bringing forth their young at any time or place that nature may require, without resorting to sheltered inland retreats. In the Okhotsk Sea, the Right Whale is found toward the northern borders in the early part of the season; later, the ships cruise in the southern quarter, about the Kurile Islands.

We find the habits of these animals, when roaming over the ocean, full of interest. They are often met with singly in their wanderings; at other times in pairs, or triplets, and scattered over the surface of the water as far as the eye can discern from the mast-head. Toward the last of the season they are seen in large numbers, crowded together. These herds are called "gams," and they are regarded by experienced whalemen as an indication that the whales will soon leave the ground. Their manner of respiration is to blow seven to nine times at a "rising," then "turning flukes" (elevating them six or eight feet out of the water), they go down and remain twelve or fifteen minutes. It is remarked, however, since these whales have been so generally pursued, that their action in this respect has somewhat changed. When frightened by the approach of a boat, they have a trick of hollowing the back, which causes the blubber to become slack, thus preventing the harpoon from penetrating. Many whales have been "missed," owing to the boat-steerer darting at this portion of the body. Having been chased every successive season for years, these animals have become very wild and difficult to get near to, especially in calm weather. The manner of propelling the boat at such times is by paddling, and when there is a breeze, by sailing, if practicable, using the oars only when it is not possible to use sails or paddles. Sometimes, during the first of the season, the animals are very wild and shy, and for days in succession the boats may be in hot pursuit without success.

Among right-whalemen there is a difference of opinion about "going on to a whale,"* whether it is best to get out of or into its wake, to avoid "gallying" it. As regards safety, some prefer to have a good breeze; then, setting all practicable

---

* "Going on to a whale" is a whaleman's term for getting near enough to dart the harpoon.

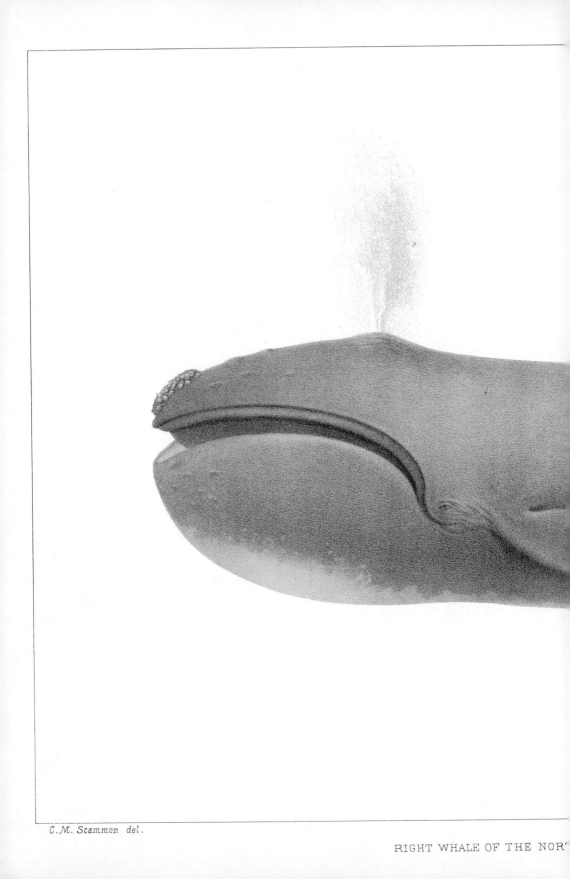

C.M. Scammon del.

RIGHT WHALE OF THE NOR

Plate XII.

ST COAST (BALÆNA SIEBOLDII ?, GRAY.)

sail, "run over" the animal to leeward, at the same time that the harpoon is thrown. The whale, after being struck, often runs to windward, thrashing its flukes in every direction. After going a short distance, it frequently stops, or "brings to," "sweeping" as it is said, "from eye to eye," and at the same time making a terrific noise called "bellowing;" this sound is compared to that of a mammoth bull, and adds much to the excitement of the chase and capture. Others will not stop until they are hamstrung, as it were, by "spading." The spading process is performed by hauling the boat near enough to cut the cords that connect the body and the flukes, either on the top or underneath, as the attitude of the animal may be. A large vein runs along the underside of the "small," terminating at the junction of the caudal fin, which, if cut, will give the creature its death-wound. The instrument used for cutting is called a "boat-spade," which may be compared to a very wide chisel, with a handle six or eight feet long. Sometimes the cords are so effectually severed that the flukes become entirely useless, and still the animal hardly slackens its speed perceptibly, showing, evidently, that its pectorals are powerful propellers. Another mode of stopping the whale is by throwing a number of harpoons, detached from the line, into the "small;" a kind of torture that would, if the bleeding victim could speak, cause it to entreat its tormentors to put an end to its misery. Yet not unfrequently, after being lacerated on every side, it holds its human pursuers at bay by assuming a vertical attitude, with flukes uppermost, which are dashed in every direction with a furious swoop, hurling sheets of spray and foaming water into the boats, and often nearly filling them. But when once "brought to" it will remain quite stationary for a few minutes, or roll from side to side, giving the officer of the boat a good opportunity to shoot a bomb-lance, or use the hand-lance with good effect, which soon dispatches it. Sometimes, however, one of these huge animals, in spite of the bomb-guns, harpoons, and all the whaling-gear combined, will, after being "fastened to," make the best of its way to windward with the boat, taking it so far from the ship as to oblige the men to cut the line and give up the chase. Of late, Greener's gun has been used to some extent in its capture. But before harpoon or bomb guns came into general use, the whalemen of the North-western Coast made such havoc among these colossal animals (which were regarded as the most vicious of their kind), as to have nearly extirpated them, or driven them to some unknown feeding-ground.

CHAPTER VII.

THE SULPHURBOTTOM WHALE.

Sibbaldius-sulfureus, *Cope*. (Plate xiii.)

The largest whale found upon the coast, and the largest known, is the Sulphurbottom. Never having had an opportunity of obtaining an accurate measurement of its proportions, we can only state them approximately. Length, sixty to one hundred feet.* Its body is comparatively more slender than that of the California Gray. Its pectorals are proportionately small, even in comparison with the Sperm Whale's, which in size and shape they very nearly resemble, being short and rounded at their extremities. Its caudal fin bears about the same proportion to the body as does that of the Finback, while its dorsal is much smaller and nearer the posterior extremity. Its head is more elongated than the Finner's; its baleen is broader at the base, the color being a jet black in several specimens we have examined, while others were of a bluish hue. The Sulphurbottom, in its food and manner of feeding, is like the other whales of its genus. It is a true rorqual, with folds beneath the anterior portion of the animal, which are a series of fine longitudinal furrows. The color of this, the greatest whale of the ocean, is somewhat lighter than the dull black of the lesser rorquals, and in some instances it is a very light brown, approaching to white; but underneath it is of a yellowish cast or sulphur color, whence the name "Sulphurbottom" is supposed to have arisen. Its coating of blubber is unevenly distributed over its body, massively covering the top of the head, but more thinly disseminated over the main portion of the trunk; while the posterior extremity, between the trunk and caudal fin, is more heavily infolded with the oily covering than all the rest.

* Captain Roys, of whaling notoriety, has kindly furnished me with the following memoranda of a Sulphurbottom whale, which was taken by him while he was in command of the barque *Iceland:*

Length, 95 feet; girth, 39 feet; length of jaw-bone, 21 feet; length of longest baleen, 4 feet; yield of baleen, 800 pounds; yield of oil, 110 barrels; weight of the whole animal, by calculation, 147 tons.

A Sulphurbottom whale is found in the Atlantic as well as in the Pacific. The Pacific species occurs at all seasons on the coasts of the Californias. During the months from May to September, inclusive, they are often found in large numbers close in with the shore, at times playing about ships at anchor in the open roadsteads, near islands, or capes, but as a general rule they do not approach vessels with the same boldness that the Finback does, although we have observed them following in a vessel's wake for several leagues. *

*Through the kindness of Doctor J. D. B. Stillman, of San Francisco, Cal., we give the following extracts from his journal of a voyage between that port and Realejo, Central America, in 1850, in relation to a Sulphurbottom which followed the ship *Plymouth*, in which the Doctor sailed, for twenty-four consecutive days. The account is as follows: "*November* 13*th:* We are witnesses of a very remarkable exhibition of the social disposition of the whale. A week ago to-day, we passed several, and during the afternoon it was discovered that one of them continued to follow us, and was becoming more familiar, keeping under the ship and only coming out to breathe. A great deal of uneasiness was felt, lest in his careless gambols he might unship our rudder, or do us some other damage. It was said that bilge-water would drive him off, and the pumps were started, but to no purpose. At length more violent means were resorted to; volley after volley of rifle-shots were fired into him, billets of wood, bottles, etc., were thrown upon his head with such force as to separate the integument; to all of which he paid not the slightest attention, and he still continued to swim under us, keeping our exact rate of speed, whether in calm or storm, and rising to blow almost into the cabin windows. He seems determined to stay with us until he can find better company. His length is about eighty feet; his tail measures about twelve feet across; and in the calm, as we look down into the transparent water, we see him in all his huge proportions. *November* 29*th:* The bark *Kirkwood* hove in sight, and bore down to speak us. When off a mile or two to leeward, our whale left us and went to her, but returned soon after. He showed great restlessness last night; and to-day, whenever we stood off on the outward tack, he kept close below us, and rose just under our quarter, and most commonly to windward, to blow. But whenever we stood toward the land he invariably hung back and showed discontent. This afternoon he left us. It is now twenty-four days since he attached himself to us, and during that time he has followed us as faithfully as a dog an emigrant's wagon. At first we abused him in every way that our ingenuity could devise to drive him off, lest he might do us some mischief; but, save some scratches he received from our ship's coppering, and numerous sloughing sores, caused by the balls that had been fired into him, no damage was received by either of us from his close companionship, though our white paint was badly stained by the impurity of his breath. We long since ceased our efforts to annoy him, and had become attached to him as to a dog. We had named him 'Blowhard,' and even fancied, as we called him, that he came closer under our quarter, when I felt like patting his glabrous sides, and saying: 'Good old fellow.' As the water grew shoaler he left us, with regret unfeigned on our part, and apparently so on his. This story of the whale is so remarkable, that were there not so many witnesses, I would not venture to tell it, lest I be accused of exaggeration. There were a number of experienced whalemen among our passengers, who said the animal was a 'Sulphurbottom.'"

It is rarely that the Sulphurbottom "bolts" or "breaches," yet, when engaged in this sprightly act, the animal presents itself in that degree of magnificence which is commensurate with its inordinate activity and immense proportions. The Sulphurbottom is considered the swiftest whale afloat, and for this reason is but seldom pursued, and still more rarely taken. Captain Thomas, of the bark *Lagrange*, in 1857, off San Bartolome Bay, caught one by first shooting a bomb-lance into a vital part; and although the whale ran a long distance before "turning up," the pursuers were enabled to keep trace of it among the large number around by its "spouting blood." When the animal was nearly exhausted, the boats approached near enough to "get fast," and the capture was completed. This individual yielded about ninety barrels of oil, and measured eighty-five feet in length. The schooner *Page*, of San Francisco, succeeded in taking several Sulphurbottom whales, near Ascension Island, the capture being made with the bomb-gun and lance. Notwithstanding that a large proportion of these whales sunk as soon as dead, the whalemen were enabled to save them, the water being of moderate depth, in consequence of which they rose to the surface before decomposition was far advanced. The size of those taken by the *Page* compared favorably with the one taken by the *Lagrange*.

Several days' trial were made in the brig *Boston*, in 1858, off Cerros Island, to capture these animals. It was in the month of July, and the sea, as far as the eye could discern, was marked with their huge forms and towering spouts. Ten were "bombed" by the best shooters, who affirmed that they "chose their chance," but as soon as the gun was discharged the whale would disappear, and that was the last trace seen of it, except a patch of foam, sometimes mixed with blood. On the last day of pursuit, toward evening, another vessel appeared in the offing, and approached within a mile or less, when the last trial bomb was fired, and the men in the boats looked eagerly to the rising of the wounded whale, but in vain. A signal was made from the approaching ship that they had seen the animal, as it "broke water" close to their vessel, when it soon rolled over dead, and sunk. The swiftness of the Sulphurbottom under water, as demonstrated at this time, appeared to make pursuit impracticable. Doubtless, several of those fired at received mortal wounds, or were killed outright, but their propensity to sink, and also to "run under water," baffled the skill of the whalers to secure them.

On a second voyage of the *Page*, six of these immense creatures were taken by the bomb-gun and lance, off the port of San Quentin, Lower California, where the moderate depth of water was favorable for the pursuit. Large numbers of them were found on this ground, where they had been attracted by the swarms of sar-

C. M. Scammon, del.

THE SULPHURBOTT

Plate XIII.

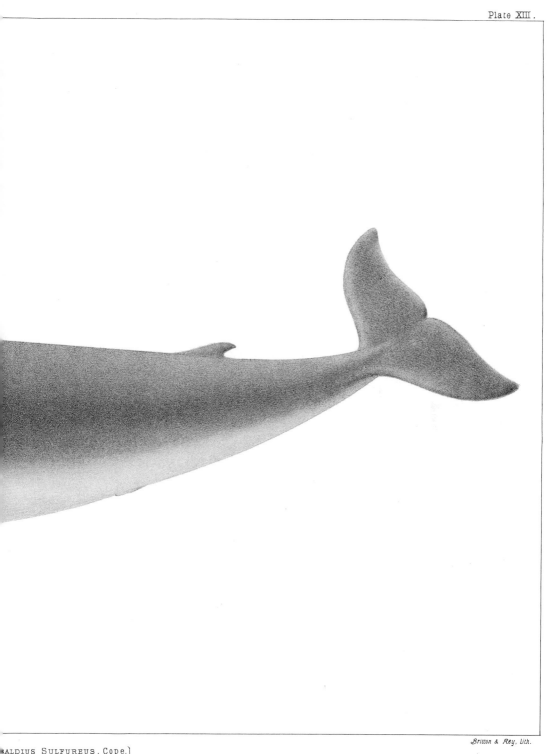

(ALDIUS SULFUREUS, Cope.)

Britton & Rey, lith.

dines and prawns with which the waters were enlivened; and the whales, when in a state of lassitude from excessive feeding, would frequently remain nearly motionless ten to twenty minutes at a time, thus giving the whaleman an excellent opportunity to shoot his bomb-lance into a vital part, causing almost instant death.

The enormous size of the *Sibbaldius sulfureus* is not easily to be comprehended by the reader, when compared even with the lesser rorquals, or the mysticetus, or the Cachalot. In 1862, the whalemen at Monterey, California, killed one of these immense animals which measured ninety-two feet in length. Before they could tow it to the station, it became "blasted;"* but on arrival, no effort was spared to strip the colossal prize of its fatty covering. Accordingly, their "purchases" were applied to roll the swollen creature over upon the beach; but in so doing, the capstan, which was firmly placed on the bank, and had lifted many a large whale, was torn up and the "falls" were parted. Finally the whalemen gave up the undertaking, and only cut off the fat that could be reached above water. In contemplating this, the greatest whale of the ocean, one can but admire its prominent characteristics, which are its enormous yet symmetrical proportions, and the muscular development which enables it to excel in velocity all its congeners, while its whole bearing indicates its superiority to all the other Cetaceans. It glides over the surface of the ocean, occasionally displaying its entire length. When it respires, the volume of its vaporous breath ascends to a height which reveals at once, to the observer, the presence of that leviathan of the deep, whose capture baffles the practical skill of the most experienced whalers. When "rounding" to descend to the depths below, it throws its ponderous flukes high above the waves, with a swoop that is well in keeping with its matchless strength and vigor.

* "Blasted" is a whaler's term for being much swollen.

CHAPTER VIII.

THE SPERM WHALE.

PHYSETER MACROCEPHALUS, *Linn.* (Plate xiv.)

This, the largest of the toothed Cetaceans, is known to English and American whalemen as the Sperm Whale, to the Germans as the Pottfisch, and to the French as the Cachalot. It widely differs from all others of its order, both in figure and habits. The fully matured animal equals, if it does not exceed, the Bowhead, or Great Polar Whale, in magnitude and in commercial value. The adult female, however, is only about one-third or one-fourth the size of the largest male. She is likewise more slender in form, and has an effeminate appearance. The time of gestation is supposed to be ten months, and she seldom produces more than one young at a birth—never more than two—and these are brought forth at any time or place that nature may demand. The new-born cub is about one-fourth the length of the mother. It obtains its nourishment from two teats, situated one on each side of the vaginal opening. In giving suck, it is said the female reclines on her side, when the calf seizes the teat in the corner of its mouth, thereby giving the milk-food immediate passage to its throat. The length of time that the young follow the dam is not known.

The largest males measure from eighty to eighty-four feet. The ponderous head is nearly one-third of the whole bulk of the animal, and over one quarter of its length. The opening of the mouth is about five-sixths the length of the head; the lower jaw, from the expansion of the condyles, contracts abruptly to a narrow symphysis, and is studded on each side with twenty-two or twenty-four strong, sharp, and conical teeth, fitting to the furrow, or cavity, in the upper jaw, which is destitute of, or contains only rudimentary teeth. The tongue, which is usually of a whitish color, "is not capable of much protrusion." The throat, however, is large, and is said to be capacious enough to receive the body of a man. The eyes are placed a little above and behind the angle of the mouth. A few inches behind the eyes are the openings of the ears, which are not over one-fourth of an inch in diameter. Above, and at the junction of the head with the body proper, is a swell called the "bunch of the neck." About midway between this protuberance and the caudal fin, is another and larger bunch, called the "hump;" then follows a succession of smaller processes along the "small," toward the posterior extremity, which is termed the "ridge." The pectorals, or side-fins, are placed a little behind and below the eyes, and in size rarely exceed six feet in length and three feet in width. The caudal fin is about six feet in breadth, and measures twelve to fifteen feet between the extremities, or about one-sixth the length of the whole animal. Unlike the baleen whales, the Cachalot has but one spiracle, or spout-hole, which is placed near the anterior and upper extremity of the head, a little upon the left side; its external form is nearly like the letter S. This fissure in the adult is ten or twelve inches in length. The color of the Sperm Whale is generally black, or blackish-brown above; a little lighter upon the sides and below, except on the breast, where it becomes a silvery gray. Some examples, however, are piebald. The oldest males are frequently well-marked with gray about the nose, or upper portion of the head, and when this is indicated, they are called "gray-headed."

In the young Sperm Whales, as in the young of all Cetaceans, the black-skin, or epidermis, is much heavier than in the adults, it being half an inch in thickness, or thereabouts, while it does not exceed a quarter of an inch on the old whale. As age advances, the skin becomes more furrowed. Beneath the black-skin lies the rich coating of fat, or blubber, which yields the valuable oil of commerce. The head produces nearly one-third of all the oil obtained. Next to and above the bone of the upper jaw (which is termed the "coach," or "sleigh"), is a huge mass of cartilaginous, elastic, tough fat, which is called the "junk." Above the "junk," on the right side of the head, is a large cavity, or sack, termed the "case," which contains oil in its naturally fluid state, together with the granulated substance known as "spermaceti." From this capacious hidden receptacle, as much as fifteen barrels of "head-matter" has been obtained. The "ambergris," which is so highly prized, is nothing more than the retained anal concretion of a diseased whale. On the left side of the cranium, above the "junk," is the breathing-passage, or nostril, of the whale. This, with the "case," is protected by a thick, tough, elastic substance called the "head-skin," which is proof against the harpoon.

We now come to the general habits of this gigantic animal, relative to its movements in the vast oceans of the globe. Among the whole order of Cetaceans, there is no other which respires with the same regularity as the Cachalot. When emerging to the surface, the first portion of the animal seen is the region of the hump; then it raises its head, and respires slowly for the space of about three seconds, sending forth, diagonally, a volume of whitish vapor, like an escape of steam; this is called the "spout," which, in ordinary weather, may be seen from the mast-head at a distance of three to five miles. In respiring at its leisure, the animal sometimes makes no headway through the water; at other times it moves quietly along at the rate of about two or three miles an hour; or, if "making a passage" from one feeding-ground to another, it may accelerate its velocity. When in progressive motion (after "blowing"), hardly an instant is required for inspiration, when the animal dips its head a little, and momentarily disappears; then it rises again to blow, as before, each respiration being made with great regularity. The number of its spoutings, when in a state of quietude, depends on the size of the animal: varying in the adult females and the younger of both sexes from the oldest and largest males. The same may be said as to the period of time it remains upon or beneath the surface of the ocean. With the largest bulls, the time occupied in performing one expiration and one inspiration is from ten to twelve seconds, and the animal will generally blow from sixty to seventy-five times at a "rising," remaining upon the surface of the sea about twelve minutes. As soon as "his spoutings are out," he pitches head-foremost downward; then "rounding out," turns his flukes high in the air, and, when gaining nearly a perpendicular attitude, descends to a great depth, and there remains from fifty minutes to an hour and a quarter.

While on a cruise in the bark *Rio Grande* around the Galapagos Islands, in 1853, a large Cachalot was captured, which yielded eighty-five barrels of oil. This animal was pursued from eleven o'clock A.M. to four P.M., during which time it spouted, or "blowed," very regularly, fifty-five times at each "rising" while on the surface, and when he descended was not visible again for fifty-five minutes. All this time he was going a direct course at the rate of three miles an hour. The smaller and younger whales, however, are not so regular in their time of remaining upon or below the surface of the water, and, as before mentioned, they spout a less number of times. They generally continue above the water one-fourth or one-fifth of the time consumed by the others, making thirty or forty spouts while up, and remaining under water twenty to thirty minutes. But when the Cachalot becomes alarmed, or is sporting in the ocean, its actions are widely different. If frightened, it has the faculty of instantly sinking, although nearly in a horizontal attitude (as the sailors say, "he can let go and go down in a jiffy"). When merely startled, it will frequently assume a perpendicular position, with the greater portion of its head above water, to look and listen; or, when lying on the surface, it will sweep

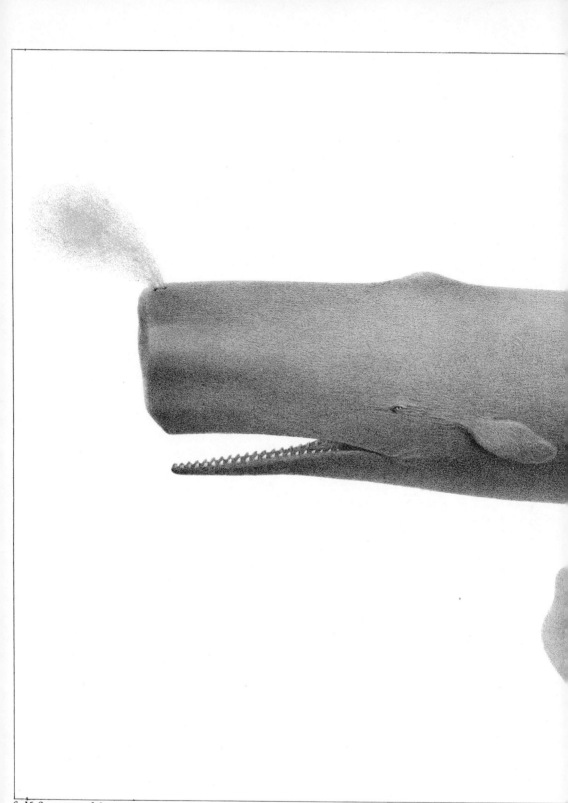

C.M.Scammon del.

SPERM WHA

Plate XIV.

(SETER MACROCEPHALUS. LINN.)

around from side to side with its flukes, to ascertain whether there is any object within reach. At other times, when at play, it will elevate its flukes high in the air, then strike them down with great force, which raises the water into spray and foam about it; this is termed "lobtailing." Oftentimes it descends a few fathoms beneath the waves; then, giving a powerful shoot nearly out of the water at an angle of forty-five degrees or less, falls on its side, or leaps bodily out in a semi-lateral attitude, coming down with a heavy splash, producing a pyramid of foam which may be seen from the mast-head, on a clear day, at least ten miles, and is of great advantage to the whaler in searching for his prey. These singular antics of the Sperm Whale are said to be performed in order to rid itself of a troublesome parasite, known among the whale-fishers by the name of "Suckfish;" but the animal is seldom infested with the parasitic crustacea which are indigenous to the rorquals and Right Whales.

Many have the impression that the Sperm Whale is found but rarely out of the limits of tropical or temperate waters, but we know that the largest Cachalots have often been taken as far south as 56° of latitude, both in the Pacific and Atlantic, and as far north in the Pacific as Cape Ommany, which is in latitude 56° 12'.

We may further add, that it is one of the few species of the larger Cetaceans which inhabit every ocean not bound with icy fetters during the rigors of winter, and although great numbers are found in the cold latitudes, they also delight to bask in the equatorial waters under a tropical sun.* It is true, however, that but few are met with in the far northern limits of the Atlantic or the Pacific, compared with the number which inhabit the great range of the southern seas. This, however, may be easily accounted for, as there is no northern thoroughfare by which these whales of passage can migrate to or from the Atlantic or Pacific, while at the south they are continually passing to and fro from ocean to ocean throughout the year.

The Cachalots are gregarious, and they are often seen in schools numbering from fifteen or twenty up to hundreds. The oldest and largest males, however, for the greater part of the year roam alone; yet there is no lack of instances where

---

* We are aware that eminent naturalists have averred that there are several species of the Sperm Whale, on the ground of their geographical distribution; and it is not within our province, nor is it our intention, to enter into any discussion relative to the question, further than to substantiate, as far as our observations go, what that excellent and practical observer, Beale, has maintained: that there is but one species of Sperm Whale "in the ocean roving," and as far as any variety is visible, it exists in every zone and hemisphere.

these monsters have been found in herds by themselves; but the usual assemblage is made up of males and females—the latter with their young. At such times two or three large bulls are in attendance, which lead the van. The female is quite solicitous for her playful offspring, and when pursued, the mother may be seen assisting it to escape by partially supporting it on one of her pectorals. The females likewise manifest much sympathy for each other, for when one of their number is attacked by the boats, they all "bring to," and remain, usually for some time, with their dying companion; by this means a number of whales are often captured from the same school. The young bulls periodically go in large herds; but, unlike the females, if one of their band is harpooned, its cowardly associates make off in great trepidation. When individually attacked, however, it makes a desperate struggle for life, and often escapes after a hard contest. Nevertheless, it is not an unusual occurrence for the oldest males to be taken with but little effort on the part of the whaler. After being struck, the animal will oftentimes lie for a few moments on the water as if paralyzed, which affords the active man of the lance opportunity to dart his weapon effectually, and complete the capture. It is said that the Cachalots are endowed with the faculty of communicating with each other in times of danger, when miles (and some observers say leagues) distant. If this be true, the mode of communication rests instinctively within their own contracted brains.

It has been the general belief that the Sperm Whale is excessively timid; but, if this is its general character, there are many exceptions among the larger males, for when attacked, they have in repeated instances turned upon their pursuers, in the most defiant manner, and their own disfigured jaws—which are their principal weapons of defense—prove that they either engage in desperate contentions with their kind, or with some unknown leviathan inhabiting the deep. Moreover, it is, we believe, a well-established fact, that ships have been sunk by the deliberate assaults of vicious, gray-headed, old Cachalots.*

* The accounts of the destruction of the American ships *Essex* and *Ann Alexander* having been published in various works pertaining to the whale-fishery, we will only briefly note them here. The *Essex* was destroyed in the South Pacific by an infuriated whale, in the year 1820, under the following circumstances. The animal was seen ahead approaching the ship at the rate of about three miles an hour, and the ship running at about the same speed, when the huge creature gave the vessel such a shock, as he came in collision, as to spring a serious leak. Then he went down and re-appeared a ship's length or two off, lashing the water into foam. After going a distance of about one-fourth of a mile, and recovering from the concussion, he returned with great velocity, and, striking the ship's bow, staved it in, which caused the vessel to sink ten minutes after. The *Ann Alexander* was sunk by a Sperm Whale on the coast of Peru, in 1851,

It is the opinion of many experienced and observing whalemen—with whom we concur—that the Sperm Whale has a higher organization than any other species of Cetacea. Its massive form is composed of bone, flesh, and sinew, which has a finer texture than that of the rorqual or the mysticetus. The latter subsists on minute crustacea and small fishes, skimmed as it were from the surface of the seas and inland waters. The mouth of the Cachalot is armed with teeth of ivory, finely set, for the purpose of prehension, and the animal is endowed with the power of descending to the remote caverns of the ocean in search of its prey, and remaining there a length of time unequaled by any of its congeners. The principal food of the Sperm Whale is familiarly named by the whalers "squid;" which includes one or more species of cuttle-fishes (cephalopods). The animal's manner of pursuing its prey is not definitely known; but several high authorities maintain, that after descending to the desired depth it drops its lower jaw nearly to a right angle with the body, thereby exhibiting its polished white teeth, which attract within its reach the swimming food, while the creature moves along through the ocean's depths; the moment its prey comes in contact with the expanded jaw,

under like circumstances to those of the *Essex.* In 1807, the ship *Union,* of Nantucket, was wrecked "by striking," says the narrator, "on a Sperm Whale." It was in the night, and the question is, whether the ship struck the animal accidentally, or whether the whale made an attack? Other disasters to vessels might be cited, which were occasioned by the attack of, or by coming in collision with, the colossal Cachalot. The ferocity of many old male Sperm Whales has been fully demonstrated by their attacks on boats, and to distinguish them from other whales they are often called "eating whales." According to the author of the *Arctic Whalemen,* an instance occurred with the boats of the ship *Citizen,* upon the Atlantic Ocean, in the year 1851, where, after the whale had been struck, lanced, and while spouting blood, he made an attack and demolished one boat, after which he gave chase to another; but the fifth boat, having been dispatched from the ship to the rescue, came up just in time to divert the animal's attention, when he turned upon it. By the dexterous management of the captain, who had come

in this relief boat, the whale was foiled in his attempt to destroy it. In the midst of the fray, the bleeding animal caught sight of the ship, which was approaching the boats under flowing sails. Instantly the enraged animal made for the vessel; while those on board, being advised of the fact, put the craft before the wind to avoid him. On the whale came; but, owing to the increased speed of the ship, he shot past the stern a few feet, and soon after went into his "flurry," and "turned up," when he was taken to the vessel, "cut in," and "tried out," yielding seventy-five barrels of oil. Another instance, somewhat similar, occurred to the boats of the bark *Athalia.* In this case, however, the whale, after staving a boat, not being content with the manner in which he destroyed it, went deliberately at the remains and chewed them into fine pieces. These instances are only mentioned as among scores of other similar cases which might be given. And we have no doubt but that many vessels which have sailed from port, and never been heard of after, have suffered wreck through Cachalots.

it is instantly crushed, and a portion or all is swallowed. This hypothesis of the mode in which the animal feeds may be correct. As to the nature of its food there is no question, for it is well known that the cephalopods are its main dependence; yet occasionally the codfish, albicore, and bonito, are laid under contribution.* But the true and natural way in which this great rover of the hidden

---

*Relative to the food of the Sperm Whale, we quote the following from Beale's interesting account of the *Sepia octopus*:

NATURE OF THE SPERM WHALE'S FOOD.

The *Sepia octopus*, or "sea squid," as it is termed by whalers, sometimes reaches an enormous size. Mr. Henry Baker, F. R. S., in the *Philosophical Transactions* for 1758, p. 777, after having given an interesting description of a specimen, sent to him for examination by the Earl of Macclesfield, states that it can, by spreading its arms abroad like a net, so fetter and entangle the prey they inclose, when they are drawn together, as to render it incapable of exerting its strength; for, however feeble these branches or arms may be singly, their power united becomes surprising; and we are assured — Nature is so kind to these animals — that if in their struggles any of their arms are broken off, after some time they will grow again, of which a specimen at the British Museum is an undoubted proof, for a little new arm is there seen sprouting forth in the room of a large one which had been lost. "It is evident," he continues, "from what has been said, that the sea polypus, or octopus, must be terrible to the inhabitants of the waters, in proportion to its size (Pliny mentions one, whose arms were thirty feet in length), for the close embraces of its arms and adhesion of its suckers must render the efforts of its prey ineffectual, either for escape or resistance, unless it be endowed with an extraordinary degree of strength." Of the smaller genera of these animals, the reader will find some interesting details, by referring to the appendix to *Tuckey's Voyage to the Congo*, vol. iii. There is also an account of a newly discovered cephalopod, in the appendix to Sir J. Ross' *Voyage to the Antarctic Regions*. A gigantic cephalopod was discovered by Drs. Bank and Solander, in Capt. Cook's first voyage, floating dead upon the sea, surrounded by birds, who were feeding on its

remains. From the parts of this specimen which are still preserved in the Hunterian Collection, and which have always strongly excited the attention of naturalists, it must have measured at least six feet from the end of the tail to the end of the tentacles. But this last we must imagine a mere pigmy, when we consider the enormous dimensions of the one spoken of by Dr. Schewediawer, in the *Philosophical Transactions*, vol. lxxiii, p. 226, whose tentaculum, or limb, measured twenty-seven feet in length; but let the doctor speak for himself. "One of the gentlemen," says he, "who was so kind as to communicate to me his observations on this subject (ambergris), also, ten years ago, hooked a Spermaceti Whale that had in its mouth a tentaculum of the *Sepia octopoda* nearly twenty-seven feet long! This did not appear its whole length, for one end was corroded by digestion, so that in its natural state it may have been a great deal longer. When we consider," says the Doctor, "the enormous bulk of the tentaculum here spoken of, we shall cease to wonder at the common saying of the fishermen, that the cuttle-fish is the largest fish of the ocean." In Todd's *Cyclopædia of Anatomy*, p. 529, treating of *Cephalopoda*, in an admirable paper by Mr. Owen, it states, that "the natives of the Polynesian Islands, who dive for shell-fish, have a well-founded dread and abhorrence of these formidable cephalopods, and one can not feel surprised that their fears should have perhaps exaggerated their dimensions and destructive attributes." The same learned writer, after having beautifully described another animal of the same order, observes: "Let the reader picture to himself the projecting margin of the horny hook developed into a long-curved, sharp-pointed claw, and these weapons clustered at the expanded terminations of the tentacles and arranged in a double alternate series, along the whole internal surface of the eight muscular feet, and he will have some idea of the formidable nature of the

C. M. Scammon del.

Britton & Rey Lith.

SPERM WHALE IN SEARCH OF FOOD.

depths seeks and devours its animal food, is still tinged with mystery. In past years it was commonly believed that the Cachalot's home was in the fathomless depths of the ocean, and that only a few stragglers were occasionally met with near coast waters of moderate depth. But we find abundant proof, and from our own observations, too, that they are met with and have been captured in waters

carniverous *Onychoteuthis.*" This species of cephalopod is thus armed with those kind of teeth at the termination of the tentacles, in order to secure the "agile, slippery, and mucus-clad fishes" on which it preys. And there is an instance recorded in Sir Grenville Temple's *Excursions in the Mediterranean*, by which we perceive that these terrible creatures sometimes prey upon men! "In those shallow waters," says Sir Grenville, "are caught great quantities of fish, by forming curved lines or palisades some way out to sea with palm branches, by which the fish that come up with the high water are detained when it recedes. The horrid polypus, which is, however, greedily eaten, abounds, and some are of enormous size. They prove at times highly dangerous to bathers. An instance of this occurred two years since. A Sardinian captain, bathing at Jerbeh, felt one of his feet in the grasp of one of these animals; on this, with his other foot he tried to disengage himself, but this limb was immediately seized by another of the monster's arms; he then, with his hands, endeavored to free himself, but these, also, in succession, were firmly grasped by the polypus, and the poor man was shortly after found drowned, with all his limbs strongly bound together by the arms and legs of the fish; and it was extraordinary, that where this happened, the water was scarcely four feet in depth!" Other species of these surprising animals, as the *Calamaries*, or "flying squid," as they are termed by the whalers, have the power of propelling themselves through the atmosphere. "There is good reason for believing," says Mr. Owen, "that some of the small, slender-bodied, subulate species of this genus are enabled to strike the water with such force as to raise themselves above the surface, and dart, like the flying-fish, for a short distance through the air." I have myself seen, very frequently, while in the North and South Pacific, tens of thousands of these animals dart simultaneously out of the water, when pursued

by the albicore, or dolphins, and propel themselves head first, in a horizontal direction, for eighty or a hundred yards, assisting their progression, probably, by a rotatory or screwing motion of their arms or tentacles, and which they have the power of thus moving with a singular velocity. This species, also, as well as the large *Onychoteuthis*, I am led to believe, often serves the Sperm Whale with food. I have seen, on several occasions, very large limbs of the latter species of squid floating on the surface of the ocean, appearing as if bitten off by some animal—most probably by the Sperm Whale—for when these remains have been seen, I have always looked most anxiously for these animals, and have never been disappointed in seeing them within a few hours afterward. One day, being on the coast of Peru, off Paita Head, as it is called, which lies in about the latitude of five degrees south, I was startled by seeing a remarkable-looking animal raising itself quickly to the surface of the sea by means of a number of very long flexible arms, which it threw about with great precision, in a rotatory or screwing-like motion, so that it appeared to move itself through the water with the same kind of action that an eight-pronged corkscrew would maintain in passing through any penetrable substance. This curious animal, however, quickly disappeared; and it was not until I explained its appearance to the captain, that I knew it to be a squid. On another occasion, while upon the Bonin Islands, searching for shells upon the rocks, which had just been left by the receding sea-tide, I was much astonished at seeing at my feet a most extraordinary looking animal, crawling toward the surf, which had only just left it. I had never seen one like it under such circumstances before; it therefore appeared the more remarkable. It was creeping on its eight legs, which, from their soft and flexible nature, bent considerably under the weight of its body, so that it was lifted by the efforts of its tentacula only, a small distance where the soundings were not over one hundred and fifty fathoms, and frequently not over sixty or seventy: for example, off San Bartolome Bay, coast of California; also about Point Abraojos on the same coast, and near Asuncion Island, which is midway between the first named points.

It has been previously remarked that the elongated under jaw of the Sperm Whale, with its bristling teeth, is its chief arm of attack and defense, and the agile manner in which the animal uses it when upon or near the surface is quite sur-

from the rocks. It appeared much alarmed at seeing me, and made every effort to escape, while I was not much in the humor to endeavor to capture so ugly a customer, whose appearance excited a feeling of disgust, not unmixed with fear. I, however, endeavored to prevent its career, by pressing on one of its legs with my foot; but although I made use of considerable force for that purpose, its strength was so great that it several times quickly liberated its member, in spite of all the efforts I could employ in this way on wet slippery rocks. I now laid hold of one of the tentacles with my hand, and held it firmly, so that the limb appeared as if it would be torn asunder by our united strength. I soon gave it a powerful jerk, wishing to. disengage it from the rocks to which it clung so forcibly by its suckers, which it effectually resisted; but a moment after, the apparently enraged animal lifted its head, with its large eyes projecting from the middle of its body, and letting go its hold of the rocks, suddenly sprung upon my arm, which I had previously bared to my shoulder, for the purpose of thrusting it into holes in the rocks to discover shells, and clung with its suckers to it with great power, endeavoring to get its beak, which I could now see between the roots of its arms, in a position to bite. A sensation of horror pervaded my whole frame when I found this monstrous animal had affixed itself so firmly upon my arm. Its cold slimy grasp was extremely sickening, and I immediately called aloud to the captain, who was also searching for shells at some distance, to come and release me from my disgusting assailant. He quickly arrived, and taking me down to the boat, during which time I was employed in keeping the beak away from my hand, quickly released me by destroying my tormentor with the boat-knife, when I disengaged it by portions at a time. This animal must have meas-

ured across its expanded arms about four feet, while its body was not larger than a large clenched hand. It was that species of *Sepia* which is called by whalers 'rock squid.'" Thus are these remarkable creatures, from the different adaptation of their tentacles, and slight modifications of their bodies, capable of sailing, flying, swimming, and creeping on shore; while their senses, if we may judge from the elaborate mechanism of their organs, must possess corresponding acuteness and perfection. But for the description of the anatomy of these animals, I must refer the reader to Mr. Owen's masterly paper on that subject, in *Todd's Cyclopædia of Anatomy*, above quoted.

Having thus quoted from Doctor Beale on the nature of the Sperm Whale's food, we will add another quotation, relative to ambergris:

Though ambergris, even during the sixteenth century, appeared to be much valued as a mercantile commodity by the English, it is curious we knew nothing of its source, and very little of the use which was made of it in other countries. In the year 1672, we find the Honorable Robert Boyle claiming the honor of having discovered its source, from a manuscript which was found on board a Dutch East-Indiaman, which had fallen into our hands by the chance of war. This precious document stated, that "ambergreese is not the scum or excrement of the whale, but issues out of the root of a tree, which tree, howsoever it stands on the land, alwaies shoots forth its roots towards the sea, seeking the warmth of it, thereby to deliver the fattest gum that comes out of it, which tree otherwise by its copious fatness might be burnt and destroyed: wherever that fat gum is shot into the sea, it is so tough that it is not easily broken from the root, unless its own weight and prising. It opens and shuts its mouth, if need be, in a twinkling, or it throws the lower jaw down to nearly a right angle with its body, or sways it from side to side at an astonishing angle, when we take into consideration the distance between the condyles at their junction with the animal's head. When the creature essays to grasp a large object on the water, it instantly rolls over to bite; but does it necessarily follow that the same attitude must be maintained when obtaining its food in the abyss beneath? Or is it impossible that this protruding jaw of massive bone and

the working of the warm sea doth it, and so it floats on the sea; there was found by a souldier seven-eighths of a pound, and by the chief two pieces, weighing five pounds. If you plant the trees where the stream sets to the shore, then the stream will cast it up to great advantage! March 1st, 1672, in Batavia." (*Phil. Trans.*, vol. viii, p. 6133.)

But notwithstanding the above statement, Doctor Thomas Brown, in his work published a few years afterward (1686), in his description of a Sperm Whale which was thrown on the coast of Norfolk, states that "in vain it was to rake for ambergriese in the paunch of this leviathan, as Greenland discoverers, and attests of experience dictate, that they sometimes swallow great lumps thereof in the sea—insufferable fetor denying that inquiry; and yet, if as Paracelsus encourageth, ordure makes the best musk, and from the most feted substances may be drawn the most odoriferous essences, all that had not Vespasian's nose might boldly swear there was a substance for such extractions;" which proves that the doctor still suspected that the ambergris was found in the Sperm Whale, although it was found by this animal floating in the sea, and swallowed by it in "great lumps!" But it was reserved for Doctor Boylston, of Boston, to enlighten mankind upon this important subject, and he therefore claims the discovery of its source in the following manner: "The most learned part of mankind are still at loss about many things even in medical use, and particularly were so in what is called ambergris, until our whale fishermen of Nantucket, in New England, some three or four years past made the discovery. Their account to me is this: Cutting up a spermaceti bull-whale, they found, accidentally, in him, about twenty pounds weight, more or less, of that drug; after which, they and other such fishermen became very curious in searching

all such whales they killed, and it has been since found in lesser quantities in several male whales of that kind, and in no other, and that scarcely in one of a hundred of them. They add further, that it is contained in a cyst or bag, without any inlet or outlet to it, and that they have sometimes found the bag empty and yet entire; the bag is nowhere to be found but near the *genital parts* of the fish. The ambergris is when first taken out moist, and of an exceedingly strong and offensive smell." This letter was written to the Royal Society in 1724. (*Phil. Trans.*, vol. xxxiii, p. 193.)

In the same year, however, we have another letter from America, written to the Royal Society by the Honorable Paul Dudley, F. R. S., who, after telling us that the old Sperm Whales carry their young ones "on the flukes of their tails, who with their fins clasp about the small, and hold themselves on," also says, "one of our country doctors tells me that the tooth of this fish (Sperm Whale) shaved or powdered, and so infused in liquor, equals the hartshorn, and has been used in the small-pox, and given to lying-in women in case of sickness, with success!—the quantity is as much as will lie upon an English shilling." Farther on in the same letter he states, "I meddle not here with the *precious* ambergris found in this whale, because I design to close the whole with that discovery." And here is his conclusion: "But truth," says he, "is the daughter of time; it is now at length found out, that *occultum naturæ* is an animal production, and bred in the body of the Spermaceti Whale. I doubt not," he continues, "but in process of time some further particulars may be procured with respect to ambergris, and I shall be proud to transmit them; in the mean time I hope the Society will accept of this first essay, and allow my poor country the honor of discovering, or at least ascertaining, the origin ivory is not sometimes employed to remove the kraken from its slimy bed? Be that as it may, however, it is our belief that all Cetaceans occasionally resort to the bottom of the ocean, sea, or inland waters, as well as rise to the surface to breathe and display their various attitudes. We also regard the Cachalot as able to descend to a greater depth and remain there a longer time than any other whale; and that it evinces, in its characteristic movements or evolutions, a superiority over all other cetaceous animals that have come under our observation.

and nature of ambergris." (*Phil. Trans.*, vol. xxxiii.)

In a paper which was read before the Royal Society by Doctor Schwediawer, in 1783, respecting the medicinal properties of ambergris, he remarks, that "if we wish to see any medical effects from this substance, we must certainly not expect them from two or three grains, but give rather as many scruples of it for a dose; though even then I should not expect much from it, as I have taken of pure unadulterated ambergris in powder thirty grains at once, without observing the *least* sensible effect from it. A sailor, however, who had the curiosity to try the effects of some recent ambergris upon himself, took half an ounce of it melted upon the fire, and found it a good purgative, which proves that it is not quite inert." (*Phil. Trans.*, vol. lxxii, p. 226.)

In 1791, the attention of the government was drawn to this subject, in order to discover if it could be more frequently found. When Captain Coffin was examined at the bar of the House of Commons on the subject, he stated that he had lately brought home three hundred and sixty-two ounces, troy, of this costly substance, which he had found in the anus of a female Sperm Whale that he had captured off the coast of Guinea, and which he stated was very bony and sickly. At the time he brought this quantity to England, the ambergris was selling for twenty-five shillings an ounce, but he stated he sold his for nineteen shillings and sixpence per ounce, to a broker, who exported it to Turkey, Germany, and France, among the natives of which it appears to have been long celebrated for its aphrodisiacal properties. "The use of ambergris," says Brande, "in Europe is now nearly confined to perfumery, though it has formerly been used in medicine by many eminent physicians. In Asia and part of Africa, ambergris is not only used as a medicine and perfume, but considerable use is also made of it in cooking, by adding it to several dishes as a spice. A great quantity of it is also constantly bought by the pilgrims who travel to Mecca, probably to offer it there, and make use of it in fumigations, in the same manner as frankincense is used in Catholic countries. The Turks make use of it as an aphrodisiac. Our perfumers add it to scented pastiles, candles, balls, bottles, gloves, and hair powder; and its essence is mixed with pomatum for the face and hands, either alone or united with musk, though its smell is to some persons extremely offensive. Ambergris may be known to be genuine by its fragrant scent when a hot needle or pin is thrust into it, and its melting like fat of a uniform consistence, whereas the counterfeit will not yield such a smell, nor prove of such a fat texture. One thing, however, is very remarkable, that a resemblance to the smell of this drug, which is the most agreeable of all the perfumes, should be produced by a preparation of one of the most odious of all substances. Mr. Homberg found that a vessel in which he had made a long digestion of human fæces, acquired a very strong and perfect smell of ambergris, insomuch that any one would have thought that a great quantity of essence of ambergris had been made in it; the perfume was so strong and offensive that the vessel had to be removed from the laboratory! (*Brande's Manual of Chemistry*, p. 594.) Ambergris appears to be nothing but the hardened fæces of the Spermaceti Whale, which is pretty well proved from its being mixed so intimately with the refuse of its food (the squids' beaks). Mr. Enderby has a fine specimen of this substance, six or seven inches long, which bears very evident marks of having been molded by the lower portion of the rectum of the whale.

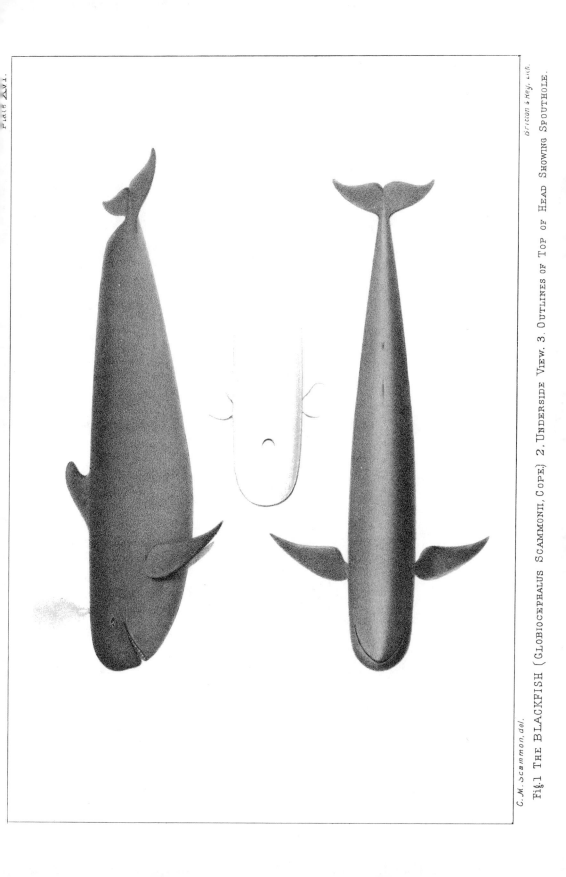

Plate XVI.

C. M. Scammon, del.

Britton & Rey, Lith.

Fig.1 THE BLACKFISH (GLOBIOCEPHALUS SCAMMONI, COPE,) 2. UNDERSIDE VIEW. 3. OUTLINES OF TOP OF HEAD SHOWING SPOUTHOLE.

CHAPTER IX.

THE DOLPHINS.

In addition to the whalebone whales, and the Cachalot, which have been described in the preceding pages as frequenting the North-western Coast of North America, many species of Dolphins are also found. Those coming under our observation are known as the Blackfish (*Globiocephalus Scammonii*), the Killer (*Orca*), the Whitefish (*Beluga*), the Bay Porpoise (*Phocæna vomerina*), the Striped or Common Porpoise (*Lagenorhynchus obliquidens*), Baird's Dolphin (*Delphinus Bairdii*), the Right Whale Porpoise (*Leucorhamphus borealis*), the Cowfish (*Tursiops Gillii*), the White-headed or Mottled Grampus (*Grampus Stearnsii*), the Bottle-nosed Grampus, the Panama Grampus, the Puget Sound Grampus, the San Diego Bay Grampus, the Square-headed Grampus, the Brown-sided Dolphin of Santa Barbara Channel, and the Narwhal (*Monodon monoceros*). All these species are covered with a coating of fat, or blubber, varying in thickness from one-half of one inch to four inches.

SECTION I.—THE BLACKFISH.

Globiocephalus Scammonii, *Cope.* (Plate xvi.)

Blackfish are generally found wherever Sperm Whales resort, but in many instances they congregate in much larger numbers, and range nearer the coast, than the regular feeding-grounds of the latter. Although subsisting almost entirely upon the same kind of food—the "squid," or *octopus*—still, at times, when schools of them visit bays or lagoons, they prey upon the small fish swarming in those shallow waters. In Magdalena Bay we have seen them in moderate numbers, appearing as much at home miles from sea as the Common Porpoise or the Cowfish. They collect in schools, from ten or twenty up to hundreds, and when going along upon the surface of the sea, there is less of the rising and falling movement than with the Porpoise, and their spoutings, before "going down," are irregular, both in number and time between respirations. If the animal is moving quickly, much of the head and body is exposed. Whalemen call this going "eye out." In low latitudes, during perfectly calm weather, it is not unfrequent to find a herd of them lying quite still, huddled together promiscuously, making no spout and seemingly taking a rest. Sometimes they assume a perpendicular attitude, with a portion of the head above the water, as does the Sperm Whale.

On the 14th of December, 1862, on the coast of Lower California, in latitude 31°, land ten miles distant, a school of Blackfish was "raised." The boats were immediately lowered and gave chase, and three fish were taken. The largest one was a male, and measured accurately as follows:

	Ft.	In.
Length	15	6
Depth of body	3	6
Circumference of body	8	9
Expansion of flukes	3	6
Breadth of flukes	1	0
From end of head to spout-holes	1	6
From end of head to eye	1	4
From end of head to dorsal fin	4	6
Length of pectorals	2	10
Erom end of head to pectorals	2	9
Extreme width of pectorals	1	0
Opening of mouth	1	4
Length of dorsal fin, along the back	2	0
Extreme length of dorsal fin, upper edge	2	4
Extreme width of dorsal fin	1	0
From notch of flukes to vent	5	0
From notch of flukes to genital slit	6	0
Extension of spout-hole across the head	0	4

The breadth of the body, just forward of the side fins, was twenty-two inches. The number of teeth on each side of the upper jaw varies from ten to twelve; in the lower one from eight to ten; the protruding parts being from one-fourth to three-fourths of an inch in length. The outline of the head shows its shape laterally, and also the spiracle, which is of half-circle shape, opening downward as the spout ascends, and closing upward when it has escaped. The jet does not rise above two or three feet, and its direction is at a right angle with the body, when not affected by the wind. From all that we can learn of their breeding habits, they bring forth their young at any time, or in any part of the ocean, as necessity may require. Off the Gulf of Dulce, coast of Guatemala, in February, 1853, a fœtus a yard long was taken from an adult measuring thirteen feet. In the same school from which this female was captured, we saw several young ones, apparently about the same size as the above mentioned fœtus, and doubtless this animal, had it not been disturbed, would have soon played in its native element. The Blackfish is taken for its oil, which is, however, much inferior to that of the Sperm Whale. The yield is small compared to its size, it being from ten to twenty-five feet in length, and producing from ten gallons to ten barrels of oil. The blubber varies in thickness from one to four inches; its color is nearly white. The flesh of the Blackfish is like coarse beef, and after being exposed to the air for a few days, then properly cooked, is by no means unsavory food, and is often used by whalemen as a substitute for the fresh meat of land animals. The same may be said of the different species of porpoises. Formerly, Blackfish were found in large numbers on the coast of Lower California, particularly about Cape St. Lucas, and up the Gulf of California; but probably, from the same cause as made mention of concerning Sperm Whales, these grounds are now seldom frequented by them.

Although the Blackfish is taken for its oil, it is not an object of pursuit by the whaler, like the balænas and the Cachalot. Sperm whalers do not lower their boats for Blackfish, when on Sperm Whale ground, unless the day is far spent, or there is little prospect of "seeing whales." The northern or polar whale-ships pay but little attention to them, except, perhaps, when passing the time "between seasons," cruising within or about the tropics. Occasionally a small vessel is fitted out for hunting the Blackfish and Sperm Whale, carrying a proportionately limited crew, thereby making the capture of this species of the smaller Cetaceans profitable. When a ship's boat is lowered for Blackfish, the chase begins as for other whales; although many masters have their boats all ready, and run just ahead of, or into a "school," with the ship, before lowering, by which means the animals are so frightened or "gallied," that they "bring to," or move slowly in all directions, giving the boats, which are instantly lowered, a good chance to "get fast." The harpoon frequently kills the fish; if not, a few darts with the hand-lance dispatch it. As soon as it is dead, the prize almost invariably sinks; and if the ship is close at hand, it is towed to the vessel at once; but if a considerable distance away, it is either made fast to the "loggerhead" at the stern of the boat, or a buoy is tied to it and left, to be afterward recovered; the boats still continuing the chase. In this way quite a number are captured from one school. The favorite resorts of Blackfish, along the coasts of North and South America, on the Pacific side, are off Guatemala, Equador, and Peru; yet their geographical distribution is occasionally extended to high northern and southern latitudes.

SECTION II.—THE ORCA, OR KILLER.

(Plate xvii.)

The Orca—a cetaceous animal, commonly known as the "Killer"—is one of the largest members of the Dolphin family. The length of the adult males may average twenty feet, and the females fifteen feet. The body is covered with a coating of white fat, or blubber, yielding a pure, transparent oil. An extremely prominent dorsal fin, placed about two-fifths of the length of the body from the end of the animal's beak, distinguishes it from all other Dolphins. In the largest species (*Orca rectipinna*) this prominent upper limb stands quite erect, reaches the height of six feet, is dagger-shaped, and frequently turns over sideways at its extremity. In the animals of more moderate size, the fin is broader at the base, less in altitude, and is slightly curved backward, while upon others it is shorter still, and broader in proportion at its junction with the back, and is more falcated.

The *Orea rectipinna*, so far as we have observed, is more slender in its proportions, and is less marked with white or light spots than the others. It is usually, in color, jet-black above and lighter below; yet many of inferior size are most beautifully variegated, the colors being almost as vividly contrasted as in the stripes of the tiger of India. Some individuals have a clear white spot, of oblong shape, just behind the eyes, and a maroon band, of nearly crescent shape, adorning the back, behind the dorsal fin, which it more than half encircles. In others, the marks behind the eyes and dorsal are of a yellowish tinge, and usually, when this occurs, a small patch of light shade borders the semicircled exterior spout-hole. The dorsal band is somewhat pointed at the centre of its convex side, and, when looked at from behind the creature, nearly assumes the form of a heart. The under side of the pectorals and the caudal fin are generally of a milk-white or cream color, bordered by a darker shade; and the nether portion of the body is white, with patches of the same color edging the sides. The head of the Orca is more pointed than that of the Blackfish (*Globiocephalus*), but less so than that of the Bay Porpoise (*Phocæna vomerina*), to which it bears a resemblance. Its eyes appear sharp and prominent in comparison with other Cetaceans, which in a modified degree indicates the animal's disposition. Its mouth is armed with strong, sharp, conical teeth, which interlock, like those of the smaller Dolphins,* and its whole

---

* In the head-bones of two specimens which we examined, the number of teeth on each of the upper and lower jaws, were, respectively, twelve and thirteen.

C.M. Scammon, del.

Lith. Britton & Rey

ORCAS OR KILLERS.
1. ORCA RECTIPINNA, COPE. 2. ORCA ATER, COPE. 3. ORCA (ATER, VAR?)

formation combines great strength with agility—if we exclude its towering upper fin, with which the largest are furnished. This protuberance, on account of its extraordinary elongation, imparts to the animal a very unwieldy appearance; and, as it vibrates in the air when the creature rolls to and fro, or makes its sidelong bounds over the waves, appears to be a great burden, and to require much effort on the part of the wearer to keep right-side up. Its two spiracles, which unite in one at their orifice, situated above and behind the eyes, are covered by a cartilaginous valve, which opens and closes on its posterior side at every respiration. The vapor or spout emitted is "low and bushy," like that of the Blackfish. The animal is entirely free from parasites, its scarf-skin being beautifully smooth and glossy.

Until recently, we were under the impression that the short-finned Killers upon the western coast of North America were inhabitants especially of the frosty regions; but recent observations prove that they frequent both the high and low latitudes. Indeed, they may be regarded as marine beasts, that roam over every ocean; entering bays and lagoons, where they spread terror and death among the mammoth balænas and the smaller species of dolphins, as well as pursuing the seal and walrus, devouring, in their marauding expeditions up swift rivers, numberless salmon or other large fishes that may come in their way. It is well known that there are several species of Orcas, incident to their wide geographical distribution, which includes every zone and hemisphere; but those we have described are, to our knowledge, found in the waters of the Pacific, in the Okhotsk and Behring seas, and through Behring Strait into the Arctic Ocean. The habits of the Killers exhibit a boldness and cunning peculiar to their carnivorous propensities. At times they are seen in schools, undulating over the waves—two, three, six, or eight abreast—and, with the long, pointed fins above their arched backs, together with their varied marks and colors, they present a pleasing and somewhat military aspect. But generally they go in small squads—less than a dozen—alternately showing themselves upon the surface of the water, or gliding just below, when nothing will be visible but their projecting dorsals; or they disport themselves by rolling, tumbling, and leaping nearly out of water, or cutting various antics with their flukes. At such times, they usually move rapidly over the surface of the sea, and soon disappear in the distance.

Both the high and low finned Orcas are found in the same school; yet we have occasionally seen those with the lowest and most falcated fins exclusively by themselves. Three or four of these voracious animals do not hesitate to grapple with the largest baleen whales; and it is surprising to see those leviathans of the deep so completely paralyzed by the presence of their natural, although diminutive, enemies.   Frequently the terrified animal—comparatively of enormous size and superior strength—evinces no effort to escape, but lies in a helpless condition, or makes but little resistance to the assaults of its merciless destroyers. The attack of these wolves of the ocean upon their gigantic prey may be likened, in some respects, to a pack of hounds holding the stricken deer at bay.   They cluster about the animal's head, some of their number breaching over it, while others seize it by the lips and haul the bleeding monster under water; and when captured, should the mouth be open, they eat out its tongue.   We saw an attack made by three Killers upon a cow whale and her calf, in a lagoon on the coast of Lower California, in the spring of 1858.   The whale was of the California Gray species, and her young was grown to three times the bulk of the largest Killers engaged in the contest, which lasted for an hour or more.   They made alternate assaults upon the old whale and her offspring, finally killing the latter, which sunk to the bottom, where the water was five fathoms deep.   During the struggle, the mother became nearly exhausted, having received several deep wounds about the throat and lips.   As soon as their prize had settled to the bottom, the three Orcas descended, bringing up large pieces of flesh in their mouths, which they devoured after coming to the surface.   While gorging themselves in this wise, the old whale made her escape, leaving a track of gory water behind.   Instances have been known, on the North-western Coast, where a band of Orcas laid siege to whales that had been killed by whalemen, and which were being towed to the ship, in so determined a manner, that, although they were frequently lanced and cut with boat-spades, they took the dead animals from their human captors, and hauled them under water, out of sight.   The Orca, however, does not always live on such gigantic food; and we incline to the belief that it is but rarely these *carnivora* of the sea attack the larger Cetaceans, but chiefly prey with great rapacity upon their young.   The Orca finds its principal food in the smaller species of its own genus, together with seals and the larger fishes, as before mentioned.   For several seasons we had watched them about the seal islands of California, and came to the conclusion that they subsisted on the fish found around the edge of the kelp which fringes the shores.   By chance, however, we were so fortunate as to take one at the island of Asuncion, and, on examining its stomach, found it filled with young seals.   At the time it was the height of the sealing season, and the beaches around the island were lined with innumerable herds; and, although there were sealing parties about the rocks from early dawn until dusk of evening, no one ever saw these savage animals molest the seals that were continually swimming about in very large numbers.   Subsequently, we had an excellent opportunity to observe them at the island of Santa Barbara, in animated pursuit of their prey. Only four of the short-finned Killers were in the band. It was a windy day, and a heavy surf beat high and spitefully against the rugged points and bluffs, which seemed to arouse both aquatic beast and bird into most unusual activity, for the gulls and eagles hovered and swooped above, watching to snatch any morsel that might drop from the murderous jaws of the pursuing Killers, who were making the circuit of the island, apparently intent on surprising any unwary seal that might be play-ing in the surge; and upon meeting with one they would instantly dive after it, or bound over the projecting rocky points in hot chase, as the surf swept over them; but as soon as they discovered our boat, they dashed their flukes in the air, and made off for the open sea. Even the largest male sea-lions endeavor to avoid the Orcas; for whenever the latter are about the rocks and islets, those howling monsters seek a safe retreat on shore.

That the Orca is possessed of great swiftness is undeniable, when we realize the fact that the numerous species of Dolphins are overtaken by them and literally swallowed alive. Eschricht, in his interesting memoir on *The Northern Species of Orca*, states that it had been known to swallow four porpoises in succession, and that thirteen of these animals, together with fourteen seals, had been found in the maw of one of these greedy creatures, which measured only sixteen feet in length. The fierce character of the Orca, and the nature of its food, necessarily bring its haunts at or near the coast; and the sounds and bays, which teem with every variety of marine animal life, are much more frequently its feeding-grounds than the periodical abodes of the balænas, which are farther out in the ocean. The vast net-work of inland waters on the western coasts of British Columbia and Alaska is a favorite resort for the Orcas throughout the year. In the fishing season we have met with them in the vicinity of the Nass River, exhibiting their variously figured dorsals and colored marks, as they made their gambols or shot out upon the surface in the chase. During the early spring months the *oulacon* literally choke the mouth of the Nass, and here the seals and porpoises congregate to fill them-selves to repletion from the myriads of those minnows; and, in turn, in obedience to the laws of nature, the Orcas are found here, pursuing and devouring the ene-mies of the "small fish."* They will sometimes be seen peering above the surface with a seal in their bristling jaws, shaking and crushing their victims, and swallowing them apparently with great gusto; or, should no other game present itself, porpoises and salmon may fill their empty maws, or a Humpback or Finback whale may furnish them an ample repast.

* "Small fish" is the common name for *oulacon*.

Farther northward, among the icy regions, the Orca delights in the pursuit and destruction of the White Whale, or Beluga, and in robbing the walrus of its helpless offspring. The tender flesh and rich fat of the White Whale furnishes them with choice food; but, as if not content with satiating their own greed, they seem to aim at the total destruction of their victims, by tearing the whole animal into fragments. Captain Holböll writes of the Greenland Killers as follows: "In the year 1827, I was myself an eye-witness of a great slaughter performed by these rapacious animals. A shoal of belugas had been pursued by these blood-thirsty animals into a bay in the neighborhood of Godhaven, and were there literally torn to pieces by them. Many more of the belugas were killed than eaten; so that the Greenlanders, besides their own booty, got a good share of that of the Killers."

It has been said that even the full-grown walrus, although armed with long tusks, is fearful of the Orca; but in relation to that, we have nothing in our notes of observation to substantiate the assertion. It is true, the ponderous creatures will crawl upon the ice with their little ones to avoid the Killers, but it seems to be only for the purpose of keeping their cherished young beyond the reach of their enemies. Sometimes the cub will mount upon its mother's back for refuge, clinging to it with instinctive solicitude. When in this apparently safe position, the rapacious Orca quickly dives, and, coming up under the parent animal, with a spiteful thud throws the young one from the dam's back into the water, when in a twinkling it is seized, and, with one crush, devoured by its adversary.

Compared with other species of the Dolphin tribe, the Orcas are not numerous, neither do they usually go in large shoals or schools, like the porpoises and Blackfish. Their mating season, or time of gestation, is a matter of conjecture; probably in this respect they are similar to the Sperm Whale. We have met with them in midwinter, in the Gulf of Georgia and along the northern coast as far as Sitka, as often as at other seasons of the year, showing plainly that they are not confined to warm latitudes, nor migrate from the colder climates during the rigorous months. They are seldom captured by civilized whalemen, as their varied and irregular movements make the pursuit difficult, and the product of oil is even less than that of the Blackfish, in proportion to their size. The Makah Indians, however, occasionally pursue and take them about Cape Flattery, in Washington Territory, as they consider their flesh and fat more luxurious food than the larger balænas, or rorquals. But, in whatever quarter of the world the Orcas are found, they seem always intent upon seeking something to destroy or devour.

SECTION III.—THE WHITEFISH, OR WHITE WHALE.

BELUGA, n. sp.? (Plate xviii, fig. 1.)

Our opportunities for observing this beautiful member of the Dolphin family have been as follows: In the Okhotsk Sea, along the coast of Eastern Siberia, during the summer of 1862; in Plover Bay (latitude 64° 26' north, longitude 173° 07' west), September, 1865; in the same place and month, 1866; and in Norton Sound, September, 1865.

Before entering into the details of its habits and the mode of its capture, we will briefly describe this inhabitant of the far north, as we have seen it, westward of the Pacific American shores; and whose haunts also include the Arctic Ocean, and the seas of Okhotsk and Behring. The animal, which is distinguished by its uniform light soft hue at maturity, resembles the *Leucorhamphus Peronii* in its symmetry of upper contour. Its linear dimensions average perhaps thirteen feet; although the largest ones considerably exceed that length. Its head is small; its prominent forehead being protected with a fatty cushion similar to that of the Blackfish. Its short oval and fleshy pectorals are placed more than one-fifth of the length of the whole animal from its muzzle, giving that portion between the head proper and the fins the appearance of a true neck. The opening of its mouth is contracted and curved upward. Both upper and lower jaws are furnished with sharp conical teeth, and among the adults the dental formulæ may be put down at $\frac{11}{8} \frac{11}{8}$, or eleven teeth on each side of the upper jaw, and eight on each side of the lower one. Its diminutive eyes are but little larger than those of the Common Porpoise. The minute orifices which constitute the ears are covered with a sort of scale that quite conceals them. Its spiracle is situated a little behind the angle of the eye. The body is full, and tapers rather abruptly toward the caudal fin, which is broad, and in expansion exceeds that of the Orca, or *Globiocephalus*. The color of the adults is invariably a yellowish white, while the very young are of a leaden or bluish black; but as these mature they become mottled, and eventually assume the soft cream-like tinge of the parent animal. This species of the Dolphin family is very rapid in its motions, and its swiftness is brought into full play when in pursuit of the numerous varieties of fishes along the sea shores or up the rapid rivers. When making prey of such bottom fish as the flounder and halibut, it often darts into shallows where it can hardly float; but, like the California Gray, in this respect, it evinces no alarm at its situation, and makes but little effort to reach a greater depth. The White Whale, like all others of this family, is fond of gathering in troops, yet we have observed that it generally advances in lines of seldom more than two or three abreast, or more frequently in single file; spouting irregularly, and showing little of its form above water. When undulating along in this manner, it often makes a noise at the moment of coming to the surface to respire, which may be likened to the faint lowing of an ox; but the strain is not so prolonged. Sometimes these animals will gambol about vessels as porpoises do; but at the slightest noise upon the water, or at the discharge of fire-arms, they instantly disappear.

Through the kindness of Captain Arnold, we are able to add the measurements of a White Whale killed at the fishery on Tigel River, Eastern Siberia. The description and proportions of the specimen alluded to are as follows:

	Ft.	In.
From tip of snout to notch of flukes	16	6
From tip of snout to corner of mouth	1	0
From tip of snout to eye	1	4
From tip of snout to spout-hole	2	2
From tip of snout to pectorals	3	8
From eye to top of head	1	2
From notch of flukes to vent	4	5
From notch of flukes to genital slit	5	9
Expansion of flukes	3	10
Breadth of flukes	1	11
Thickness of flukes	0	3
Round the body in largest place	9	10
Length of pectorals	1	11
Width of pectorals	1	3
Thickness of blubber	0	4

Sex, male; color, white. Color of blubber, yellowish white; yield of oil, one hundred gallons.

At this place the animal ascends the river a distance of thirty miles,* where it is captured with the harpoon and lance as in ordinary whaling; but in other estuaries which branch from the northern seas it is taken in nets, during the season from June to September. Large numbers are captured by the natives of those coasts, and the oil obtained is to them a valuable article of commerce. In winter, the fat of the White Whale is considered a luxurious dish for the table, and the lean flesh supplies ample food for the sledge-dogs.

---

* Dall gives an account of a beluga being taken by the Russians, in 1863, at Nulato, on the Yukon River, about seven hundred miles from the sea.

SECTION IV.—THE BAY PORPOISE.

PHOCÆNA VOMERINA, *Gill.* (Plate xviii, fig. 2, 3, 4.)

This peculiar species of Dolphin is the least in size of the entire whale tribe inhabiting the Pacific North American Coast. When fully matured it may attain the length of six feet, but those we have had opportunity to measure fell considerably short of these dimensions. Usually the adults are not more than four and one-half feet between linear extremes. The body of the male is jet black above, a little lighter below; and while the female is of the same color above, it is lighter on the sides, with a narrow black streak running from the corner of the mouth to the pectorals, and the lower portion of the animal is of a milky whiteness, yet the pectoral and caudal fins are black underneath, or of a dark gray. Occasionally, however, both males and females are found with the larger portion, or the whole, of their dorsal and caudal fins white. The former are of triangular shape, and placed very nearly midway between the animal's extremities. The caudal fin varies much in its contour, sometimes being quite broad and straight on its posterior edge, which is slightly notched in the centre; in other specimens the caudal lobes are lunate, and united present a forked appearance. Its pectorals are extremely small and placed low. Its head is somewhat pointed, but destitute of the slender, elongated beak of the *Delphinus Bairdii*, and the Right Whale Porpoise. The anterior portion of the animal resembles that of both the Orca and the White-headed Grampus. Its eyes are placed about two inches behind the corner of the mouth, and nearly in a line with it. Its ears are two inches from the eyes, and these minute orifices would not be noticed by the casual observer, as they are less than a sixteenth of an inch in diameter. The spiracles are placed a little forward of the eyes, and unite in one where they pass through the fleshy part of the cranium. The valve which covers them is convex on its posterior side. When the animal respires this valve is turned downward. Both upper and lower jaws are furnished with teeth, which in the adults are thin, flat, and broadest near their summits. In one example, a female four feet long, taken at San Francisco, California, the number was $\frac{2\,6}{2\,4}$, and in another, $\frac{2\,4}{2\,4}$. In a male, four feet eight inches in length, taken in Port Townsend Bay, Washington Territory, the number was the same as last mentioned.

The following measurements and memoranda were carefully taken from a male specimen obtained at Port Townsend, Washington Territory, April 28th, 1869:

	Ft.	In.
Length	4	8
Greatest girth (behind pectorals)	3	2
Girth at the vent	1	4
From tip of snout to pectorals	1	0
Length of pectorals	0	8
Width of pectorals	0	$2\frac{3}{4}$
From tip of snout to dorsal fin	2	0
Length of dorsal fin, along the back	0	9
Height of dorsal fin	0	$3\frac{1}{2}$
Expansion of caudal fin	1	2
Greatest breadth of each lobe	0	5
From tip of snout to genital slit	2	1
From tip of snout to vent	3	4
Opening of mouth	0	$3\frac{1}{2}$
From tip of snout to eyes	0	6
From tip of snout to spout-hole	0	5
Depth of small at junction with caudal fin	0	3
Depth of small at the vent	0	7
Thickness of blubber	0	1

Another specimen, a female, taken at San Francisco, California, during the summer of 1872, was examined and measured, with the following results:

	Ft.	In.
Length	4	0
Greatest girth (behind pectorals)	2	$3\frac{1}{2}$
From tip of snout to pectorals	0	11
Length of pectorals	0	6
Width of pectorals	0	$2\frac{3}{4}$
From tip of snout to dorsal fin	1	9
Height of dorsal fin	0	4
Length of dorsal fin along the back	0	9
Expansion of caudal fin	1	0
Breadth of each lobe of caudal fin	0	4
Depth of small at junction with caudal fin	0	3
Thickness of small at junction with caudal fin	0	$1\frac{1}{8}$
From tip of snout to corner of mouth	0	4
From tip of snout to eyes	0	6
From tip of snout to spiracle	0	$5\frac{1}{2}$
From tip of snout to ears	0	8
From notch of caudal fin to vent	1	4
From notch of caudal fin to genital slit	1	5
From notch of caudal fin to teat slit	1	6
Thickness of blubber	0	$0\frac{3}{4}$

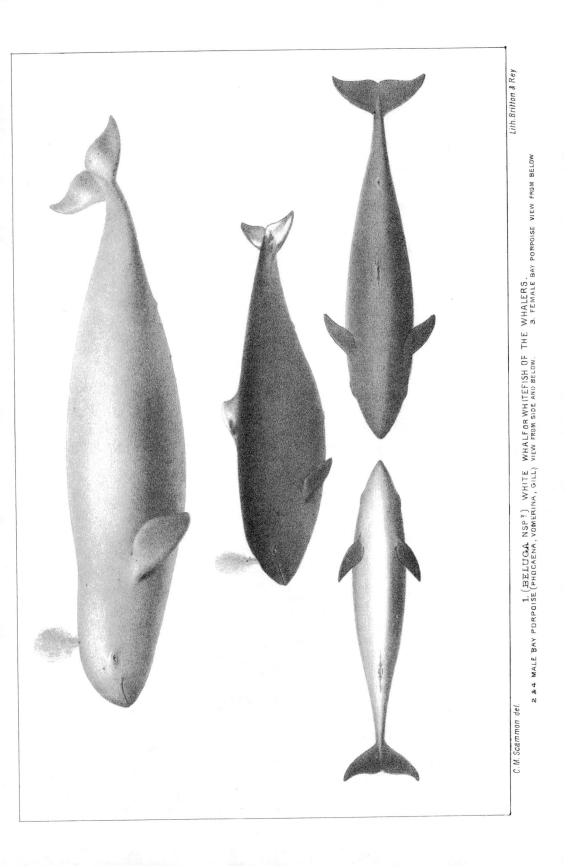

C.M. Scammon del.

Lith.Britton & Rey

1. (BELUGA, NSP?) WHITE WHAL OR WHITEFISH OF THE WHALERS.
2 & 4 MALE BAY PORPOISE (PHOCAENA, VOMERINA, GILL) VIEW FROM SIDE AND BELOW.   3. FEMALE BAY PORPOISE VIEW FROM BELOW

Color of body, black above, lighter on the sides, and white below; under side of caudal and pectoral fins, black.

The coating of fat or blubber which covers the Bay Porpoise, is either of a yellowish white or pearl color, and in thickness, varies from one-half of an inch to an inch and a half.

The habits of this animal differ from those of other species found in the open sea or along the coast. Their favorite resort seems to be in the discolored waters, between the limits of the pure ocean element and the fresh rivers. They are rarely seen far from either side of these boundaries. Our observation proves that they are found as far south as Banderas Bay, and about the mouth of the Piginto River, on the coast of Mexico (which estuary is in latitude $20° 30'$), and as far north as the Columbia River, latitude $46° 16'$. In the winter season they are seen off Astoria, and in Cathlamet Bay, twenty miles above; but during the spring and summer, when the river is fresh to its mouth, and in some instances for miles at sea, they leave the Columbia, following in the vein of mixed water. They are never found in large schools; but occasionally six or eight may be seen scattered about, appearing on the surface alternately, sometimes singly, or two or three at the same instant. Neither do they make those playful gambols and leaps that the larger dolphins do, their general habit being to make a quick puff and turn as soon as they appear above water, apparently choosing the darkness below rather than the light above. It is not from shyness, however, for they are met with about roadsteads and harbors, among shipping, and frequently play their odd turnings close to vessels under way, or at their moorings. By night, when at anchor, we have known them to play about the vessel's rudder; but this may be regarded as an unusual occurrence. Sometimes they are seen among the breakers, on the bars fronting harbor mouths, darting through or along the crests of the rollers as if excited into unusual action by the dashing waves surrounding them. They feed upon small fish, and are occasionally taken in the seines that are hauled along the shores of San Francisco Bay by the Italian fishermen. The northern Indians frequently capture them about the inland waters, during the clear, calm weather of the summer months. At such times they come up and lie quite motionless, for a brief interval, upon the glassy surface of the water, as if basking; then the wily savage, who is on the watch, silently paddles his canoe within gunshot, and fires a ball through the animal's brain; this, of course, kills it instantly, and it generally floats a sufficient length of time to enable the pursuer to obtain his prize, which is regarded as a great delicacy, and a time of feasting in his lodge quickly follows.

SECTION V.—THE STRIPED OR COMMON PORPOISE.

LAGENORHYNCHUS OBLIQUIDENS, *Gill.* (Plate xix, fig. 2.)

This species of the smaller dolphins varies but little in its general proportions from Baird's Dolphin, except in its back fin, which is more falcated and slender, and its snout, which is more blunt. In point of color it is greenish black on the upper surface, lightened on the sides with broad longitudinal stripes of white, gray, and dull black, which in most examples run into each other, but below it is of a pearly or snowy white. The posterior edge of the dorsal fin is tipped with dull white or gray, and sometimes the flukes are marked in the same manner.

We have observed that this species has a wider range, congregates in larger numbers, and exhibits more activity, than any other of the Dolphin family. They are seen, in numbers varying from a dozen up to many hundreds, tumbling over the surface of the sea, or making arching leaps, plunging again on the same curve, or darting high and falling diagonally sidewise upon the water, with a spiteful splash, accompanied by a report that may be heard at some distance. When a brisk breeze is blowing they frequently play about the bow of a ship going at her utmost speed, darting across the cutwater and shooting ahead, or circling around the vessel, apparently sporting at ease. In calm weather they are sometimes seen in immense shoals, leaping, plunging, lobtailing, and finning—in fact, exhibiting an endless variety of attitudes—and at the same time the whole assemblage moves swiftly in various directions, as if enjoying a general frolic.

While on a cruise in the U. S. Revenue cutter *Wayanda*, during the month of October, 1872, we had an opportunity of witnessing, at midnight, the gambols of an immense herd of these active and rapacious animals. The sea was quite smooth, and not a breath of wind was stirring. At first we could hear a harsh rustling sound, as if a heavy squall of wind, accompanied with hail, was sweeping over the otherwise tranquil sea; and, as the moon burst through the clouded sky, we could see a sheet of foam and spray surging toward us. In a few moments the vessel was surrounded by myriads of these Common Porpoises, which, in their playful movements, for the space of one hour, whitened the sea all around as far as the eye could discern, when they almost instantly disappeared.

The Striped Porpoises are often seen in considerable numbers about the large bays and lagoons along this coast, that have no fresh water running into them. They abound more along the coasts where small fish are found than in mid-ocean, as they principally prey upon the smaller finny tribes; and to obtain them shoot swiftly through the water, seizing the object of pursuit with the slightest effort. Occasionally a large number of them will get into a school of fish, frightening them so much that they will dart around in all directions, taking no regular course to escape their pursuers, and finally get so bewildered as to lose nearly all control over their movements. At such times the Striped Porpoise is manifestly the "sea swine," filling itself to repletion.

In perfectly calm weather they are sometimes seen huddled together on the glaring surface, their heads slightly raised, or reclining a little on their sides, as if resting from their constant activity; but such instances are not frequent. Generally they are seen in great numbers rushing over and through the undulating sea, exhibiting their active habits and propensity to roam over an unlimited extent of ocean.

SECTION VI.—BAIRD'S DOLPHIN.

DELPHINUS BAIRDII, *Dall.* (Plate xix, fig 1.)

This Dolphin inhabits the Pacific North American coast, in common with other varieties which abound in those waters. At a distance it much resembles the Common Porpoise of fishermen and sailors; but it differs in several points from that species. We were so fortunate as to obtain two female specimens off Point Arguello, in the fall of 1872, from which we obtained the following notes. Apparently, both individuals were adults, and nearly the same size and weight. The body of the *Delphinus Bairdii* is more slender, and its snout more elongated and rounded, than that of the Striped or Common Porpoise, and may be compared to the bill of a snipe. Its teeth are slender, conical, and slightly curved inward. Its dorsal fin is more erect and less falcated than that of the *Lagenorhynchus obliquidens*, while the pectorals are nearly of the same shape and comparative proportions; but the caudal fin is less in breadth, and greater in proportionate expansion. Its back, immediately forward of the dorsal fin, is somewhat concave, so that when taking a side view the upper contour appears lower before than behind the fin. Its varied colors are, top and sides of head, black; sides of body behind the vent, and both sides of pectorals and flukes, a greenish black; a black patch around the eye, with a white streak passing forward above the mouth; a continuous black streak from the side of the under jaw to the anterior edge of the pectorals; sides, behind the eye, gray—the upper boundary of this color being somewhat above the plane of that organ, beginning to curve downward just behind the dorsal fin, and meeting both white and black marks between the vent and the flukes, in or near the mesial line on the under side of the body; a lanceolate white patch extending on the ventral side, from the middle of the under jaw to the anterior angle of the vulvæ; a narrow white strip extending from the corner of the mouth backward, on each side, slightly arched above the pectoral, and then curving downward gradually, the two meeting below in the region of the vent. Another, still narrower and somewhat obscure, starts at the same place with the last, but is soon lost in the white ventral patch before alluded to. Appended are the dimensions, in feet and inches, of the examples above mentioned:

	No. 1.	No. 2.
Total length of animal	6 $7\frac{1}{2}$	6 9
Anterior edge of pectorals	1 0	1 0
Posterior edge to angle of truncation	0 8	0 $8\frac{1}{2}$
Breadth of pectorals	0 $3\frac{1}{4}$	0 $3\frac{3}{4}$
Expansion of flukes	1 6	1 $5\frac{1}{2}$
Longitudinal width	0 5	0 6
Height of dorsal fin	0 7	0 $7\frac{1}{2}$
Length of dorsal fin along the back	0 $8\frac{1}{2}$	1 0
Tip of beak to anterior edge of pectorals	1 8	1 8
Tip of beak to anterior edge of dorsal fin	3 0	3 1
Tip of beak to corner of mouth	0 $11\frac{1}{2}$	1 $0\frac{3}{4}$
Tip of beak to eye	1 1	1 $1\frac{3}{4}$
Tip of beak to spiracles	1 2	1 3
Width of spiracles	0 $1\frac{1}{8}$	0 $1\frac{1}{8}$
Notch of flukes to vent	1 $8\frac{1}{2}$	1 11
Notch of flukes to teats	1 $1\frac{1}{2}$	1 2
Length of vulva and genital slit	0 4	0 5
Circumference behind pectorals	3 $1\frac{1}{2}$	3 0
Circumference at genitalia	2 $3\frac{1}{2}$	2 $1\frac{1}{2}$
Circumference before the dorsal fin	3 4	3 3
Height from eye to top of head (straight line)	0 $3\frac{3}{4}$	0 $4\frac{1}{2}$
Height from eye to under side of throat (straight line)	0 4	0 4
Height from pectorals to top of back (straight line)	0 9	0 10
Height from corner of mouth to top of head (straight line)	0 $4\frac{1}{2}$	0 $4\frac{3}{4}$
Height from corner of mouth to underside of throat (straight line)	0 3	0 3
Height of small close to the flukes	0 3	0 4
Centre of eye to ear (one inch below eye)	0 2	0 2

Weight of animals (avoirdupois), respectively, one hundred and one hundred and sixty-one pounds; weight of brain, two pounds.

The *Delphinus Bairdii* may be considered symmetrical in its proportions. It moves through the water with great swiftness and grace.

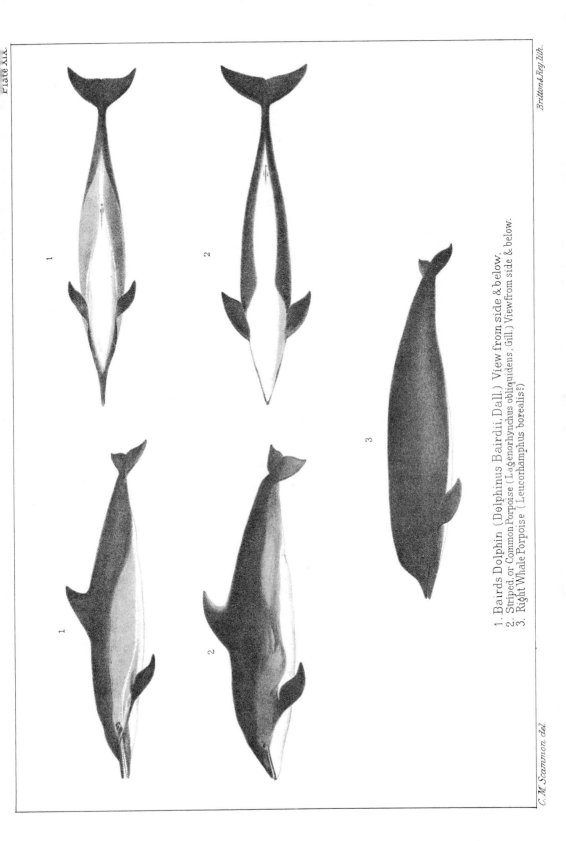

Plate XIX.

1

2

1

2

3

1. Bairds Dolphin (Delphinus Bairdii, Dall.) View from side & below.
2. Striped, or Common Porpoise (Lagenorhynchus obliquidens, Gill.) View from side & below.
3. Right Whale Porpoise (Leucorhamphus borealis?)

C. M. Scammon del.

Britton & Rey, lith.

SECTION VII.—THE RIGHT WHALE PORPOISE.

LEUCORHAMPHUS BOREALIS, *Peale.* (Plate xix, fig. 3.)

The Right Whale Porpoise of the western coast of North America, in habit and form, is nearly the same as the Right Whale Porpoise of the southern hemisphere (*Leucorhamphus Peronii*), but it is not so beautifully marked, in vivid contrast, with pure white and jet black, as the latter; the former being black above and lighter below, with but little of its lower extremities banded with white. The *Leucorhamphus borealis* is not usually met with in large numbers, and is seldom found in shallow bays or lagoons. We have seen them as far south as San Diego Bay, on the California coast, and as far north as Behring Sea; showing plainly, that the two species of the same genus have a feeding-ground which embraces at least the western coast of North and South America.

SECTION VIII.—THE COWFISH.

TURSIOPS GILLII, *Dall.*

This porpoise is larger than the Striped or the Right Whale species, and is known by the name of Cowfish. It is longer also in proportion to its girth, and its snout is somewhat contracted. Its teeth are much larger, straight, conical, and sharply pointed, but less in number. A specimen taken at Monterey, in 1871, had $\frac{24}{24}\frac{24}{24}$. The animal also differs in color, it being black all over, lightened a little below. This description is based upon two momentary observations—the first at San Bartolome Bay, in 1853, and the second in Ballenas Lagoon, in 1859. The habits of the Cowfish, as observed on the coasts of California and Mexico, are strikingly different from that of the true porpoises. It is often remarked by whalemen that they are a "mongrel breed" of doubtful character, being frequently seen in company with Blackfish, sometimes with porpoises, and occasionally with Humpbacks, when the latter are found in large numbers on an abundant feeding-ground. They are met with likewise in the lagoons along the coast, singly, or in pairs, or in fives and sixes—rarely a larger number together—straggling about in a vagrant manner through the winding estuaries, subsisting on the fish that abound in those circumscribed waters. At times they are seen moving lazily along under the shade of the mangroves that in many places fringe the shores; at other times lying about in listless attitudes among the plentiful supplies of food surrounding them.

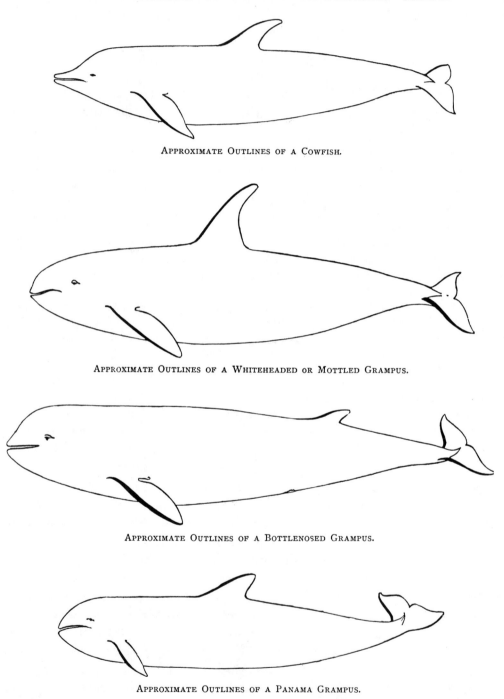

APPROXIMATE OUTLINES OF A COWFISH.

APPROXIMATE OUTLINES OF A WHITEHEADED OR MOTTLED GRAMPUS.

APPROXIMATE OUTLINES OF A BOTTLENOSED GRAMPUS.

APPROXIMATE OUTLINES OF A PANAMA GRAMPUS.

GRAMPUSES.

Of this group of the *Delphinidæ*, which has been observed along the Pacific North American Coast, there is but little known; they are commonly distinguished by the names given in the list of the dolphins found upon this coast. Our personal knowledge of these obscure animals is so limited that we have hesitated whether or not to mention them; but after due consideration we submit the following remarks:

SECTION IX.—THE WHITEHEADED OR MOTTLED GRAMPUS.

Grampus Stearnsii, *Dall.*

The average length of the Whiteheaded or Mottled Grampus may be ten feet. Its muzzle terminates in a rounded point, and very nearly resembles that of the *Phocæna vomerina*. Its dorsal fin is narrow, quite high, and slightly falcated; hence the animal is sometimes taken for the *Orca ater*, and its general appearance and movements through the water are very similar to those of that animal. Its individual marks vary more than any other species of the toothed whales of the coast. While the prevailing color is very dark, approaching to black, the head and anterior portion of the body—as far as the pectorals in some examples—are white, in others it is only partially so; and frequently they are seen more or less mottled with light gray to the region of the dorsal fin. They are gregarious, and congregate frequently in large schools; at other times two or three, or even a solitary individual, will be met with, wandering about the coast or up the bays in quest of food, which consists of fish and several varieties of crustaceans. It is rarely taken, as it is extremely wild and shy.

SECTION X.—THE BOTTLENOSED GRAMPUS.

The Bottlenosed Grampus is probably the largest of the Dolphin family of Cetaceans. Its color approaches nearer to brown than black. The fin on the back is comparatively small, angular in shape, with the longest side attached to the body, and placed much nearer the caudal fin than on other species of the same genus.

The name "Bottlenose" is said to have been given it by reason of the head resembling the upper portion and neck of a junk-bottle; if so, from our observation of it (which was many times, from the vessel's deck or masthead), in its different natural positions, the bottle must have been one with a very large but exceedingly short neck; still the comparison is not, perhaps, inappropriate. The largest of this species are not less than twenty-five feet long, and otherwise are similar in their proportions to the Blackfish. The head appears to be of a shape between that of the *Globiocephalus* and the *Phocæna vomerina*, having a short rounded beak. The habits of the Grampus are such as nearly preclude capture, and little is known of its peculiarities. Two or three are generally seen together, "rounding" to go down as soon as they come to the surface of the water and spout, and when next rising may be beyond view. An exception to this, however, occurred in July and August, 1856, on the coast between Cape St. Lucas and Cerros Island, at which time we saw large numbers of them going in schools, ten, twenty, or thirty together, nearly all being of the largest growth; their actions were a good imitation of a school of small Cachalots — spouting several times when up, and only remaining down the usual time of Sperm Whales of their apparent size. Several fruitless trials were made to capture one. In two instances the harpoons were fastened effectually, and the consequence was that the animals immediately went down with great velocity, each in its descent taking a line one hundred and fifty fathoms long, almost before the boats' crews knew what they were about. It is said, however, that they have been taken with comparatively little difficulty, where the boats were supplied with lines upwards of three hundred fathoms long. The oil produced by the Bottlenose is reputed to be equal in quality to that of the Sperm Whale, and the yield is in a similar ratio to that from the Blackfish and Killer.

SECTION XI.—THE PANAMA GRAMPUS.

In March, 1853, off Panama Bay, on board the bark *Rio Grande*, we captured what were supposed to be two small Blackfish; but, on making an examination, it was decided that they were a species of grampus. Our notes are as follow:

Length of largest specimen, ten feet. Back fin placed as on a Blackfish. Upper end of dorsal more pointed than that of the *Globiocephalus*—the whole fin was very nearly the form of that of the Striped or Common Porpoise. Body less in circumference in proportion to length than that of the Blackfish. Form of head somewhat pointed, approaching to a beak. Color, a uniform jet black. Average thickness of blubber, about an inch; its color is quite red, and the oil retained the same hue after extraction, and appeared watery. The jaws were furnished with sharp, straight, conical teeth.

These animals are found in large schools, and move over the surface of the sea in the same manner as the *Globiocephalus*.

SECTION XII.—THE PUGET SOUND GRAMPUS.

In Port Townsend Bay, Washington Territory, June 19th, 1868, a great number of small whales, evidently a species of grampus, were seen gamboling, in squads of six or eight individuals, whose movements were similar to those of the Blackfish (*Globiocephalus*). They were likewise of the same jet black color; but the dorsal fin was narrower, very pointed, and placed about one-fourth of the animal's length from its flukes. So far as our observations go, the Puget Sound Grampuses are not numerous, and they are but rarely seen about the inland waters of Washington Territory, which is the only place where we have met with them.

SECTION XIII.—THE SAN DIEGO BAY GRAMPUS.

Of this individual Cetacean, our observations have been confined exclusively to those frequenting the Bay of San Diego, where the animals are seen passing into and out of the estuaries connecting with the main lagoon. The distinguishing mark peculiar to this species, is its broad, triangular, and prominent dorsal fin, which is placed about midway between its extremities, and is slightly falcated. Nothing is definitely known about the animal's dimensions. As seen when undulating over the water, it exhibits the ordinary movements of the Cowfish. Its length may be approximated at twelve or fifteen feet; otherwise its proportions of body are nearly the same as those of the *Orca ater*. Its color is black above, with more or less white beneath. It feeds on fish, for which purpose it ascends the estuaries. Repeated attempts have been made to secure one of the creatures, and during the chase they have been approached so near as to allow good views of their proportions upon the surface of the water; but their shyness and rapid movements have thus far precluded every effort to capture them.

SECTION XIV.—THE SQUAREHEADED GRAMPUS.

The conflicting descriptions given of this animal forbid an exact delineation. Some observers say it has nearly the form of the Sperm Whale—especially its head, which is square and extremely bulky. Others aver that its mouth, which "lays low," terminates in a short beak, with a high square forehead. Our own observations have been confined to distant views of them from the masthead or from the deck; yet they have afforded considerable opportunity to note their movements, which are very nearly an imitation of the smaller Sperm Whales. Their spouting and "turning of flukes," which are performed with characteristic regularity, have deceived many an expert whaleman, and repeatedly the boats have been lowered in pursuit of them, the animals having been mistaken for Cachalots. The Squareheaded Grampuses, however, frequently remain longer upon and underneath the surface of the water than the Sperm Whales, and seldom, if ever, go in large schools, as do the Cachalots and Blackfish. In this respect they have more the habits of the Orcas. They are said to yield a superior quality of oil, but in small quantity, compared to their size.

SECTION XV.—THE BROWNSIDED DOLPHIN OF SANTA BARBARA CHANNEL.

Although the knowledge we possess of this dolphin is very meagre—having discovered the animal after the natural history part of this work had been prepared for the press—still it is thought advisable to submit a description, however brief it may be. While lying at anchor off the town of Santa Barbara, May 16th, 1873, a school of what we took to be the Striped or Common Porpoises, was seen playing around the vessel. Their irregular movements, and the unusual length of time they remained upon the surface of the water, afforded an opportunity to study them. Their forms were apparently the same as that of the Striped or Common Porpoise, except that the dorsal fin is of the triangular shape which is present with Baird's Dolphin, and the color on its sides is brown, while its back is of a dull black; hence it has been given the provisional name of the Brownsided Dolphin. With regard to the habits of the animal, we observed one peculiar feature: that of darting through the thick beds of kelp which fronted the shore. Really they seemed to delight in sporting among it, and occasionally one of the band would be seen leaping clear of the water, taking with it long sprays of the *fucus.* All our efforts to capture one proved unavailing; but enough was seen to convince us that they were an undescribed species.

SECTION XVI.—THE NARWHAL.

MONODON MONOCEROS, *Linn.*

Although the Narwhal is but rarely met with in that part of the Arctic Ocean accessible to the whalemen who pass through Behring Strait, yet, beyond question, it is an occasional visitor to those icy waters, and even to the neighboring shores of eastern Siberia. We have it authentically stated by a trader and traveler in Siberia, that the aborigines of that frozen coast have a superstitious dread of the casual visits of the Narwhal, and when one is seen by a single native, it is regarded as an ill omen, and the beholder either immediately puts an end to his existence, or he becomes a prey to evil forebodings, which ultimately bring the poor victim to an untimely end. The tusks of the Narwhal have been exchanged in barter by the inhabitants of that portion of north-eastern Asia bordering the Arctic Ocean, and, as articles of traffic, have passed from one party to another, till they have finally reached the trading-posts on the northern shores of the Okhotsk Sea. Captain Arnold, who was engaged in a trading expedition from San Francisco to the Okhotsk coast, in 1868, obtained at Tavisk Bay a very fine tusk of a Narwhal, which measured eight feet in length, including the root, which was fifteen inches. The tusk at its base was seven and a half inches in circumference, and tapering to its extremity, where its diameter was one-half of an inch. From its junction with the head, its whitish and polished surface exhibits a uniform twist, which adds much to its symmetrical beauty. Relative to the natural history of the Narwhal, we can state nothing from our own observations, but make the following extracts from Godman's monograph of the animal, which is based entirely upon the observations of the renowned Scoresby: "The Narwhal, when fully grown, measures from thirteen to fourteen feet in length, exclusive of the tusk, and at the thickest part, which is two feet behind the fins, the circumference is about eight or nine feet. The part of the body anterior to the fins and head is paraboloidal; the middle portion of the body is almost cylindrical; the posterior portion, to within three or four feet of the tail, is somewhat conical; thence a ridge, commencing both at the back and belly; the section becomes first an ellipse, and then a rhombus at the junction of the tail. The back and belly ridges run half-way or more across the tail; the ridges of the tail run the same way along the body, and form ridges on the sides of the rump. The back appears depressed and flat, three or four feet posterior to the neck. The head forms about one-seventh of the whole length of the animal, being small, blunt, and round. The mouth is small and incapable of much extension, having a wedge-shaped under lip. The eyes are only one inch in their largest diameter, and are placed on a line with the opening of the mouth at about thirteen inches from the snout. The opening of the ear, situated six inches behind the eye on the same horizontal line, is of the diameter of a small knitting-needle. The spiracle, or blow-hole, is situated immediately over the eyes, and is a singular semicircular opening about three and one-half inches in diameter, and one inch and a half in length. The fins are twelve or fourteen inches long, and six or eight broad, and placed at one-fifth of the length of the animal from the snout. Where fixed to the body, the fin is elliptical. In the adult Narwhal, the ground is wholly white, with dark-gray or blackish spots. These spots are of a roundish or oblong form; on the back, where they seldom exceed two inches in diameter, they are the darkest and most crowded together. On the sides these spots are fainter, smaller, and more open. On the belly they are extremely faint and few. A close patch of brownish-black, without any white, is often found on the upper part of the neck, just behind the blow-hole. The sucker Narwhals are almost uniformly of a bluish-gray, or slate color. Very old individuals become almost white. The remarkable peculiarity of the Narwhal is its long, spiral, ivory tusk, which grows from the left side of the inferior portion of the upper jaw, sometimes to the length of ten feet or more. This tusk is generally covered with a dark, greasy incrustation above, while below and at the point it is kept white by use. In addition to this external tusk, peculiar to the male, there is another on the right side of the head, about nine inches long, imbedded in the skull. In females, as well as in young males, in which the tooth does not appear externally, the rudiments of two tusks are generally found in the upper jaw." *

The food of the Narwhal is said to consist of molluscous animals, and sometimes fish, although the creature is destitute of teeth exclusive of its tusks. The Narwhal is considered a harmless animal, but active and possessed of considerable swiftness; yet, when on the surface of the water for the purpose of respiration, it

---

* Scoresby, in his Greenland voyage, killed a female Narwhal having an external horn four feet three inches long, twelve inches of which were imbedded in the skull. It had also, as usual, a milk-tusk nine inches long, which was of conical form and obliquely truncated at the thickest end, and without the knot formed in many of the milk-tusks. The horn was on the left side of the head, and the spiral was dextrorsal.

frequently lies motionless for several minutes. The Narwhal is captured by shooting it with a rifle, or it is taken with the harpoon and lance, as are other whales. The blubber of the body yields a fine quality of oil. The Greenlanders and Esquimaux utilize the whole creature. The flesh is devoured as excellent food; the oil is burned in their moss lamps; the intestines are manufactured into lines and garments; and the tusks are fashioned into spears and other weapons.

PART II.

PINNIPEDIA.

PART II.—PINNIPEDIA.

INTRODUCTION.

A VARIETY of marine animals inhabit the western coast of North America which are scientifically classed under the head of *Pinnipedia*, but familiarly known under the general name of Seals. Those described in the following monograph are enumerated, and their technical names given, at the conclusion of the catalogue appended to this work.

All the pinnipedes periodically inhabit both the water and the land adjacent. Their food consists of fish, crustaceans, and various other marine invertebrates found about the shores, and of sea-fowls. All the different species of pinnipedes bring forth and suckle their young in a similar manner to other mammals. The general form of the animal is elongated, with quite full anterior proportions, exclusive of the head and neck. The posterior part of the body is tapering, and terminates at the junction with the hind limbs. Their appendages for locomotion are commonly called flippers. The anterior, or side ones, nearly correspond to the fore limbs of carnivorous animals; and, in some species, they take closely the form of the pectorals of Cetaceans. Where one set of flippers is furnished with claws, or nails, the other is nearly or quite destitute of them; and, whether it be the anterior or posterior members which are thus armed, it is these of which the animal principally makes use in its movements upon the land. These flippers are very flexible, and seem much better suited for propulsion in the water than for terrestrial locomotion. The body of the animal is usually covered with short and bristly hair; but in some few species their inner coating is a thick, rich fur, with long, glistening hairs over all. The geographical distribution of the pinnipedes is unlimited, the family being distributed in different groups over every zone and both hemispheres.

It is difficult to produce a satisfactory figure of a seal, for the reason that in its various attitudes the animal materially changes its contour. In one position its neck becomes somewhat slender and elongated, and its head appears comparatively small; while in another posture the creature seems distorted into a swollen form throughout. Hence we shall introduce a few illustrative figures in addition to the plates which represent the general forms of these animals.

CHAPTER I.

THE SEA ELEPHANT.

MACRORHINUS ANGUSTIROSTRIS, *Gill.* (Plate xx, fig. **1, 2.**)

Among the varieties of marine mammals which periodically resort to the land, no one attains such gigantic proportions as the Sea Elephant. This animal, which was sometimes called the Elephant Seal, and known to the old Californians as the *Elefante marino,* had a geographical distribution from Cape Lazaro, latitude 24° 46′ north, longitude 112° 20′ west, to Point Reyes, latitude 38° north, longitude 122° 58′ west on the coast of California; and, strange as it may appear, we have no authentic accounts of this species of amphibious animal being found elsewhere in the northern hemisphere. At the south, however, about Patagonia, Tierra del Fuego, and numerous islands in both the Atlantic and Pacific, and the Crozets, Kerguélen, and Herd's Islands, in the high latitudes of the Indian Ocean, have been points where the Sea Elephants have gathered in almost incredible numbers, and where hundreds of thousands of them have been slain by the seamen, pursuing their prey in those distant regions.

The sexes vary much in size, the male being frequently triple the bulk of the female; the oldest of the former will average fourteen to sixteen feet; the largest we have ever seen measured twenty-two feet from tip to tip. The following measurements (in feet and inches) and notes were taken of two large females and one new-born pup, obtained on the coast of Lower California:

	No. 1.	No. 2.
Length from tip to tip	9 0	10 0
Round the body behind fore flippers	5 10	5 9
Length of tail	0 2	0 2½
Breadth of tail at root	0 2	0 2½
Length of posterior flippers	1 7	1 10
Expansion of posterior flippers	1 8	1 8
Length of fore flippers	1 5	1 2
Width of fore flippers	0 6	0 6

	No. 1.		No. 2.	
Round extremity of body at root of tail	1	6	1	7
From tip of nose to corner of mouth	0	7	0	8
Opening of mouth	0	4½	0	4½
From tip of nose to eye	0	8	0	9
From tip of nose to fore flippers	2	7	3	0
Length of fissure between the eye lids	0	0	0	1¾

	New-born Pup.	
Length from tip to tip	4	0
Length of posterior flippers	0	7½
Length of fore flippers	0	7
Breadth of fore flippers	0	2½
From tip of nose to side flippers	1	6
From tip of nose to eye	0	4
From eye to ear (the minute opening of which is barely perceptible)	0	2
From tip of nose to corner of mouth	0	4½
Opening of mouth	0	3

The posterior flippers of the Sea Elephant are very nearly like those of the Leopard Seal, except that they are clawless. The fore flippers, however, are furnished each with five nails, which, in shape, somewhat resemble those of the human hand, but in color they are a dull black; the longest in the two adult examples examined measured one and a half inches. The two teats of the smaller animal were twenty inches from the posterior termination of the body. In the larger one they were two feet and three inches from the root of the tail, which is extremely short and pointed. The whiskers on each side of the face, in both specimens, numbered from thirty-five to forty, the longest of which were seven inches; their color was of a dark brown tipped with a lighter shade. Eight or ten bristle-like hairs were present upon or near the upper lid of the eye, and constituted the eyebrows. The pup, whose measurements are given above, had forty-six whiskers on one side of its face, and forty-two on the other, and ten frizzly hairs over each eye. Its color was a dark brown, or nearly a chestnut shade.

The color of the adult Sea Elephant is a light brown, when its thin short hair is grown to full length; but, immediately after shedding, it becomes like that of the land elephant, or of a bluish cast. The average thickness of its skin is fully equal to that of the largest bullock. A fat bull, taken at Santa Barbara Island, by the brig *Mary Helen*, in 1852, was eighteen feet long, and yielded two hundred and ten gallons of oil. Round the under side of the neck, in the oldest males, the animal appears to undergo a change with age; the hair falls off, the skin thickens and becomes wrinkled—the furrows crossing each other, producing a checkered

Plate XX.

C. M. Scammon, del.

SEA-ELEPHANT. (MACRORHINUS ANGUSTIROSTRIS.) GILL.
1. MALE. 2 FEMALE.

From Photo. by Watkins

SEA-LION (EUMETOPIAS STELLERI.) GILL.
1 MALE. 2 FEMALE.

surface—and sometimes the throat is more or less marked with white spots. Its proboscis extends from opposite the angle of the mouth forward (in the larger males) about fifteen inches, when the creature is in a state of quietude, and the upper surface appears ridgy; but when the animal makes an excited respiration, the trunk becomes more elongated, and the ridges nearly disappear. The mouth is furnished with teeth similar to those of the Sea Lion. The adult females average ten feet in length between extremities. They are destitute of the proboscis, the nose being like that of the common seal, but projecting more over the mouth. Their canine teeth are shorter, smoother below the sockets, larger at the base, and hollow nearly to the upper point. The sailors on a voyage to the Sea Elephant grounds, not having a supply of tobacco pipes, made them of these teeth, and the quills or leg bones of the pelican; the former furnishing the bowls, and the latter the stems.

The habits of the huge beasts, when on shore, or loitering about the foaming breakers, are in many respects like those of the Leopard Seals. Our observations on the Sea Elephants of California go to show that they have been found in much larger numbers from February to June than during other months of the year; but more or less were at all times found on shore upon their favorite beaches, which were about the islands of Santa Barbara, Cerros, Guadalupe, San Bonitos, Natividad, San Roque, and Asuncion, and some of the most inaccessible points on the main-land between Asuncion and Cerros. When coming up out of the water, they were generally first seen near the line of surf; then crawling up by degrees, frequently reclining as if to sleep; again, moving up or along the shore, appearing not content with their last resting-place. In this manner they would ascend the ravines, or "low-downs," half a mile or more, congregating by hundreds. They are not so active on land as the seals; but, when excited to inordinate exertion, their motions are quick—the whole body quivering with their crawling, semi-vaulting gait, and the animal at such times manifesting great fatigue. Notwithstanding their unwieldiness, we have sometimes found them on broken and elevated ground, fifty or sixty feet above the sea.

The principal seasons of their coming on shore, are, when they are about to shed their coats, when the females bring forth their young (which is one at a time, rarely two), and the mating season. These seasons for "hauling up" are more marked in southern latitudes. The different periods are known among the hunters as the "pupping cow," "brown cow," "bull and cow," and "March bull" seasons; but on the California coast, either from the influence of climate or some other cause, we have noticed young pups with their mothers at quite the opposite months. The continual hunting of the animals may possibly have driven them to irregularities. The time of gestation is supposed to be about three-fourths of the year. The most marked season we could discover was that of the adult males, which shed their coats later than the younger ones and the females. Still, among a herd of the largest of those fully matured (at Santa Barbara Island, in June, 1852), we found several cows and their young, the latter apparently but a few days old.

When the Sea Elephants come on shore for the purpose of "shedding," if not disturbed they remain out of water until the old hair falls off. By the time this change comes about, the animal is supposed to lose half its fat; indeed, it sometimes becomes very thin, and is then called a "slim-skin."

In the stomach of the Sea Elephant a few pebbles are found, which has given rise to the saying that "they take in ballast before going down" (returning to the sea). On warm and sunny days we have watched them come up singly on smooth beaches, and burrow in the dry sand, throwing over their backs the loose particles that collect about their fore limbs, and nearly covering themselves from view; but when not disturbed, the animals follow their gregarious propensity, and collect in large herds.

The mode of capturing them is thus: the sailors get between the herd and the water; then, raising all possible noise by shouting, and at the same time flourishing clubs, guns, and lances, the party advance slowly toward the rookery, when

CLUB AND LANCE USED IN THE CAPTURE OF THE SEA ELEPHANT.

the animals will retreat, appearing in a state of great alarm. Occasionally an overgrown male will give battle, or attempt to escape; but a musket-ball through the brain dispatches it; or some one checks its progress by thrusting a lance into the roof of its mouth, which causes it to settle on its haunches, when two men with heavy oaken clubs give the creature repeated blows about the head, until it is stunned or killed. After securing those that are disposed to show resistance, the party rush on the main body. The onslaught creates such a panic among these peculiar creatures, that, losing all control of their actions, they climb, roll, and tumble over each other, when prevented from farther retreat by the projecting cliffs. We recollect in one instance, where sixty-five were captured, that several were found showing no signs of having been either clubbed or lanced, but were smothered by numbers of their kind heaped upon them. The whole flock, when attacked, manifested alarm by their peculiar roar, the sound of which, among the largest males, is nearly as loud as the lowing of an ox, but more prolonged in one strain, accompanied by a rattling noise in the throat. The quantity of blood in this species of the seal tribe is supposed to be double that contained in an ox, in proportion to its size.

After the capture, the flaying begins. First, with a large knife, the skin is ripped along the upper side of the body its whole length, and then cut down as far as practicable, without rolling it over; then the coating of fat that lies between the skin and flesh—which may be from one to seven inches in thickness, according to the size and condition of the animal—is cut into "horse-pieces," about eight inches wide, and twelve to fifteen long, and a puncture is made in each piece sufficiently large to pass a rope through. After flensing the upper portion of the body, it is rolled over, and cut all around, as above described. Then the "horse-pieces" are strung on a raft-rope (a rope three fathoms long, with an eye-splice in one end), and taken to the edge of the surf; a long line is made fast to it, the end of which is thrown to a boat lying just outside of the breakers; they are then hauled through the rollers and towed to the vessel, where the oil is tried out by boiling the blubber, or fat, in large pots set in a brick furnace for the purpose. The oil produced is superior to whale oil for lubricating purposes. Owing to the continual pursuit of the animals, they have become nearly if not quite extinct on the California coast, or the few remaining have fled to some unknown point for security.

Thus far, we have been writing of the Sea Elephant and manner of capturing it on the islands and coasts of the Californias; and, although thousands of the animals, in past years, gathered upon the shores of the islands contiguous to the coast, as well as about the pebbly or sandy beaches of the peninsula, affording full cargoes to the oil-ships, yet their numbers were but few, when compared with the multitudes which once inhabited the remote, desolate islands, or places on the main, within the icy regions of the southern hemisphere; and even at the expense of digression, we have thought it well to give an account of the animal in those regions. Several geographical points have already been mentioned, and among these Kerguelen Land, or Desolation Island, and Herd's Island, are the great resorting-places of these animals at the present day. The last-named place is in latitude 53° 03' south, and longitude 72° 30' to 73° 30' east. Its approximate extent is sixty miles. Its shores are somewhat bold, broken, and dangerous to land upon; no harbor being found that is secure for the smallest vessel. In the smoothest time, when landing, the boat's crew are obliged to jump into the water, to hold and steady the boat, that it may not be staved on the beach, or swept out by the receding undertow. In fact, a heavy surge always beats upon those frozen, rock-bound shores, varied only by the combing seas, that dart higher yet up the precipitous cliffs, when urged on by the oft-repeated gales that sweep over the southern portions of the Indian Ocean.

Captain Cook, the celebrated explorer, on his voyages of discovery in the *Resolution*, when he visited Kerguelen Land, called it the Island of Desolation, on account of its barren and uninhabitable appearance, although it possessed fine harbors, where the hardy mariner could rest securely with his ship during the violent winter storms. But not so at Herd's Island. The Sea Elephant oil-ship, breasting the changing winds and waves to procure a cargo, is officered by the most fearless and determined men, who have had experience in whaling, sealing, or Sea Elephant hunting in those rough seas. The majority of the men are shipped at the Cape de Verde Islands, they being of a muscular race, who have proved themselves to be excellent hands for the laborious work. The ship, when first sent out, is provided with a "double crew," and is accompanied by a small vessel, of a hundred tons or less, for a "tender." On arriving at the island, the ship is moored with heavy chains and anchors, and every other preparation is made for riding out any gale that may blow toward the land. The sails are unbent, all the spars above the topmasts are sent down, and, with the spare boats, are landed and housed during the "season," which begins about the middle of November, and ends in the middle of February. Quarters are provided for that portion of the ship's company which is assigned to duty on shore. The habitation is a small hut, properly divided off into apartments—one for the mates, one for the steerage officers, and another for the men. This dwelling is no larger than necessity demands. Its walls are built of the detached pieces of lava, or bowlders, nearest at hand; rough boards and tarred canvas, supplied from the ship, form the roof, which must be made waterproof and snow-proof. During the day, light is admitted to each room through a single pane of glass, or a spare deck or side light—perhaps found among the rubbish on board the vessel; and doors are made after the fashion of "good old colony times," with the latch-string ever swinging in the wind. In this dank habitation, planted between an iceberg on one side and a bluff volcanic mountain on the other, these rough men of the sea at once adapt themselves to their several situations, and all the discipline is maintained that they would be subject to if on board ship. The high surf at this island renders it impracticable to haul off the blubber in "rafts," as at Desolation Island and on the coasts of the Californias:

hence it is usually "minced" (the "horse-pieces" cut into thin slices) and put into tight casks to prevent any waste of the oil; then, when a smooth day comes, they are rolled down the beach, and pulled through the rollers by the boats; or the tender is anchored near shore, a line is run to the vessel, and the casks hauled alongside, hoisted in, and transferred to the ship, where the oil is tried out and "stowed down" in the usual manner.

As soon as the season is over—or, rather, when the time has come for the ship to leave, either for home, or to find shelter in some harbor at the Island of Desolation—the shore-party is supplied with provisions, all the surplus articles that were landed are re-embarked, the heavy anchors are at last weighed, and amid hail, snow, and sleet, the ship under her half-frozen canvas bounds over the billows, and soon disappears in the offing.

The vessels having departed, the officers and men left on the island resume their daily occupations. Usually the number is divided into two "gangs," stationed at separate places, where clusters of huts have sprung up for the use of those belonging to the different vessels, who have from time to time made it a temporary abiding-place. Try-works are built, and a shanty is erected for a cooper's shop. These two habitable spots are known as "Whisky Bay" and "The Point;" the former being a slight indentation of the shore-line, where the Elephants in countless numbers were found by the first vessel visiting there, which, as report says, had a supply of "old rye" stowed in her run. The captain, in the heat of his successful prosecution of the arduous business of procuring a cargo, gave his men permission to "splice the main brace strong and often," so long as the work went briskly on; and it is humorously told that this noted landing-place was "christened" at the cost of barrels of the beverage, thus securing to it a name as lasting as that of the prominent headland on the borders of the Okhotsk Sea, well known to whalemen as "Whisky Bluff." From day to day the separated parties, living some thirty miles apart, hunt the animals for leagues along the shores, with the varied success incident to season or circumstances; and, although on the same island, the face of the country is so broken—being rent into deep chasms, walled in as it were by giddy, shelving heights, making it impossible to travel, even on foot, far inland toward its extremities, and the shores hedged in by sharp ridges of basalt, stretching out into the sea—the two divisions know nothing of each other until the vessels return, which is frequently after an absence of from eight to twelve months, and during that time a thousand or more barrels of oil may have been collected.

Notwithstanding the hardships and deprivations that are undergone to make a successful voyage, there is no lack of enterprising merchants ready to invest their capital in any adventure when there is a prospect of ultimate gain; and no ocean or sea where there is a possibility of navigating appears too perilous for the adventurous seamen to try their luck upon. The very fact of the voyage being fraught with danger and difficulty tends to stimulate them to action. And in this remote part of the world of which we have spoken, that was unknown to the early explorers, as well as to those who have more recently voyaged toward the Antarctic continent—and for the geographical position of which we are indebted to the enterprise and nautical skill of those of our countrymen who commenced the life of a sailor by "coming through the hawse-holes"—we find that rival parties are left on its bleak shores, who, when opposed the one to the other, watch with greater care every movement that may be made, than the coming and going of the creatures which are the objects of pursuit. Many a war of words has arisen, with the brandishing of club and lance in the strife; but, like the pioneer California miners, when left to rely on their own good sense for self-government, there was little to fear but that all laws made would be simple, just, and strictly adhered to. When parties from different vessels are located on the same beach, the custom is for all to work together when killing the animals, as well as when skinning and cutting the blubber from the bodies into "horse-pieces." These are thrown into one or more piles; after which, the men of each party are ranged in squads, and each one, in turn, draws a piece from the heap, until all is disposed of. These divisions are made whenever the animals are found and killed in any considerable numbers; and, if far from the rendezvous, the blubber is "backed," or rolled in casks to the main depot. "Backing" is the stringing of eight or ten pieces on a pole, which is carried on the shoulders of two men; but if a cask is used, three men are allotted to each one of six or eight barrels' capacity, to roll which the distance of two miles is allowed to be a day's work. While the ship is away, homeward bound, or returning to the island for another cargo, the tender may be at Desolation Island, picking up what scattering Elephants can be found upon shores that once swarmed with millions of those huge beasts; or a short whaling-cruise is made, until the time comes for commencing operations at the island.

Hunting for the scattering animals about the shores of Desolation Island, "between seasons," is the most exposed and solitary pursuit either in the whale or seal fishery. The tender takes a detachment of the crew, and plies along the island coast, landing one or two men on each of the best beaches, with a supply of water and provisions; a tent or shanty is erected, partly of wood, partly of canvas; and the skins of the Elephants furnish the floor, couch, and covering of the temporary habitation. Here the banished hunter or hunters rest at night, after the fatigues of ranging along the shores, killing and flaying the animals met with, and transporting the blubber to a place of deposit, where it is buried, to prevent the gulls from devouring it, until taken aboard. As the season returns at Herd's Island, the vessels are usually "on the ground;" the treacherous surf is again passed and repassed in the light, frail whale-boats, landing the fresh crew from home, who relieve those who have thus literally "seen the elephant." The time passes quickly away, in the toil and excitement of killing and flensing; and again the floating fragment of the world departs for the land of civilization, leaving her last crew from home to pass an Antarctic winter, amid the solitudes of icebergs and the snow-covered peaks of the mountain land. No passing sail is seen to break the monotony of their voluntary exile; even many varieties of sea-birds found at Desolation Island do not deign to visit them. Multitudes of penguins, however, periodically resort to the island, and their eggs, together with the tongues of the Sea Elephants, and one or two kinds of fish, furnish a welcome repast for all hands, by way of change from that substantial fare called "salt-horse" and "hardtack." Beside the close stoves in their apartments, which are heated with coal from the ship, or the fat of the Elephant pups, and the flickerings of a murky oil-lamp, the long winter evenings are passed in smoking and playing amusing games—"old sledge" and "seven-up" being favorites—and the reckless joking that circulates among adventurers who make light of ill-luck, and turn reverses into ridicule.

The extent and value of the Sea Elephant fishery, from its commencement up to the present date, is not definitely known, as the ships engaged in the enterprise, when whaling and sealing was at its height in the southern ocean, were also in pursuit of the valuable fur-bearing animals, as well as the Cachalot and the balæna; hence their cargoes were often made up of a variety of the oils of commerce. We have reliable accounts, however, of the Sea Elephant being taken for its oil as early as the beginning of the present century. At those islands, or upon the coasts on the main, where vessels could find secure shelter from all winds, the animals have long since been virtually annihilated; and now they are only sought after in the remote places we have mentioned, and these points are only accessible under the great difficulties that beset the mariner when sailing near the polar regions of the globe. Enough data are at hand, nevertheless, to show that hundreds of thousands of the animals, yielding as many barrels of oil, have been taken from Desolation and Herd's Islands, by American ships, which for many years have maintained a monopoly of the business.

CHAPTER II.

THE SEA LION.

(Plate xxii, fig. 1, 2.)

Among the numerous species of marine mammalia found upon the Pacific Coast of North America, none excite more interest than the Sea Lion; even the valuable and almost domesticated Fur Seal of the Pribyloff group of islands fails to equal it in utility to the Aleutians, who depend upon it not only as a staple article of food, but obtain, by the sale of its silky skin, their foreign luxuries of every nature. But the Fur Seal (*Callorhinus*) dwells only periodically in isolated places, while the Sea Lion, although having an extended geographical range, is a frequenter, not only of remote and secluded places, but also of thickly inhabited coasts; entering inland bays and rivers; at times disporting among the shipping, and quite frequently making some detached rock or reef, contiguous to the busy shore, a permanent abode, where it seems to enjoy its approximate union with civilization. The Sea Lion is known, among naturalists, as belonging to the sub-family *Trichophocinæ*, of which there are three genera, and several varieties, said to be distributed as follows: *Otaria jubata*, found on the southern coasts and islands of South America; *Eumetopias Stelleri*, which inhabits the coasts and islands of the North Pacific, from California and southern Kamschatka northward; *Zalophus Gillespii*, found on the coasts and islands of the North Pacific, from Lower California and southern Japan northward; *Zalophus lobatus*, of the Australasian seas.* To whatever genus of the *Trichophocinæ* the animals may belong, their general habits, so far as I have had opportunity to observe, are the same; the only difference being that those among their number who migrate north or south, conform, in some respects, to the various situations they may be placed in between the equatorial and polar regions.

---

* The classification and geographical distribution here given, are based upon the authority of the valuable work of J. A. Allen, on the Eared Seals, lately published; with an account of the northern Fur Seals, by Captain Charles Bryant.

We are acquainted, however, with only two genera,* one of which (*Otaria jubata*) inhabits the coast of South America, and the other (*Eumetopias Stelleri*) we have met with between the tropical lines of the Pacific, from the Galapagos Islands— which are situated about the equator—northward on the west coast of North America nearly to Behring Strait, and westward to the Island of Saghalien on the coast of eastern Siberia. The first-named genus has a short, rounded head, prominent above the eyes, and a shaggy mane, which imparts a resemblance to the king of beasts; hence the appropriate name, Sea Lion, which was given it when first described.

The *Eumetopias Stelleri* is of more symmetrical proportions than the *Otaria jubata*, and very nearly resembles the Fur Seal, more particularly the males; and,

* Since the publication of the article "About Sea Lions," in the *Overland Monthly* of September, 1871, we have had opportunity of making additional observations upon these animals at the Farallone Islands, where we saw the largest females we have ever met with on the California coast. Hence, what we have formerly taken to be the *Eumatopias Stelleri* may prove to be the *Zalophus Gillespii?*; but, if such be the fact, both species inhabit the coast of California, at least as far south as the Farallones. Moreover, both species, if we may be allowed the expression, herd together in the same rookeries. On making a series of observations upon the outward forms of Sea Lions, it will be found that a confusing variety exists in the figures of these very interesting animals, especially in the shape of the head: some having a short muzzle, with a full forehead; others with forehead and nose somewhat elongated; and still others of a modified shape, between the two extremes.

Within the past five years, several observers have assured me that the Sea Lions of the north, particularly those of St. Paul's Island, Behring Sea, were much larger than those on the coast of California; but this information proves to be incorrect, for the same observers, after visiting the island a second time, and investigating the matter more thoroughly, have arrived at the conclusion that the male Sea

Lions there found will rarely exceed eleven feet in extreme length; while on the coast of California, animals of that length are frequently met with, and, as before stated, there is no lack of cases where the animals have reached the length of twelve feet, and an instance is known, as stated by Professor Davidson, of the U. S. Coast Survey, where the specimen measured fifteen feet from tip to tip. In any event, there is no further question about the northern Sea Lions exceeding in size the Sea Lions of California, as those inhabiting the last-named region are at least fully equal in magnitude to their congeners of the north. The accompanying figures may convey a better idea of their forms than a written description.

Doubts have been expressed as to the migratory habits of the Sea Lion; but we are fully convinced that there are individuals, at least, among all the northern herds, that change from the cold latitudes to the tropics, as we have killed several of the animals upon the southern coast of California, during the month of June, in which were found arrow or spear heads, such as are used by the northern sea-coast natives. Professor Davidson states that in June, 1870, a spear-head, such as is used by the natives of Alaska, was found in a large male Sea Lion, taken at Point Arenas, in latitude 39°, on the coast of California.

MALE SEA LION SLEEPING.

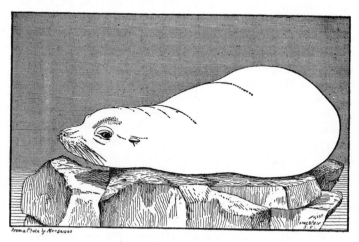

MALE SEA LION WAKING.

APPEARANCE OF A MALE SEA LION WHEN ROARING.

FEMALE SEA LIONS OF ST PAUL'S ISLAND.

at a distance, it is difficult to distinguish between a fully matured Fur Seal and a Sea Lion of ordinary size. The extreme length of the full-grown male Sea Lion of the north may be set down at sixteen feet from tip of nose to end of posterior flippers, and yield of oil at forty gallons; but it is seldom they are found measuring twelve feet from tip of nose to tip of tail, and the individual yield of oil throughout the season would not exceed ten gallons. Its greatest circumference would not be over eight feet, and its weight about one thousand pounds. Its head and neck are more elongated, and the latter is destitute of the mane which is characteristic of the Lion of the southern seas. Its mouth is armed with strong, glistening, white teeth. Its projecting upper lip is furnished, on each side, with strong, flexible whiskers, which are generally of a white, or yellowish-white color, some of which grow to the length of eighteen inches. When the animal is either excited by curiosity or anger, its eyes are full of expression; and at such times they appear large, but when the creature is dozing, these members have quite the opposite appearance. Its ears are cylindrical at the root, tapering to a point, are covered with short, fine hair, and lie nearly in a line with the body. Its limbs, which are incased with a sort of thick shagreen, combine the triple functions of legs, feet, and fins, and are far better adapted to locomotion in the watery element; where, when excited, its movements are swift and graceful, while on the land, the creature's imposing, though awkward traveling, requires great effort. Its body is covered with short, coarse, shining hair. The color of the adult males is much diversified; individuals of the same rookery being quite black, with scattering hairs tipped with dull white, while others are of a reddish brown, dull gray, or of light gray above, darker below. The adult female is not half the bulk of the male, and its color is a light brown. One of the average size, taken at Santa Barbara Island, coast of California, in the spring of 1871, measured six feet four inches from tip of nose to tip of posterior flippers, and weighed one hundred and eighty-two pounds.

We submit the following measurements, etc. (in feet and inches), of a full-grown male Sea Lion (No. 1), taken at the Farallone Islands, July 17th, 1872; of an adult female Sea Lion (No. 2), taken at Santa Barbara Island, coast of California, April 12th, 1871; and of a male Sea Lion (No. 3), about ten months old, taken at the last-named island, April 4th, 1872:

	No. 1.	No. 2.	No. 3.
Length of animal from tip of nose to tip of posterior flippers,	12 0	6 4	4 10
Length of posterior flippers....................................	2 2	1 1	0 11½
Breadth of posterior flippers (expanded).....................	0 9	0 8	
Round the body behind the pectorals.......................	7 0	3 3	2 8

	No. 1.	No. 2.	No. 3.
From tip of nose to pectorals	5 0	2 1	1 9
Length of pectorals	2 6	1 4	1 3
Breadth of pectorals	1 4	0 6	0 4½
Distance between extremities of pectorals	10 0		
From tip of nose to eye		0 3¾	0 $3\frac{1}{14}$
From tip of nose to ear		0 8	0 7
Length of ear	0 1½	0 1¼	0 1
Girth of body at root of posterior flippers		1 6	0 11½
From tip of nose to root of tail			3 10½
From tip of nose to corner of mouth		0 4½	0 3½
From end of lower jaw to corner of mouth		0 3	0 2½
Length of tail	0 7	0 2	0 2½
Length of longest whiskers	1 6	0 6	0 5½
Length of longest claws on posterior flippers	0 1¼		
Breadth of longest claws on posterior flippers	0 0⅜		
From root of tail to genital slit	1 2		0 6
From root of tail to hind teats		1 2	
From root of tail to forward teats		1 10	
Distance between the two hind teats across the belly		0 5	
Distance between the two forward teats across the belly		0 8	
Thickness of blubber	0 1	0 0¾	0 0½

Number of whiskers on each side of the face: No. 1, thirty-one; No. 2, thirty-five; No. 3, thirty-six and thirty-five.

Three other males were measured at the same time of the first example, which varied but little in their proportions. The number of claws on posterior flippers of No. 1 were five, three of which were rudimentary. In the adult female example, (No. 2) the blubber was half an inch thick on the back, and one inch on the belly.

The following are the measurements, etc. (in feet and inches), of a female Sea Lion (No. 1), supposed to be a yearling, taken at Santa Barbara Island; and of a new-born female Sea Lion pup, (No. 2), taken at the same island, May 3d, 1873:

	No. 1.	No. 2.
Length of animal from tip of nose to tip of posterior flippers	4 10	2 4
Length of posterior flippers	0 11	0 5½
From tip of nose to root of tail	3 10½	1 11
Length of tail	0 2½	0 1½
From tip of nose to pectorals	2 0	0 10½
Length of pectorals	1 2½	0 7
Breadth of pectorals	0 4½	0 3
Girth of body behind pectorals	2 7	1 3
Girth of body at junction with posterior flippers	1 1	0 6¾

	No. 1.	No. 2.
From tip of nose to corner of mouth	0 3¼	0 2
From end of under jaw to corner of mouth	0 2	
From tip of nose to eye	0 3	0 1¾
From tip of nose to ear	0 6	0 4
Length of ear	0 1¼	
Thickness of blubber	0 0¾	0 0¼

In the first example, the whiskers on each side of the face numbered thirty-five and thirty-six; length of the longest whisker, four and three-eighths of an inch. The color of the second example was black above, a little lighter below, with scattering hairs of light brown or dull white. It had three rudimentary claws on each pectoral; and five claws on posterior flippers, two of which were rudimentary. Weight of animals, respectively, eighty and ten and a half pounds.

We give also several zincographic illustrations, which may afford a better idea of the different forms of the animals in varied attitudes, as well as their facial expression when sleeping, waking, and when in a state of excitement, which is manifested by howling or roaring.

Both males and females have a double coating of fat or blubber, lying between the skin and the flesh of the body. These coatings are separated by a thin layer of muscular tissue. The fat yields the oil of commerce, although inferior in quality to that of the Sea Elephant. The young pups, or whelps, are of a slate or black color, and the yearlings of a chestnut brown. An erroneous impression generally prevails relative to the size of the Sea Lion, which is considered, by many, to be of mammoth proportions. And, when describing the larger species of mammalia found in the vast ocean, there is a manifest propensity to magnify them until transformed into huge monsters, like the whale of the ancient voyagers, which "wore nine hundred foot long," or that distinguished specimen of the seal family, honored with the name of "Ben Butler," who, with his troop, holds possession of Seal Rock, off the cliffs of San Francisco, and that has been estimated at the great weight of two thousand pounds.

The habits of the Sea Lion exhibit many striking features. It not only dwells near the Arctic and Antarctic latitudes, but it basks upon the glittering sands under an equatorial sun. On approaching an island, or point, occupied by a numerous herd, one first hears their long, plaintive howlings, as if in distress; but, when near them, the sounds become more varied, and deafening. The old males roar so loudly as to drown the noise of the heaviest surf among the rocks and caverns; and the younger of both sexes, together with the "clapmatches," croak hoarsely, or send forth sounds like the bleating of sheep or the barking of dogs;

in fact, their tumultuous utterances are beyond description. A rookery of the matured animals presents a ferocious and defiant appearance; but usually, at the approach of man, they become alarmed, and, if not opposed in their escape, roll, tumble, and sometimes make fearful leaps, from high precipitous rocks, to hasten their flight. Like all others of the seal tribe, they are gregarious, and gather in the largest numbers during the "pupping season," which varies in different latitudes. On the California coast it is from May to August, inclusive, and upon the shores of Alaska it is said to be from June to October; during which period the females bring forth their young, nurse them, associate with the valiant males, and both unite in the care of the little ones, keeping a wary guard, and teaching them, by their own parental actions, how to move over the broken, slimy, rock-bound shore, or upon the sandy, pebbly beaches, and to dive and gambol amid the surf and rolling ground-swells. At first the pups manifest great aversion to the water, but soon, instinctively, become active and playful in the element; so, by the time the season is over, the juvenile creatures disappear with the greater portion of the old ones; only a few of the vast herd remaining at the favorite resorts throughout the year. During the pupping season, both males and females, so far as we could ascertain, take but little if any food, particularly the males; though the females have been observed to leave their charges and go off, apparently in search of subsistence, but they do not venture far from their young ones. That the Sea Lion can go without food for a long time is unquestionable. One of the superintendents of Woodward's Gardens informed me, that in numerous instances they had received Sea Lions into the aquarium, which did not eat a morsel of nourishment during a whole month, and appeared to suffer but little inconvenience from their long fast.

As the time approaches for the annual assemblage, those returning or coming from abroad are seen near the shores, appearing wild and shy. Soon after, however, the females gather upon the beaches, cliffs, or rocks, when the battles among the old males begin for the supreme control of the harems; these struggles often lasting for days, the fight being kept up until one or both become exhausted, but is renewed again when sufficiently recuperated for another attack; and, really, the attitudes assumed, and the passes made at each other, equal the amplifications of a professional fencer. The combat lasts until both become disabled, or one is driven from the ground, or perhaps both become so reduced that a third party, fresh from his winter migration, drives them from the coveted charge. The vanquished animals then slink off to some retired spot, as if disgraced. Nevertheless, at times, two or more will have charge of the same rookery; but, in such instances, frequent defiant growlings and petty battles occur. So far as we have observed upon the

Sea Lions of the California coast, there is but little attachment manifested between the sexes; indeed, much of the Turkish nature is apparent. But the females show some affection for their offspring: yet, if alarmed when upon the land, they will instantly desert them, and take to the water. The young cubs, on the other hand, are the most fractious and savage little creatures imaginable, especially if awakened from their nearly continuous sleeping; and frequently, when a mother reclines to nurse her single whelp, a swarm of others will perhaps contend for the same favor.*

To give a more extended and detailed account of the Sea Lions, we will relate a brief sketch of a sealing season on Santa Barbara Island. It was near the end of May, 1852, when we arrived; and, soon after, the rookeries of "clapmatches," which were scattered around the island, began to augment, and large numbers of huge males made their appearance, belching forth sharp, ugly howls, and leaping out of or darting through the water with surprising velocity; frequently diving outside the rollers, the next moment emerging from the crest of the foaming break-

---

* It is positively asserted by the natives of St. Paul's Island, Behring Sea, that the female Sea Lion of that locality suckles the male pup the second year. Special Agent Bryant, who has passed several seasons upon this island, has informed us that he has investigated the matter as far as practicable, and gives credit to the assertion. There would seem to be nothing improbable about the young Sea Lion suckling the second year, as the fact of yearlings of land mammals doing likewise is fully established. But whether the female Sea Lion, of a year's growth, is denied the nourishment which is afforded to the male, would seem a critical question; yet, if such is the fact, this may account for the great discrepancy of size between the adult males and females.

Although a digression from, yet in a sense corroborative of, the habits imputed to the Sea Lion, in nursing its young, we will mention facts which have just come to our knowledge, through the whalemen at Monterey Bay, California, which present nearly a parallel case with that of the Sea Lions. On the 1st of October, 1873, the whalers captured a cow whale of the Humpback species; also a calf that was with

her, which was judged to be about one year old. That this yearling was the offspring of the captured female, there can be no question, as she followed close to the calf (which was first harpooned) until it was nearly lifeless; and when the exhausted creature was about to expire, the mother made an effort to support it by holding it upon the surface of the water with her head. These solicitous manifestations on the part of the female are regarded as unquestionable evidence, that the young whale in question was her cherished offspring. As soon as it expired, the mother turned to make her escape, but while in this act, she was "harpooned" and "bombed," killing her almost instantly. Both whales were towed to the station; and when the calf was cut in, it was found to be a male; and on flensing the mother, a well-grown fœtus was found in her, which proved, in this instance, that the yearling whale not only follows its dam, but during that period the mother associates with the adult males, and again becomes pregnant before separating from her former calf. At the time of the capture of the two whales above mentioned, an adult bull was in their company, which was also captured.

ers, and waddling up the beach with head erect, or, with seeming effort, climbing some kelp-fringed rock, to doze in the scorching sunbeams, while others would lie sleeping or playing among the beds of sea-weed, with their heads and outstretched limbs above the surface. But a few days elapsed before a general contention, with the adult males, began for the mastery of the different rookeries, and the victims of the bloody encounters were to be seen on all sides of the island, with torn lips, or mutilated limbs and gashed sides; while, now and then, an unfortunate creature would be met with, minus an eye, or with the orb forced from its socket, and, together with other wounds, presenting a ghastly appearance. As the time of "hauling up" drew near, the island became one mass of animation; every beach, rock, and cliff, where a seal could find foot-hold, became its resting-place; while a countless herd of old males capped the summit, and the united clamorings of the vast assemblage could be heard, on a calm day, for miles at sea. The south side of the island is high and precipitous, with a projecting ledge hardly perceptible from the beach below, upon which one immense Sea Lion managed to climb, and there remained for several weeks—until the season was over. How he ascended, or in what manner he retired to the water, was a mystery to our numerous ship's-crew, as he came and went in the night; for "Old Gray"—as named by the sailors—was closely watched in his elevated position during the time the men were engaged at their work on shore.*

None but the adult males were captured, which was usually done by shooting them in the ear or near it; for a ball in any other part of the body had no more effect than it would in a grizzly bear. Occasionally, however, they are taken with the club and lance, only shooting a few of the masters of the herd. This is easily accomplished with an experienced crew, if there is sufficient ground back from the beach for the animals to retreat. During our stay, an instance occurred, which not only displayed the sagacity of the animals, but also their yielding disposition, when hard pressed in certain situations, as if naturally designed to be slain in numbers equal to the demands of their human pursuers. On the south of Santa Barbara

* Relative to the Sea Lions leaping from giddy heights, an incident occurred at Santa Barbara Island, the last of the season of 1852, which we will here mention. A rookery of about twenty individuals was collected on the brink of a precipitous cliff, at a height at least of sixty feet above the rocks which shelved from the beach below; and our party were sure in their own minds, that, by surprising the animals, we could drive them over the cliff. This was easily accomplished; but, to our chagrin, when we arrived at the point below, where we expected to find the huge beasts helplessly mutilated, or killed outright, the last animal of the whole rookery was seen plunging into the sea.

Island was a plateau, elevated less than a hundred feet above the sea, stretching to the brink of a cliff that overhung the shore, and a narrow gorge leading up from the beach, through which the animals crawled to their favorite resting-place. As the sun dipped behind the hills, fifty to a hundred males would congregate upon the spot, and there remain until the boats were lowered in the morning, when immediately the whole herd would quietly slip off into the sea and gambol about during the day, returning as they saw the boats again leave the island for the ship. Several unsuccessful attempts had been made to take them; but, at last, a fresh breeze commenced blowing directly from the shore, and prevented their scenting the hunters, who landed some distance from the rookery, then cautiously advanced, and suddenly, yelling, and flourishing muskets, clubs, and lances, rushed up within a few yards of them, while the pleading creatures, with lolling tongues and glaring eyes, were quite overcome with dismay, and remained nearly motionless. At last, two overgrown males broke through the line formed by the men, but they paid the penalty with their lives before reaching the water. A few moments passed, when all hands moved slowly toward the rookery, which as slowly retreated. This maneuvre is called "turning them," and, when once accomplished, the disheartened creatures appear to abandon all hope of escape, and resign themselves to their fate. The herd at this time numbered seventy-five, which were soon dispatched, by shooting the largest ones, and clubbing and lancing the others, save one young Sea Lion, which was spared to ascertain whether it would make any resistance by being driven over the hills beyond. The poor creature only moved along through the prickly pears that covered the ground, when compelled by his cruel pursuers; and, at last, with an imploring look and writhing in pain, it held out its fin-like arms, which were pierced with thorns, in such a manner as to touch the sympathy of the barbarous sealers, who instantly put the sufferer out of its misery by the stroke of a heavy club. As soon as the animal is killed, the longest spires of its whiskers are pulled out, then it is skinned, and its coating of fat cut in sections from its body and transported to the vessel, where, after being "minced," the oil is extracted by boiling. The testes are taken out, and, with the selected spires of the whiskers, find a market in China—the former being used medicinally, and the latter for personal ornaments.

At the close of the season—which lasts about three months, on the California coast—a large majority of the great herds, both males and females, return to the sea, and roam in all directions in quest of food, as but few of them could find sustenance about the waters contiguous to the islands, or points on the mainland, which are their annual resorting-places. They live upon fish, mollusks, crustaceans, and sea-fowls; always with the addition of a few pebbles or smooth stones, some of which are a pound in weight.* Their principal feathery food, however, is the penguin, in the southern hemisphere, and the gulls in the northern; while the manner in which they decoy and catch the *gaviota* of the Mexican and Californian coasts, displays no little degree of cunning. When in pursuit, the animal dives deeply under water and swims some distance from where it disappeared; then, rising cautiously, it exposes the tip of its nose above the surface, at the same time giving it a rotary motion, like that of a water-bug at play. The unwary bird on the wing, seeing the object near by, alights to catch it, while the Sea Lion, at the same moment, settles beneath the waves, and at one bound, with extended jaws, seizes its screaming prey, and instantly devours it.

A few years ago great numbers of Sea Lions were taken along the coast of Upper and Lower California, and thousands of barrels of oil obtained. The number of seals slain exclusively for their oil would appear fabulous, when we realize the fact that it requires on an average, throughout the season, the blubber of three or four Sea Lions to produce a barrel of oil. Their thick, coarse-grained skins were not considered worth preparing for market, in a country where manual labor was so highly valued. At the present time, however, they are valuable for glue-stock, and the seal-hunter now realizes more comparative profit from the hides than from the oil. But while the civilized sealers, plying their vocation along the sea-board of California and Mexico, destroy the *Leon marino*, for the product of its oil, skin, testes, and whiskers, the simple Aleutians of the Alaska region derive from these animals many of their indispensable articles of domestic use. It appears an

* The enormous quantity of food which would be required to maintain the herd of many thousands, which, in former years, annually assembled at the small island of Santa Barbara, would seem incredible, if they daily obtained the allowance given to a male and female Sea Lion, on exhibition at Woodward's Gardens, San Francisco, California, where the keeper informed me that he fed them regularly, every day, forty pounds of fresh fish. Since these animals have taken up their abode in the ponds of the gardens, the male has become quite expert in catching food within his jaws, as it is thrown to him or near him, while lying upon a pile of rocks in the centre of the pond. Sometimes a piece of sturgeon, upon which fish the animals are chiefly fed, would be thrown in the water near by; and, although it would sink out of sight from the surface, the huge beast would make a bound from the rocks, and diving, would instantly recover it and again return to his elevated position; or when a morsel lodged upon the rocks, he would seize and devour it in a moment, and in the same manner as the animal picks up a crab, with his mouth, from the slimy rocks of the ocean, and instantly bolts it. The female was fed in the water; and as the food was thrown from side to side in the aquarium, the animal would dart through the element with surprising velocity to receive it.

instructive fact in the order of Providence, that the northern belt of coast is clothed with gigantic forests, and swarms with terrestrial animals of the chase, whereby the natives of the wooded regions find means of transport across the inland waters, and ample clothing from the skins of the animals which range through their hunt-ing-grounds, while the thousand islands which diversify the shore between the capes of Mendocino and Ommany are but sparsely inhabited by the *Eumetopias*, and those found are turned to little account by the semi-aquatic savage. But on the seal islands of Alaska, where the only timber at hand is drifted from the great rivers draining the wooded main-land, or borne by the Kamschatka branch of the Kuro Siwo, we find rookeries of the largest Sea Lions met with upon the shores of the Pacific, gathered with the great herds of Fur Seals which constitute the chief wealth of Alaska; and although the two species differ in their character, still they are found peacefully occupying the same or adjacent breeding-grounds. The Aleutians even aver that the Sea Lion and the Fur Seal sometimes cohabit together.

The principal rookery of Sea Lions on St. Paul Island is near its north-east point; and to this place the natives resort, between the toils of the Fur Seal season, to make their annual "drive" to their village, which is clustered about the slope and glen of the opposite shore. This "drive," to the good-natured Aleuts, is what the buffalo-hunt has been to the red-skins on the plains of the Platte, or *matanza*-time with the old Californians; for the party starts out as on a sporting foray, and at night they stealthily get between the herd of Sea Lions and the water; then, with professional strategy, they manage to "cut out" six or eight of the largest at a time, and drive them a short distance inland, where they are guarded until a band of two or three hundred are assembled. Formerly the implement used in driving was a pole with a small flag at the end; but, since our adopted country-folk have become more Americanized, that Yankee production, a cotton umbrella, has been substituted, and it is said that any refractory *siutch* in the "drive" is instantly subdued by the sudden expansion and contraction of an umbrella in the hands of a pursuing native.

To collect the desired number for the yearly supply involves several days; therefore a throng of villagers, it is said, sets out prepared with everything needful for the campaign. As the work of driving goes on only at night, the day is passed in sleeping and cooking their food by smoldering fires of drift-wood and seal-fat, sheltered by their umbrellas, or a sort of tent contrived by spreading blankets and garments over whales' ribs in lieu of tent-poles—never forgetting in their repast the fragrant *chi*, which is quaffed in numberless cups from the steaming *sam-o-var*. At length, the whole troop of animals being assembled, a flash of umbrellas here and there, with the call of the herdsmen, brings all into moving phalanx. But the time for driving must be either at night, after the dew is fallen, or upon a dark, misty, or rainy day; as the thick mat of grass that covers the land must be wet, in order that the animals may easily slip along in their vaulting gait over the green road to their place of execution. Under the most favorable circumstances, the march does not exceed six miles in twenty-four hours; and it being a distance of four leagues or more to the village, three days and nights, or more, are spent before they arrive at the slaughtering place. There they are allowed to remain quiet for a day, to cool their blood, which becomes much heated by the tedious journey; after which, they are killed by shooting. The dead animals are then skinned, and their hides packed in tiers until fermented sufficiently to start the hair, when they are stretched on frames to dry, and eventually become the covering or planking for the Aleutian *baidarkas* and *baidarras*. The fat is taken off and used for fuel, or the oil is rendered to burn in their lamps. The flesh is cut in thin pieces from the carcass, laid in the open air to dry, and becomes a choice article of food. The sinews are extracted, and afterward twisted into thread. The lining of the animal's throat is put through a course of tanning, and then made into boots, the soles of which are the under covering of the Sea Lion's fin-like feet. The intestines are carefully taken out, cleaned, blown up, stretched to dry, then tanned, and worked into water-proof clothing. The stomach is emptied of its contents, turned inside out, then inflated and dried for oil-bottles, or it is used as a receptacle for the preserved meat; and what remains of the once formidable and curious animal is only a mutilated skeleton.

Crossing Behring and the Okhotsk seas, to the coasts of Siberia, including the peninsula of Kamschatka and the island of Saghalien, the mode of capture by the natives changes from that of the eastern continental shores. The inlets and rivers of these Asiatic regions swarm with salmon from June to September, and at this season the seals follow, and prey upon them as they ascend the streams. The natives then select such places as will be left nearly bare at low tide, and there set their nets—which are made of seal-thongs—to strong stakes, so placed as to form a curve open to the confluence of the stream. These nets are similar to gill-nets, the meshes being of a size to admit the seal's head—which gives free passage to the shoals of fish—and the pursuing animal, as soon as entangled in the net, struggles forward in its efforts to escape, but is held firmly in the meshes, where it remains till low water, when the natives, in their flat-bottomed skin-boats, approach and dispatch the victim with their rude bone implements. As the season becomes warm, the animals of both sexes congregate in their favorite rookeries, and the females climb to the most inaccessible places among the rocks and crags, to bring forth and nurture their offspring. But here they are hunted by the natives accustomed to the use of fire-arms, who shoot them for the skins of the young ones, which are used for clothing.

In this region also, during the spring and fall, after the "net-sealing" is over, great numbers of Sea Lions are captured upon the floating ice, with gun or spear; and during the rigorous months, the seal-hunters cut through the congealed mass what they term "breathing-holes." Through these the seals emerge to the frosted surface, and, if the sun peers through the wintery clouds, the creature, warmed into new life, may stroll hundreds of yards away; the watchful hunter, secreted behind a cake of ice or a bank of snow, rushes out from his covert, and places a covering over the hole, effectually preventing the animal's escape, and then dispatches it with knife and spear. Its skin is stripped off, scraped clean, closely rolled, and laid away until the hair starts—this process is called "souring;" then the hair is scoured off, and the bare hide is stretched to season—a process usually requiring about ten days—when it is taken down and rubbed between the hands to make it pliable; this completes the whole course of dressing it. The prepared hides are then converted into harness for the sledge-dogs and reindeer, and water-proof bags; if wanted for the soles of moccasins, or to cover their skin-boats, they are dried with the hair on, and become nearly as stiff as plates of iron. The blubber of the animals, if killed in the fall or winter, is preserved by freezing, and is used for food, fuel, and lights, as desired; while the same part of those taken during the spring and summer is put in the skins of young seals, and placed in earthen vaults, where it keeps fresh until required for consumption. The residue of the animal is tumbled into a reservoir, sunk below the surface of the ground, where it is kept for the winter's supply of food for the dogs, which live upon the frozen flesh and entrails of the seals, whose skin furnishes the tackle by which they transport the primitive sledge over the snow-clad wastes of Siberia and Kamschatka.

In the southern regions, the Sea Lion is but rarely pursued by the aborigines; for the Fuegians, who are so little elevated above the beast, have no means of capturing the animal, as have the Aleuts and Koraks of the north; and those degraded types of humanity, who wander about the shores of Tierra del Fuego, partake of the same food as do the amphibious herds. But the Patagonians are sometimes found clothed in long mantles of Sea Lion skins, and the seal is otherwise utilized by them. Along the coasts of Chile and Peru, the inflated skins of the Sea Lion are frequently used instead of the wooden *balsa*, or catamaran. The vast herds of these marine animals, to the far north and south, do not materially diminish, as they are hunted by the natives solely for domestic consumption; but those on our California shores will soon be exterminated by the deadly shot of the rifle, or driven away to less accessible haunts.

CHAPTER III.

THE BANDED SEAL.

HISTRIOPHOCA EQUESTRIS, *Gill*. (Plate xxi, fig. 1, 2.)

Of this beautifully marked animal, which attains the length of six or eight feet, there is but very little known. Its geographical distribution is said to extend eastward to Amoor land. It is found upon the coast of Alaska, bordering on Behring Sea, and the natives of Ounalaska recognize it as an occasional visitor to the Aleutian Islands. It is said to be found in greater numbers on the Asiatic coast than on the American. In April, 1852, we observed a herd of seals upon the beaches at Point Reyes, California; these, without close examination, answered to the description given by Gill, which is as follows: "The species is remarkable for color as well as structural peculiarities. The male is at once recognizable by the color, and this may be said to be a chocolate brown, except (1) a band of whitish yellow, bent forward toward the crown around the neck; (2), an oval ring of the same color on each side, encircling the fore feet and passing in front just before them; and (3) another band, also bent forward above, behind the middle of the trunk. There is considerable variation in extent of these bands, and sometimes the puribrachial rings are more or less confluent with the posterior band. The females are simply whitish yellow, or have very indistinct traces of the pastmidian band." Although we are quite confident the seals we saw on Point Reyes were the same as those described by Gill, still it is a remarkable fact that we have never seen this species on the coast of California since. The Russian traders, who formerly visited Cape Romanzoff, from St. Michael's, Norton Sound, frequently brought back the skins of the male *Histriophoca*, which were used for covering trunks and for other ornamental purposes.

Plate XXI.

C.M.Scammon, del.

BANDED SEAL. (HISTRIOPHOCA EQUESTRIS) GILL.
1.MALE _ 2.FEMALE

C.M.Scammon, del.

FUR SEAL. (CALLORHINUS URSINUS.) GRAY
1 MALE _ 2 FEMALE

CHAPTER IV.

FUR SEALS.

THE NORTHERN FUR SEAL (CALLORHINUS URSINUS, *Gray.*)   (Plate xxi, fig. 1, 2.)

The Fur Seals have so wide a geographical range—extending nearly to the highest navigable latitudes in both the northern and southern hemispheres—and are found assembled in such countless numbers at their favorite resorts, that they become at once a source of great commercial wealth; and, among marine mammalia, they are the most interesting we have met with. Captain Fanning—one of the noted sealing-masters in early times—distinguished the different ages and sexes as follows: "Full-aged males, called 'wigs;' the females, 'clapmatches;' those not quite so old, 'bulls;' all the half-grown of both sexes, 'yearlings;' the young of nearly a year old, called 'gray' or 'silvered pups;' and before their coats are changed to this shade, called 'black pups.'"

The color of the full-grown males, or "wigs," is dark brown—with scattering hairs of white about the head, neck, and anterior portion of the body—and, in some instances, nearly approaches to black. At a distance, it is difficult to distinguish between an old "wig" and a full-grown male Sea Lion of the California coast, the former being frequently found measuring nine feet from tip of nose to extremity of posterior flippers.

The "clapmatches" average fully one-half the length of the largest "wigs," and the greater portion of them are of a silver-gray color; the very oldest, however, are dark brown on the back and sides, with scattering white hairs over all. The fur is reddish brown inside. The thick mixture of black, glistening hairs imparts the dark hue to the oldest animals, and the white hairs on the younger ones give them the silvery lustre. Both old and young are of lighter shade underneath, particularly about the pectorals and posterior portions of the body. The layer of fat, or blubber, between the skin and flesh, may average one and a half inch in thickness, varying according to the time the animal has been on shore—it being very fat when the season begins, and very lean when the season is over, which changes the animal's appearance considerably from its former robust condition. When in full flesh, the adult females weigh about eighty-five pounds.

Following are measurements of five female Fur Seals, taken at the mouth of the Strait of San Juan de Fuca, in the spring of 1869:

	No. 1.		No. 2.		No 3.	
Length of animal from tip of nose to tip of tail.............	4	0	4	7	4	0
Length of tail...	0	1½	0	2	0	1½
Length of posterior flippers................................	1	4	1	6	1	4
Extreme width of posterior flippers when expanded	0	8	0	8	0	7
From end of posterior flippers to nails or claws on same	0	6			0	6
Length of nails or claws..................................	0	0¾			0	0¾
From tip of nose to ear...................................	0	6¼	0	6½	0	6
Length of each ear	0	1¼	0	1½	0	1¼
Length of under jaw.......................................	0	2	0	2½	0	2
From tip of nose to eye...................................	0	2½	0	2¾	0	2½
Length of fissure between the eyelids......................	0	1½				
From tip of nose to pectorals.............................	1	11	2	0	1	10
Length of each pectoral...................................	1	2	1	2	1	2
Width of each pectoral....................................	0	5	0	5	0	4¼
Circumference of body just behind pectorals................	2	7	3	0	2	5

	No. 4.		No. 5.	
Length of animal from tip of nose to tip of tail....................	4	9	3	6
Length of tail..	0	2	0	1½
Length of posterior flippers......................................	1	5	1	3
Breadth of posterior flippers when expanded			0	7
From end of posterior flippers to nails...........................	0	3		
Length of nails on posterior flippers	0	0¾		
From tip of nose to pectorals.....................................			1	4
Length of pectorals...	1	2	1	1
Width of pectorals	0	5	0	4½
From tip of nose to ear..			0	6
Length of each ear			0	1½
From tip of nose to eye..			0	2½
Length of under jaw...			0	2
Circumference of body just behind pectorals.......................	3	1	2	2½

The succeeding figures afford a general illustration of the forms, or proportions, of the animals, when in various attitudes. The zincograph (No. 1) of the full-aged male gives a good representation of the animal's anterior figure, as well as imparting, to some degree, the surly expression ever present with those veterans who have fought for prestige upon the rookeries many successive seasons. No. 2 is an excellent representation of a female head when seen in that position. No. 3 affords a good idea of the outline of the head (side view), and the expression of the harmless mother, who bears her offspring, and submits to the harsh treatment of her male companion and master, without manifest complaint or resistance.

No. i.—Full-Aged Male Fur Seal, St. Paul's Island. (*Drawn by Elliott.*)

Nos. 4 and 5 represent the relative proportions of a female, (view from side and below, which were drawn from a dead animal, verified by measurements. No. 6 illustrates the familiar attitudes of Fur Seals of both sexes, more especially the younger animals, or those supposed to be three or four years old.

It is very rarely that the "clapmatch" has more than one pup. Out of twenty-two individuals examined, not one was found with twins; and the Indians about Fuca Strait say they never have seen two fœtuses in the same seal. They have, however, two teats each side of the belly, nearly on a line with the corners of the mouth and the posterior limbs. While taking measurements of some "clapmatches" at the summer village of Kiddy Kubbit, situated near the mouth and on the south side of the strait, where the animals lay in one of the large lodges, the women were engaged in skinning them and trying out the oil from the blubber. The question arose, whether a Fur Seal ever had more than one pup at a birth. A bevy of squaws discussed the subject with great spirit, raising such a din about our ears that nothing else could be heard; at last, a herculean *kloochman* clutched a knife, and slashing into the seals, brought forth one pup only from each individual, and, with a knowing look as well as a multitude of words, gave us to understand that this examination, together with past experience in the matter, was proof positive that the offspring of this species of mammalia did not come in pairs.

The time of gestation has been supposed to be about nine months, but later observations at the seal islands of Behring Sea prove it to be at least ten months, or more. The pups, when first born, are about one-third the length of the mother. They are covered with a thick mat of coarse fur, which changes to a finer texture and lighter shade as the animals mature. The time of bringing forth the young ("pupping season"), on the coast of California, is from May to August, including a part of both months; on the coast of Patagonia, and the latitudes near Cape Horn, from October to March.

The flippers of the Fur Seal are destitute of hair, being covered with tough, black skin, similar to shagreen, which is very flexible about the terminations of their extremities; the side limbs are shaped much like the fins of the smaller Cetaceans; the posterior ones have each five distinct toes, or digits, and three nails, or claws, project from their upper sides, four inches or more from their tips, according to the size and age of the animal. The tail is extremely short, and pointed. The ears are quite pointed also, slanting backward, and are covered with short, fine hair. The head, in proportion, is longer and sharper than that of the Leopard Seal. The number of whiskers on each side of the face may average twenty; they are of different shades, from blackish brown to white, and frequently attain the length of seven inches. The eyes are invariably dark and glistening, and have a human-like expression.

The intrinsic value of the animal does not depend upon the price of its skin alone; for the layer of fat adhering to it yields the oil of commerce, and supplies light and heat to the natives in their dismal winter quarters. The flesh, likewise, affords them a staple article of food. Fanning, as well as other early voyagers, speaks of the flesh of the Fur Seal pups, when six weeks old or more, as being

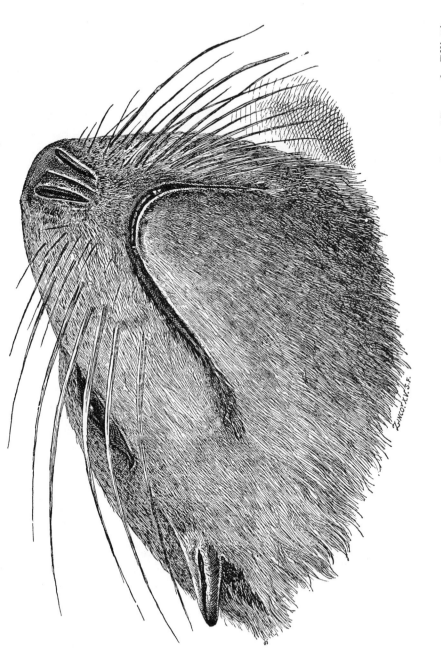

No. 2.—HEAD OF FEMALE FUR SEAL, VIEWED FROM BELOW, TWO-THIRDS NATURAL SIZE. (*Drawn by Elliott.*)

equal to the best mutton, if properly cooked. Notwithstanding, after repeated trials, we confess our preference for the latter. The hearts and livers of young seals, whether of the Fur or Hair species, are excellent; but we would advise those fond of fresh meat not to witness the killing of the animals and the extraction of those choice portions of them. The employés of the Russian-American Company frequently salted seal meat for ship's use, when a supply of beef could not be obtained.

The habits of the Fur Seals differ in several respects from those of the numerous Hair species. One of their most remarkable traits is their extended geographical range. To give a clear idea of their varied haunts as regards climate and diversity of locality, we may mention the following as among their favorite resorting-places: The coast of Patagonia, west coast of Africa, Falklands, New South Shetlands, South Georgia, southern coast of Chile, island of Masafuero, Lobos Islands (on the coast of Peru), Galapagos Islands (off the coast of Ecuador), the islands of Desolation, Crozets, and St. Paul's in the Indian Ocean, and St. Paul and St. George islands (Behring Sea), and Robin and Jonas islands in the Okhotsk Sea. Thus it will be seen that these curious animals are inhabitants of the antipodes of the globe, and bask in a tropical sun as well as endure the rigors of the icy regions of the Arctic and Antarctic.

Some idea may be had of their numbers in former years, when on the island of Masafuero, on the coast of Chile—which is not over twenty-five miles in circumference—the American ship *Betsey*, under the command of Captain Fanning, in the year 1798,* obtained a full cargo of choice skins. It was estimated at the time

---

* At the present day, when the American ships that double Cape Horn, and the Cape of Good Hope, are magnificent types of naval architecture compared with those of the early voyages, a reminiscent note, relative to the *Betsey*, her owners, commander, and ship's company, is of peculiar interest, as portraying the character of all those who, at that period, entered so practically yet enthusiastically into commercial pursuits. "In the early part of the month of May, 1797," writes Captain Fanning, "it was the good fortune of the author to meet at New York with Captain John Whetten, a gentleman distinguished as an able navigator, and at the time in command of the ship *Ontario*, in the China trade. With him originated, and with him also was the project first discussed, of fitting out a suitable vessel, which should proceed to the South Seas, there to procure a cargo of Fur Seal skins, and with this cargo thence to cross the Pacific for the Canton market, where the article was well ascertained to be greatly in demand, and held at prices that furnished good grounds upon which to hope that a very handsome profit would be realized. Another great inducement held out in favor of the attempt, was the probability that Captain Whetten himself, in the *Ontario*, would be at Canton at about the period of the arrival there (which would be in our fall part of the year, say the month of September, October, or November) of any vessel shortly fitted out. The intimate knowl·

No. 3.—Head of Female Fur Seal, side view, two-thirds Natural Size. (*Drawn by Elliott.*)

that there were left on the island at least five hundred thousand seals. Subsequently, there were taken from the island but little short of one million skins.

The seal fishery was extensively prosecuted for many years by our countrymen. The sealing fleet on the coast of Chile alone, in 1801, amounted to thirty vessels, many of which were ships of the larger class, and nearly all were under the American flag. Up to the present day, American vessels are the pioneers in the most remote and unexplored regions, wherever the migratory animals are to be found in sufficient numbers to induce that class of our seamen who are fond of a sportsman's life, in addition to that of sea-faring, to embark in the enterprise.

In the midst of the Crimean War, an enterprising firm in New London, Connecticut, fitted out a clipper bark, which was officered and manned expressly for a

edge Captain Whetten had of the manner of doing business with these people, and the great assistance he could afford, being conversant in all their intricate trade, and in the purchasing of silks and other articles for the New York market, as our homeward cargo, were certainly such arguments as were well calculated to increase the confidence of success in the contemplated voyage. This was an opportunity not to be left unimproved; and to one naturally possessed of an ambitious and aspiring mind, with a strong attachment to a seaman's profession, increased as it had been, since my first visit to the South Seas, by a perusal of the voyages of such circumnavigators as Drake, Byron, Anson, Bouganville, Cook, and others, the hope of being able to add some new discoveries to the knowledge already in the possession of man relating to those seas, and the no less flattering hope of realizing a fortune should the enterprise be well conducted and successful in its termination, were sufficient to bind me to exert myself in bringing about this desired voyage. Every view was encouraging; but funds were necessary, and to raise these without delay, I applied to that upright and liberal merchant, Mr. Elias Nexsen, with whom also to consult and advise upon the best means of securing the early fitting-out and sailing of the enterprise. To the information and encouragement given by Captain Whetten,

was added my own strong confidence in its practicability, and the flattering results that such an adventure held forth. The plan met with his entire approval, and after some conversation with Captain Whetten, on 'Change that day, in the afternoon of the same he made the offer of his brig, the *Betsey*, then in port. She was New York built, a little short of one hundred tons, and an excellent vessel of her class. 'If she will answer,' said he, 'I will put her into the business, and at whatever price, upon a minute inspection, her value shall be ascertained to be, I will take the one-half in the adventure of the vessel, and her outfits.' I was unable," adds the captain, "to take more than one-eighth myself, but the remaining three were, by the evening of the same day, taken by other friends, and thus the whole amount required to insure the sailing of the vessel was made up. An inventory was taken, agreeably to the understanding at the commencement, by which the value of the vessel was ascertained, and made satisfactory to all concerned. In less than a month from the time the enterprise was first entertained, the *Betsey* sailed from New York, to stop at New Haven (the native place of Mr. Caleb Brintnall, the first officer, a great disciplinarian), and afterward at Stonington, to obtain and complete her complement of men, in all twenty-seven; for it had been concluded to be the

No. 4.—Side View of Female Fur Seal.

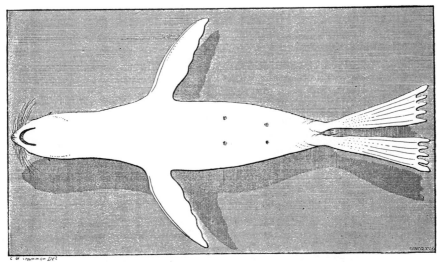

No. 5.—View of Female Fur Seal from below.

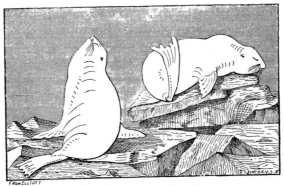

No. 6.—Attitudes of Fur Seals.

sealing voyage in the Okhotsk Sea. The captain was a veteran in the business, and many thought him too old to command, but the result of the voyage proved him equal to the task. The vessel proceeded to Robin Island—a mere volcanic rock, situated on the eastern side of the large island of Saghalien. Many outlying rocks and reefs are about it, making it dangerous to approach, and affording but slight shelter for an anchorage. Here the vessel (of about three hundred tons) lay, with ground-tackle of the weight for a craft of twice her size. Much of the time fresh winds prevailed, accompanied by the usual ugly ground-swell; and, in consequence of her being long, low, and sharp, the deck was at such times frequently flooded; nevertheless, she "rode out the whole season, though wet as a half-tide rock," and a valuable cargo of skins was procured, which brought an unusually

most judicious policy, to select the greatest proportion of them from the New England States. Having obtained the number of hands required for the *Betsey*, on the 13th day of June, 1797, the vessel was got under way, and proceeded to sea, from Stonington, Connecticut. When off Watch-hill Point, (situated about nine leagues to the northward of Montague Light, on the east end of Long Island) she was brought to, in order to discharge the pilot, and the occasion was embraced, as the best suited to ascertain the minds and inclinations of the seamen. All hands were therefore mustered on deck, aft, and liberty was given to all such as were disinclined to proceed on the voyage—to all those who were unwilling to encounter the dangers, privations, and sufferings, usually attendant on similar expeditions—now to return with the pilot. Notwithstanding this, no one seemed so inclined, but all, to a man, answered, their desire was to proceed on the voyage, confirming the same by three hearty cheers. And here it may be remarked, that a more orderly and cheerful crew never sailed round the world in any vessel. The pilot accordingly returned by himself. At six P.M. we took our departure from Block Island, with a fine breeze from the southwest." On their passage to the Cape de Verde Islands, as related on the ship's log, "At four P.M. fell in with a mast; sent the boat to tow it alongside;

hoisted it on deck, to be made to answer any purpose that future emergency might require." "While on the passage to the Cape de Verdes, by the expressed wish and counsel of the officers, it was thought advisable to alter the rig of the *Betsey*, and change her into a ship. This, it was supposed, and afterward ascertained to be the fact, would be greatly to our advantage; for while laying off and on at the seal islands, to procure our cargo of Fur Seal skins, the cabin-boy alone could tend and work a mizzen-topsail, who certainly would be altogether unable to do anything with the heavy boom of a brig's fore-and-aft mainsail. At this place the alteration was carried into effect; the mizzen-mast, top, spars, rigging, sails, etc., were already in readiness, and the armorer, at his forge erected on shore, forged and made the chains and all the other requisite iron-work, so that the mast was stepped, sails bent, and the *Betsey* rigged into a ship all ready for sea, in five days' time. This was accomplished without one dollar extra expense to the owners." The *Betsey*, having obtained supplies at the Cape de Verdes, sailed on the 23d day of July, 1797, for the Falkland Islands, where she arrived October 19th of the same year. Not finding Fur Seals there in any considerable numbers, it was decided to double Cape Horn and make the best of their way to the Island of Masafuero; accordingly they sailed high price in the European market, on account of the regular Russian supply being cut off in consequence of the war. This is only given as one instance of the many that may be related of sealing life.

The "season," as understood by sealers, is the time the animals collect in herds, or rookeries, on shore: the females to bring forth their young, and copulate with the vigorous males, while the valiant old bulls guard the rookeries, until all again return to the sea, and migrate to some unknown quarter. A few days before the main body arrive, a number of old "wigs" come up as if to see that all is right. Frequently the innumerable herd have been seen, in the southern hemisphere, from the high elevations of mountainous islands, as far as the eye could distinguish at sea, leaping and plunging like a shoal of porpoises until nearing the

from the Falkland Islands December 8th, 1797, and arrived at their destination January 20th, 1798. On the 5th day of April following, having obtained a full cargo of selected seal-skins, the little vessel with her valuable freight departed for China. On the passage thence, through the trade winds, the ship was unrigged and rigged again from deck to truck, which incident Captain Fanning makes mention of as follows: "Previous to the ship's departure from New York, a sufficient quantity of rope for a new gang of standing rigging had been taken on board; this had been prepared, during our leisure hours heretofore, and fitted, in readiness to go over the mast-head when necessary. For several days past the trade wind had not veered more than two points, blowing directly on our stern, so that all the sails which would be of service, could be set on one mast. This was a most favorable opportunity for replacing our old rigging with the new; we, therefore, hit upon the expedient of stripping one mast at a time, and accordingly commenced with the foremast, securing it well by purchases and tackles at the hounds, before letting up the lower rigging; afterward, putting the new suit on the lower-mast, topmast, etc., and then setting all taut up preparatory to spreading sail upon it. As soon as everything was completely ready, this was done, and the mainmast served in a like man-

ner. Our carpenter and armorer were first-rate workmen, and had made a set of machinery, by means of which, from the old rigging, we laid a new set of running rigging throughout; thus equipped, our ship, as respected her rigging, was in a far better condition than when she left the United States." We will add, that the *Betsey* was an armed vessel, which carried "eight four-pounders, of iron, and two brass long six-pounder guns," with a ship's company of twenty-seven officers and men. This pigmy ship arrived safely at Canton, and disposed of her valuable furs to great advantage. A China cargo was purchased, and when received on board, the vessel sailed for home by the way of the Cape of Good Hope. In passing through the Straits of Sunda, the vessel was attacked by a fleet of twenty-nine piratical proas, which were badly punished by her gallant crew. Continuing on her course, the *Betsey*, which sailed as a brig upon a voyage of adventure the 13th day of June, 1797, returned to her home-haven on the 6th day of April, 1799, transformed into a full-rigged ship, having accomplished one of the most successful sealing voyages of those days. Furthermore, the author states "he believes it to be the first American vessel, manned and officered wholly by native-born citizens, that ever sailed around the world from the port of New York."

shore; then, passing through the surf, they collect upon the beaches, and divide into families, or rookeries, as far as practicable.   These families, or divisions, are guarded by the "wigs," who can only maintain their authority and position at the expense of frequent pitched battles with others of their sex who may attempt to displace them.   They also keep a watchful eye over the numerous "clapmatches" under their charge; and should one attempt to take to the water, she is immediately driven back, and frequently suffers from the savage bites of her master for attempting to escape.   It is no unusual occurrence, in the height of the season, to see two full-grown "wigs" fight by the hour, exhibiting much tact in their assaults upon each other, both endeavoring to gain advantage by some adroit movement—at times making a savage lock with their mouths, or seizing each other by the fore flippers, or gashing necks and bodies with their sharp, tusk-like teeth. Sometimes we have seen several old males together on a separate beach, who were cut in every direction, and apparently had retired from the main herd, being unable to continue the fight in consequence of wounds received.

Frequently, many thousands of seals congregate on the same island.   They prefer remote, isolated situations, often upon barren rocks or islands, the shores of which are surrounded by a high surf, in which they delight to play.   They sometimes ascend high, precipitous rocks, where it is next to impossible for man to follow them.   Their food consists of fish and a variety of other marine productions, and small stones or pebbles are found in their maws.   When a great number are collected on shore, their barking and howling is almost deafening; and when passing to leeward of a seal island, the odor arising from it is anything but pleasant.

We have before spoken of the wide geographical distribution of the Fur Seals, and of their gregarious propensities.   We may add, likewise, from our own observation as well as the expressed opinion of several experienced sealing-masters, that their natural migrations extend over a great expanse of the ocean; and if they are unusually disturbed in their favorite haunts for several successive seasons, they are quite sure to seek some distant or unknown place, where they can congregate unmolested by man.

The females have great affection for their young, which may be more manifested on a coast where, by almost constant hunting from year to year, they have become wild and shy.

On one of the San Benito Islands, on the coast of Lower California, we once watched with interest a "clapmatch" and her pup, which was but a few weeks old.   She approached the shore cautiously, with her little one nestling about her; and while "hauling" upon the beach, she was constantly on the lookout, but at the same time caressing and endeavoring to quiet the object of her care, with a fondness almost human. All being still about the shore save the "wash" along the beach, she soon lulled it into quietness, and both lay huddled on a shelving rock, enjoying the warmth of a midday sun. Now and then a heavier swell than usual would roll in, varying the otherwise monotonous sound, when instantly the mother would raise her head and gaze with glaring eyes to make sure that there was no cause for alarm; then again she would resume her former posture, with her pup hugged to her breast by one of her pectorals, as if to sleep.

Some small sticks being at hand, we broke one, to see what effect so slight a noise might have upon them. The instant it snapped, the young one uttered cries of alarm, and the mother yelped defiantly; they soon, however, became quiet again, and we were on the point of leveling the rifle, when accidentally an old "wig" was caught sight of, lying on a high rock not far distant: taking sure aim we fired, then turned to observe the movements of the "clapmatch" and her little one. With a bound or two she reached the water, but returned again to urge her young one off as best she could; soon both were in their chosen element, and disappeared around a rocky point—and that was the last seen of them.

Our observations having been confined almost exclusively to the Pacific Coast, and chiefly between Chile and Alaska, what may follow, in addition to personal knowledge, has been obtained from the most reliable sources within our reach.

In former times, when Fur Seals abounded, they were captured in large numbers with the ordinary seal-club in the hands of the sealer, who would slay the animals "right and left" by one or two blows upon the head. A large party would cautiously land to leeward of the rookery, if possible; then, when in readiness, at a given signal all hands would approach them, shouting, and using their clubs to the best advantage in the conflict. Many hundreds were frequently taken in one of these "knock-downs," as they were called. As soon as the killing was over, the flaying commenced. Some sealers became great experts in skinning the animals; and the number of skins one would take off in the course of an hour would be a decidedly fishy story to tell. However, to flay fifty seals in a day would be regarded as good work. It will be readily seen that a sealing-ship's crew, numbering twenty or more, would make great havoc among a seal rookery in very short time; and it is no matter of surprise that these valuable fur-bearing animals soon became comparatively scarce. As early as 1835, about Cape Horn, Patagonia, and other points in the Antarctic regions, men were left to "watch out" and shoot the animals as one or more came on shore.

Both officers and men have been frequently landed from sealing-vessels on barren islands, rocks, or points, which would appear quite inaccessible to any but sealers or sea-elephant hunters, by reason of the heavy surf and surge about them; and where men occasionally have perished of starvation or thirst, by not receiving the needful supplies from the ship, which might have been wrecked before the time for her return.　One can hardly imagine more desolate habitations than the Diego Ramirez, off Cape Horn, or the Crozets and Prince Edward's Islands, in the Indian Ocean; but these places are no more forbidding in point of gloomy climate, isolation, and barrenness, than scores of others that might be mentioned, where men were left for months with or without a boat, as occasion required.

On the coast of California, many beaches were found fronting gullies, where seals in large numbers formerly gathered; and as they there had plenty of ground to retreat upon, the sealers sometimes drove them far enough back to make sure of the whole herd, or that portion of them the skins of which were desirable.

On the North-western Coast, south of the Aleutian Islands, but few Fur Seals are taken, and those are chiefly caught by the Indians with spears of native manufacture—the fishing being almost entirely confined to the mouth of Juan de Fuca Strait, and the contiguous coast of the Pacific.

The Indian seal-fishers are among the tribes inhabiting the coast from Gray's Harbor to the southern part of Vancouver Island.　The seals appear on the coast some years as early as the first of March, and more or less remain till July or August; but they are most plentiful in April and May.　During these two months, the Indians devote nearly all of their time to sealing, when the weather will permit.

It is but a few years since the Indians have turned their attention to taking seals solely to procure their skins and oil for barter; and what may seem surprising, it is but a few years since the animals have been known to resort to the vicinity of the strait in such large numbers.　We have it from the most reliable source, that there were but a few dozens of Fur Seal skins taken annually by the Indians, from 1843 to 1864; after which period, the number of skins sold by them at Victoria, Vancouver Island, Nee-ah Bay, and points on Puget Sound, has steadily increased, up to 1869, when the number in the aggregate amounted to fully five thousand skins.

When going in pursuit of seals, three or four natives embark in a canoe at an early hour in the morning, and usually return the following evening.　The fishing-gear consists of two spears, which are fitted to a pronged pole fifteen feet in length; to the spears a line is attached, which is fastened to the spear-pole close to, or is held in the hand of, the spearman when he darts the weapon.　A seal-club is also provided, as well as two seal-skin buoys—the latter being taken in the canoe to be used in rough weather, if necessary; or if a seal, after being speared, can not be managed with the line in hand, a buoy is "bent on," and the animal is allowed to take its course for a time. Its efforts to escape, by diving repeatedly, and plunging about near the surface of the water, soon exhaust the animal somewhat; and when a favorable time is presented, the spearman seizes the buoy, hauls in the line until within reach of the seal, and it is captured by clubbing. But, generally, the line is held in the hand when the spear is thrust into the seal; then the pole is instantly withdrawn, and the canoe is hauled at once to the floundering creature, which is dispatched as before described. Indians from the Vancouver shore frequently start in the night, so as to be on the best sealing-ground in the morning. This locality is said to be south-west of Cape Classet, five to fifteen miles distant.

Frequently, during the early part of the day, in the spring months, fresh winds come from the eastward, causing a rough, short sea in the whirling currents about the mouth of the strait. At such times these seal-fishers, or hunters, squatting in their canoes—which have a skin buoy lashed on each side of the bow—present not only a comical, but perilous appearance, they being continually drenched with salt water by the toppling seas, and the canoes making as great a diversity of bounds and plunges as do the seals themselves.

In Behring Sea, the islands of St. Paul and St. George are now the main resorting places of the Fur Seals, although in former years Copper Island swarmed with these periodical visitors; considerable numbers were also inhabitants of Behring Island, as well as several of the more isolated points in the Aleutian chain. The Aleutians, under the direction of officers of the Russian-American Company, were employed in taking the seals. Under the judicious management of the Russians, the animals did not decrease in numbers, and, to a certain extent, they became tamed, for they returned periodically to the islands, and brought forth and nurtured their young; and it was the custom to drive thousands of them inland, that their capture might be more easily accomplished. The loud moanings of the animals when the work of slaughtering is going on beggars description; in fact, they manifest vividly to any observing eye a tenderness of feeling not to be mistaken. Even the simple-hearted Aleutians say that "the seals shed tears."

Our observations about the mouth of the Strait of Juan de Fuca lead us to believe that the unusually large number seen in the vicinity during the past two years are a portion, at least, of the great herd that resort to St. Paul and St. George. One reason for this conclusion is, that no adult males are found with them. This would naturally follow the careful course adopted by the Russians of sparing the females, in order to propagate the stock. Moreover, this female herd—

for, almost invariably, those of the band which had been taken by the Indians were females—are found to have fœtuses in them that must necessarily be brought forth in the course of a month or two, which would probably be about the time they would arrive in that far northern region. The Indians unanimously affirm that they come from the south and go to the north. It is quite certain that they do not resort to any islands in or near the strait, or the adjacent coast. As near as can be ascertained, the main body pass by the mouth of the strait during the months of March and April and a part of May, after which comparatively few are seen; scattering ones, however, remain till the close of summer, as before mentioned. But where these countless herds of fur-bearing animals resort to in winter seems a mystery. All we know is, that at the proper seasons of the year they come on shore plump and fat, the females have their young, and all remain about the land until the little ones are sufficiently matured to migrate.

At the expense of being prolix, we quote the following from the notes of Captain Bryant,* whose stay upon the Island of St. Paul, Behring Sea, afforded him ample opportunity to study the habits of the *Callorhinus ursinus:*

"The Fur Seals resort to the Pribyloff Islands during the summer months for the sole purpose of reproduction.† Those sharing in these duties necessarily remain on or near the shore until the young are able to take to the water. During this considerable period the old seals are not known to take any food. These, and no others, occupy the rookeries (or breeding-grounds) with the females.

"The breeding-rookeries, which are frequented exclusively by the old males and females, with their pups, occupy the belt of loose rocks along the shores between the high-water line and the base of the cliffs or uplands. The old male appears to return each year to the same rock, so long as he is able to maintain his position.‡ The native chiefs affirm that one seal, known by his having lost one of his flippers, came seventeen successive years to the same rock. Those under six years are never allowed by the old ones on these places. They usually swim in the water along the shore all day, and at night go on the upland above the rookeries, and spread themselves out, like flocks of sheep, to rest.

* See *Bulletin of the Museum of Comparative Zoology*, Harvard College, Cambridge, Mass., Vol. II, No. 1—"On the Eared Seals," by J. A. Allen.

† Some observers say that they shed their fur.

‡ Subsequent observations prove that these animals do not invariably return every year to the same rookery, or island. We are informed by Captain Earskin, of the Alaska Commercial Company's service, that some young seals which were marked upon St. Paul's Island during the season of 1872, were found the year following on St. George's Island.—C. M. S.

"Wherever a long, continuous shore line is occupied as a breeding-rookery, neutral passages are set apart at convenient distances, through which the younger seals may pass from the water to the upland, and return, unmolested.

"Constant care is necessary lest thoughtless persons incautiously approach the breeding-grounds, as the stampede of the seals that would result therefrom always destroys many of the young. The old males are denominated by the natives *Seacutk* (married seals). These welcome the females on their arrival, and watch over and protect them and their young until the latter are large enough to be left to the care of their mothers and the younger males. Those under six years old are not able to maintain a place on the rookery, or to keep a harem, and these are denominated *Holluschuck* (bachelors). These two classes of males, with the full-grown females, termed *Motku* (mothers), form the three classes that participate in the duties of reproduction.

"By the first to the middle of April the snow has melted from the shore, and the drift ice from the north has all passed. Soon after this period, a few old male seals make their appearance in the water near the island, and after two or three days' reconnoissance, venture on to the shore and examine the rookeries, carefully smelling them. If the examination is satisfactory, after a day or two a few climb the slopes and lie with their heads erect, listening. At this time, if the wind blows from the village toward the rookeries, all fires are extinguished, and all unnecessary noises avoided. These scouts then depart, and in a few days after, small numbers of male seals of all ages begin to arrive. The old patriarchs soon take their places on the rookeries, and prevent the younger males from landing. They thus compel them to either stay in the water or go to the upland above. In locating, each old male reserves a little more than a square rod of space to himself and his ten or fifteen wives.

"Male seals continue to arrive in small numbers daily, a few of which are yearlings; those two, three, four, and five years old arrive in about equal proportions. Those older than this are more numerous than the younger, each one of which battles his way to his old place on the rookery, or, taking a new one, prepares to contend for it in case the owner comes to take it. As they acknowledge no right but that of might, the later comer has to select again, or fight for his rights on his chosen spot.

"About the 15th of June the males have all assembled, the ground being then fully occupied by them, as they lie waiting for the females to come. These appear in small numbers at first, but increase as the season advances, till the middle of July, when the rookeries are all full, often overlapping each other.

"Many of the females, on their arrival, appear desirous of returning to some particular male, and frequently climb the outlying rocks to overlook the rookeries, calling out, and listening as if for a familiar voice. Then changing to another place, they do the same again, until some 'bachelor' seal, swimming in the water, approaches and drives her on shore, often compelling her to land against her will. Here comes in the duty of the 'bachelor' seals. They swim all day along the shore, escorting and driving the females on to the rocks as fast as they arrive. As soon as a female reaches the shore, the nearest male goes down to meet her, making meanwhile a noise like the clucking of a hen to her chickens. He bows to her and coaxes her, until he gets between her and the water, so that she can not escape him. Then his manner changes, and with a harsh growl he drives her to a place in his harem. This continues until the lower row of harems is nearly full. Then the males higher up select the time when their more fortunate neighbors are off their guard, to steal their wives. This they do by taking them in their mouths and lifting them over the heads of the other females, and carefully placing them in their own harem, carrying them as cats do their kittens. Those still higher up pursue the same method, until the whole space is occupied. Frequently a struggle ensues between two males for possession of the same female, and both seizing her at once, pull her in two, or terribly lacerate her with their teeth. When the space is all filled, the old male walks around, complacently reviewing his family, scolding those who crowd or disturb the others, and fiercely driving off all intruders. This surveillance always keeps him actively occupied. In two or three days after landing, the females give birth to one pup each, weighing about six pounds. It is entirely black, and retains this color for the whole season. The young are quite vigorous, even at birth, nursing very soon after they are born. The mother manifests a strong attachment for her own offspring.

"In a few days after the birth of the young, the female is ready for intercourse with the male. She now becomes solicitous of his attentions, and extends herself on the rocks before him. Owing to the position of the genital organs, however, coition on land seems to be not the natural method, and only rarely, perhaps in three cases out of ten, is the attempt to copulate under such circumstances effectual. In the meantime, the four and five year old males are in attendance along the shore. When the jealous lord is off his guard, or engaged in driving away a rival, a female will slip into the water, and an attentive 'bachelor' seal follows her some distance from shore. Then, breast to breast, they embrace each other, turning alternately for each other to breathe, the act of copulation sometimes continuing from five to eight minutes. When the female again returns to the shore, she is treated with indifference by all the males. By the middle of August, the young are all born, and the females are again pregnant. The old males, having occupied their stations constantly for four months, without food, now resign their charge to the younger males, and go some distance from shore to feed.

"The fact of their remaining without food seems so contrary to Nature, that it appears to me proper to state some of the evidences of it. Having been assured by the natives that such was the fact, I deemed it of sufficient importance to test it by all the means available. Accordingly I took special pains to examine daily a large extent of the rookery, and note carefully the results of my observations. The rocks on the rookery are worn smooth and washed clean by the spring-tides, and any discharge of excrement could not fail to be detected. I found, in a few instances, where newly-arrived seals had made a single discharge of red-colored excrement, but nothing was seen afterward to show that such discharges were continued, nor any evidence that the animals had partaken of food. I also examined the stomachs of several young ones, killed by the natives for eating, and always without finding any traces of food in them. The same was true of the few nursing females killed for dissection.

"About the 20th of July, the great body of the previous year's pups arrive, and occupy the slopes with the younger class of males, and they continue to be mixed together during the remainder of the season. The two-years-old females, which pair with the young males in the water near the island, also now associate with the other females. The pups are five weeks old when the old females go off to feed; they go with the mothers to the upland, but keep by themselves. The pups born on the lower edge of the rookery, where the surf breaks over them occasionally, learn to swim early, but the larger portion of them do not take to the

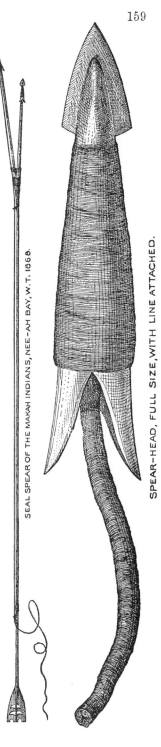

SEAL SPEAR OF THE MAKAH INDIANS, NEE-AH BAY, W.T. 1868.

SPEAR-HEAD, FULL SIZE, WITH LINE ATTACHED.

water until later, and many have to be forced in by the parents. Once in, however, they soon love to sport in it. The young are taught to swim by the old males on their return from feeding.

"By the last of October, the seals begin to leave the islands in small companies, the males going last, and by themselves. In November, the young seals (as I was informed by the natives, my own observations ending in August) stop to rest a few days on the Aleutian Islands, and at Ounalaska the natives obtain several hundred skins annually.

"Manner of Killing the Seals.—It will be recollected that I have described the younger seals as spreading out on the slopes above the rookeries to rest at night. A party of men approach these places armed with clubs, and quietly creep between the seals and the shore. When ready, the men start up with a shout at a given signal, and drive the seals inland in a body. When at a sufficient distance from the rookery, they halt to screen the flock of as many as possible that are too old for killing, only those that are two and three years old yielding prime skins ; the fur of those older is too coarse to be marketable. The screening is done by driving the seals slowly forward in a curve; the older, sullenly holding back, force the more timid forward, when the men, opening their ranks, let them pass through and return to the shore. The remainder of the flock is then driven to the killing-ground, though still containing many too old to be of value.

"It is necessary to drive the flock some distance from the breeding-ground, as the smell of the blood and the carcasses disturbs the seals. Another object is, to make the seals carry their own skins to the salt-house ; hence it is sometimes necessary to drive them six or seven miles. The driving has to be conducted with great care, as the violent exertion causes the seals to heat rapidly, and, if heated beyond a certain degree, the fur is loosened, and the skin becomes valueless. In a cool day they may be driven one mile and a half per hour with safety. When arrived at the killing-ground, a few boys are employed to keep them from straggling, and they are thus left to rest and cool. Then from seventy to one hundred are separated from the flock, surrounded, and driven on each other, so that they confine themselves by treading on each other's flippers. Those desired for killing are then easily selected, and quickly dispatched by a blow on the nose. When these are killed, the remainder are allowed to go to the nearest water, whence they immediately return to the place from which they were driven. This operation is repeated until the whole flock is disposed of. The work of skinning is performed by all the men on the island, and everyone participating in it is allowed to share in the proceeds.

"As the seals are not wholly at rest until the females arrive, great care is necessary in selecting the time and place from which to drive. These points are determined by a head-man, who assumes the whole control of this part of the business. In the month of May, only the small number required by the natives for food are driven. In June, when the seals are more numerous, they are driven and killed for their skins, although the percentage of prime skins is at this time very small, often not twenty per cent. of the whole flock driven. About the middle of July, the females go off into the water, and there is a period of general rest among all the seals, during which time the natives desist entirely from killing for ten to fifteen days. At the close of this period, the great body of yearling seals arrive. These, mixing with the younger class of males, spread over the uplands, and greatly increase the difficulty of killing properly. Up to this time, there having been no females with the seals driven up for killing, it was only necessary to distinguish ages; this the difference in size enables them to do very easily. Now, however, nearly one-half are females, and the slight difference between these and the younger males, renders it necessary for the head-man to see every seal killed, and only a strong interest in the preservation of the stock can insure the proper care. September and October are considered the best months for taking the seals.

"Besides the skin, each seal will yield one gallon and a half of oil, and the linings of all the throats are saved and salted as an article of trade to other ports in the territory, these being used by the natives for making water-proof frocks to wear in their skin-canoes when hunting the sea-otter or fishing. These parts have no very great commercial value, though they are considered by the natives as indispensable to them.

"Mode of Curing the Skins.—The skins are all taken to the salt-houses, and are salted in kenches, or square bins, the skins being spread down, flesh-side up, and a layer of salt spread over them. They remain thus packed for thirty or forty days, when they are taken from the bins; the salt is removed, and the skins are folded together, the flesh-side in, and sprinkled as they are folded with a quantity of clean salt. They are then ready for shipment.

"Number of Seals frequenting the Island.—There are at least twelve miles of shore-line on the island of St. Paul's occupied by the seals as breeding-ground, with an average width of fifteen rods. There being about twenty seals to the square rod, gives one million one hundred and fifty-two thousand as the whole number of breeding males and females. Deducting one-tenth for males, leaves one million thirty-seven thousand and eight hundred breeding females. Allowing one-half of the present year's pups to be females, this will add half a million of breeding females to the rookeries of 1872, in addition to those now there, while the young of last year and the year before are also to be added. This estimate does not include the males under six years of age, these not being allowed on the rookeries by the older males, nor the yearlings. If we now add those frequenting St. George's Island, which number half as many, and make a very liberal discount for those that may be destroyed before reaching maturity, the number is still enormous. It will also be seen that the great importance of the seal-fishery is not to be calculated from the basis of its present yield, since each year adds to its extent, as with proper care the number can be increased until both islands are fully occupied by these valuable animals.

"Prices Paid for the Skins at the Islands, and their Value in Europe.—The Russian Company allowed the natives the value of ten cents per skin. This was the pay they received for their labor of killing, curing the skins, and delivering them alongside the vessel, ready for shipment, the company finding salt and magazines in which to salt them.

"The parties who took advantage of the interval between the transfer of the territory and the enacting and enforcement of the law of the 27th of July, 1868, to kill and purchase of the natives, paid twenty-seven cents per skin, and had they been allowed to trade the present year, would have bidden forty cents apiece for them. To this is to be added the cost of salt, buildings, and the expense of the agency on shore. Their market value was at that time five dollars, so that, after a liberal allowance for incidental expenses, the profit must be very large. Previous to 1866, these skins were worth only three dollars each, but, owing to recent improvements in their manufacture, they have become fashionable for ladies' wear, and soon after the transfer of the territory to the United States the price rose to seven dollars. At this time, the Russians had one hundred thousand on hand, which were forwarded to London, the only market for seal-skins in the raw state, and the only place where they are dressed. The different parties which sealed on the islands in the summer following the purchase, took two hundred thousand, which so overstocked the market that they are now [1871] worth only three or four dollars.

"The agents of the Russian Fur Company aimed to control this branch of the fur trade in Europe by regulating the supply. To do this they sent orders a year in advance to have such a number killed as in their judgment the market might need, always keeping at the same time one year's supply on hand. At the time of the sale of the territory, the annual yield was estimated at eighty thousand skins. The opinion of the men who have the special care of the seals is, that it has reached one hundred thousand, and that the killing yearly of this number will in no way check their increase.*

"USE OF THE FLESH BY THE NATIVES.—The flesh of the seal constitutes the principal food of the inhabitants, they killing, from time to time, such numbers as are necessary for that purpose. Before the seals leave in autumn, a number are killed sufficient for their winter's supply. The carcasses are allowed to freeze, and in this state they keep them until the return of the seals in the spring. The flesh of the yearling seal is somewhat darker than beef; it is juicy and tender, but lacks the sweetness and flavor of beef, and is less firm and nutritious. In highly seasoned dishes, it is relished by nearly all who partake of it. The soldiers on the island preferred it to salt rations. A five-weeks-old pup roasted is esteemed a great luxury."

---

*At the present time (fall of 1873), the number of Fur Seals taken annually may be put down at one hundred and forty-five thousand, which are obtained at the places following: At St. George's and St. Paul's islands, Behring Sea, one hundred thousand; at Copper and Behring islands, twenty-five thousand; on the coasts of California and Washington Territory, at Robin Island (Okhotsk Sea), at the South Shetland Islands, and about Cape Horn and other places, twenty thousand. The price of the skins in Europe may average nine dollars, from which deduct ten per cent. for expenses, making the home price of each skin about eight dollars, and bringing the net value of the fishery up to $1,174,500 yearly.

CHAPTER V.

THE LEOPARD SEAL.

Phoca Pealii,?* *Gill.* (Plate xxii, fig. 1.)

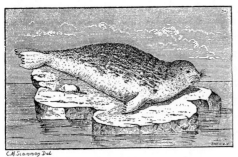

C.M. Scammon Del.
MOVING ATTITUDE OF A LEOPARD SEAL, ON SHORE.

This species of *Phoca*, known under the local name of Leopard Seal, inhabits, according to our observation, the western coast of North America and the contiguous northern region as far as the most western islands of the Kurile chain. The adult animals we have met with in different latitudes, were, to all outward appearances, of the same form and of the same modified colors. The places of observation were Plover Bay, coast of Eastern Siberia, 1865; coast of Upper California, 1852; coast of Lower California, 1856; Strait of Juan de Fuca, 1869. The skeleton of the one examined at Plover Bay was forwarded to the Smithsonian Institution, through our friend W. H. Dall, who assumed charge of the scientific enterprise connected with the Western Union Telegraph Expedition, after the death of the lamented Kennicott. The Leopard Seal in its proportions may be regarded as under-sized. It never exceeds six feet in length; and its thick body, with its short limbs, gives the animal a bloated appearance, which seems ill adapted to much activity. Its head is short, broad, and rounded; the eyes are large, full, and expressive, with five coarse, bristle-like hairs placed on a curve one inch above the edge of the upper lid, which constitute the eyebrows. It has thirty to thirty-five whiskers on each

* W. H. Dall, who has had considerable opportunity to observe upon these seals, is under the impression that several species of them exist upon this coast, in which opinion we concur; but, whether such is the fact or not, we will state that, so far as our observation has extended, the habits of these seals, both north and south, are the same.

Plate XXII.

C. M. Scammon, del.

LEOPARD SEAL.(Phoca Pealii ♀) Gill.

From Wolf.

SEA-OTTER.(Enhydra Marina.)Fleming.

side of the face, which protect or screen the mouth. The ears are merely openings in the surface of the skin, which are placed one and a half inches behind the eyes. Both side and posterior flippers are covered with the same thick short hair as the body, and each one is furnished with five sharp, slender claws, those on the pectorals being the longest, the principal of which measure one linear inch. The posterior flippers, when relaxed, may be three and a half inches in breadth, but are capable of expansion to ten. Two orifices in lieu of teats, placed two and a half inches apart, are situated on the lower portion of the belly, and nine inches forward from the origin of the tail. The tail is about three inches long, and is thick and fleshy. The color of the animal varies but little from a light gray, thickly mottled with dull black on the back and half-way down its sides, then changing to a dingy white underneath, with here and there distinct spots of darker shades. About the throat and breast, the creature at a distance looks to be of a uniform dull white.

The following measurements in feet and inches, and weights, were taken of two adult females caught at Smith's Island, Juan de Fuca Strait, in the months of February and March, 1869:

	No. 1.		No. 2.	
Length of animal from tip of nose to tip of tail	3	10	3	8
From tip of nose to fore flippers	1		1	
Length of fore flippers	0	6	0	7
Length of posterior flippers	0	9	0	8
Length of tail	0	3	0	$2\frac{1}{2}$
From tip of nose to eye	0	3	0	$2\frac{1}{2}$
From tip of nose to ear			0	4
From tip of nose to corner of mouth	0	$2\frac{1}{4}$	0	$2\frac{1}{2}$
Distance between the eyes			0	2
Circumference of body immediately behind side flippers	2	$6\frac{1}{2}$	2	3

Weight of No. 1, sixty pounds; weight of No. 2, fifty-six pounds. The time of gestation with the Leopard Seals is supposed to be nine months. We have met with the new-born pups about Puget Sound in the months of July and August; on the coast of California, in June and July.

The thick coating of white fat which infolds the body produces the purest oil of any of the pinnipedes. The Leopard Seal is endowed with no little sagacity, and, although exceedingly wary, it displays considerable boldness. It is found about outlying rocks, islands, and points, on sand-reefs made bare at low tide, and is frequently met with in harbors among shipping, and up rivers more than a hundred miles from the sea. We have often observed them close to the vessel when under way, and likewise when at anchor, appearing to emerge deliberately from the depths below, sometimes only showing their heads, at other times exposing half of their bodies, but the instant any move was made on board, they would vanish like an apparition under water, and frequently that would be the last seen of them, or, if seen again, they would be far out of gun-shot.

The animals come ashore more during windy weather than in calm, and in the night more than during the day; and they have been observed to collect in the largest herds upon the beaches and rocks, near the full and change of the moon. They delight in basking in the warm sunlight, and when no isolated rock or shore is at hand, they will crawl upon any fragments of drift-wood that will float them. Although gregarious, they do not herd in such large numbers as do nearly all others of the seal tribe; furthermore, they may be regarded almost as mutes, in comparison with the noisy Sea Lions. It is very rarely, however, any sound is uttered by them, but occasionally a quick bark or guttural whining, and sometimes a peculiar bleating is heard when they are assembled together about the period of bringing forth their young. At times, when a number meet in the neighborhood of rocks or reefs distant from the main land, they become quite playful, and exhibit much life in their gambols, leaping out of the water or circling around upon the surface.

Its terrestrial movements, however, are quite different from those of the Sea Lion, having a quick, shuffling, or hobbling gait, only using its pectorals to draw itself along with, while a small portion of the animal's belly alternately rests upon the ground, the posterior part of the body, including the hind flippers, being turned a little upward. The head and neck are slightly elevated, also, when the animal is in its land-traveling attitude, but the creature is not so erect as, nor does it present the imposing appearance of, the Sea Lion, in its habits upon the shore. Its food is principally fish, and its rapacity in pursuing and devouring the smaller members of the piscatory tribes is quite equal, in proportion to its size, to that of the Orca. When grappling with a fish too large to be swallowed whole, it will hold and handle it between its fore flippers, and, with the united work of its mouth—which is armed with incisors, canines, and molars—the wriggling prize is demolished and devoured as quickly, and much in the same manner, as a squirrel would eat a bur-covered nut.

The animal is easily tamed, and very soon becomes attached to its keeper. We have had several young ones on board ship, and in every instance it was but a few weeks before they would follow, if permitted, the one who had especial charge of them, and when left solitary, they would express discontent by a sort of mournful bleating. A very interesting specimen of the Leopard Seal is on exhibition at Woodward's Gardens. This little favorite has been a resident of that popular and interesting resort for over three years, and, although a female, as we were informed, is honored with the title of "Commodore." The animal generally makes its appearance close at hand whenever within hearing, if called by name, and when its keeper appears on the lawn, to feed the pelicans, black swans, and other aquatic birds, which are its companions in the artificial pond, the Commodore does not wait to be invited, but, knowing as well as its keeper the meal-hour, is on the watch, and the moment the food-bearer is seen, the little creature—which is not over four feet long—lifts itself out of the water over the curb-stones and waddles quickly to its master's side, then holding up its head with mouth wide open, receives the choice morsels of fish which drop from his hand.

Leopard Seals are very easily captured when on shore, as a single blow with a club upon the head will dispatch them. The Indians about Puget Sound take them in nets made of large hemp-line, using them in the same manner as seines, drawing them around beaches when the rookery is on shore. They are taken by the whites for their oil and skins, but the Indians and Esquimaux make great account of them for food. The last-mentioned eat them, as they do nearly every article of sustenance, with or without cooking, but the natives of Puget Sound singe them before a fire until the hair is consumed and the skin becomes crisp, after which it is cut up and cooked as may best suit their relish.

CHAPTER VI.

THE SEA OTTER.

(Plate xxii.)

The most valuable fur-bearing animals inhabiting the waters of the North-western Coast of North America are the Sea Otters. They are found as far south as twenty-eight degrees north latitude, and their northern limits include the Aleutian Islands. Although never migrating to the southern hemisphere, these peculiar amphibious animals are found around the isolated points of southern Kamschatka, and even to the western Kuriles, a chain of islands that separates the Okhotsk Sea from the north-eastern Pacific. The length of the full-grown animal may average five feet, including the tail, which is about ten inches. The head resembles that of the Fur Seal. The eyes of the Sea Otter are full, black, and piercing, and exhibit much intelligence. The color of the female, when "in season," is quite black; at other periods, it is a dark brown. The males are usually of the same shade, although, in some instances, they are of a jet, shining black, like their mates. The fur is of a much lighter shade inside than upon the surface, and, extending over all, are scattering, long, glistening hairs, which add much to the richness and beauty of the pelage. Some individuals, about the nose and eyes, are of a light brown, or dingy white. The ears are less than an inch in length, quite pointed, standing nearly erect, and are covered with short hair. Occasionally, the young are of a deep brown, with the ends of the longest hairs tipped with white, and, about the nose and eyes, of a cream color.

The mating season of the Sea Otter is not known, as the young are met with in all months of the year; hence, it is reasonable to suppose they differ from most other species of fur-bearing marine mammalia in this respect. The time of gestation is supposed to be eight or nine months.

The hind feet, or flippers, of the animal are webbed, much like the seal's. Its fore legs are short, the fore paws resembling those of a cat, being furnished with five sharp claws, as are the posterior flippers.

The oldest and most observing hunters about Point Grenville (in latitude 47° 20′) aver that the "Sea Otter is never seen on shore unless it is wounded." Nevertheless, we have accounts of their being found on the Aleutian Islands when the Russians were first engaged in the fur trade, and the animals are still occasionally taken, while asleep upon the rocks. We quote the following from Coxe's work on *Russian Discoveries between Asia and America, and the Conquest of Siberia,* published in 1780: "Of all these furs, the skins of the Sea Otters are the richest and most valuable. These animals resort in great numbers to the Aleutian and Fox islands; they are called by the Russians *Boobry Morfki,* or sea beavers, on account of the resemblance of their fur to that of the common beaver. They are taken four ways: struck with darts as they are sleeping upon their backs in the sea; followed by boats and hunted down until they are tired; surprised in caverns, and taken in nets." They are possessed of much sagacity, have great powers of scent, and are exceedingly imbued with curiosity. Their home is nearly as much in the water as that of some species of whales; and as whalers have their favorite "cruising-grounds," so, likewise, do the Otter-hunters have their favorite hunting-grounds, or points where the objects of pursuit are found in greater numbers than along the general stretch of the coast. About the sea-board of Upper and Lower California, Cerros, San Geronimo, Guadalupe, San Nicolas, and San Miguel islands, have been regarded as choice places to pursue them; and farther northward, off Cape Blanco, on the Oregon coast, and Point Grenville and Gray's Harbor, along the coast of Washington Territory. At the present day, considerable numbers are taken by whites and Indians about those northern grounds. Thence, to the northward and westward, come a broken coast and groups of islands, where the animals were, in times past, hunted by the employés of the Hudson's Bay Company and Russian-American Company, and where they are still pursued by the natives inhabiting those rock-bound shores. These interesting mammals are gregarious, and are frequently seen in bands numbering from fifty up to hundreds. When in rapid movement, they make alternate undulating leaps out of the water, plunging again, as do seals and porpoises. They are frequently seen, too, with the hind flippers extended, as if catching the breeze to sail or drift before it.

They live on clams, crabs, and various species of crustacea, and sometimes small fish. When the Otter descends and brings up any article of food, it instantly resumes its habitual attitude—on the back—to devour it. In sunny days, when looking, it sometimes shades its eyes with one fore paw, much in the same manner as a person does with the hand. The females rarely have more than a single one at a birth—never more than two—which are "brought forth upon the kelp," say the white hunters, that abounds at nearly all points known as their favorite resorting-places. The mothers caress and suckle their offspring seemingly with much affection, fondling them with their fore paws—reclining, in their usual manner—and frequently uttering a plaintive sound, which may have given rise to the saying that "Sea Otters sing to quiet their young ones," and gives some credence to the suggestion that the human-like actions of the animal originated the story about mermaids. But when they are startled, they rise perpendicularly half their length out of the water; and if their quick, sharp eyes discern aught to cause alarm, the cubs are seized by the mouth, and both mother and offspring instantly disappear under water. Males and females are sometimes seen curled up in such shapelessness as to present no appearance of animal form. When in this posture they are said to be sleeping.

Sea Otters are rarely seen far from shore, their home being among the thick beds of kelp near the beach, or about outlying rocky reefs and islets. Point Grenville, however, seems to be an exception, as there is no kelp in sight from the shore.

Pursuit and Capture.—About the period of the establishment of Fort Astoria, near the mouth of the Columbia River, and for many succeeding years, the Sea Otter hunters along the coasts of California and Oregon were made up from nearly all the maritime nations of Europe and America, as well as from the different tribes of natives that dwelt near the sea-shore. Those of the former were hardy spirits, who preferred a wild life and adventurous pursuits, rather than civilized employment. The distance coasted in their lightly constructed boats, the stealthy search for the game, and when discovered, the sharp-shooting chase, gave these hunting expeditions a pleasant tinge of venture. Moreover, the taking of Sea Otters on the coasts of the Californias was prohibited by the Mexican government, and the hunters were aware that, if detected, the penalty would be severe; hence, they ever kept a watchful eye on all vessels seen, which were carefully avoided or cautiously approached.

A peculiar sort of boat is used by the hunters, called an "Otter-canoe." It is fifteen feet long, nearly five wide, and eighteen inches deep. It is sharp at each end, with flaring sides, and but little sheer. Still, these boats are excellent "sea-goers," and are regarded as unsurpassed for landing through the surf, their shape being peculiar. So, likewise, are the paddles for propelling them, which are short, with very broad blades—they being better adapted for use in the thick beds of kelp. The outfit, when going on a cruise, is limited to nearly the barest necessities. Three men usually go in one boat—two to paddle, and one to shoot; the latter having two or three favorite rifles, with a supply of ammunition. A little tea, coffee, sugar, flour, or ship-bread, is provided, adding pipes and tobacco, and, as a great luxury, perhaps a keg of spirits completes their equipment.

All being in readiness, they leave the quiet waters of the harbor, and put to sea, following the general trend of the land, but at times making a broad deviation, to hunt about some islands, miles from the main-land. When an Otter is seen within rifle-shot, instantly the hunter fires; and if only wounding the animal, it dives under the water, but soon re-appears, to be repeatedly shot at until killed. Sometimes, three boats will hunt together. Then they take positions, one on each side, but in advance of the third, and all three in the rear of where the animal is expected to be seen. It is only the practiced eye of the experienced men that can detect the tip of the animal's nose peering above water, and frequently disguised by a leaf of kelp. Occasionally, a large band is met with. Then every exertion is made to keep them within the triangle formed by the boats; and, at such times, a deal of rapid and sharp shooting ensues, and many a bullet sings through the air, or skips over the water, almost as near the pursuers as the animals pursued. However, six, eight, or a dozen Otters are sometimes secured before the main body disperses; and it is rarely any accident occurs by reckless firing.

From day to day, if the weather is pleasant, they cruise in search of the animals—landing to pass the night at different places well known to them, behind some point or rock that breaks the ocean swell. The landings are made by watching the successive rollers as they break upon the beach, and when a favorable time comes, the boat, under dexterous management, glides over the surf with safety to the shore. It is then hauled up clear of the water, and turned partially over for a shelter, or a tent is pitched. A fire is made of drift-wood, or, if this fail, the dry stalks of the cactus, or a bunch of dead chaparral, serves them; and, if their provisions should be getting short, an excursion is made up some one of the many ravines or intervals—perhaps to a stagnant water-pool, where the deer and antelope in that arid region resort to quench their parching thirst. The unerring rifle brings one to the ground, when out comes the hunter's knife, and cutting the choice pieces from the creature, he sallies back again to camp, and soon has the venison broiling over the coals, and, in due time, it is added to their evening meal, which is partaken of with hearty relish; then follow the pipes, which are enjoyed as only those men of free and easy life can enjoy them. Relieved from all care, these adventurers talk of past exploits or frolics, and finally roll themselves in their blankets for a night's invigorating sleep in the open air. At daybreak they are all awakened by the screams of sea-birds and the barking of coyotes, attracted by the scent of the encampment. The morning repast over, they again embark in their cockle-shell boats, launch through the surf, gain the open sea, and paddle or sail along the shores in search of "Otter signs." But the scarcity of Otters on the old hunting-grounds has developed the character of these fearless hunters, who, in order to still maintain their game-life, have again reluctantly taken to their pigmy sea-craft—a small vessel of forty tons—in which they have stretched across the Pacific to the western Kuriles (the extreme geographical limit of the breeding-grounds), and now successfully pursue them around those rugged islands during summer, returning again to the California shores with their rich booty as winter approaches.

HUNTING FROM THE SHORE.—From San Francisco northward, as far as Juan de Fuca Strait, the hunting is chiefly prosecuted by shooting the animals from the shore; the most noted grounds being between Gray's Harbor and Point Grenville —a belt of low coast, lying within the parallels of 46° and 48°, north latitude.

The white hunter builds his two log-cabins; one, near the southern limits of his beat, and the other at its northern terminus near Point Grenville. During the prevalence of the southerly winter gales he takes up his quarters at the last-named station, as the game is found there more frequently; but when the summer winds sweep down from the north he changes his habitation, and pursues the animals about the breakers of Gray's Harbor. From early dawn until the sun sinks beneath the horizon, the hunter, with rifle in hand and ammunition slung across his shoulder, walks the beach on the lookout for "a shot." The instant one is seen, crack goes the rifle; but it is seldom the animal is secured by one fire. A Sea Otter's head bobbing about in the restless swell is a very uncertain mark; and if instantly killed, the receding tide or adverse wind might drift the animal seaward: so that, even if it eventually drift to shore, it may be far out of sight from the hunters by day, or be thrown on the rocks by the surge during the night, and picked up by some of the strolling Indians who run the beach in quest of any dead seal or Otter that may come in their way.

The difficulty in shooting from the shore, when the marksman stands nearly on a level with the ever-changing swell, has always been an aggravating annoyance; to avoid which, the hunters now use a sort of ladder, or, as it may be termed, two ladders, joined near the upper ends by a hinge, spreading at the lower ends, forming a triangle—when placed on the beach or in the edge of the water—on which the hunter climbs in order to gain elevation. The ladders are made of light material, so that they can be easily carried at any time, should the sea be ruffled by a local wind or waves from seaward. When an Otter is seen, up go the ladders, and up goes the hunter to the topmost round, and fires. The shot is repeated very quickly, if the first does not take effect; and ball after ball is sent after the animal, until it is far out of reach. It is estimated that the best shooters average at least twenty-five shots to every Otter obtained, and that about one-half the number killed are secured by the rightful owners; but, when once in their possession, it is quickly fleeced of its valuable skin, which is stretched on the walls of the cabin to dry. It is no unusual occurrence for the hunter to pass a week traveling up and down the beach, and he may shoot sixty or more rounds, and, perhaps, kill several Otters; but, owing to "bad luck," not one may be secured—the carcass either drifting to sea, or to shore, possibly, with the flowing night-tide, and the object so patiently and eagerly sought for is at last stealthily appropriated by some skulking savage.

Notwithstanding their propensity to purloin, the Indians of the North-western Coast not only occasionally shoot the Sea Otters, as do the whites, but in the months of July and August, when calm weather prevails, they capture them by night. A small canoe is chosen for the purpose, and the implement used to capture the animals is a spear of native make, composed of bone and steel, fitted to a long pole by a socket. Four chosen men make the crew for the canoe. Near the close of day, a sharp lookout is kept for any band of the animals that may have been seen from the shore, and their position accurately defined before beginning the pursuit. All being in readiness, as the shade of evening approaches, they launch their pigmy craft upon the calm sea, and three men paddle in silence toward the place where the Otters were seen, while the fourth takes his station in the bow. He is either a chief, or some one distinguished in the chase. He watches intently for the sleeping Otters. As soon as one is descried, the canoe is headed for it, and, when within reach, the spear is launched into the unwary creature. In its efforts to escape, it draws the spear from the pole. There is a small but strong cord connecting the spear and pole, which admits them to separate a few feet, but does not free the Otter. The animal dives deeply, but with great effort, as the unwieldy pole greatly retards its progress. The keen-eyed savage traces its course, in the blinding darkness, by the phosphorescent light caused by the animal's transit through the water; and when it rises upon the surface to breathe, it is beset with clubs, paddles, and perhaps another spear, and is finally dispatched, after repeated blows or thrusts. The conflict arouses the whole band, which instantly disappear; so that it is seldom more than one is secured. As soon as the hunt is over, the animal is brought on shore, the skin taken off and stretched to dry, and, when ready for market, the lucky owner considers himself enriched to the value of ten or fifteen blankets, and the flesh is devoured as a choice article of food.

The mode of capturing the Sea Otters between Point Grenville and the Aleutian Islands varies with the different native tribes inhabiting that coast. The Aleutians, dressed in their water-proof garments, made from the intestines of seals, wedge themselves into their *baidarkas* (which are constructed with a light, wooden frame, and covered with walrus or seal skin), and, donning their hunting-caps, plunge through the surf that dashes high among the crags, and, with almost instinctive skill, reach the less turbulent ground-swell that heaves in every direction. These aquatic men are so closely confined by the narrow build of their boats, and keeping motion with them, too, that their appearance suggests the idea that some undescribed marine monster had just emerged from the depths below. Once clear of the rocks, however, the hunters watch diligently for the Otters. The first man that gets near one darts his spear, then throws up his paddle by way of signal; all the other boats forming a circle around him, at some distance. The wounded animal dives deeply, but soon returns to the surface, near some one of the *baidarkas* forming the circle. Again the hunter that is near enough hurls his spear and elevates his paddle, and again the ring is formed as before. In this way the chase is continued until the capture is made. As soon as the animal is brought on shore, the two oldest hunters examine it, and the one whose spear is found nearest its head is entitled to the prize.

The number of Sea Otter skins taken annually is not definitely known, but from the most authentic information we can obtain, the aggregate for the past three years has been five thousand, one thousand of which came from the Kurile Islands; and, valuing each skin at fifty dollars, amounts to the sum of two hundred and fifty thousand dollars.

Whether these very valuable fur-animals have decreased in numbers within the past few years, is questionable. The hunting of them on the coast of California is no longer profitable for more than two or three hunters, and we believe of late some seasons have passed without any one legitimately engaging in the enterprise; notwithstanding, off Point Grenville, which is an old hunting-ground, sixty Otters were taken by only three hunters during the summer of 1868—a great annual increase over many past years. It is said the Russian-American Company restricted the number taken yearly by the Aleutian Islanders, from whom the chief supply was obtained, in order to perpetuate the stock. Furthermore, may it not be that these sagacious animals have fled from those places on the coasts of the Californias where they were so constantly pursued, to some more isolated haunt, and now remain unmolested?

ALEUTIAN ISLANDERS' SEA OTTER CANOE, OR BAIDARKA, WITH HUNTERS ENGAGED IN THE CHASE.

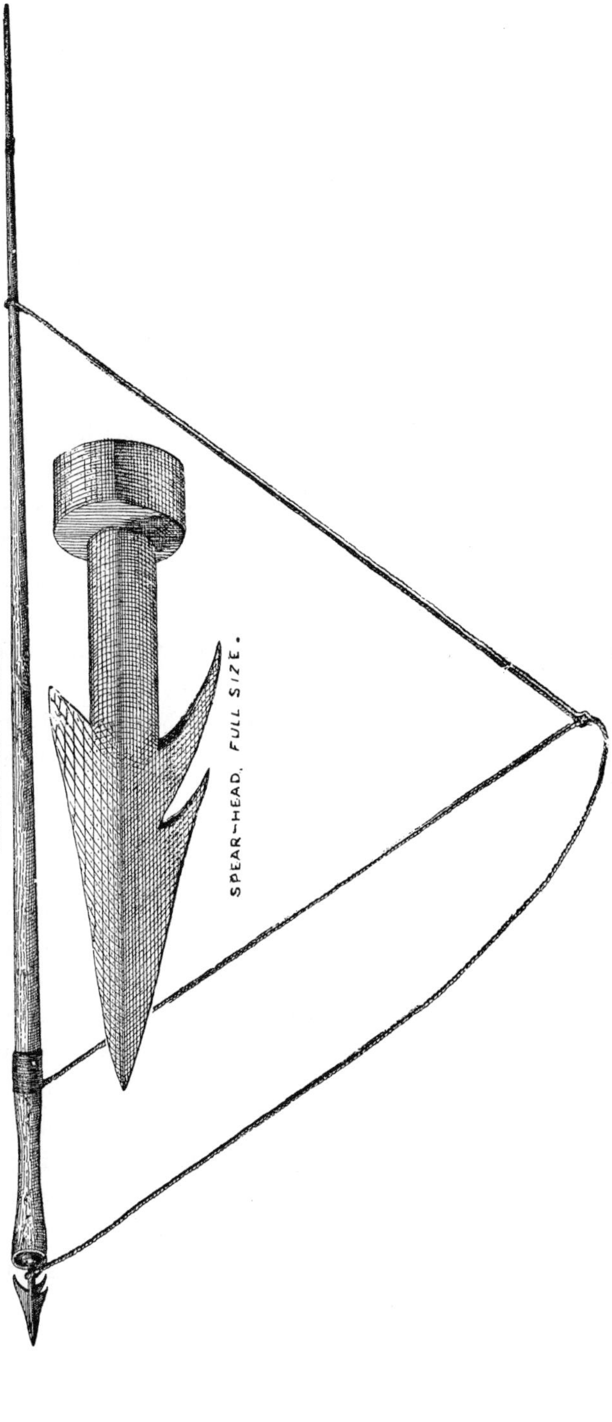

ALEUTIAN ISLANDER'S SEA-OTTER SPEAR.

SPEAR-HEAD. FULL SIZE.

CHAPTER VII.

THE WALRUS.

Rosmarus obesus, *Illiger.*

Eminent naturalists have remarked that the Walrus, or Sea-horse, appears to be the connecting link between the mammals of the land and those of the water. This bulky and unwieldy animal when on shore has some resemblance to the seal, yet differs materially in its proportions, as well as in its elephant-like tusks. The Walrus attains the size of the largest Sea Lion, and measures from ten to fourteen feet in length, and about eight feet in circumference. Its head is rounded, small (when compared with the anterior portion of the body), and flattened in front. Its eyes are diminutive in size, and deeply set; the small orifices of the ears are about three inches behind, and two inches below the eyes. The cheeks are studded with four or five hundred spines or whiskers, some of which are rudimentary, while others grow to the length of three or four inches. They are transparent, curved, abruptly pointed, and about the size of a straw, but not twisted, as has been stated by some writers. Its neck is short, and its unwieldy body is largest about the chest. Its posterior is abrupt.

By the courtesy of Mr. H. W. Elliott, we present on the following page figures of the Walrus, copied from his excellent sketches, executed at St. Paul's Island, Behring Sea, in 1872. The tusks of the Walrus are not only a means of defense, but are used in obtaining food, and in mounting the ice-floes, when the shore is not accessible. The canine teeth, as they are sometimes called, may average two feet in length, including the root, which is imbedded in the jaw six or eight inches. Yet some individuals have been taken with tusks two and a half to three feet in length, and each weighing from ten to twenty pounds. In shape they are somewhat bowing, and slightly hollowed, notched, and ridgy at their bases. At their junction with the skull, they are about three inches asunder; they project at an obtuse angle from the upper jaw, and, in some instances, meet at their extremities; while others grow perpendicular to each other, or turn outward on each side. There is considerable diversity in their length, shape, and size, even in the full-grown tusks, some being very short and stout, while others are elongated and slender. The Walrus has no sharp incisors like the seal. The nostrils are placed on the superior portion of the snout, through which the animal appears to inspire, and expires through its mouth, as it dips its head below the surface, blowing up the water into spray, in such a manner as to resemble the spout of a whale. Never having had an opportunity of taking detailed measurements of the Walrus, we quote from the most reliable authorities: "Its fore feet, or flippers, are from two to two and a half feet in length, and about twelve inches in breadth; they are webbed, and the under sides are protected by a tough skin, a quarter of an inch or more in thickness. The posterior flippers are from two to three feet long, and are

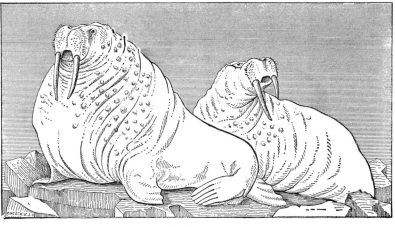

WALRUSES.

capable of expansion at their extremity nearly equal to their length; each toe is furnished with a small nail." The skin of the animal is thick and somewhat spongy, but exceedingly tough. The hair that covers it in most adult individuals is short and of a dark brown; yet there is no lack of examples where it is of a much lighter shade, or a light but dingy gray. Unlike others of the seal tribe, the animal is abundantly infested with vermin. Under the skin lies the coating of fat which yields oil—it is from two to three inches in thickness. The appearance of the fully developed Walrus in the water, with its long tusks, which seem like an incumbrance, has a striking contrast with that of the common seal. The young, however, before its cumbrous canines protrude, resembles the latter in general form, but is of a black color. On land the Walrus is comparatively inactive and clumsy in its movements; but in the water its motions are easy and vigorous. Its geographical distribution quite encircles the globe in that colder belt of the northern hemisphere, above the latitude of 45°, and but few individuals are met with south of 47° north. In Behring Sea they are found as far south as the shores of the peninsula of Alaska, and in the Pacific Ocean about several of the islands which fringe the central coast of Alaska Territory. They feed upon shell-fish and other submerged marine productions. The Walrus is gregarious, being sometimes found in herds upon the ice, and at the proper season the animals collect upon the beaches, or they clamber upon rocky islets in remote places. They are said to be monogamous, but we are of the opinion that they are not exclusively so. The season when the sexes seek each other is in the last of the spring months, or the first of the summer. The time of gestation is about nine months. The mother and her offspring manifest a stronger mutual affection than we have observed in any other of the marine mammals; and the cub seeks her protection, clinging to her back whenever there is cause for alarm,* and she will at all times place herself between the foe and her helpless charge. Frequently has she been known to clasp to her breast the terrified little one, embracing it with her fore flippers, while receiving mortal wounds from the whaleman's lance. A male, and a female with her cub, are often seen together; yet herds of old and young, of both sexes, are met with, both in the water and upon the ice. When undisturbed they are quite inoffensive, but if hotly pursued they make a fierce resistance; their mode of attack is by hooking their tusks over the gunwales of the boats, which may overturn them, or they strike a blow through the planking, which has repeatedly been the means of staving and sinking them. Captain Lyon remarks: "Mr. Shirer described the fury of the wounded animals as being quite outrageous; but those which were unhurt quickly forsook their suffering companions." There may have been instances of a combined attack of Walruses on besieging boats; but like all other marine mammals which have been continuously pursued, they soon become wary, and when there is cause for alarm they give warning to their neighboring associates by loud

---

* Captain T. W. Williams, a whaling master of much experience and observation, states, that on one voyage to the Arctic Ocean, a female Walrus was captured two miles from the ship, and the young cub kept close to the boats that were towing its dead mother to the vessel; and when arrived, made every effort to follow her as she was being hoisted on board. A rope with a bowline was easily thrown over it, and the bereaved creature taken on deck, when it instantly mounted its mother's back and there clung with mournful solicitude, until forced by the sailors to again return to the sea; but even then it remained in the vicinity of the ship, bemoaning the loss of its parent by uttering distressful cries.

roarings, or if asleep, by pecking at them with their tusks, when all make a pre-
cipitate retreat from the ice, or they will tumble and roll over the rocks or rough
ground, if on shore, in their flight to the sea, unless detained with their young.
"The chase of the Walrus is of great antiquity; accordingly, we find that Ohthere,
a Norwegian, about the year 890 gave an account of it to Alfred the Great, having,
he says, 'made a voyage beyond Norway for the more *commodite* of fishing horse-
whales, which have in their teeth bones of great price and excellence, whereof he
brought some at his return to the King.'"

The capture of the Walrus is made both upon the water and land. It is
stated that a Greenlander will never venture on the encounter alone, nor without
the assistance of three or four expert comrades. They employ a harpoon, which,
however, from the toughness of the skin, is fixed with difficulty, and hence it is
not so easy an operation as the striking of a whale. When the instrument holds,
the animal is allowed to swim about until it is wearied; they then try to secure it
and kill it with lances. But even under these circumstances the process is not an
easy one; the creature, as we have stated, getting roused and fighting a hard battle.
It is necessary, according to Zorgdrager, to make a selection. Accordingly, the
fishers aim at the eyes, which obliges the animal to turn its head, and then the
fatal blow is aimed at the breast. "In this crisis," remarks Scoresby, "the best
defense against these enraged animals is sea-sand, which, being thrown into their
eyes, occasions partial blindness and obliges them to disperse; then the captured
one becomes a more easy prey." According to Lord Sheldham's account of the
capture of Walruses upon the land in early times, the hunters, armed with spears,
and under cover of night, with trained dogs, made an effort to partially disperse
the main herd; then falling upon detachments of the animals, which, being bewildered in the darkness, were then slain in large numbers. Godman relates that
one of the Esquimaux modes of killing the Walrus in summer is, when perceiving a
large herd asleep on the floating ice, they paddle to some other piece near by,
which is small enough to be moved. On this they lift their canoes, and then bore
holes, through which they fasten their lines; and when every thing is prepared,
they quietly paddle their ice-float toward the herd, each hunter sitting by his own
spear and line. "When arrived at the place where the animals lie snoring, each
man, if so disposed, strikes a different one, though two generally attack the same.
The stricken creature instantly makes great effort to escape, but, although he tumbles into the water, he is held by the spear-lines which are made fast to the ice.
As soon as the victim becomes wearied, the hunter launches his canoe, and at a
safe distance spears him to death." According to our observation, the manner of

capturing the animals by the natives about the eastern coast of Behring Sea, and in the Arctic Ocean, is by shooting them when on shore with a rifle, and pursuing them when in the water with spears and lances. In approaching the animal in their skin-boats, a paddle formed from a slab of whalebone is employed to gently beat the surface of the sea, which is thought to serve as a kind of decoy to the creature; and when within reach, the spear, with a line of walrus hide attached, is thrust into the object of pursuit, and subsequently it is dispatched by being pierced with knives and other sharp instruments. But the natives of the Pribyloff Islands, and also those of the peninsula of Alaska (who have become excellent marksmen), shoot them with heavy muskets.

Great numbers of Walruses are found about the waters of the Arctic uniting with Behring Straits, and in Behring Sea, and innumerable herds still resort in the summer months to different points on the southern or central coasts of Alaska, particularly at Amak Island and Point Moller, on the northern shore of the Alaskan peninsula. Within the last ten years many of these animals have been destroyed by the whalers, both in the Arctic and Behring Seas. The mode of capture was by shooting them when upon the ice with Spencer rifles, or, if in the water, by harpooning and lancing them. To the natives of the coasts where the Walrus frequents, the animal is of indispensable value. The flesh supplies them with food; the ivory tusks are made into implements used in the chase, and for other domestic purposes, as well as affording a valuable article of barter; and the skin furnishes the material for covering their summer habitations, planking for their *baidarras*, harness for their dog-teams, and lines for their fishing-gear. But the savage native and the civilized fisherman and sailor are not the only enemies of the Walrus. The polar bear seeks them in its prowlings, and when meeting with a herd, the huge beast selects and seizes one of the smallest individuals with his capacious jaws, and the resisting struggles of the poor victim to free itself are quickly suppressed by repeated blows with bruin's paws, which cause almost instant death. The murderous beast then quickly tears the skin from the body by means of his long, sharp claws, when the remains are devoured. That carnivorous animal of the cetacean order, known as the Orca, or Killer, also watches for the young cubs of the Walrus, and if there is floating ice at hand, the mother with her charge clambers upon it to avoid the pursuer; if this fails, however, the cub will mount the mother's back as the only place of refuge. But the Killer is rarely baffled in obtaining the object it seeks by this mode of the mother's protection, for the pursuing animal dives deeply, and then comes head up under the old Walrus, with such force as to throw the cub from the dam's back into the water, when it is instantly seized and swallowed by its adversary. Instances have been known, however, where the Orca has paid dearly for its murderous temerity, as the enraged Walrus, when bereft of her young, will sometimes strike her tusks into her foe with such effect as to cause a mortal wound or instant death.

Among the numerous enemies of the Walrus, it is to be regretted that the whalers are included, they having been driven to the necessity of pursuing them on account of the scarcity of Cetaceans. Already the animals have suffered so great a slaughter at their hands that their numbers have been materially diminished, and they have become wild and shy, making it difficult for the Esquimaux to successfully hunt them, in order to obtain a necessary supply of food. It is stated that there has been much suffering among those harmless people of the far north, on account of this source for supplying themselves with an indispensable article of sustenance being to an alarming extent cut off.

According to *The Friend*, published at Honolulu, March 1st, 1872, the whalers first began to turn their attention to Walrus-catching about the year 1868, and the work has continued up to the present time. Usually, during the first part of every season there has been but little opportunity to capture whales, they being within the limits of the icy barrier. Hence, much of the whalers' time during the months of July and August has been devoted to capturing the Walrus; and it is estimated that at least sixty thousand of these animals have been destroyed by the whale-fishers in the Arctic Ocean and Behring Sea during the last five years, which produced about fifty thousand barrels of oil, with a proportionate amount of ivory.

PART III.

THE AMERICAN WHALE-FISHERY.

PART III.—THE AMERICAN WHALE-FISHERY.

CHAPTER I.

ORIGIN AND ANCIENT MODE OF WHALE-FISHING.

BEFORE entering upon the history of the American Whale-fishery, we will introduce a few remarks relative to the origin and prosecution of whaling in other quarters of the world. If we go back to the time of the early Grecian sailors, and follow through the maritime history of every nation, there appears to be no positive record as to the time when, or place where, whale-fishing originated. In the collection of various whaling and exploring voyages which we have perused, nearly all the authors agree that the Basques and Biscayans were the first to capture whales as a regular commercial pursuit. Eminent writers, however, maintain that the Norwegians were the first to pursue those leviathans of the deep, and that they carried on a fishery long before any other European nation. It may be possible that the Norwegians were the first who made the whale-fishery a legitimate business. This, however, seems to be very doubtful, when we look to the shores of Japan and Chinese Tartary, where, ever since we have been in possession of any reliable knowledge of that region and its inhabitants, we know that the Japanese and Tartars have successfully pursued the whale in large boats from their shores. Among the American authorities relative to the foreign whale-fishery is the Hon. J. Ross Browne, who, having had recourse to the Congressional Library at the time of compiling his *Etchings of a Whaling Cruise, and History of the Whale-fishery*, has given, in the appendix to that work, a concise and somewhat chronological account of whaling commerce, beginning as early as 887, and following down to the present century, from which we shall quote numerous statistics of that eminent writer, as also extracts from the works of other authors.

"As early as 887, according to Anderson (in his *Historical and Chronological*

Deduction of the Origin of Commerce), or, as Hakluyt thinks, about 890, 'Our excellent King Alfred' received from one Octher [Ohthere?], a Norwegian, an account of his discoveries northward on the coast of Norway; a coast which seems to have been before very little, if at all, known to the Anglo-Saxons. There is one very remarkable thing in this account; for he tells King Alfred 'that he sailed along the Norway coast, so far north as commonly the whale-hunters used to travel;' which shows the great antiquity of whale-fishing; though undoubtedly then, and long after, the use of what is usually called whalebone was not known; so that they fished for whales merely on account of their fat or oil. Octher, after giving a very curious description of the country inhabited by the Finmans, proceeds to say, 'he visited this country also with a view of catching horse-whales, which had bones of very great value for their teeth, of which he brought some to the king; that their skins were good for making ropes for ships. These whales are much less than other whales, being only five ells long. The best whales were caught in his own country, of which some were forty-eight, some fifty yards long. He said that he was one of six who had killed sixty in two days.'"*

"These horse-whales, spoken of by Octher, were what we call sea-horses, and the Dutch, sea-cows, or *morses*. It is probable that the length of the whales caught in his own country is greatly exaggerated. Beale quotes from many of the ancient writers instances of extraordinary exaggerations of this kind, and doubts whether any whales were ever seen of a greater length than eighty or ninety feet, even admitting they were once found of larger growth than any now seen or captured. The earliest authentic data that I have been able to find respecting the origin of the whale-fishery, as a regular and permanent branch of trade, is that furnished by M'Culloch in his *Commercial Dictionary;* which, although little more than a condensation from the works of Anderson, Macpherson, and others, is of a more reliable character than any similar compilation I have met with. At the time

---

* This would seem incredible; but when we investigate the statement, it is found that Ohthere was a Flemish writer. Hence, instead of reckoning ells at three feet, we put them down at twenty-seven inches, which would make the largest whale one hundred and twelve feet long. As to the killing of sixty whales in two days, by six men, as stated by Ohthere, Scoresby (*Arctic Regions*, Vol. II, page 9) gives a very plain account, in a note, of how this assertion might be truthful; which is as follows: "The Honorable Daines Barrington, in the account of Ohthere's voyage, published in his *Miscellanies*, translates the passage, containing his exploit in the whale-fishery, in the words, 'he had killed some six; and sixty in two days.' But, conscious of the unintelligibleness of the sentence, he observes, in a note, that *syxa*, he conceives, should be a second time repeated here, instead of *syxtig*, or sixty; it would then only be asserted that six had been taken in two days, which is much more probable than sixty."

the inhabitants of Massachusetts were making their first attempts in the capture of the whale (about 1650), the Biscayans had already extensively engaged in that business; the Dutch and the English had followed their example; the Russian Company had obtained an exclusive charter for it, and many other nations of Europe had directed their attention to the northern fisheries."

"It is probably true, as has been sometimes contended," says M'Culloch, "that the Norwegians occasionally captured the whale before any other European nation engaged in so perilous an enterprise. But the early efforts of the Norwegians were not conducted on any systematic plan, and should only be regarded in the same point of view as the fishing expeditions of the Esquimaux. The Biscayans were certainly the first people who prosecuted the whale-fishery as a regular commercial pursuit. They carried it on with great vigor and success in the twelfth, thirteenth, and fourteenth centuries. In 1261, a tithe was laid upon the tongues of whales imported into Bayonne, they being there a highly esteemed species of food. In 1388, Edward III relinquished to Peter de Puayanne a duty of six pounds sterling a whale, laid on those brought into the port of Biarritz, to indemnify him for the extraordinary expenses he had incurred in fitting out a fleet for the service of his majesty. This fact proves beyond dispute that the fishery carried on from Biarritz at the period referred to must have been very considerable indeed; and it was also prosecuted to a great extent from Cibourre, Vieux Boucan, and subsequently from Rochelle and other places. The whales captured by the Biscayans were not so large as those that are taken in the Polar Seas, and are supposed to have been attracted southward in the pursuit of herrings. They were not very productive of oil, but their flesh was used as an article of food, and the whalebone was applied to a variety of useful purposes, and brought a very high price."

In 1554, Pierre Belon writes concerning the Right Whale, or at least one of the baleen whales, as follows: "The animal which we call the whale (baleen) was named by the ancient Greeks, *phalene;* by the Latins, *balena;* and is designated by the Italians as the *capodoglio* (oil-head). It is generally considered to be the largest of all fishes, as may well be supposed from the size of the bones and ribs of the animal, which is enormous, so that they have been much wondered at when exhibited. It is for this reason that some have called it the *Cete.* There is no ground for believing that the whale has two large horns on its head, as some have drawn this animal; but there is a kind of tube on the upper part of the head, which does not, however, rise above the skin, and the existence of which only becomes apparent when the animal throws out the water through it, which has been taken in by the muzzle. This it does sometimes with such violence that ships have been capsized by it" (the jet of water). "It is also believed that the whale, like the porpoise and the dolphin, jumps entirely out of the water in order to take breath, and even that it has been heard blowing from a great distance off. This fish has neither hair nor scales, but is covered with smooth, hard, black, and thick skin, or hide, under which there is a layer of fat fully a foot in thickness, and this is what is sold during Lent. The tongue is marvelously large, and excellent eating; and it is customary to salt and preserve it, as is also done with all the rest of the flesh of this fish. And that which is called whalebone (*coste de balene* — literally, whale's ribs), with which ladies nowadays make their corsets and stiffen out their dresses, and which the beadles of some churches carry as wands — these are certain pieces cut off and drawn out from that which serves as eye-lids for the whale, and which covers his eyes, and which is furnished at its extremity with a kind of long, stiff hair. This is what the Latins call the *pretentures*, and which they say enables the animal to direct his course through the sea. As far as the other exterior and interior parts of the whale are concerned, they clearly resemble those of the sea-hog, and, making allowance for size, those of the porpoise and dolphin."

Although this writer in some points gives us a very erroneous account of the whalebone whale, yet in a general view it is an intelligible description of the animal; and it also establishes the fact that the animal's baleen, fat, and flesh were utilized at that period, the former being used as at the present day to distort the figures of women in their dress, and the latter was esteemed as luxurious food. The author's figure of the balæna is almost entirely in error, yet it is hardly more so than the representations of the same animal which may be found in popular works of the present century. We continue to quote from M'Culloch:

"This branch of industry among the Basques and Biscayans ceased long since, and from the same cause that has occasioned the cessation of the whale-fishery in many other places — the want of fish. Whether it was that the whales, from a sense of the dangers to which they exposed themselves in coming southward, no longer left the icy sea, or that the breed had been nearly destroyed, certain it is that they gradually became less numerous in the Bay of Biscay, and at length ceased almost entirely to frequent that sea; and the fishers being obliged to pursue their prey upon the banks of Newfoundland and the coasts of Iceland, the French fishery rapidly fell off. The voyages of the Dutch and English to the Northern Ocean, in order, if possible, to discover a passage through it to India, though they failed of their main object, laid open the haunts of the whale. The companions of Barentz, who discovered Spitzbergen in 1596, and of Hudson, who soon after explored the same seas, represented to their countrymen the amazing number of whales with which they were crowded.* Vessels were in consequence fitted out for the northern whale-fishery by the English and Dutch, the harpooners and a part of the crew being Biscayans. They did not, however, confine their efforts to a fair competition with each other as fishers. The Muscovy Company obtained a royal charter, prohibiting the ships of all other nations from fishing in the seas round Spitzbergen, on pretext of its having first been discovered by Sir Hugh Willoughby. There can, however, be no doubt that Barentz, and not Sir Hugh, was its original discoverer; though, supposing that the fact had been otherwise, the attempt to exclude other nations from the surrounding seas on such a ground was not one that could be tolerated. The Dutch, who were at that time prompt to embark in a commercial pursuit that gave any hope of success, eagerly entered on this new career, and sent out ships fitted equally for the purposes of fishing and of defense against the attacks of others. The Muscovy Company having attempted to vindicate its pretensions by force, several encounters took place between their ships and those of the Dutch. The conviction at length became general that there was room enough for all parties in the northern seas; and in order to avoid the chance of coming into collision with each other, they parceled Spitzbergen and the adjacent ocean in districts, which they respectively assigned to the English, Dutch, Hamburgers, French, Danes, etc. The Dutch, thus left to prosecute the fishery without having their attention diverted by hostile attacks, speedily acquired a decided superiority over all their competitors. When the Europeans first began to prosecute the fishery on the coast of Spitzbergen, whales were everywhere found in vast numbers. Ignorant of the strength and stratagems of the formidable foe by which they were now assailed, instead of betraying any symptoms of fear, they surrounded the ships and crowded all the bays. Their capture was, in consequence, a comparatively easy task, and many were killed which it was afterward necessary to abandon, from the ships being already full. While fish were thus easily obtained, it was the practice to boil the blubber on shore in the north, and fetch home only the oil and whalebone; and perhaps nothing can give a more vivid idea of the extent and importance of the Dutch fishery in the middle of the seventeenth century, than the fact that they constructed a considerable village (the

---

* Doctor Lindeman states in his work upon the whale-fishery (*Die arktische Fischerei der Deutschen Seestädte*, 1620 *to* 1868), "in the thirteenth and fourteenth centuries the Hanseatic cities carried on war with Denmark on account of interference with their whale-fisheries on the coast of Jutland." He further mentions, that "the first English whaling-ships were sent out from Hull in 1598, to the coasts of Iceland and the region of the North Cape."

houses of which were all previously prepared in Holland, on the isle of Amsterdam), on the northern shore of Spitzbergen, to which they gave the appropriate name of Smeerenberg (from *smeeren*, to melt, and *berg*, a mountain). This was the grand rendezvous of the Dutch whale-ships, and was amply provided with boilers, tanks, and every sort of apparatus required for preparing the oil and bone. But this was not all. The whale-ships were attended with a number of provision-ships, the cargoes of which were landed at Smeerenberg, which abounded during the busy season with well-furnished shops, good inns, etc., so that many of the conveniences and enjoyments of Amsterdam were found within about eleven degrees of the Pole! It is particularly mentioned that the sailors and others were every morning supplied with what a Dutchman regards as a very great luxury, hot rolls for breakfast. Batavia and Smeerenberg were founded nearly at the same period, and it was for a considerable time doubted whether the latter was not the more important establishment. (*De Reste, Histoire des Pêches, etc.,* tome i, p. 42.)

"During the flourishing period of the Dutch fishery, the quantity of oil made in the north was so great that it could not be carried on by the whale-ships, and every year vessels were sent out in ballast to assist in importing the produce of the fishery. But the same cause which had destroyed the fishery of the Biscayans ruined that which was carried on in the immediate neighborhood of Spitzbergen. Whales became gradually less common, and more and more difficult to catch. They retreated first to the open seas, and then to the great banks of ice on the eastern coast of Greenland. When the site of the fishery had thus been removed to a very great distance from Spitzbergen, it was found most economical to send the blubber direct to Holland. Smeerenberg was, in consequence, totally deserted, and its position is now with difficulty discernible. When in the most flourishing state, toward 1680, the Dutch whale-fishery employed about two hundred and sixty ships and fourteen thousand sailors."

Frederic Marten, who made a voyage to Spitzbergen and Greenland during the summer of 1671, gives a quaint account of the British whalers at that period, from which we extract the following:

"We set sail the 15th of April, 1671, about noon, from the island of Elbe. The name of the ship was *Jonas in the Whale*, Peter Peterson, of Frisland, master." Having arrived at Spitzbergen, the writer continues: "On the 5th of June, in the forenoon, it was moderately cold and sunshiny, but toward noon darkish and cloudy, with snow and great frost. We saw daily many ships sailing about the ice. I observed that as they passed by one another, they hailed one another, crying *Holla!* and asked each other how many fish they had caught, but would not stick sometimes to tell more than they had. When it is windy, that they could not hear one another, they waved their hats to signifie the number caught. But when they have their full freight of whales, they put up their great flag as a sign thereof; then if any hath a message to be sent, he delivers it to them. On the 12th of July we had a gloomy sun—sunshine all day. We saw but very few whales more, and those we did see were quite wild, that we could not come near them. That night it was so dark and foggy that we could hardly see the ship's length. We might have got sea-horses enough, but we were afraid of losing our ships, for we had examples enough of them that had lost their ships, and could not come to them again, but have been forced to return home in other ships. When after this manner any have lost their ships, and can not be seen, they discharge a cannon from the ship, or sound the trumpets or hautboys, according as they are provided in their ships, that the men that are lost may find their ships again."

As to the mode of capturing and flaying the *mysticetus*, as well as the process of extracting the oil from the blubber, the narrator gives the following description, under the headings respectively of "How they Catch the Whale," "What they do with the Dead Whale," and "Of the Trying out of the Train-oyl from the Fat."

"First, it is to be observ'd, that when it's like to be a good year to catch whales in, there is many *white-fish* to be seen before: but where we see many *seales*, there we do not expect to meet with many *whales;* for they say, that they eat up the food of the whale, wherefore the whales will not stay in such empty places, but go to find out better, and so come to *Spitzbergen*, for there, at the shoar, we see great plenty of the small sea-snails, and perhaps some other small fish. They are caught after the following manner: When they see whales, or when they hear them blow or spout, they call in to the ship, *Fall, fall;* then every body must be ready to get into the long-boat that he doth belong to; commonly six men go into every long-boat, and sometimes seven, according as the long-boats are in bigness; they all of them row until they come very near unto the whale; then doth the harpoonier arise, who sits always before in the boat, where the harpoon, or the sharp iron made like unto an arrow fixed to a stick, doth also lie on the foremost board of the long-boat, which the seamen call the *Staffen*, that is, the broad piece of wood that cometh up before the boat from the bottom, and stands up higher than all the rest. But when the whale runs strait down towards the bottom underneath the water, then he doth draw the rope very hard, so that the upper part of the long-boat is even with the surface of the water; nay, he would certainly pull it down to the bottom, if they should not give him rope enough. This he doth commonly where the sea is deepest; and this doth require an incredible force to draw so many hundred fathoms of rope under water. This gives me occasion to remember, that when we on the 27th of April, in the year 1672, did fling out our lead, near St. Kilda, behind Scotland, into the sea, where it was one hundred and twenty fathom deep, when the weather was calm, and when we would pull it up again, it was so heavy that twenty men had much to do to heave it. The harpoonier taketh his harpoon, and holds the point, or the iron thereof, together with the rope or line of five or seven fathom long, about an inch thick, and is laid up round like a ring, that it may not hinder the harpoon when it is flung, for as soon as he doth fling or dart the harpoon, this line follows; for it is more pliable than the rest that are fastened to it, wherewith they pursue the whale. It is made of the finest and softest hemp, and not daubed with tar, but it doth swell in the water, and so it grows hard. The harpoonier darts his harpoon with the right hand at the fish. When the whale is hit with the harpoon, all the men that are in the long-boat turn themselves about and look before them, and they lay their oars nimbly upon the sides of the long-boat. There is a man in the long-boat, whose business it is to look after the rope; for in each of these long-boats there is a whole heap of lines, between the two seats or benches; this heap is divided into three, four, or five parts, and each of them is of eighty, ninety, to one hundred fathoms long. The first of them is ty'd to the fore-runner, or small line; as the whale runs under the water, they tye more and more line to it, and if in one boat there should not be enough, they make use of those that are in the other long-boats. These ropes or lines are thicker and stronger than the fore-runner, and are made of strong and tough hemp, and tarr'd over. The line-furnisher, or the man that doth look after the ropes, and also the other men that are in the long-boat, must have great care that the ropes or lines may not be entangled when they run out so swift, or that they may not run towards the side of the long-boat, for then the long-boat would be overset, and many men lose their lives, if other long-boats were not near to their assistance. The line must run just before, in the middle of the long-boat, that is called the *Stave* by the seamen, and by reason of this strong and violent motion, the wood and rope would be set on fire. But to prevent this, the harpoonier hath a wet rag ty'd to a stick (like unto a mop) ready at hand, wherewith he wets the wood without ceasing. The other three men that are in the long-boats take also care of the lines, as well when they are let out, as when they are taken in again; and when they can not hold it with their hands, they wind it about the staves of the boat, and so they do stop it from going any further. Another, that is called the steer-man, stands behind in the long-boat, and steers the boat with an oar, and he takes great care, and minds the rope, to see which way it runs out, for if it doth go towards either side, and doth not run just before over the stave, he so guides the boat, that it may run exactly out before. The whale runs away with the long-boat as swift as the wind. If the harpoonier can, he doth dart the harpoon just behind the spout-hole of the whale, or in the thick fat of his back, where they also do launce him, for that maketh him spout blood sooner than if wounded in any other place, and die sooner than if you should launce them into their belly, or through the guts. The first whale we caught spouted blood in such a quantity, that the sea was tinged by it wherever he swam, whereunto the *Mallemucks* flock'd in great numbers, as I have mentioned before. They also launce the whales near their privy-parts, if they can come at it; for if they are run in there, it doth pain them very much; nay, even when they are almost dead, if you run in your launce thereabout, it causes the whole body to tremble. For the most part they do not much mind where they launce or push them; for there is no time to take deliberation, but they strike at him as well as they can. But about the head the harpoon can do him no hurt, because the fat is but very *thin* there on the bones, which the whales know as well as we; for when they find themselves in danger, so that they can not escape the harpoon, they rather leave their head than their back undefended, for there the harpoon breaks out easier, and so the whale gets away, like one that hath no mind to fight any longer. The use of the harpoon is, to tye, as it were, the whales with them, that they may not run away. It is shaped like an arrow before: it hath two sharp beards, they are sharp at the edge, and have a broad back, like unto a hatchet that is sharp before and blunt behind, or on the back, so that it may not cut with its back, for else it would tear out, and all your labour would be lost. The iron handle is thicker behind than before, and it is hollow, whereinto they put the stick. Before this hollow part, the fore-goer is fasten'd or ty'd, that is to say the foremost rope. Those are the best harpoons that are made of clean and fine steel, and are not hardened too much, so that you may bend it without snapping, for oftentimes two hundred pounds are lost (for a midling whale is esteem'd at so much) in a minute's time for want of a good and well-temper'd harpoon. The wooden stick is fastened within the iron collet or funnel of the harpoon, with packthread wound all about the iron; somewhat higher up, about two spans off, there is a hole made through the stock. The harpoon is light behind, and heavy towards the point, or before, like an arrow, that is made heavy before with iron, and light behind with feathers, so that fling it which way you will, it doth fall always upon the point. Through this hole cometh a piece of packthread, wherewith the end of the fore-runner is fastened to the handle or stock of the harpoon, but this is soon torn off, and it serveth for nothing more after the harpoon sticks in the body of the whale; neither is the wooden handle of any further use, and so it doth soon come out from the iron. When the whale is struck with the harpoon, all the other long-boats row out before, and take notice which way the line doth stand, and some-times they pull at the rope or line. If it is stiff and heavy, the whale doth draw it still with his might; but if it doth hang loose, so that the long-boat is before and behind equally high out of the water, then the men pull in the rope again, and the rope-giver layeth it down in very good order, round, and one row above the other, that if the whale should draw on again, he may have it ready to give him without being entangled. Here is also this to be observed, that if the whale runs upon the level, they must not give him too much rope, for if he should turn and wind himself much and often about, he might easily wind the rope about a rock or heavy stone, and so fasten it to it, and so the harpoon would come out, and all the labour would be lost, which hath often hapned, and we ourselves lost one that way. The other long-boats that are towed behind, wherein the men look all before them, and sit still, and let the whale draw them along. If the whale doth rowl upon the ground, so that the long-boats or sloops lye still, they draw their lines in again by degrees, and the rope-master doth lay them down again in their proper places, as they had been laid before. When they kill the whale with launces, they also pull their lines in again, untill they come near to the whale, yet at some distance, that the others may have room to launce. But they must have great care, that all the lines of every sloop may not be cut off together, because some whales sink, and others do swim even with the water when they are dead, which nobody can tell beforehand, whether they will do one or the other. The fat ones do not sink presently after they are fresh killed, but the lean ones sink immediately after they are dead, but after some few days they come up again, and swim on the water. But it would be too long a while for a man to stay till he cometh up again, and the sea is never so quiet that one can stay long in the same place; and where the sea is quiet, and without waves, there the stream doth carry the ships and the ice along together, so that we should be forced to leave the whale unto others, that would find him dead some days after. 'Tis true, this is the easiest way to catch whales, but it is very nasty and stinking work; for long and white maggots grow in their flesh, they are flat, like unto worms that breed in men's bellies, and they smell worse than ever I smelt anything in my life. The longer the whale lies dead in the water, the higher he doth swim above it; some swim a foot high above the water, others to their middle, and then they do burst easily, and give a very great report. They begin immediately to stink, and this encreases hourly, and their flesh boils and ferments like unto beer or ale, and holes break in their bellies, and their guts come out. If any man is enclined to sore eyes, this vapor inflames them immediately, as if quicklime was flung into them. But when the live whales rise and swim again, some of them are astonish'd, others wild or stark mad. To those that are wild we come softly or gently from behind, as we do when we are going to trapan them; for when the wind is down, the weather calm, and air serene, so that the sea doth not foam or roar, the whales hear immediately the striking of the oars.

"If many small ice-sheets lye near to one another, so that we can not follow the whale with our sloops or long-boats, we fetch in our line with all might and strength, and if with one or more pulls we can fetch out the harpoon, it is well, if not, we chop off the rope or line. The whale is best and surest struck with a harpoon when he spouts water, as is already said above, for we do observe, that when they lie still and very quiet, that they then listen, and are sometimes under, and sometimes above water, so that their back doth not quite dry, and before we are aware of it he flings up his tail behind out of the sea, and so bids us good-by. The whales may easily be caught when the air is very serene and clear, and the sea quiet, and where there float neither great nor small ice-sheets, so that we may go in between them with our boats or sloops, to follow them; for at the ice-fields the whales do commonly lye and rub themselves at them, perhaps by reason of the lice that bite them. Besides, against the ice-sheets the sea beats, dashes, and foams, with small curling waves, so that the whales do not observe nor mind the striking of the oars, and so they are easily struck with the harpoon. It is very dangerous to kill a female, chiefly when she is big with young, for they defend themselves very long, and are harder to be kill'd than a male one. Oftentimes the long-boats wait six or seven hours, nay, a whole day, for a whale, before they see one.

"Where great quantity of small ice is crowded together, there it is also very dangerous, and hard to come to the whale, for he is so cunning, that when he perceives where the ice is he retires thither immediately. The harpoonier stands at the head of the long-boat, and doth draw on the rope, to try whether it is heavy or light; if it feels heavy, so that we are afraid that it will pull the boat under water, then we give him more rope; if he runs strait out before, he draweth the sloops after him. If he doth run underneath a great ice-field, the harpoonier taketh a knife in his hand, which they call the chopping-knife, and if the ice-field be hollow, or spongy, or full of holes in the middle, so that the whale can fetch breath underneath it, and the rope is not long enough to follow him, and if the ice be several miles long, they draw the rope in as much as possibly they can, until it be strait, and then he chops it off, loosing the piece of the rope whereon the harpoon is fastened, that sticketh in the body of the whale, yet not without great loss, for oftentimes they run away with the lines that belong to five and more sloops. It happens very often, that they run to the ice with the long-boats, so that they dash against it, as if they would break it into pieces, which also very often happens. But when the whale rises again, they oftentimes fling one or two more harpoons into him, according as they find he is tired more or less; then he dives under water again. Some swim or run even all along on the water, and they play with their tail and fins, so that we must have great care that we may not come too near them. When the whales fling their tails about in this manner, they wind the line about their tail, so that we need not to fear the harpoon tearing out, for then they are ty'd strong and firm enough with the rope. After they are wounded, they spout with all their might and main, so that you may hear them as far off as you may a cannon; but when they are quite tired, it cometh out only by drops, for he hath not strength enough to force the water up, and therefore it sounds as if you held an empty mug or bottle under water, and the water runs into it. And this sound is a certain sign of his feebleness, and that he is going to expire. Some whales blow blood to the very last, after they have been wounded, and these dash the men in the long-boats most filthily, and dye the sloops red as if they were painted with a red colour; nay, the very sea is tinged red all along where they swim. Those whales that are mortally wounded heat themselves, that they reek while they are alive, and the birds sit on them, and eat on them while they are still alive. When the whales blow up the water, they fling out with it some fattish substance that floats upon the sea like sperm, and this fat the *Mallemucks* devour greedily, of which several thousands attend him, so that a whale often hath more attendants than a king hath servants. Sometimes also the harpoons break out; then often long-boats of other ships attend, and as soon as they see that the harpoon is come out, they fling their own into him, and the whale is theirs, altho' the first harpoon hath almost kill'd the whale, yet if he doth get loose, the second party claims him, and the first must look for another. Sometimes at the same time two harpoons, belonging to two several ships, are struck into the whale; such ones are divided equally, and each one hath half: the other two, or three, or more sloops, as many as there is of them, wait for the whales coming up again, and when they see that he is tir'd, they kill him outright with launces. In doing this is the greatest danger, for the first that do fling the harpoon into him are drawn along by the whale, and are at a good distance from him, but those that kill him with launces are as well upon his body as at his sides, according as the whale turns and winds himself, and they receive many severe blows. Here the steerman must take care to observe how the whale runs and turns himself about, that the harpoonier may reach him with his launces; all the other men in the sloops row diligently, sometimes forwards, and sometimes backwards, which they call rowing on and striking, and when the whale lifts up himself out of the water, he commonly doth strike about with his tail and fins, that the water dasheth up like dust. A long-boat he values no more than dust, for he can beat it all into shatters at a blow; but a great ship is too hard for him, and if he strikes against it with his tail, he feels it more than the ship, for he doth so paint the ship with his own blood, that it maketh him very feeble. A good steerman is next unto the harpoonier most useful in the sloop; he steers with one oar and doth look out before; the other four men turn their back to the head, and look towards the stern, therefore doth the steerman and harpoonier always cry, row on, or strike, that is to say, row near to the whale, or else keep farther off. The launces have a wooden stick or handle above two fathoms long, or somewhat shorter than a pikestaff; the iron thereof is commonly a fathom long, and pointed before like unto a pike; it is made of steel or tough iron, that it may bend without breaking. For after you have made a deep hole in his body with your launces, you poke into it with them one way and the other way, as they do when they poke for eels, but if he doth get one or more out of your hands, you take another, for every sloop hath at least five, six, or seven, and yet sometimes he has them all out of three, four, or more boats sticking in his body.

"After the whale is killed they cut off his tail; some keep the tail and fins, and hang them up at the outside of their ship, for that defends them from the ice when it presseth upon the ship. The tail hinders the boat in its course, because it doth lye across, and that is the reason why they cut it off. Before the tail they fasten a piece of a rope, and at the other end at the stern of the last sloop. There is in all four or five sloops fastened to one another behind, and so they row one behind the other to the great ship. When they have brought the whale to the ship, they tye it with ropes fast to the ship; that part where the tail is cut off they fasten to the fore-part of the ship, and the head towards the stern, about the middle, near the great shrouds of the mainmast on the larboard of the ship; it is seldom that a whale doth reach farther than from the poop to the middle of the ship, except the vessels are very small. By the larboard is to be understood that side of the ship that is at your right hand as you go from before towards the stern; but that side of the ship that is on your right hand as you go from the stern towards the fore-part is called star-board, because you go from the steer forward.

"Whoever of the ships' crews sees a dead whale, cries out *Fish mine*, and therefore the merchants must pay him a ducat, for his care and vigilance. Many of them climb often up into the mast, in hopes to have a ducat, but in vain. When the dead whale is thus fastened to the ship, two sloops hold on the other side of the fish or whale, and in each of them doth stand a man or boy, that has a long hook in his hands, wherewith he doth hold the boat to the ship, and the harpoonier stands before in the sloop, or upon the whale, with a leathern suit on, and sometimes they have boots on. Underneath the hook are some sharp nails fixed, that they may be able to stand firm, for the whale is very slippery, so that one may easily fall, as upon slippery ice. These two men that cut the fat off have their peculiar wages for it, viz: about four or five rix-dollars. First, they cut a large piece from behind the head, by the eyes, which they call the *Kenter-piece*, that is as much as to say the winding-piece; for as they cut all the other fat all in rows, from the whale towards the end, so they cut this great kenter-piece larger and wider than all the rest. This piece, when it is cut round about from the whale, reaches from the water to the cradle, (that is the round circle that goeth round about the middle of the mast, and is made in the shape of a basket), from whence you may guess at the bigness of a whale. A strong and thick rope is fixed to this kenter-piece, and the other end is fixed underneath the cradle, whereby the whale is as it was born up out of the water, that they may come at it, and by reason of the great weight of the whale, the ship leans towards that side. One may judge how tough the fat is, for in this piece an hole is made, through which the rope is fastened, yet not deep into the fat, wherewith they turn the fish at pleasure. Then, as is before said, they cut another piece down hard by this, that is also hauled up to the ship; and then in the ship they cut it into less pieces about a foot square. These two men have in their hands, as well as those that stand on the whale, long knives, wherewith they cut these square pieces. These knives are, with their hafts, about the length of a man; and the more the fat of the whale is loosened, just as the hide is flea'd from an ox, the higher must they pull up the fat with their pulleys, that they may cut it the easier. And when they have drawn up this fat, the men take it to them into the ship, and loosen the rope that it was fastened unto. The rope is fastened with a ring whereinto they put a great iron hook, which is fastened to a strong tackle, and also sometimes, before in the ship, are fix'd two other tackle, wherewith all the fat is drawn up into the ship. In the ship stand two men, with hooks as long as a man, wherewith they hold the great piece of fat, which the two men cut into square pieces with their long knives. By them stands another, that hath a short hook with a ring in his hands, which he thrusts into the pieces of fat that are cut square, and puts it upon the bench or dressing-board, where it is cut by others into less pieces. The two first men with their long knives, that cut the large pieces of fat, stand near the larboard of the ship, at that side where the whale is fix'd, and the other men, that afterwards cut it into less pieces, stand on the other side call'd starboard. When it is a good time to catch whales, and they will not lose it, they tow sometimes several fish behind their ship, and catch more; and they cut only the great pieces of fat of them, and fling them underneath into the ship. But when they have no more vessels to put their fat into, they sail into an harbor; or if it be calm weather, and not windy, they stay in the sea, and fasten themselves to a sheet of ice, and so they drive along with the stream. The other men cut the fat into small pieces, on a table; on the further side of the table is a nail fastened, whereunto they fasten a hook, which they put into the fat, that it may may lye steddy when they cut it into small pieces; the fat is tough to cut, wherefore it must lie firm. That side whereon the skin is they lay undermost, and so cut the fat from it by pieces. The knives wherewith they cut the fat into small pieces are less than the other, about three foot long with their hafts. They all cut from them that they may not be bedaubed with the fat, which might occasion a shrinking-up and lameness of the sinews of their hands and arms. One of them cuts the soft and tough fat into small pieces with a long knife; this man they call the *chopper*, and he is mightily daubed, wherefore he doth hang about him all sorts of rags and clouts he can get. The fat of some whales is white, of others yellow, and of some red. The white fat is full of small sinews, and it does not yield so much oyl as the yellow. The yellow fat that looks like butter is the best. The red and watery fat cometh from dead whales, for in the place where the fat runs out the blood settles in its room, and yields the worst and least oyl. Before the table is a gutter made of two boards nailed together, whereinto the small or minced fat is flung; by it stands a boy that shuffles the fat by degrees into a bag that is fixed to the end of the gutter, and is like unto a pudding-bag, so that it reaches down into the ship; out of this bag the fat runs down into a tub or wooden funnel, which they put upon empty vessels, or cardels, as they call them, and the men that are below in the ship fill them with it, and so it is kept until they try it up into train-oyl. When the fat is cut off from one side of the whale, before they turn him they cut out the whalebone in one entire piece ; and this is so heavy that all the ship's crew hath enough to do to pull it up. They make use, for that purpose, of a peculiar sort of hooks, two whereof they fix on the sides, and one on the middle of it, very well provided with strong tackle, and afterwards they cut out the whalebone of the other side of the fish, and draw it up also with pulleys into the ship, where it is cut into such pieces as they bring it hither in. The whalebone doth only belong to the owners of the ship, and the others that run their hazard, whether they catch few or many whales. The rest, which take their pay by the month, receive their money when they come home, whether they have caught many or none, and the loss or gain falls upon the merchants. The hooks that they crane up the whalebone withal, are made on purpose for it, like a beam of a pair of scales ; on each end are two sharp points, which they knock in between the whalebone ; in the middle of the beam is fastened a long handle with a ring, whereon the ropes are fastened ; on this handle there are fixed two other crooked hooks like bird's claws ; in the ring where the ropes are fastened is another crooked hook, at the top fastened by a ring, such a one as we make use of here when we wind anything up by a crane ; but in the middle between these two hooks is fastened another rope, which keeps the lowermost hook steddy ; the two hindmost points are knocked into the whalebone behind, and the two foremost short ones before, which hold the whalebone fast between them when it is wound or pulled up.

"The dead whales, when the fat is cut off of them, they let float, and are the food of the birds of prey when they are hungry ; but they had rather have dead whales that have still their fat left on them. The white bear is generally not far off, whether there be any fat left on them or no, and look like dogs that only feed upon carrion, and at that time their white fur is turned into a yellow colour, and at the same time they shed their hair, and their skins are worth very little. Where a dead whale is near, we see it by the birds, whereof are many, and also the white bears discover it, chiefly in the spring, when but few whales are caught, for then they are greedy of their prey ; afterwards, when many whales float on the sea, they have their bellies full, and we do not find so many by a whale, because they are dispersed.

"Formerly the Dutch did try out their train-oyl in Spitzbergen, at Smeerenberg, and about the Cookery of Harlingen, where still, for a remembrance, all sorts of tools belonging thereunto are to be seen, whereof I have made mention before. The Frenchmen try up their train-oyl in their ships, and by that means many ships are burnt at Spitzbergen; and this was the occasion of the burning of two ships in my time. They try out their train-oyl at Spitzbergen, that they may load the more fat in their ships; and they believe it to be very profitable, for they go their voyage upon part, that is to say, they receive more or less, according to what they catch: but I do not account it wisdom to fill up the room of the ship with wood, where they might stow vessels. But our countrymen, as I told you before, put the fat into the vessels, wherein it doth ferment just like beer; and I know no instance that ever any vessel did fly in pieces, although they are stopt up very close, and so it becometh for the greatest part train-oyl in them. Of the fresh fat of whales, when it is burnt out you lose twenty in the hundred, more or less, according as it is in goodness. At the place where they try up the fat into train-oyl, near Hamburg, they try up the fat out of the vessels into a great wooden trough or tub, and out of this two men empty it into a great kettle that stands near it, that doth hold two cardels of fat, that makes one hundred and twenty, one hundred and thirty, and sometimes one hundred and forty gallons. Underneath this copper that is made up with bricks they put the fire, and so they boil it, and try it up into train-oyl, as you try up other fat. This copper is very well secured, as the dyers' coppers use to be; it is very broad and flat, just like a frying-pan made of copper. When the fat is well tryed or fryed out, they take it out of the pan with small kettles, into a great sieve, that the liquid only may run through; the rest is thrown away. This sieve stands over a great tub, which is above half filled with cold water, that the hot train-oyl may be cooled, and that what is unclean and dirty of the blood and other soil may fall to the bottom, and only the clear train-oyl swim at the top of the water, like other oyl. In this great tub or trough is a small spout or tap, which doth run out over another as big as a tub, out of which the train-oyl runs into another tub, when it is almost ready to run over, which is also filled with cold water to the middle, wherein it is more cooled, and becomes clearer, and more refined than it was before. In this trough is another spout, through which the train-oyl runs into the warehouse into a vatt, whereout they fill it into cardels or vessels. Some have but two tubs. A cardel or hogshead holds sixty-four gallons. A true train-oyl barrel doth hold thirty-two gallons. The greaves they try up the second time, and make brown train-oyl out of it; others that think it not worth their while, fling them away."

Having submitted a brief sketch of primitive European whaling commerce, deduced from the most reliable papers and publications accessible to us, we will now enter upon an account of the American whale-fishery.

CHAPTER II.

THE AMERICAN WHALE-FISHERY.

The American Whale-fishery began as early as 1614. According to Captain John Smith, the enterprise was prosecuted by the colonists along the New England coast prior to that date, and it was among the first pursuits of the colonial inhabitants of New York and Delaware.* The right of whale-fishing "was guaranteed by the Royal Charter of 1629 to the proprietors of Massachusetts, as being within their waters."† Yet, according to Cheever, "the first person that is *recorded* to have killed a whale, among the people of New England, was one William Hamilton, somewhere between 1660 and 1670;"‡ and as early as 1700 they began to fit out vessels from Cape Cod and Nantucket, to "whale out" in the deep sea for sperm whales. These treasures of the ocean were of great value to the early settlers, both commercially and in a domestic point of view. One John Higginson, of Cape Cod, writes: "We have a considerable quantity of whale-oil and bone for exportation." Even in those primitive times, among the few inhabitants of the coast who were engaged in the exciting adventure, it was not without its strifes, for, in 1692, Mr. Higginson, one of the spiritual advisers of those days, and Timothy Lindall, wrote to Nathaniel Thomas:§

"Sir, we have been jointly concerned in *seuerall* whale voyages at Cape Cod, and have sustained *greate* wrong and injury by the unjust dealing of the inhabitants of those parts, especially in two instances; yᵉ first was when Woodbury and company, in our *boates*, in the winter of 1690, killed a large whale in Cape Cod harbour. She sank, and after rose, went to sea with a harpoon, warp, etc., of ours, which have been found in the hands of Nicholas Eldridge. The second case is this: Last winter, 1691, William Edds and company, in one of our *boates*, struck a whale, which came ashore dead, and by yᵉ evidence of the people of Cape Cod was the very whale they killed. The whale was taken away by Thomas Smith, of Eastham, and unjustly detained."

Annals of Salem, vol. ii, p. 223.

†Vide *Annals of Salem*, vol. ii, p. 223.

‡*Whale and his Captors*, p. 23.

§*Annals of Salem*, vol. ii, p. 223.

These remarks show that shore-whaling was pursued at the Cape previous to 1690. About 1748, the whales, having been driven from the contiguous shores, were pursued farther seaward in sloops and schooners of fifty tons, each of which had a company of thirteen men, and lowered two boats in the chase. In 1765, the whale-fishery from Boston and adjacent ports amounted to one hundred small vessels,* which cruised as far to the northward and eastward as the Straits of Belle Isle, the Gulf of St. Lawrence, and to the Western Islands. But at the island of Nantucket, or among the Nantucket men, originated the grand whaling enterprise which has reached every accessible point around the world.† The colonists who had come hither to settle were, like all other New Englanders of their time, made up of those characteristic spirits, who believed in God, and maintained the right of worshiping Him according to the dictates of their own convictions. Moreover, they were inured to frugal habits, but were alive to industry and adventure. Their first whaling from the island was in boats from the shores, which occurred as early as 1690.‡ A tall spar was erected, upon which the whalemen in turn ascended to watch for whales. As soon as the spout of the animal was seen in the distance, the signal was given, when immediately the boats were manned, launched through the surf, and with sturdy stroke they plied their rudely fashioned oars, and away flew the primitive whaling squadron, which was soon invisible from the island hamlet. The capture being made, the prize was towed to the beach and stripped of its blubber, which was transported in carts to the try-houses, where the oil was extracted and put into casks ready for market. The shore-whaling continued for over fifty years, but eventually it was abandoned, for the same reason that the Spitzbergen and Smeerenberg fisheries were — the scarcity of whales near

---

* *Annals of Salem*, vol. ii, p. 225.

† J. Hector St. John, who published a book in 1793, entitled *Letters from an American Farmer*, gives many interesting facts concerning the Nantucket people and the whale-fishery of the period, from which we extract a few paragraphs. Relative to the children, he says:

"At school they learn to read, and to write a good hand, until they are twelve years old; they are then in general put apprentices to the cooper's trade, which is the second essential branch of business followed here; at fourteen, they are sent to sea, where in their leisure hours their companions teach them the art of navigation, which they have an opportunity of practicing on the spot. They learn the great and useful art of working a ship in all the different situations which the sea and wind so often require; and surely there can not be a better or a more useful school of that kind in the world. Then they go gradually through every station of rowers, steersmen, and harpooners; thus they learn to attack, to pursue, to overtake, to cut, to dress their huge game: and after having performed several such voyages, and perfected themselves in this business, they are fit either for the counting-house or chase."

‡ *Hunt's Merchants' Magazine*, vol. iii, p. 364.

the coast. As early as 1712 or 1713, sloops of thirty-eight to fifty tons were fitted out from Nantucket, for voyages east to Newfoundland and south to the Gulf Stream. They had two boats each, and were manned with a crew of twelve or thirteen men, half of the number being natives.* In some instances the whole company, except the captain, were Indians; and the "Nattick" language was, in a great measure, adopted on board.† With these vessels, thus manned, and with the addition of an occasional representative of the African race, the fishery was successfully pursued up to 1746,‡ when larger ones, schooners and brigs, from one hundred to one hundred and thirty tons, were employed. These more capacious whaling craft stretched across the Atlantic, in their voyages, to the coast of Africa, traversed the Banks of Newfoundland, and contended with the ice of Baffin's and Hudson's bays, in search of their mammoth prey, and in open seasons reached the latitude of 81°.

According to Ricketson's *History of New Bedford*, the founder of that city, Joseph Russell, Esq., was the first to engage in the whale-fishery at that point, which dates back to 1755. In 1765, he, with others, employed in the enterprise the sloops *Nancy, Polly, Greyhound*, and *Hannah*, each of which was about fifty tons burden. Their cruises were extended during the milder months of the year as far south as the "Capes of Virginia." In these primitive voyages, the oil was not extracted from the blubber until the vessel's return, when the hoy-like craft was hauled broadside upon the shore, and an ox-cart was the means of transporting

---

* Pitkins mentions that the American whaling-fleet, in 1731, amounted to thirteen hundred tons. — *Pitkins on Commerce*, p. 43.

† It has been stated by several writers that the American colonists followed up the Indian mode of capturing the whale, by first striking it with a harpoon having a log of wood attached to it by a line, even as late as the commencement of the Sperm Whale fishery. It is quoted that the Hon. Paul Dudley stated: "Our people formerly used to kill the whale near the shore, but now they go off to sea in sloops and *whale-boats*. Sometimes the whale is killed by a single stroke, and yet at other times she will hold the whalemen in play *near half a day together*, with their lances; and sometimes they will get away after they have been lanced and spouted thick blood, with irons in them, and drags ("droges") fastened to them, which are thick boards about fourteen inches square." It was considered presumption to attempt to capture the huge creatures "in small boats, and by the aid of lines, from the end of which was attached the harpoon, by which they could draw themselves to the harpooned whale whenever they wished to destroy it with the lance." We are of the opinion, however, that the colonial whalers did not follow the Indian mode of whale-fishing; for it is well known that the British whalers, as early as 1670, used the line attached to the boat, and, so far as the drags or "droges" are concerned, they are used at the present day in cases of emergency.

‡ *Hunt's Merchants' Magazine*, vol. iii, p. 356.

Plate XXIII.

A WHALING SCENE OF 1763.

the reeking fat from the vessel to the "try-houses." This was the custom with all the whalers of those times.*

About 1770, other vessels of larger tonnage were added to the whaling squadron,† which extended their voyages, like the Nantucket-men, across the Atlantic. Among them were the New Bedford brigs *Patience* and *No Duty on Tea*. In September, 1791, the ship *Rebecca*, owned by those veteran merchants, Joseph Russell & Sons and Cornelius Howland, was among the first, if not the first, of American whalers which doubled Cape Horn and obtained a full cargo in the Pacific. The chronicler states: "Although the *Rebecca* was only one hundred and seventy-five tons, she was considered a very large vessel, and was visited as an object of wonder." Thus began the commercial enterprise at New Bedford—or, as the town was first named, Bedford—which has since become, and still is, the whaling metropolis of the world. Between the years 1771 and 1775, Massachusetts alone employed annually, in the northern whale-fishery, one hundred and eighty-three vessels, tonnaging thirteen thousand eight hundred and twenty tons; and one hundred and twenty-one vessels, with an aggregate burden of fourteen thousand and twenty tons, were engaged in the southern fishery,‡ and many places along the sea-board of New England, as well as towns

---

* The plate facing this page, representing a whaling-scene of 1763, was copied by permission from the celebrated painting by William H. Wall. The author of the *History of New Bedford* describes it in his work, from which we extract the following: "Upon the shore lies keeled over on her side one of the small vessels then employed for whaling; the model of the craft, a sloop, indicates a primitive idea of naval architecture. By the side of this sloop, but otherwise concealed from view, is seen the sail of another vessel, with the union-jack of old England drooping from the mast-head. The river lies peacefully outstretched, with a view of Palmer's Island and the shore along by the 'Smoking Rocks,' and Naushon in the distance. Where now stand our wharves and warehouses, the primeval forest trees are seen extending their roots to the water's edge. In the foreground of the picture, and that which will be to most its chief interest, is seen a group of the early inhabitants of New Bedford, busily employed. Under an old shed is seen the try-pot, with its attend-

ants; and also the jaw of a whale thrown upon the roof;" and between the shed and the sloop may be seen the ox-teams, hitched to a sort of sled (in lieu of the ordinary wheeled cart), on which the whale-fat is transported in casks to the try-works. "More conspicuous, and nearer the beholder, stands one man in a red shirt with a patch on the breast, pouring oil from a long-handled dipper into a wooden-hooped barrel; another handling over the blubber; and still more prominent, a fine-looking fellow is coopering a barrel, in conference with an Indian, who, with his baskets and moccasins for sale or barter, is seated upon a broken mast. Farther on, seated upon the frame of a grindstone, and giving directions to a colored man, who is holding his master's horse by the bridle, is seen, in his broad-brimmed hat and Friendly coat, the founder of New Bedford and father of her whale-fishery, Joseph Russell."

† *History of New Bedford*, p. 59.

‡ See *Hunt's Merchants' Magazine*, vol. iii, p. 366.

farther north and south, became whaling-ports. The subjoined table gives the number of American vessels annually engaged in the enterprise, with the amount and value of oil taken each year from 1762 to 1770, inclusive:

Year.	No. Vessels.	No. of Barrels.	Value of Imports.
1762.	78	9,440	$102,518 40
1763. *	60	9,238	100,324 68
1764.	72	11,983	131,135 38
1765.	101	11,512	125,020 32
1766.	118	11,969	129,983 24
1767.	108	16,561	179,852 46
1768.	125	15,439	167,667 54
1769.	119	19,140	462,996 60
1770.	125	14,331	346,666 89
	906	119,613	$1,746,165 51

About 1774,† the fleet was augmented by still larger vessels,‡ some of which crossed the equator, and obtained full cargoes upon that noted ground called the "Brazil Banks," while others cruised around Cape Verde Islands or the West Indies,

* Scoresby, in his account of the *Whale-Fishery of the British Colonies in America*, states that there were eighty vessels employed in the American fisheries during the year 1763.

† *History of Nantucket*, p. 233.

‡ St. John, in his *Letters*, published in 1793, which have previously been referred to, thus describes the mode of whale-fishing at that time: "The first proprietors of Nantucket, or rather the first founders of this town, began their career of industry with a single whale-boat, with which they went to fish for cod; the small distance from their shores at which they caught it, enabled them soon to increase their business, and those early successes first led them to conceive that they might likewise catch the whales, which hitherto sported undisturbed upon their banks. After many trials and several miscarriages, they succeeded: thus they proceeded, step by step; the profits of one successful enterprise helped them to purchase and prepare better materials for a more extensive one: as these were attended with little costs, their profits grew greater.

"The south sides of the island, from east to west, were divided into four equal parts; and each part was assigned to a company of six, which, though thus separated, still carried on their business in common. In the middle of this distance they erected a mast, provided with a sufficient number of rounds, and near it they built a temporary hut, where five of the associates lived, whilst the sixth, from his high station, carefully looked toward the sea, in order to observe the spouting of the whales. As soon as any were discovered, the sentinel descended, the whale-boat was launched, and the company went forth in quest of their game.

"It may appear strange to you that a vessel so slender as an *American whale-boat*, containing in the Gulf of Mexico, Caribbean Sea, or upon the coast of the Spanish Main. Soon after, they extended their voyages to the South Atlantic, around the Falkland Islands, and to the coast of Patagonia, where Fur Seal skins and Sea Elephant oil were sometimes obtained. In such instances these whaling and sealing expeditions were called "mixed voyages." "Between the years 1770 and 1775," according to

six diminutive beings, should dare to pursue and to attack, in its native element, the largest and strongest fish that Nature has created. Yet by the exertion of an admirable dexterity, improved by a long practice, in which these people are become superior to any other whalemen; by knowing the temper of the whale after her first movement, and by many other useful observations, they seldom fail to harpoon it, and to bring the huge leviathan on the shores. Thus they went on, until the profits they made enabled them to purchase larger vessels, and to pursue them farther, when the whales quitted their coasts. * * By degrees they went a-whaling to Newfoundland, to the Gulph of St. Laurence, to the Straits of Belleisle, the coast of Labrador, Davis's Straits, even to Cape Desolation, in 70° of latitude ; where the Danes carry on some fisheries, in spite of the perpetual severities of that inhospitable climate. * * Would you believe that they have already gone to the Falkland Islands, and that I have heard several of them talk of going to the South Sea! Their confidence is so great, and their knowledge of this branch of business so superior to that of any other people, that they have acquired a monopoly of this commodity.

"Such were their feeble beginnings, such the infancy and progress of their maritime schemes; such is now the degree of boldness and. activity to which they are arrived in their manhood. After their examples several companies have been formed in many of our capitals, where every necessary article of provisions, implements, and timber, are to be found. But the industry exerted by the people of Nantucket hath hitherto enabled them to rival all their competitors;

consequently this is the greatest mart for oil, whalebone, and spermaceti on the continent.

"The vessels most proper for whale-fishing are brigs of about one hundred and fifty tons burden, particularly when they are intended for distant latitudes; they always man them with thirteen hands, in order that they may row two whale-boats; the crews of which must necessarily consist of six, four at the oars, one standing on the bows with the harpoon, and the other at the helm. It is also necessary that there should be two of these boats, that if one should be destroyed in attacking the whale, the other, which is never engaged at the same time, may be ready to save the hands. Five of the thirteen are always Indians; the last of the complement remains on board to steer the vessel during the action.

"As soon as they arrive in those latitudes where they expect to meet with whales, a man is sent up to the mast-head; if he sees one, he immediately cries out, '*Awaite pawana*' (here is a whale); they all remain still and silent until he repeats '*Pawana*' (a whale), when in less than six minutes the two boats are launched, filled with every implement necessary for the attack. They row toward the whale with astonishing velocity; and as the Indians early became their fellow-laborers in this new warfare, you can easily conceive how the *Nattick* expressions became familiar on board the whale-boats. Formerly it often happened that whale-vessels were manned with none but Indians and the master; recollect also that the Nantucket people understand the Nattick, and that there are always five of these people on board.

"There are various ways of approaching the

Macy's *History of Nantucket*, "the whaling business increased to an extent hitherto unparalleled. In 1770 there were a little more than one hundred vessels engaged, and in 1775 the number exceeded one hundred and fifty, some of them large brigs." The following table briefly exhibits the state of the fishery from 1771 to 1775 (showing the annual average), which at that period was prosecuted chiefly from Massachusetts, although Sag Harbor had three sloops cruising for whales in high northern latitudes as early as 1760 :*

Ports from which the equipments were made.	Northern Fishery, vessels.	Tonnage.	Southern Fishery, vessels.	Tonnage.	Seamen employed.	Barrels of Sperm Oil taken.	Barrels of Whale Oil taken.
Nantucket................	65	4,875	85	10,200	2,025	26,000	4,000
Wellfleet................	20	1,600	10	1,000	420	2,250	2,250
Dartmouth	60	4,500	20	2,000	1,040	7,200	1,400
Lynn....................	1	75	1	120	28	200	100
Martha's Vineyard	12	720	..	....	156	900	300
Barnstable..............	2	150	..	....	26	240	....
Boston.................	15	1,300	5	700	260	1,800	600
Falmouth, Barnstable Co.	4	300	..	....	52	400	....
Swanzey................	4	300	..	....	52	400	....
Total	183	13,820	121	14,020	4,059	39,390	8,650

The first voyage made across the equinoctial line into the South Atlantic was by the brig *Amazon*, of Nantucket, under the command of Uriah Bunker, who returned with a "full ship" April 19th, 1775.†

whales, according to their peculiar species; and this previous knowledge is of the utmost consequence. When these boats are arrived at a reasonable distance, one of them rests on its oars, and stands off, as a witness of the approaching engagement; near the bows of the other the harpooner stands up, and on him principally depends the success of the enterprise. He wears a jacket closely buttoned, and round his head a handkerchief tightly bound; in his hands he holds the dreadful weapon, made of the best steel, marked sometimes with the name of their town, and sometimes with that of their vessel; to the shaft of which the end of a cord of due strength, coiled up with the utmost care in the middle of the boat, is firmly tied; the other end is fastened to the bottom of the boat. Thus prepared, they row in profound silence, leaving the whole conduct of the enterprise to the harpooner and to the steersman, attentively following their directions. When the former judges himself to be near enough to the whale, that is, at the distance of about fifteen feet, he bids them stop; perhaps she has a calf, whose safety attracts all the attention of the dam, which is a favorable circumstance; perhaps she is of a dangerous species, and it is safest to retire, though their

* Thompson's *History of Long Island*, vol. i, p. 349.   † Sanford's *Letters*.

The breaking-out of the Revolutionary War paralyzed the whaling commerce, which nearly proved ruinous to all those who were embarked in it. Nantucket, at that time, had one hundred and fifty vessels. But on the return of peace it was resumed, and but few years elapsed before it was again pursued with great vigor. The first whale-ship that ventured into the Pacific was sent by the Nantucket colony of whaling-men from England, in 1787,* and the first officer of the vessel, Archelus Hammond, struck the first Sperm Whale known to have been captured in that ocean.

In the year 1789, a gentleman from Cape Cod, who had returned from service in the East India Company, having seen Sperm Whales near Madagascar, communicated the fact to some of the Nantucket whalemen, who, profiting by the knowledge, in due time dispatched ships to that coast, which proved to be a rich whaling-ground. From 1787 to 1789, inclusive, the American Whale-fishery was prosecuted from the ports, and to the extent set forth in the following statement :†

Ports from which the equipments were made.	Northern Fishery, vessels.	Tonnage.	Southern Fishery, vessels.	Tonnage.	Seamen employed.	Barrels of Sperm Oil taken.	Barrels of Whale Oil taken.
Nantucket..............	18	1,350	18	2,700	487	3,800	8,260
Wellfleet, and other ports at Cape Cod..........	12	720	4	400	212	....	1,920
Dartmouth and N. Bedford	45	2,700	5	750	650	2,700	1,750
Cape Ann..............	..	....	2	350	28	....	1,200
Plymouth..............	1	60	..	....	13	100	....
Martha's Vineyard.......	2	120	1	100	39	220	....
Boston................	6	450	..	....	78	360	....
Dorchester and Wareham..	7	420	1	90	104	800	....
Total	91	5,820	31	4,390	1,611	7,980	13,130

In 1791,‡ six whale-ships were fitted out at Nantucket for the Pacific—the first that ever sailed from the United States for those distant grounds. Their

ardor will seldom permit them; perhaps she is asleep; in that case he balances high the harpoon, trying in this important moment to collect all the energy of which he is capable. He launches it forth—she is struck: from her first movement, they judge of her temper, as well as of their future success. Sometimes, in the immediate impulse of rage, she will attack the boat, and demolish it with one stroke of her tail; in an instant the frail vehicle disappears,

* *Proceedings American Antiquarian Society,* No. 57, p. 28–29.

† *Hunt's Merchants' Magazine,* vol. iii, p. 370.

‡ *Proc. American Antiquarian Society,* p. 29.

names were the *Beaver, Washington, Hector, Warren, Rebecca,* and *Favorite,* and the names of their captains were those characteristic ones among the settlers of the islands, as follows: Worth, Bunker, Brock, Barnard, Meader, and Folger. These ships were only two hundred and fifty tons burden, dull sailers, having no copper on their bottoms, and but scantily fitted with whaling appliances or provisions. The scene of their first exploits was upon the coast of Chile. These pioneer voyages, through the persistent daring of the hardy men who led them, were eminently successful, which induced the people of the neighboring settlements of other New England ports to extend their whaling commerce, and but few years passed before a numerous fleet were plying over those rough waters. Gradually, however, they extended their cruises toward the more distant but smiling regions of the tropics. As early as 1800,* American whalers were plowing the sparkling waters along the coast of Peru, and their keels cut the equatorial line, north and south, in the Pacific. A favorite cruising-ground was from the Spanish Main, westward, around the Galapagos Islands. There a rich harvest rewarded them, where they labored in a genial climate, with an almost uninterrupted succession of fine breezes and pleasant weather. At certain seasons, north of the equator, the north-east trades blew fresh, and at the south they would frequently increase to a brisk gale; but these periodical breezes, compared with the heavy gales of the Atlantic and the tedious weather about Cape Horn, served only to enliven them into renewed activity under the heated rays of a tropical sun, when in pursuit of the vast herds of Cachalots which were met with, bounding over or through the crested waves. During these long voyages, it became unavoidably necessary to occasionally go into port, in order to "recruit ship." When arrived at these places of supply, good store of fresh meat, water, and vegetables was laid in, and the ship's company were allowed to pass, in turn, a few days of liberty on shore. In due time those ports along the coast of Chile and Peru, which were suited to the requirements of the adventurers, became famous places of resort for American whale-ships. The principal ones were

and the assailants are immersed in the dreadful element. * * At other times she will dive and disappear from human sight; and everything must then give way to her velocity, or else all is lost. Sometimes she will swim away, as if untouched, and draw the cord with such swiftness, that it will set the edge of the boat on fire by the friction. If she rises, before she has run out the whole length, she is looked upon as a sure prey. The blood which she has lost in her flight weakens her so much, that if she sinks again, it is but for a short time; the boat follows her course, with an almost equal speed. She soon re-appears; and, tired at last with convulsing the element, which she tinges with her blood, she dies, and floats upon the surface."

* Nantucket paper.

Talcahuano and Valparaiso, in Chile, and Payta, Callao, and Tumbez, in Peru. At these places usually could be obtained any needed recruits, and the picturesque scenery, blended with those sunny climes, together with the charms of the beautiful women, made their periodical visits to the coast peculiarly attractive, and wrought an entire temporary change from the life on "blue water." The abrupt and lofty group of islands—the Galapagos—which extend into both latitudes from the equator, and the little island of Cocos, situated in the rainy region on the border of Panama Bay, were frequently visited, and became more familiar to the whalemen, in many instances, than their Atlantic homes. Every ragged mountain and verdant valley of the former were traversed in hunting the *galapago*, or "elephant terrapin," which furnished them with ample supply of the most delicious meat, and the latter was resorted to for fresh water, which was dipped from cascades flowing out of their natural reservoir beyond the wooded bluffs. And upon the rocks about the beach of Chatham Bay, rudely chiseled, are the records of those pioneer whale-fishers, together with the dates of the visits of transient vessels, from the pigmy shallops of Drake's time to the magnificent national ships of the present century. The War of 1812 caused another cessation in American whaling, yet it was revived simultaneously with the declaration of peace; and, as early as 1815, ships were in pursuit of the balænas amid the icy regions of the north and south, and the Cachalots in both hemispheres. Not unfrequently American whalemen were the discoverers and pioneers to distant islands and coasts when engaged in their legitimate pursuits; and they were often the first to display our national flag in commercial marts remote from their home havens. In this connection we will mention the fact that, in 1792,[*] at the peak of the ship *Washington*, of Nantucket, under the command of George Bunker, was hoisted the first American ensign ever spread to the breeze in the port of Callao. Characteristic of the life they led, the love of adventure tempted the whalers to turn their prows even from the sunny shores of Peru, and, with flowing sheets, they coursed over the Pacific until, in latitude 5° to 10° south, and longitude 105° to 125° west, the objects of pursuit were found in countless numbers, whose huge forms blackened the waves, and whose spoutings clouded the air as far as the eye could discern. This discovery was made by Captain George W. Gardner, in the ship *Globe*, of Nantucket, in 1818.[†] The captain named it the "Off-shore Ground," and ere long this circumscribed spot in the ocean was whitened by the sails of fifty ships.

Captain Winship, of Brighton, Massachusetts, reported to his friends at Nantucket, that on a voyage from China to the Sandwich Islands, he had seen large

---

[*] *Proceedings American Antiquarian Society*, No. 57, p. 29.   [†] Nantucket paper.

numbers of Sperm Whales on the coast of Japan.   Upon this information, in 1820, ships were dispatched to what is now known as the Japan Ground.   The two first to arrive were the Nantucket ship *Maro*, Captain Joseph Allen, and the English ship *Enderby*, which was commanded by Frederick Coffin, of Nantucket.   Here they were successful in soon filling their vessels with sperm oil, and two years after there were more than thirty ships upon that coast.   About this period nearly the whole coast of western North America, as far as the land known as New Albion, was traversed by the sperm-whalemen, and it is said that more than a hundred ships were literally spanning the North Pacific in their eager search between the two continents for the coveted Cachalots.   In 1828, four ships were sent from Nantucket to cruise for Sperm Whales off the coast of Zanzibar, around the Chychile Islands, and about the mouth of the Red Sea; and one of the number, with the very appropriate name of *Columbus*, through the skill and energy of the captain, sailed up the Red Sea in quest of the objects of pursuit.

But while the explorations and the chase for both the Cachalot and the Right Whale were being vigorously prosecuted in the North and South Atlantic, and through the temperate and torrid zones, not only by American whalemen, but by vessels wearing the flags of the principal maritime nations of Europe, those remote and forbidding latitudes of the Indian Ocean and the South Pacific had received due attention.   As far back as 1803, ships were cruising around Kurguélen Land for Right Whales, in the season, and sometimes a portion of their crews were engaged in sealing along the surf-beaten shores of Desolation and the Crozet islands, making up "mixed" but profitable voyages.   Subsequently the coasts of New Zealand and New Holland (now Australia), became prolific whaling-grounds. Yet, with all the vast extent of both sea and ocean known to the whalemen for prosecuting their vocation, there were adventurous spirits among them who were ever in deep study and eager for a new field of pursuit, and plying their vessels to the far north in the Pacific, an unparalleled success awaited them.   In the year 1835,[*] the American ship *Ganges* took the first Right Whale on the Kodiak Ground. This was the beginning of the great whaling of the North-western Coast; and in 1839 the fleet of the United States engaged in whaling numbered five hundred and fifty-seven vessels, which were distributed among the Northern Atlantic ports in the proportions set forth in the subjoined table.   In 1842 the number was six hundred and fifty-two.   At this time the foreign whaling-fleet amounted to two hundred and thirty sail, and the combined fleet of the world, engaged in the enterprise, numbered eight hundred and eighty-two ships, barks, brigs, and schooners.

[*] *Vide* Nantucket paper.

Places where owned.	Ships and Barks.	Brigs and Schrs.	Amount of Tonnage.	Places where owned.	Ships and Barks.	Brigs and Schrs.	Amount of Tonnage.
New Bedford....	169	8	56,118	Portsmouth.....	1	..	348
Fairhaven.......	43	1	13,274	Newport........	9	2	3,152
Dartmouth......	3	..	874	Bristol..........	5	1	1,782
Westport	5	4	1,443	Warren.........	18	3	6,075
Wareham.......	2	2	904	Providence......	3	..	1,086
Rochester.......	5	10	2,615	New London....	30	9	11,447
Nantucket	77	4	27,364	Stonington......	7	5	2,912
Edgartown......	8	..	2,659	Mystic..........	5	3	1,797
Holmes' Hole....	3	1	1,180	Sag Harbor.....	31	..	10,605
Fall River......	4	3	1,604	Greenport.......	4	1	1,414
Lynn..........	4	..	1,269	New Suffolk....	1	..	274
Newburyport....	3	..	1,099	Jamesport	1	..	236
Plymouth.......	3	..	910	Bridgeport......	3	..	913
Salem	14	..	4,265	New York.......	3	..	710
Boston..........	..	1	125	Hudson..........	8	..	2,902
Dorchester......	2	..	581	Poughkeepsie ...	6	..	2,043
Falmouth.......	8	..	2,490	Cold Spring.....	2	..	629
Provincetown....	..	1	172	Wilmington.....	5	..	1,578
Portland........	1	..	388	Newark.........	1	..	366
Wiscasset.......	1	..	380	....	..	..	....

In 1846, the American force engaged was six hundred and seventy-eight ships and barks, thirty-five brigs, and twenty-two schooners, aggregating two hundred and thirty-three thousand one hundred and eighty-nine tons, valued at $21,075,000. At the same time, all the investments connected with the business are said to have been at least $70,000,000, and seventy thousand persons derived their chief support from the whaling interests. The first Bowhead Whales taken in the North Pacific, or in Behring Sea, were by the American ships *Hercules*, Captain Ricketson, and *Janus*, Captain Turner, which were on the coast of Kamschatka in 1843. In 1847, Bowheads were discovered in the Okhotsk Sea; and in 1848, Captain Royce, in the bark *Superior*, of Sag Harbor, was the first to pass through Behring Strait, and capture the *Balæna mysticetus* of the Arctic Ocean. From 1846 to 1851, inclusive, the whale-fishery of the United States may be regarded as having been in its most flourishing condition, the average number of vessels annually employed for these years being six hundred and thirty-eight, with an aggregate tonnage of two hundred and two thousand two hundred and seventy-two tons. This immense fleet was scattered around the world, plying upon the well-known cruising-grounds, which were familiarly named as follow:

SPERM WHALE GROUNDS: *Atlantic Ocean and contiguous waters.*—Around the Azores or Western Islands; about the Cape de Verde Islands; the Charleston Grounds; north of the Bahama Islands; in the Gulf of Mexico; in the Caribbean Sea; about the West India Islands; on the coast of Africa; and the Carrol Ground, which is a space of ocean situated between the island of St. Helena and the coast of Africa.

SPERM WHALE GROUNDS: *Indian Ocean and neighboring waters.*—To the south of Madagascar, and between that island and Africa; off the northern end of Madagascar; along the coast of Arabia, including the mouth of the Red Sea; on the coast of Java; Malacca Straits; on the north-western coast of Australia; on the southern coast of Australia, and between it and Tasmania or Van Dieman's Land.

SPERM WHALE GROUNDS: *Pacific Ocean and adjacent waters.*—The On-shore Ground, which includes the whole extent of ocean between the southern boundary of Chile and the northern limits of Peru, and west to the island of Juan Fernandez and the Gallapagos group; the Off-shore Ground, which extends to latitude 5° and 10° south of the equator, and from longitude 90° to 120° west; off Cape Horn; around the Sandwich Islands; in the vicinity of the Society Islands; in the vicinity of the Fiji Islands; in the vicinity of the Navigator Islands; about the King's Mill group; about and to the south of the equator, from the coast of Ecuador to the King's Mill group; across the South Pacific between the latitudes of 21° and 27°; across the North Pacific between the latitudes of 27° and 35°; off the Bashee Islands; off the east coast of New Zealand; on the Middle Ground between Australia and New Zealand; Sooloo Sea; China Sea; on the coast of Japan, and between it and the Bonin Islands; on the North-western Coast of America; on the coast of Upper and Lower California. Sperm Whales are also found in as high latitudes as 60° south and 50° to 60° north. All these whaling-grounds, it will be seen, were the resorting-places of the Sperm Whales, and consequently of their captors, nearly all of them being in the temperate or tropical latitudes; but the Right Whales' feeding-grounds are chiefly in the colder regions, although some of their resorts were upon coasts or banks in common with their congeners. The principal grounds, however, of the Right and Polar Whales were designated as follows:

NORTHERN RIGHT WHALE GROUNDS: *Including those of the Bowhead or Polar Whale.*—On the Atlantic coast of North America, from Newfoundland south to the Bahama Islands; on the North-western Coast of North America, which includes Behring Sea; on the coast of Kamschatka; the Okhotsk Sea; the Japan Sea; the Gulf of Tartary; through Behring Sea into the Arctic Ocean, and as far north as the icy barrier, which, in some seasons, was found beyond Point Barrow; in Hudson's Bay; in Baffin's Bay; in Davis Straits; on the Coast of Greenland; about Spitzbergen.

SOUTHERN RIGHT WHALE GROUNDS. — On the Brazil Banks; on the coast of Africa; on the coast of Patagonia; around the Falkland Islands; the Tristan Ground, which was around the island of Tristan d'Acunha in the South Atlantic; around Gough's Island; around St. Paul's, the Crozet and Kerguélen islands; coast of New Holland; south coast of Chile; coast of New Zealand; off the Cape of Good Hope. Many of the whaling-grounds mentioned have long since been abandoned, as the animals pursued have been literally exterminated by the harpoon and lance; and many of the names to the grounds are only given in the familiar appellations of whalers, which embrace large tracts of ocean, sea, or gulf, within the limits of which, in many cases, are found choice feeding-grounds where the animals congregate. This is well-known to all careful observers, and is a fact that proves the theories establishing the legitimate resorts of whales on purely scientific principles, in connection with the ocean currents, to be erroneous. These places can only be known, or have been discovered, by practical observation; and many a ship has been filled with oil by cruising on a favorite spot, while others but a few leagues distant, on the same general ground, may have met with indifferent success. Besides the Cachalots and the Right Whales, two species of the rorquals were occasionally pursued, which are known as the Humpback, and the California Gray or Devilfish; the former are found broadcast over the waters of the globe, but many have been taken in some of the bays on the coasts of Africa, Chile and Peru, Central America and California, about the Rosemary Islands, and at Tongataboo (one of the Friendly group); and the latter were, and still are, taken on the coast of California, in the Arctic Ocean, and Okhotsk Sea. With the Humpbacks and California Grays, may be mentioned the Blackfish, which were sometimes taken on Sperm Whale grounds; these, included with the Right Whales and Cachalots, were all the different species of Cetaceans sought after by the whalers.*

---

* The great rorqual, commonly called the Sulphurbottom, has been occasionally taken on the coast of California of late years, but as yet no really successful mode of capturing this, the greatest of great whales, has been devised. The manner of capturing those obtained on the coast, is given with the description of the animal in this work.

CHAPTER III.

SHIPS, OUTFITS, AND MANNER OF TAKING THE WHALE.

It is the general impression among those unacquainted, that a successful whaling-voyage is inordinately remunerative; or rather, that a "full ship" insures great profit. This, however, does not always follow, for the success of the American Whale-fishery is due, first, to the economical but efficient manner in which the ships were fitted out for their long and tedious voyages; secondly, the perseverance and good management of the captains and chief officers, and, when the voyage terminated, the disposition of the "catch" to the best advantage.

There has been as great a revolution in the mode of killing whales during the past twenty years, as there has been in the art of naval warfare; were it not for this, but few whalers would now be afloat; and the "well-'pointed" whale-ship of the present day, in all her appliances, shows a corresponding improvement when compared with the whaler of the seventeenth century. Relative to those olden-time vessels, we quote the following from *Macy's History of Nantucket*: "The ship *Beaver*, of two hundred and forty tons, sailed from Nantucket on a whaling-voyage to the Pacific Ocean, in the year 1791. The whole cost of said ship fitted for the voyage, together with the cargo, amounted to $10,212. She carried seventeen men, manning three boats of five men each, which left two, called ship-keepers, on board the ship when the boats were out in pursuit of whales. The principal part of her cargo, when fitted for sea, consisted of four hundred barrels iron-hooped casks (the remainder, about fourteen hundred barrels, were wooden-hooped), forty barrels salt provisions, three and a half tons of bread, thirty bushels of beans and peas, one thousand pounds of rice, forty gallons of molasses, and twenty-four barrels of flour. All the additional provisions during the voyage were two hundred pounds of bread. The ship was seventeen months out, and was the first belonging to the island that returned from the Pacific Ocean." The ships of the present time which engage in whaling are from three hundred to five hundred tons, and when ready for a three years' voyage, their estimated value may be set down as ranging from $30,000 to $60,000. The variety and quantity of articles which go to make up the entire outfit of a first-class whaler, would swell a list too lengthy to be mentioned here.* But instead of the small boats, pulling four oars each, as did those of the *Beaver*, the modern ship lowers four boats with five oars each to pull; and two or three spare boats are taken on board as a reserve; and instead of the old style windlass, which was "hove 'round" with handspikes, they now have the patent purchase. The try-works, which in former times smoked the whole ship's company when "boiling-out oil," are now so fitted with portable pipes, as to carry the smoke clear of the decks; in fact, there is hardly a fixture, or an implement, pertaining to the "outfit," that has not been improved upon, which will be further described in subsequent pages.

History is replete in portraying the toils and hazards of the whaleman; but very little is said about the merchant who embarks his capital in this branch of industry, which to no little extent is a game-pursuit of chance; and the irksome detail of preparing a whale-ship for sea is only known to those who have had the trial of it. The success of this particular branch of our national commerce may be directly traced back to the persistent efforts of those sterling business gentlemen, who have been, or still are, the leading merchants of the chief whaling-ports of the United States. And first and pre-eminent among them were the Rotches of Nantucket,† and the Russells and Rodmans of New Bedford. Yet there are scores of

---

* For a detailed list see Appendix.

† A reminiscence of Mr. William Rotch, who was the great leader in the early days of American whaling commerce, may be interesting, as relating to his business career both in England and France. After the Revolution, Mr. Rotch, found his losses to be very heavy on account of the war, and the Nantucket-men experiencing great difficulty in prosecuting whaling to any profit, owing to the vexatious restrictions of England relative to the import of oil and whalebone, induced the distinguished pioneer whaling merchant to visit England, hoping by direct personal communication with the British Government that some arrangement might be brought about to lessen the burdens of himself and his compeers. Accordingly, he, with his son Benjamin, fitted out the ship *Maria*—which was commanded by one of the favorite captains, William Mooers; and both father and son sailed from Nantucket,

for London, the 1st of July, 1785, where they arrived on the 24th of the same month. Among Mr. Rotch's influential friends in London was Robert Barclay, and this gentleman introduced him to Henry Beaufoy, a member of Parliament, and that dignitary presented him to the Chancellor of the Exchequer, the great imperial William Pitt (then about twenty-seven years of age). Mr. Pitt received him with great politeness, and listened attentively to Mr. Rotch's remarks, which are reported to have been as follow:

"'When the war commenced, we declared against taking any part in it, and strenuously adhered to this determination, thus placing ourselves as a neutral island. Nevertheless, you have taken from us two hundred sail of vessels —valued at one million dollars—unjustly and illegally! Had the war been founded on a general declaration against America, *we* should have been included, but it was predicated on a *rebel-*

mercantile gentlemen, who followed in the same field, that have emulated them in every point of thorough business transactions connected with the enterprise. Among the most distinguished, we will mention the Howlands, Parkers, Robinsons, Bournes, Swifts, Joneses, Allens, Woods, Wings, Knowleses, and Tuckers, of New Bedford; the Coffins, Starbucks, Sanfords, and Gardiners, of Nantucket; also, the names of Williams, Barnes, Chapel, Havens, Perkins, and Smith, of New London; and the leading men of Fairhaven—Church, Whitwell, Gibbs, Jenney. And Provincetown, one of the oldest whaling-ports in New England, which is distinguished for its numerous fleet of small vessels, has upon her record the Cooks and Nickersons. Stonington speaks of her Williams and Trumbull; Edgartown of her Osborne and Worth; Greenport of her Ireland, Wells, and Carpenter; Warren of its Childs and Johnson; Westport of its Hicks and Wilcox. Sag Harbor had her Deerings, Howells, Huntings, Sleights, and Browns; Mystic her Mallory, Randall, Smith, and Ashley; and Mattapoisett her Barstow.

---

lion! consequently, none could have been included in it but such as were in arms, or those who were aiding such. We have done neither! As a proof of our being without the reach of your declaration, you sent commissioners to restore peace to America, in which, any province, county, or town, that should make submission and receive pardon, should be reinstated in its former situation. As we had not offended, we had no submission to make, nor pardon to ask, and certainly it is very hard if we do not stand on better ground than those who have offended; consequently, we remained a part of your dominions until separated by the peace!' After a long pause, Mr. Pitt replied: 'Undoubtedly you are right, sir. Now, what can be done for you?' 'I answered him,' said Mr. Rotch, 'that in the present situation of things, the principal part of our inhabitants must leave the island. Some would go into the country, and a part would remain, and continue their legitimate business, and I wish to continue the whale-fishery wherever it can be pursued to advantage; therefore, my chief business before this nation is, to ascertain if the fishery is an object worth giving such encouragement for a removal to England

as the subject deserves.' Thus our conversation ended, and I withdrew with my friend Harry Beaufoy.

"The subject was laid before the Privy Council, as the secretary, Stephen Cotterel, sent me a note, soon after this conversation, saying the Council would sit at an early day, when they would hear what I had to say. I waited for that early day a month, and then I waited on Secretary Cotterel to know what occasioned delay? His answer was, that so much business lay before the Council, that they had not time or had not been able to attend to it, but would soon. Thus I waited, not desiring to leave town lest I should be called for. This state of things continued for more than four months, during which time I received several, what I called unmeaning, court messages, such as 'They were sorry they were not able to send for me,' etc., etc. I then desired them to appoint some person for me to confer with, that the matter might be brought to a close. This was done, but unhappily Lord Hawkesbury was the person. A greater enemy to America could not be found, I believe, in that body, nor hardly in the nation. I waited on him, and informed him what en-

We speak of the whaling merchants as being not of that class who anticipated large profits and quick returns, but only a legitimate compensation for their labors, and a fair interest upon the capital invested in the voyages, which required from one to four years' time to accomplish; and often, though the expedition terminated unsuccessfully, the ship was again sent out on another voyage, trusting that continued perseverance would bring about final success, which in many cases was fully realized. There are over one thousand different articles required to complete the outfit of a first-class whale-ship, many of them of trifling value to be sure, yet all important to the success of the voyage. Then there are the officers and crew to be shipped, "on a lay." The latter may be without much difficulty obtained from the shipping agents; but to select and engage a set of officers, of the highest character and undoubted skill in their profession, is not so easy a matter, and it is but rarely accomplished. If half their number are really "crack whalemen," the voyage will usually be a successful one, if whales are found in sufficient numbers.

couragement I thought would induce a removal, which I estimated at one hundred pounds sterling transportation for a family of five persons, and one hundred pounds sterling settlement — say twenty thousand pounds sterling, for a hundred families. 'Ah!' said he, 'that is a great sum! and at this time, too, when we are all endeavoring to encourage our own expeditions.' I replied, 'Thou mayst think it a great sum for this nation to pay—I think two-thirds of it a great sum for you to have taken from me as an individual, unjustly and illegally!' We had a long conversation, and I left him, to call again in a few days, which I did. I then added to my demand the liberty to bring thirty ships— American ships—for the fishery. 'O, no!' said he, 'that can not be; our carpenters must be employed.' I mentioned that we had some ships that were built before the war, 'those can surely be admitted?' 'No; they must be British-built.' 'Will it be any advantage, if an emigration takes place, for the emigrants to bring property with them?' I replied. 'Yes, certainly.' 'If they can invest their money in articles that will be worth double here to what they are at home, will that be any additional advantage to

this country?' 'Yes!' 'Then why not bring ships, when two of ours will not cost one of yours?' 'O! we don't make mercantile calculations; 'tis seamen we want!' 'Then, surely, two of our vessels will answer your purpose better than one of yours, as they will make double the number of seamen, which is the thing aimed at?' He saw that he was in a dilemma, out of which he could not reason himself, and struggled through with some violence. He had made his own nice calculations of eighty-seven pounds ten shillings for transportation and settlement of a family, and said he, 'I am about a fishery bill, and want to come at something I can insert!' My answer was, 'Thou canst go on with thy fishery bill. Thy offer is no object to me!' 'Well, Mr. Rotch, you will call on me again in two or three days?' 'I see no necessity for it.' 'But I desire you would.' 'If thou desirest it, perhaps I may call.' However, he let me rest but one day, before he sent for me again. He had the same story over again, but I told him it was unnecessary to enter again upon the subject. I then informed him that I had heard a rumor that Nantucket merchants had agreed to furnish France with a quantity of

When the ship is nearly in readiness for her voyage, she leaves the wharf, and is anchored in the offing, to complete her necessary requirements. When the last article is taken in, the crew and officers embark, the pilot goes on board, and the managing agent informs the captain that the vessel is ready to sail; he gives him his general instructions for the voyage, shakes him by the hand, and wishes him a "full ship" and a safe return; and he (the agent) feels relieved to get the expedition temporarily off his hands; but not so the captain, for he keenly feels his responsibility. A long, anxious, and tedious voyage is before him; if successful, he may return to be amply rewarded for his toils; if unfortunate, he meets with reproach and an empty purse. But there is no time for dallying, and he acknowledges the compliments of his employer, bids him a hurried good-by, steps into the waiting boat, and repairs on board. The pilot gives his orders, the ship speeds away under a press of canvas, and at length she is plunging and reeling on the broad expanse of waters. The pilot is now the only connecting link between them

oil. He stepped to his bureau and took out a file of papers, from which he *pretended* to read an entire contradiction of the report, though I was satisfied there was not a line there on the subject. I said 'it was only a vague report that I heard, and I can not vouch for the truth of it, but we are like drowning men, catching at every straw that passes by. Therefore, I am determined to go to France and see what it is. If there be any such contract, sufficient to retain us at Nantucket, neither you, nor any other nation can have us; and if it is insufficient, I shall endeavor to enlarge it.' 'Ah!' said he, 'Quakers go to France?' 'Yes, but with regret!' I then parted with Lord Hawkesbury for the last time.

"I immediately embarked with my son Benjamin, for Dunkirk, where I drew up my proposals and sent them to Paris, not wishing to proceed farther until I found the disposition of the French Court. They sent for us to come immediately. We lost no time in answering the summons, and proceeded at once to Paris. The Master of Requests, who was the proper minister to receive our proposals and make his remarks on the several articles, had examined them

and made his remarks accordingly. The proposals were:

"'1st. A full and free enjoyment of religion according to the principles of the people called Quakers.'

"To which he annexed, '*Accordé!*'

"'2d. An entire exemption from military regulations of every kind.'

"To this he annexed the following just remarks: 'As they are all peaceable people and meddle not with the quarrels of princes, neither internal nor external, this proposition may be granted.'

"The other proposition related to the regulation of the whale-fishery.

"We next proceeded to the several ministers, five in number, at Versailles. First, to Calonne, Comptroller of Finance. We gave our reasons for not taking off our hats on being introduced to them all. Calonne replied: 'I care nothing for your hats, if your hearts are right.' Next, we went to the aged Vergennes, Minister of Foreign Affairs; then to the Marshal de Castro, Minister of Marine; then to the Prince of Rubec, Generalissimo of Flanders; at last, to the Intendant of Flanders—who all agreed to my pro-

and the shore. He gives the word to "haul aback," bids a hasty farewell, jumps into his boat, and returns to his secure and quiet haven. Quickly the order is given on board to "fill away," and before the fresh, fair wind the floating fragment speeds with swelling sails, and soon the receding land, teeming with blissful life and plenty, sinks from view beneath the undulating waves.

Sea life is such a change from that on shore, one fully realizes the transition; and the monotony, as well as the thrilling incidents associated with a sailor's career, have been so often and so vividly portrayed, it would be useless to attempt here to add any new features; hence, we shall only give a somewhat terse account of the present manner of conducting a whaling voyage. The company of a four-boat whale-ship number at least thirty-five persons, viz.: a captain, four mates, a cooper, a carpenter, four boat-steerers, a cook, and a steward, with twenty-two men and boys. When the vessel is making a passage, the officers and crew are divided into two watches, with the exception of the captain, and in some instances

posals. We then returned to Paris, and were to visit Versailles to take leave according to the etiquette of the Court.

"Before we set out, one of the ministers asked us if we did not wish to visit the palace. We excused ourselves, as we did not think curiosity would justify us, if our plain way would give offense. While we remained in Paris, we received a note from the minister, saying he had spoken to the King, 'who gave full liberty to the Nantucket Friends (they avoided the name of 'Quaker!' when they found it was given in reproach) to visit the palace, both its public and private apartments, when he was out—which happened almost every day.' To view the private apartments was a great privilege not often granted, except to persons of note. But unfavorably for us, the King did not happen to be out on the day we went to take our leave, which was a disappointment; but we went through the public apartments and into the Chapel! When we hesitated at the latter, the officer insisted on our entering in our own way, showing us everything remarkable, and pointing out the place occupied by the royal family in time of mass, etc.

"We now took leave, and returned to London. After I was gone to France, Lord Hawkesbury became alarmed, and inquired of Harry Beaufoy, and asked him if I had gone to France. He replied in the affirmative. 'Why has he gone there?' 'For what you or any other man would have gone; you would not make him an offer worthy his acceptance. He will now try what can be done in France!'

"Alexander Champion wrote to me (I suppose at Lord Hawkesbury's request) to inform me that he had made provision for us in his fishery bill, and inserted liberty for us to bring in forty ships instead of thirty! which I had demanded, he having forgotten the number; but it was too late. This letter was brought to our apartments, and we understood the bearer to inquire if a Dutch gentleman resided there. He was answered in the negative, and my letter was lodged in a small letter-office, always an appendage to a large hotel. The very evening it was brought to me, we left Paris.

"We now returned to London. I was soon sent for by George Rose, who was one of Pitt's secretaries. He inquired if I had contracted with France? I told him, 'No! I did not come to make any *contract!* Propositions were the chief mate, who stand no watch, but are up at any time of night, if occasion require, and throughout the day. The two watches are designated as the starboard and port, the second mate being officer of the starboard, and the third mate of the port watch. There being four boats, there are as many mates, or "boat-headers," one of which has charge, or, as it is termed, heads each boat, except when the captain chooses to go in his own boat, which is the starboard one; at such time, the fourth mate acts as boat-steerer. The chief mate's is the port boat, the second mate's the waist boat, and the third mate's the bow boat. All the boats are suspended from tall, stout wooden davits, with two cranes under each for the keel to rest upon; the last mentioned three usually hoist on the port side of the ship, and the captain's on the opposite quarter. Besides the boat-header, there is a boat-steerer and four men, who complete the crew. The boat-steerers are shipped as such; but the men for each boat are selected from the hands, having due regard to their physical strength, activity, and intelligence, and the remainder of the

the extent of my business.' 'You then are at liberty to agree with us, and I am authorized by Mr. Pitt to tell you, that you may make your own terms!' I told him it was too late! 'I made very moderate proposals to you, but could not obtain anything worth my notice. I went to France, and sent forward my proposals, which were doubly advantageous to us, compared with what I offered your government. They considered them a very short time, and on my arrival in Paris, were ready to act. I had separate interviews with all the Ministers of State necessary to the subject, who all agreed to, and granted my demands.' He still insisted that I was not bound to France, and I should make my own terms. But all in vain; the time had passed over! Lord Litchfield also sent for me on the same subject, but was soon convinced that it was too late. The minority came to me for materials to attack Lord Hawkesbury, but I refused to supply them."

It was at one of these interviews that Mr. Pitt, or his majesty George III, asked Mr. Rotch what equivalent would be given in return for all these favors now sought from his government. "I am going to give England and his majesty

the services of our young men from my native place—the island of Nantucket." And fully was this assertion verified in subsequent years. Nantucket-men went to England, and her great supremacy in whaling was carried forward by these promised whalers; and for years she held sway through all difficulties in this branch of commerce in Europe. The island was well represented in London by more than five hundred ship-masters, the last of whom (Wm. Swain, Esq.) died in 1868, upwards of ninety-two years of age.

Mr. Rotch's son Benjamin was left in Dunkirk as a partner of his son-in-law, Samuel Rodman, who resided at Nantucket. Ships were soon after fitted out from Nantucket, on distant whaling voyages, manned and officered by Nantucket-men, who, after filling their vessels, repaired to Dunkirk, where their oil and whalebone found a ready market for France and Holland. The business was pursued with great energy by Mr. Rotch and his associates. All their ships came from America with the necessary outfits for their voyages, as they could not be easily obtained in France. Many artisans immediately connected with the business left Nantucket with their families to take up their residence in Dunkirk.

company are termed "ship-keepers." Due care is taken, as far as practicable, that two boats' crews shall be in the same watch, so that in the event of meeting with whales on the passage to the cruising-grounds, they may be immediately lowered in pursuit. But usually a few days pass, after getting to sea, before a perfect organization of all hands can be obtained; for a portion of them being green, are generally so debilitated or entirely prostrated by sea-sickness, and a majority of the old sailors so demoralized by their last excessive potations of "parting drinks," that little can be accomplished under such circumstances. But it is not long before Jack gets a sufficiency of substantial food, instead of being soaked with the vile stimulants of a sailor boarding-house, and the work of "fitting ship" for whaling begins in good earnest. The hold is "broken out," and casks containing lines, cutting-gear, harpoons, lances, etc., are unheaded, and their contents laid under contribution as may be required. The cutting-gear, which consists of heavy tackles, pendants, etc., is to be overhauled or fitted anew, and the implements belonging to the try-works must be looked after; but the first and most important duty is the proper fitting of the boats. It may be a matter of surprise, even to an old whaleman, when he sees before him the number of things required to fit out a modern whale-boat, which is only twenty-eight or thirty feet in length, and

Mr. Rotch with his wife and children remained in France through all the troublesome times of the Revolution of 1792, and suffered much in his business, which had become extensive in the fishery and in the importation of other oils into France. Mr. Rotch had seen that a war between England and France was inevitable. With these views, he began early in 1793 to make arrangements for leaving France and returning to Nantucket. Going over to London on his way home, he found that two of his ships had already been captured full of oil, and condemned by the British Government as French prizes; but being present with the authorities, he was able to recover them again through his English friends. "My going to France," said he, "to pursue the whale-fishery, so disappointed Lord Hawkesbury that he undertook to be avenged upon me for his own follies; and, I have no doubt, gave directions to his cruisers to take any of my ships that they might meet going to France. For, when the ship *Ospray*

was captured by the king's ship, the officer sent on board to examine her papers, said to the captain: 'You will take this vessel in, sir; she belongs to Mr. Rotch.'"

Mr. Rotch, with many other Americans, embarked secretly from Dunkirk in a ship bound for America, but he and his family were landed in England, where, he remarked, "I had the comfort of receiving these ships of mine four months after I left France."

On the 24th of July, 1794, Mr. Rotch, with his family, embarked in the ship *Barklay*, and after a passage of sixty-one days, arrived at Boston. They soon proceeded to Nantucket, where they remained one year, after which they removed to New Bedford. Here he died May 28th, 1828. Through a long and eventful life of usefulness, he was greatly beloved and respected, and was deeply lamented when he departed for the spiritual world, at the advanced age of ninety-four years.

six feet wide. It is sharp at both ends, with flaring sides, and is of a model that insures great swiftness, as well as the qualities of an excellent sea-boat. At the bow (or "head," as whalers usually term it) is a groove, in which is placed a metal sheave, over which the line runs; near the end and upper edges of the groove, a slender pin, of tough wood or whalebone, passes across through holes above the line, to prevent it from flying out when running. This groove is called the "chocks." About three feet from the stern is the "clumsy-cleet," a stout thwart with a rounded notch on the after side, in which the officer or boat-steerer braces himself by one leg against the violent motion of the boat, caused by a rough sea, or the efforts of the whale while being "worked upon." The space between the clumsy-cleet and the chocks is covered with a sort of deck, six inches below the gunwales, and is called the "box," or "box of the boat." Five thwarts, or seats, for the accommodation of the rowers, are placed at proper distances apart, between the clumsy-cleet and stern sheets; and opposite each rowlock, near the bottom of the boat, is a well-fastened cleet, to receive the end or handle of the oar, which is called a "peak-cleet;" and when fast to a whale, or when the crew are resting, the end of the oar is placed in the hole of this cleet, while the heavy portion still rests in the rowlock, thereby elevating the blade far above the water. About four feet of the stern is decked over, through the forward part of which, a little to one side, is placed the loggerhead, shaped like a post with a large head, which projects six or eight inches above the gunwales, and by this log-gerhead the line is controlled when the boat is fast to the object of pursuit. The equipment belonging to a modern whale-boat consists of one mast and yard, or sprit, one to three sails (but usually a jib and mainsail), five pulling-oars, one steering-oar, five paddles, five rowlocks, five harpoons, one or two line-tubs (into which the line is coiled), three hand-lances, three short-warps, one boat-spade, three lance-warps, one boat-warp, one boat-hatchet, two boat-knives, one boat-waif, one boat-compass, one boat-hook, one drag, one grapnel, one boat-anchor,* one sweeping-line, lead, buoy, etc., one boat-keg, one boat-bucket, one piggin, one lantern-keg (containing flint, steel, box of tinder, lantern, candles, bread, tobacco, and pipes), one boat-crotch, one tub-oar crotch, half a dozen chock-pins, a roll

---

* The full equipment as here enumerated, is modified to suit the particular branch of whaling pursued, as for instance, in deep-sea whaling there is no use for the anchor, and in sperm whaling the sweeping-line, buoy, etc., are not required; while in California Gray whaling in the bays or lagoons, the anchor is indispensable, and the grapnel, sweeping-line, lead, and buoy, are of much service. But many other articles are left out or supplied to a limited extent, so that the boat may be as light as possible, and work easily and quickly in shallow water.

Plate XXIV

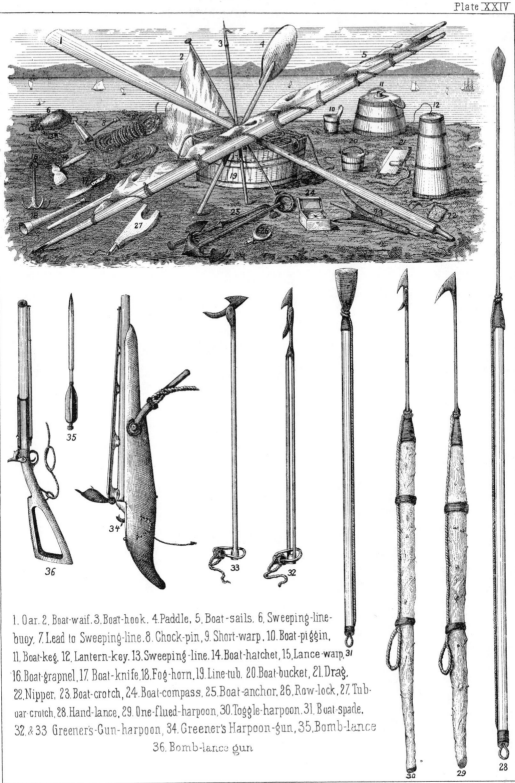

1. Oar. 2. Boat-waif. 3. Boat-hook. 4. Paddle, 5. Boat-sails. 6. Sweeping-line-
buoy. 7. Lead to Sweeping-line. 8. Chock-pin. 9. Short-warp. 10. Boat-piggin.
11. Boat-keg. 12. Lantern-key. 13. Sweeping-line. 14. Boat-hatchet, 15. Lance-warp.
16. Boat-grapnel, 17. Boat-knife. 18. Fog-horn. 19. Line-tub. 20. Boat-bucket, 21. Drag,
22. Nipper, 23. Boat-crotch, 24. Boat-compass, 25. Boat-anchor, 26. Row-lock, 27. Tub-
oar-crotch, 28. Hand-lance, 29. One-flued-harpoon, 30. Toggle-harpoon, 31. Boat-spade,
32. & 33 Greener's-Gun-harpoon, 34. Greener's Harpoon-gun, 35. Bomb-lance
36. Bomb-lance gun

C. M. Scammon, del.   Lith. Britton & Rey. S. F.

IMPLEMENTS BELONGING TO A WHALE BOAT.

of canvas, a paper of tacks, two nippers, to which may be added a bomb-gun and four bomb-lances; in all, forty-eight articles, and at least eighty-two pieces. The oars, sails, and paddles, of course, are to propel the boat, yet we may say that the two last mentioned are of much more importance now than formerly, by reason of the objects of pursuit becoming more wary. The rowlocks confine and support the oars in their proper places when rowing; the harpoons with the line are the instruments used to fasten the boat to the whale; the line-tub holds the line; the hand-lances are used in killing the whale after being harpooned; the lance-warp, when connected to the lance-pole, is hitched to the clumsy-cleet to prevent its loss when darted at the whale; the boat-warp is the painter to the boat; the short-warps are to connect the second harpoon to the main line when a second iron is thrown into the animal; the boat-spade is for cutting the cords about the "small" of the victim, or that portion of the body which connects with the flukes, crippling it, thereby retarding its progress through the water; the boat-hatchet and knives are to cut the line should it get foul and endanger the boat, when fast; the boat-waif is a small flag, used as a signal, or placed in a dead whale to indicate its whereabouts. The boat-hook is one of those indispensable implements, which is put to a variety of uses, but especially to hook up a whale's fin or stray lines, or to hold the boat in position; and the boat-compass is used to find the true course to any object not visible from the boat. The "drag" is for "bending on" to the line to assist in impeding the whale when running, or is fastened to the line when compelled to let it go from the boat. With the grapnel, the dead animal's flukes, or its head, are hauled up, in order to cut a hole and reeve the tow-rope, or to hook up lines which can not be reached with the boat-hook; and the sweeping-line, lead, and buoy, are used for getting the fin and fluke chains on to the whale when alongside the ship, or otherwise. The boat-keg is for carrying a supply of fresh water. The boat-bucket and piggin are for bailing the boat. The lantern-keg is for holding in reserve a small supply of bread, a lantern, and fire-works, in case the boat should be caught out at night, that the crew may be able to set a light to indicate to the ship their whereabouts, and in extreme necessity to have a small supply of food, with the luxury of a quid of tobacco or a smoke of a pipe. The boat-crotch is to rest the end of the iron or lance-pole on; it ships in a hole through or on the side of the gunwale. The tub-oar crotch is to receive the tub-oar and raise it above the line-tub, when the boat is fast to a whale; the chock-pins are to keep the whale-line in the chock. The canvas and tacks are to cover holes which may be staved in the boat; the nippers are several layers of canvas stitched together, and are used for holding on to the line when it is swiftly running out. The bomb-gun and lances are for killing the whale at a greater distance than could be done with the hand-lance; it does good execution within a range of twenty-five yards. Greener's harpoon-gun is also used by whalers to some extent, and quite successfully when the sea is smooth. It is similar to a small swivel-gun. The barrel is three feet long, with a bore of one inch and a half; when stocked and complete, it weighs seventy-five pounds. The harpoon, four and a half feet long, is projected with considerable accuracy to any distance under eighty-four yards. It is mounted on the bow of the boat, and was formerly fired by the boat-steerer, who pulls the "harpooner oar." This was the old Scotch plan, the gun being first used by the Scotch whalers; but at the present time it is more successfully managed by the officer in charge of the boat, who takes the boat-steerer's place for the time being.

The whale-boat being properly equipped, the crew take their places as follows: the officer in charge (or boat-header) in the stern, who steers the boat with the steering-oar, which is usually twenty-two feet long; the boat-steerer, who pulls the oar farthest forward, which is called the harpooner-oar, its length being usually seventeen feet, and who also darts the harpoon, and after the boat is fast changes ends with the boat-header and steers the boat, while the latter attends to killing the whale. The next man is called the "bowman," with an oar seventeen and a half feet in length, and besides his general duties he attends to the line when "bowing-on." The next man is the "midship-oarsman," whose oar is eighteen feet in length; then comes the "tub-oarsman," with an oar the same length as that of the bowman, whose special duty is to see that the line runs clear from the tub. The last is the "after-oarsman," who is the lightest of the crew, and pulls a correspondingly light oar; his particular duties are to attend the line as it is hauled in and coiled in the stern-sheets, or when it is "paid out," and to bail the boat. The whole outfit of the boat has two general and rather indefinite names, "boat-gear" and "craft;" but the word "craft" applies particularly to the weapons immediately used in the capture.

When the boat is lowered for the chase, the line (which is nicely coiled in the tub or tubs, as the case may be) is placed between the two after thwarts. The men being seated in their proper places, the line from the tub is taken aft around the loggerhead, then forward over the oars, and a few fathoms of it are coiled in the box of the boat; it is then termed a "box-warp." Two harpoons are placed at the head of the boat, the staves or poles of which rest in the "boat-crotch." The end of the box-warp is made fast to the "first iron;" the "second iron" is connected with the main line by a bowline in the end of a short-warp

which is bent on to the second iron. The lances
are in their places at the head of the boat, on the
starboard side ; the boat-spade on the side opposite ;
the boat-hatchet and a knife in their proper places
in the head of the boat, and the other knife ready
at the stern.

When pursuit is made, the whale is approached
in the most cautious manner, to avoid "gallying"
it. If necessary, the oars are used ; but in calm
weather the paddles are resorted to, as pulling with
the oars is adopted only when sails or paddles can
not be made available. When nearly within darting distance, which is about three fathoms, the
order is given to the boat-steerer to "stand up."
At this command he instantly springs to his feet,
and seizing the harpoon, darts it into the whale ;
if opportunity offers, the second iron is also thrown
before the animal gets out of reach. When the
harpoons are darted, word is given to "stern all,"
and the oarsmen make every effort to force the
boat astern, in order to be well clear of the animal
in its painful convulsions from the first wounds received. Notwithstanding every precaution is taken,
it is by no means an unusual occurrence to have
the boat staved by the whale when harpooned.
Should the boat be much injured, the line is cut,
or a drag or buoy is bent on to the end of it, and
all is let go. The boat nearest the whale usually
continues the pursuit ; the next boat pulls for the
one that has become disabled, and rescues the
crew.

When struck, the whale may attempt to escape
by running ; if so, every exertion is made by the
boats' crew to haul up to the animal so as to shoot
a bomb into it, or work upon it with a hand-lance ;
or if the creature descends to the depths below,
which is called "sounding," every effort is made to

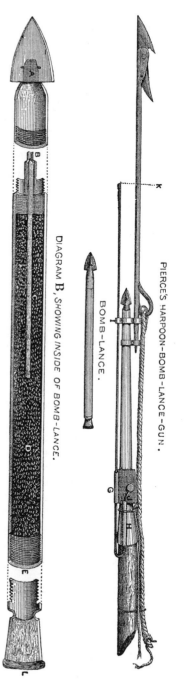

DIAGRAM B, *SHOWING INSIDE OF BOMB-LANCE.*

BOMB-LANCE.

PIERCE'S HARPOON-BOMB-LANCE-GUN.

check the movement by holding on to the line, or by slowly slacking it.   In this maneuvre the boat is occasionally hauled bow under water.   Sometimes all the line is taken out almost instantly, when it is cut to prevent the boat from being taken down, and the whale escapes.   At other times the animal will "bring to;" that is, it will stop and roll from side to side, or thrash the water with its ponderous flukes and fins, when the boat may be pulled within bomb-shot, and the creature dispatched by one or more of these missiles.

Hand-lancing for the purpose of killing a whale is now going rapidly out of practice, and the same may be said relative to boat-spades, and "loose irons" to stop a whale from running.   By the use of "Pierce's bomb-lance,"* the Bowhead or Polar Whale is now frequently captured in the Arctic Ocean, close to the

* It is a matter of surprise that so ingenious an invention for killing whales has no appropriate name, the whole apparatus being only known as "Pierce's bomb-lance;" hence, to facilitate description, we will give it the provisional designation of Pierce's Harpoon-bomb-lance Gun. The weapon, which is of brass, is fourteen inches long in the barrel, and the square portion inclosing the lock, together with the socket which receives the iron-pole or harpoon-staff, increases its linear dimensions to about one and a half feet. On one side, and near the muzzle of the gun, are two lugs with holes, which receive the end of a harpoon, to which the whale-line is attached. On the other side is a steel rod bent in the form of a staple, at the socket end of the gun, which passes through tubes attached to the socket and lock-case, as represented at G and H (in the illustration upon the preceding page), then, passing through a hole in the lug at I, it extends past the muzzle about ten inches. Upon the upper part of the rod, at J, rests the trigger to the lock. The whole apparatus, exclusive of the lines and iron-pole, weighs about ten pounds. This weapon is loaded with a light charge of powder, and projects, when discharged, a bomb-lance sixteen inches long, and seven-eighths of an inch in diameter. The lance is loaded with powder, which is ignited by a percussion-cap placed upon a nipple

at B, as seen in diagram B, at the end of the cylinder (which is connected with the point of the lance by a screw); this nipple (at B) unites with a time-fuse that leads to the powder with which the bomb is charged. One end of a small line is "seized" to the socket of the gun, then "stopped" along the iron-pole with twine — the other end being fast to the boat, in order that the instrument may be recovered after being thrown and discharged. The whale-line is also stopped along the pole, or it is secured by beckets. The manner of using the gun, is to dart it by hand from the boat, and when the harpoon penetrates the whale beyond the line K, the steel rod (which holds the trigger to the lock) comes in contact, and is pushed back, thereby springing the hammer against a percussion-cap which rests upon a nipple in the breech of the gun, by means of which it is fired off, sending the bomb-lance into the whale; and at the same time the concussion brings a plunger (which is held temporarily by a wooden pin within the head of the lance, as seen at A) upon the cap at B, the flash of which, communicating with the time-fuse imbedded in the powder contained in the cylinder, causes the bomb to explode, usually killing the whale instantly; and the harpoon being already fastened in the body of the animal, it may be easily secured.

icy barrier, as that weapon shoots an explosive missile into the animal at the same time the harpoon is fastened.

Mention has been made in the preceding pages of the manner of standing watches, and the general routine of duty on board the ship when making a passage; but it is only when they arrive on the cruising-ground that systematic whaling really begins. The ship's company, or that portion of it who "stand a watch," is divided into what are called "boat's-crew watches," each watch remaining on deck its allotted time between dark and daylight, and during the day one-half of the ship's company alternate (which is called "watch and watch"), unless whaling is going on, when all hands are engaged. A day's routine of a whale-ship's duty, when on whaling-ground, begins at a very early hour. All hands are called in time to get breakfast by sunrise, after which all required sail is set, the decks are washed off, and the lookouts are stationed at the mast-heads. If a four-boat ship, an officer and a boat-steerer stand at the main-topgallant cross-trees, two men at the fore-topgallant mast-head, and one at the mizzen-topgallant mast-head, who are relieved every two hours, as also are the men at the wheel, who steer the ship. Should no whales be seen through the day, at sunset all hands are called to shorten sail, when the light sails are furled, the mainsail taken in, the topsails reefed, and the watch is set for the night. But should whales be "raised," the hours of rest are governed entirely by the amount of necessary work to be performed. From sun to sun the boats may be engaged in the exciting chase; and the few ship-keepers left on board strain every muscle to work the vessel and make the required signals. This is no easy matter when the wind is fresh and the vessel is being continually maneuvered, as the pursuing boats change their positions. An endless variety of signals are used in the whaling-fleet in connection with the capture of a whale, more especially when there is a large fleet cruising on the same ground, for then the signals from each ship are kept private, in order to gain advantage in the pursuit.

The ship-keeper in charge of the vessel may be the captain. At present few whaling-masters make a practice of going in their boats; while formerly it was the custom for the captain to be first in the water when lowering for whales. In such cases, the person left in charge of the ship was either chosen from among the crew, or he was shipped for that particular duty. In any event, his services are important, for the safety of the boats or the capture of the whale may depend upon his vigilance and good management. The boats being down, the object of pursuit can be seen but a comparatively short distance, while from the ship's mast-head an extensive view is obtained; hence, when the boats are away, the person in charge of the vessel takes his station at the main-topgallant cross-trees, where a sharp watch is kept, both on the whales and boats. When the whales are upon the surface of the water, a flag is usually hoisted at the main-topgallant mast-head; and when they go down, the flag is lowered; and to indicate their bearing from the ship, the following signals are made with the sails: "Whales on the weather bow," weather clew of the fore-topsail or fore-topgallantsail is hauled up; "Whales on the lee bow," lee clews of the same sails are taken up; "Whales on the weather beam," weather clew of main-topsail or topgallantsail up, and generally with a waif* pointed to windward; "Whales on the lee beam," lee clew of

MAST-HEAD WAIF.

the same sails up; "Whales ahead," jib down; "Whales between the boats," flags at the fore and main mast-heads; "Come on board," flag at the peak; "Boat stove," flag at the fore and mizzen mast-heads. In sperm-whaling during light weather, the crews sometimes go a long distance from the vessel, at least ten or twelve miles; but this is not the regular practice. In right-whaling, however, it is expected that the ship and boats will keep near enough together to communicate by signals, unless enveloped in fog, rain, or snow, which occurs in high latitudes, where this species of balæna are chiefly sought; and the moment a bank of fog obscures the vessel, the rule is to "haul aback," if practicable, or in other words, to keep the ship as near the same position as possible where she was last seen by the people in the boats; who, having previously taken the bearings, find their way back by the aid of the compass, and the sounding of horns, or the firing of guns from the vessel; or, if the boats are caught out at night, lights are set, and sometimes a fire is made on the "back arches" of the try-works, by which means the whole ship is illuminated, when every spar glistens in relief upon a dark, misty background, with the sails flapping against the masts as the ship rolls and tumbles over the sea, or the swelling canvas yields to the dank blasts that are sweeping by in fitful moaning sounds, as if to render the scene more ghastly. From the time a whale is discovered until the capture is made, and the animal cut in, the scene is one of laborious excitement. If the whale is first seen spouting, the man

* The mast-head waif is a light pole six or eight feet long, with a hoop fastened at the end covered with canvas; it is sometimes called a "yonder" by English whalers.

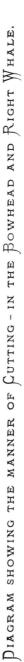

DIAGRAM SHOWING THE MANNER OF CUTTING - IN THE BOWHEAD AND RIGHT WHALE.

on the lookout calls out, "There she blows;" if breaching, he calls out, "There she breaches;" if turning flukes, he reports, "There goes flukes." Instantly the officer of the deck, or the captain, inquires, "Where away?" when he is immediately answered, "Right ahead," or "On the beam," or "Two points on the beam," or quarter, as the case may be. The next question is, "How far off?" which is quickly answered. If near by, should it be calm weather, all hands are called, the ship is hauled aback, if necessary, and the boats are immediately dropped into the water for the chase; if a long distance off, and a good breeze is blowing, all sail is set to reach the locality of the object of pursuit before lowering. The capture being made (should there be a commanding breeze), the ship is run alongside the whale; or if it be calm, the animal is towed to the vessel. Then the fluke-chain or fluke-rope is fastened (as at A, in the diagram showing the manner of cutting-in the

BLUBBER-HOOK AND FIN-CHAIN.

Bowhead and Right Whale), and is then hauled in through the fluke-chain chock, which is at the bow, and well secured to the sampson-post, the head of the animal being toward the stern. The cutting-tackles, which comprise two heavy purchases, are then sent aloft, and shackled to chain or rope pendants at the mainmast-head, where they are placed in position by rope guys from the foremast-head, and the falls of the cutting-tackles are then taken forward to the windlass. The cutting-stage, which is so constructed as to admit of the officers standing upon it immediately over the carcass when using the cutting-spades, is put over the side and lowered into position; meanwhile, the rest of the cutting-gear is being got in readiness, which consists of toggles, spades, boarding and leaning knives, gaffs, pikes, blubber-hooks, head-straps, fin-chain, throat-toggle, head-axes, etc. If the prize be a Right Whale, or Bowhead, the fin-chain is put on the fin, as at B (in

Plate XXV.

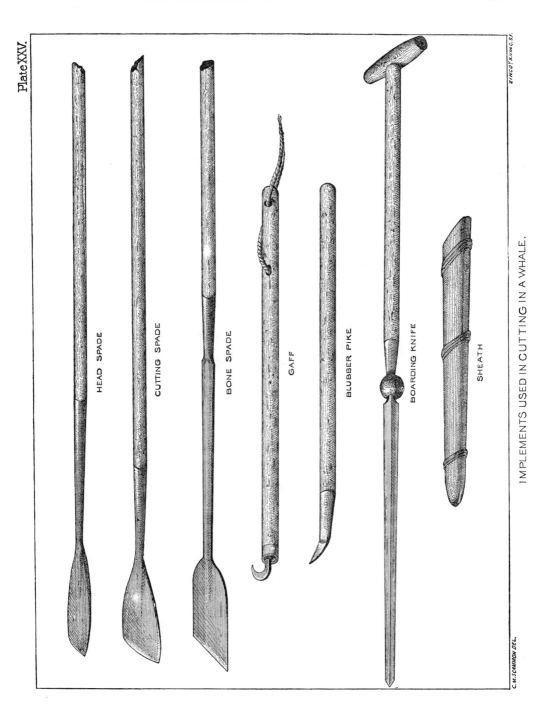

HEAD SPADE

CUTTING SPADE

BONE SPADE

GAFF

BLUBBER PIKE

BOARDING KNIFE

SHEATH

IMPLEMENTS USED IN CUTTING IN A WHALE.

C.M. SCAMMON DEL.

ZINCOT X V DE C. ST.

diagram of Bowhead); one of the cutting-tackles is then hooked or shackled into the ring at H; the fall to the tackle is then taken to the windlass and hove taut, which brings the whale fairly on its side; then, with a cutting-spade, a hole is cut in the root of the lip at F, and a scarf is cut along the lower jaw-bone from E to D. A blubber-hook being shackled to the second cutting-tackle, it is over-

HEAD-STRAP.

hauled down, and hooked into the hole in the lip, and the tackle is then hauled taut by means of the windlass, and a man with a cutting-spade cuts the lip from the jaw-bone as it is being hoisted up; and when coming to the end of the jaw, near D. it is cut off and hove in on deck. A scarf is then cut through the blub-

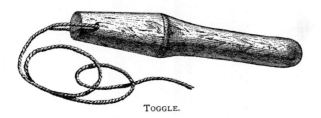

TOGGLE.

THROAT-CHAIN TOGGLE.

ber, across one side of the head forward of the eye, around under the fin, and across the body; and the fin is then raised by the first cutting-tackle, which is the starting-point of the first blanket-piece; the "knuckle-joint" being disconnected from the shoulder-blade with the "piece" from the body by cutting the tendons, which connect between the flesh and the blubber. This is called "leaning up;" and when the piece is hove up, so as to bring the whale's back up, the "head-strap" is rove through the spout-holes between the skull-bone and the blubber, as seen in the diagram at GG; then with an axe the skull is cut through to the spout-holes, on one side. This being done, the blanket-piece is raised still higher, and the other cutting-tackle is hooked to the head-strap and hove taut; when the skull-bone is cut on the other side, and the head with the baleen attached is hove up and lowered on deck. As soon as the piece comes high enough to fasten the tackle under the fin, the order is given to "board," which is done in the following manner: The second tackle, which took in the head, now being free and again ready for use, a boat-steerer or officer cuts a hole in the blanket-piece well down to the plank-sheer, and through this hole the strap of the tackle is thrust, and a heavy wooden glut, called a toggle, is passed through the thimble of the block-strap (as seen in the accompanying figure), which secures it firmly to the blanket-piece and completes the "board." Then the order is given to "take to and heave away," when the fall of the tackle is taken around the windlass and hauled taut, the men at the windlass-brakes heave upon the tackle until the second blanket-piece is raised two feet or more above the plank-sheer, and the first is cut off and lowered down the main-hatch into the blubber-room. The second blanket-piece is then hove up, until the whale again lies on its side, when the other lip is taken in by the same process. The carcass is now turned back down, by heaving up on the piece, and in doing this, the throat-blubber is cut clear from that of the trunk; and with a spade, a hole is made through both the throat and tongue, when the throat-chain toggle is inserted at C, as seen in the diagram. The tackle being hooked to the ring of the chain, the throat is cut from the flesh that adheres to it as it is drawn up, and when hoisted high enough, it is lowered on deck, or into the blubber-room. Then the body-blubber is cut in spiral folds—as represented in the diagram by diagonal lines—and rolled off down to the dotted lines behind the vent, where the whole flesh of the carcass is cut through; and the backbone being unjointed, the main portion

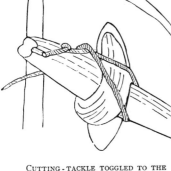

CUTTING-TACKLE TOGGLED TO THE BLANKET-PIECE.

of the mutilated remains of the animal floats clear of the ship, or it sinks to the depths beneath. The residue of the fatty covering of that portion of the creature known as the small, is soon stripped. The flukes are cut off close to the fluke-chain, and the chain hauled in, which completes the *modus operandi* of cutting-in a whalebone whale. The animal having been cut in, the head, being on deck, is next cleared away. This is done by stripping the blubber from the skull-bone; then, with spades and axes, the baleen or bone is cut, with the gum, from the jaw, in sections of several layers, and stowed below, where it remains until an opportunity occurs, in fine weather, to again take it on deck, when the slabs are separated and the gum scraped off; after which they are washed and dried, and when packed in bundles, are ready for market.

But the cutting-in of a Sperm Whale differs materially from that of the whalebone whale, although it would appear that the latter was forced into nearly every conceivable posture, during the systematic process of mutilation in order to obtain its covering; yet, in addition, the lifeless form of the Sperm Whale is made to assume a nearly vertical attitude during the course of flensing, as it was wont to do when filled with animation. The first procedure after the animal is fastened to the ship by the fluke-chain and head-rope, is to cut a hole through the blubber, between the eye and fin, at A, as seen in the accompanying outline sketch; then, after cutting the scarfs on each side and around the end of the first blanket-piece, a blubber-hook, attached to one of the cutting-tackles, is inserted into the hole at A, and the piece raised by means of the tackle until the whale is rolled on its side; then the line of separation between the upper jaw and junk is cut, as from L to C, and if a large whale, the line of separation is cut between the junk and case, as from B to E, and a cut is made across the root of the case from E to F; a scarf is also made around the root of the lower jaw, from near the corner of the mouth to G. A chain-strap is then put on the jaw near H, and hooked or shackled to the second cutting-tackle, and raised by that purchase; while the other tackle, attached to the piece, is slackened off if need be, so as to let the whale roll upon its back; when, by means of the tackle attached, and by cutting away the tongue and the adhering flesh, the jaw is wrenched from its socket, and placed on deck. This being accomplished, the first tackle, which is attached to the piece, is hove up by means of the windlass until the whale is rolled over to its opposite side, when the lines of separation are cut to correspond to those made opposite; holes are then morticed through the head close to the upper jaw-bone near I, at the end of the junk near J, and at the root of the case near K, and through these holes straps are rove, and lines are made fast to those of the junk and case. The second cutting-tackle is then hooked in the strap which is around the upper jaw at I; the fluke-chain is slackened off, and the first tackle fastened to the piece is lowered, when all hands heave on the head-tackle, forcing the whale down again, and thus bringing the creature's head up, and the body nearly to a vertical position. The officers upon the cutting-stage, with their keen spades, cut away between the bones and junk from L to C; and the enormous weight of the whole fatty mass of the head hanging down, opens the gash between

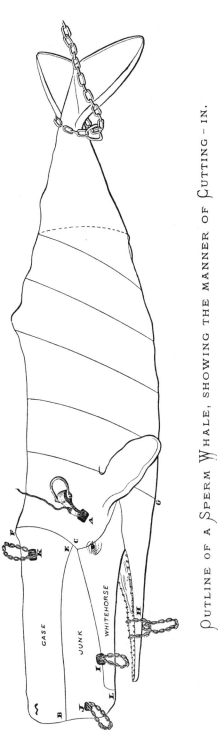

OUTLINE OF A SPERM WHALE, SHOWING THE MANNER OF CUTTING-IN.

it and the skull-bone; then, cutting across the end of the junk and root of the case, from E to F, completes the process of cutting off the head, which is temporarily made fast to the ship's quarter. The fluke-chain is then hauled in again, and the blubber is rolled from the body in the same manner as that of a baleen whale, until coming to the region of the small, when it is unjointed just behind the vent, and the remaining posterior portion of the animal is hoisted on board in one mass. The head, as it is termed, is then hauled to the gangway, and one of the tackles is hooked into the junk-strap at J, and by means of this cutting-tackle purchase, the head is taken in whole, if the whale is under forty barrels; but if over that size, it is raised sufficiently out of the water to cut the junk from the case, when it is hoisted on deck. The case is then secured by one or both tackles, hove up to the plank-sheer, and an opening is made at its root, of a suitable size to admit the case-bucket, when the oil is bailed out, or the whole case is hove in on deck before being opened, which finishes the cutting-in of a Sperm Whale.

The entire blubber being now on board, preparations are immediately made for trying-out the oil. The blanket-pieces are cut into horse-pieces, which are about fifteen or eighteen inches long, and six or eight inches in breadth and thickness. Any flesh termed "lean," or "fat-lean," that may adhere to the horse-pieces, is cut off with leaning-knives; and being thus prepared, the blubber is transported in

MINCING KNIFE.

strap-tubs to the mincing-horse—where the ordinary two-handled knife is used--or else is taken to the mincing machine, where it is cut crosswise into slices a quarter of an inch to a half inch in thickness; then it goes into a large mincing-tub, which completes its preparation for boiling. From the mincing-tub it is pitched into the try-pots with the blubber-fork, where the oil is extracted by boiling. During this process, the minced blubber is frequently stirred, to prevent it from burning and settling to the bottom of the pots; and when the scraps are sufficiently browned to show that the oil is well tried out, they are skimmed off with the skimmer into a receptacle called the scrap-hopper, and, after the oil drains from them, they furnish an abundant supply of fuel for the fires.

From the pots, the oil is bailed with the bailer into a large copper tank called a cooler; from the cooler, it passes through a cock into the deck-pot; and from the deck-pot the casks are filled. When a cask is full, it is rolled off and headed up, and in rough weather it is lashed to the ship's rail for greater security. The oil, after passing through the cooler and deck-pot, is still very hot, if the blubber is being tried out rapidly; and for this reason, the casks, when first filled, require the constant attention of the cooper, as the hoops have to be frequently driven, to prevent leakage. The oil taken from the case of the Sperm Whale is sometimes put into casks without boiling; but, usually, it is carefully scalded with the junk and a portion of the hump, and when put into casks, it is known as head, or head-matter. After the oil becomes cool, it is run through a hose into empty casks, which have been prepared with great care, and securely stowed in the hold, or they are lowered and stowed after being filled on deck.

The whole "fare" having been stowed down, the decks are cleaned up, and with lye (which is leeched from cinders and ashes taken from the furnaces of the try-works), the ship is thoroughly washed, as well as the soiled clothing of the

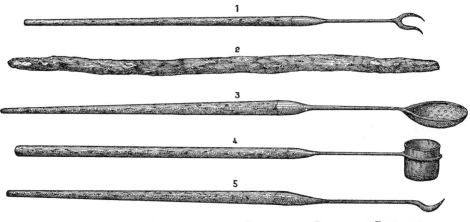

1. BLUBBER-FORK. 2. STIRRING-POLE. 3. SKIMMER. 4. BAILER. 5. FIRE-PIKE.

crew, when everything fore and aft again wears an aspect of order and cleanliness. Notwithstanding the great labor involved in obtaining the oil from a whale after its capture, ships have often been filled in a very short space of time. In former years, it was no unusual occurrence for both sperm and right whalers to get "blubber-logged," which is the expression used when as many whales are caught at one time as can possibly be cut in and tried out; and at the present day, in the Arctic Ocean, whales are so scarce, that, in order to secure a good catch, if opportunity presents, as it may the last of the season, the whole between-decks of the ship is frequently filled with blubber before much boiling is done. At such times, it is necessary to drive the work, and often eighty or one hundred barrels of oil have been tried out and stowed down in twenty-four hours, and in a few weeks many an empty ship has been filled, or has secured a good catch.

CHAPTER IV.

AMERICAN WHALING COMMERCE.

It has ever been a subject of interest to us to contemplate the advancement of commerce by sea, from the time of the barbarian sailors up to the present century, when every ocean is teeming with magnificent models of naval architecture, which are the pride of maritime nations. Yet, is there any sea-faring pursuit recorded in history which has displayed a more legitimate, energetic, and intelligent character than the whale-fishery? To be cast upon the ocean, far from land, in an open boat, is considered a perilous situation; but what may it be regarded, when, in a slight, frail hoy, like the whale-boat, we find the primitive whalemen in the same situation, attacking, with rude weapons, these monsters of the deep upon their own feeding and breeding grounds? Moreover, these adventurous men were successful in making their captures, and, after patient toil by day and night, brought their colossal prizes over the water to their village shores. With such impetuous daring did they pursue their precarious calling, that but few years elapsed before the whales of value were driven from the borders into mid-ocean, where they were pursued in mere shallops of thirty to fifty tons, into which the crews were crowded; and when a sufficient number of captures had been made to supply a full fare of blubber, the pigmy vessels returned to the home shores, apparently transformed into a mass of slimy whale-fat, above which peered the weather-worn sails. And, as years passed on, in still larger ships, they pressed forward, contending with every danger incident to the life of a sailor, upon unknown waters and in unhealthy climes, until a voyage around the world became as legitimate in the course of their professional lives, as was the launching of boats through the surf to pursue the game near shore, over a hundred years before.

As the fishery increased, several of the larger whaling-ports became distinguished for pursuing some particular branch of this commerce. Nantucket was noted for its sperm whalers, who performed long voyages, maintained excellent discipline, and their ships, being generally confined to the temperate or tropical latitudes during their cruises, were examples of cleanliness and good management.

Plate XXVI.

Provincetown has ever been foremost with her numerous fleet of plum-puddingers, or, in whaling phrase, "plum-pu-dn-rs," which are small vessels, employed on short voyages in the Atlantic Ocean. New Londoners have been, and still are, renowned for prosecuting the Right Whale fishery, in the rough waters of high latitudes, and pursuing the Sea Elephant about the forbidding shores of Kerguelen's Land, the Crozets, and Hurd's Islands, situated far south in the Indian Ocean; and also in contending with the northern ice and snow of Davis Strait and Hudson's Bay, in search of the Bowhead and the White Whale. Sag Harbor and Stonington likewise employed many of their ships in the northern and southern Right Whale fishery; and New Bedford, in the course of her absorption of the greater portion of the whaling commerce of the United States, prosecuted the enterprise in its various branches all over the ocean world, by availing herself of the services of many of the best whaling-masters and officers from other quarters, thus combining the highest energy and skill for the successful prosecution of the fishery. But, with all the judicious management of the merchants, and the unparalleled vigor and tact put forth by the seamen, our whale-fishery, as previously stated, has been for years on the decline; and the first famous whaling-port of America—Nantucket—which once boasted of her hundred fine ships, has now disposed of her last whaler—the *R. L. Barstow*—at that port of recruit, Payta, which is as familiar to all sperm-whalemen as that of Tumbez, where they went for supplies of sweet potatoes, after obtaining their onions at the former place. Sag Harbor, which in 1850 had twenty-three whalers, the majority of which were of large class, now has only two small brigs, which are employed on the Atlantic. Stonington, Mystic, Greenport, Warren, Cold Spring, Seppican, Wareham, Fall River, Falmouth, Holmes' Hole, Providence, Newport, Lynn, Quincy, Mattapoisett, Yarmouth, and Somerset, altogether mustered, in 1850, a fleet of ninety-two sails; but, according to the *Whalemen's Shipping List*, published at New Bedford, February 4th, 1873, there is not a single vessel engaged in whaling from any one of those ports. Of the forty-eight vessels comprising the New London fleet of 1850, there are left on the list of February 4th, 1873, only twenty. Fairhaven, in 1850, had forty-six whaling-vessels, of which only five are retained in the business. Provincetown's squadron of Atlantic cruisers, in 1850, numbered sixteen vessels, which tonnaged in the aggregate 1,871 tons; it had in February, 1873, nineteen vessels, whose capacity amounted to 1,561 tons. Edgartown, in 1850, had five large whalers in the Pacific, and one brig in the Atlantic; in 1873, only three remained, two of which were in port; and Westport, which had a squadron of fifteen vessels in 1850, now (1873) has only eight. The great fleet of New Bedford, in 1850, numbered two hundred and thirty-seven, which were principally whalers of the larger class. It now has (1873) one hundred and twenty-nine. San Francisco, in 1853, had ten vessels in the business, but the present year there is but one legitimate whaling-craft sailing from that port. It may be regarded as a singular coincidence, that Boston and New York, which repeatedly, in former years, attempted, but failed, to successfully establish the whaling business at either port, have now (February 4th, 1873) six small vessels in the Atlantic and one in the Pacific whale-fishery. Marion has three small schooners, Beverly one brig, Dartmouth two ships, San Francisco one bark, which make up the whole American whaling-fleet of the present day, consisting of twenty-six ships, one hundred and twenty-five barks, twelve brigs, and thirty-eight schooners—in all, 47,378 tons.

The following prices have been taken from the *Merchants' Magazine*, and the *Whalemen's Shipping List* of November, 1840; also from J. Ross Browne's work:

AVERAGE PRICES OF OIL (PER GALLON) AND BONE (PER POUND), FROM 1835 TO 1872, INCLUSIVE.

Year.	Sperm Oil.	Whale Oil.	Bone.	Year.	Sperm Oil.	Whale Oil.	Bone.
1835............	$0 84	$0 36	$0 24	1854............	$1 48¾	$0 58⅝	$0 39¼
1836............	88	44	25	1855............	1 77	71	45¼
1837............	82	33	22	1856............	1 62	79½	58
1838............	85	32	19	1857............	1 28⅓	73¼	96¾
1839............	1 00	35	19	1858............	1 21	54	92¼
1840............	1 02½	30	18	1859............	1 36¼	48½	85
1841............	1 00	30½	19	1860............	1 41½	49⅛	80¼
1842............	94	31¾	19⅔	1861............	1 31½	44¼	66
1843............	73	33¾	23	1862............	1 42½	59⅓	82
1844............	63	34½	35¾	1863............	1 61	95¼	1 53
1845............	90½	36½	40	1864............	1 78	1 28	1 80
1846............	88	32⅞	33⅝	1865............	2 25	1 45	1 71
1847...	87⅞	33¾	34	1866............	2 55	1 21	1 37
1848............	1 00½	36	31	1867............	2 33½	73¼	1 17½
1849............	1 09	40	31¾	1868............	1 92	82	1 02½
1850............	1 20½	49	34½	1869............	1 78	1 01¾	124
1851............	1 27¼	45¼	34½	1870............	1 35½	67¼	85
1852............	1 23¾	68⅔	50¾	1871............	1 35	60	70
1853............	1 24¾	58⅛	34½	1872............	1 45¼	65½	1 28½

Following, we give a tabular statement of the condition of the fishery for thirty-eight years, beginning in 1835 and ending in 1872, inclusive:

Years.	Number of Ships and Barks.	Number of Brigs.	No. Schrs. and Sloops.	Aggregate Tonnage.	Barrels of Sperm Oil.	Barrels of Whale Oil.	Pounds of Bone.	Value of Imports.
1835.	483	8	9	145,120	172,683	120,649	965,192	$ 6,168,997 92
1836.	488	9	10	150,269	132,130	131,176	1,028,773	5,733,536 21
1837.	490	9	10	150,969	181,724	219,138	1,753,104	7,357,553 31
1838.	495	25	30	159,723	131,856	227,016	1,783,848	6,157,037 52
1839.	498	100	78	169,983	150,000	230,000	Not Rendered.	7,544,250 00
1840.	510	40	9	171,196	157,791	207,908	2,000,000	9,775,062 60
1841.	535	41	9	191,767	159,304	207,348	2,000,000	7,684,087 70
1842.	542	43	9	195,833	165,637	161,041	1,600,000	6,829,788 90
1843.	578	40	9	198,754	166,985	206,727	2,000,000	6,497,587 64
1844.	595	41	11	200,147	139,594	262,047	2,532,445	6,523,384 ·61
1845.	643	35	18	218,655	157,917	272,730	3,167,142	9,128,235 67
1846.	678	35	23	233,189	95,217	207,493	2,276,939	5,553,817 52
1847.	670	31	22	230,218	120,753	313,150	3,341,680	7,807,865 20
1848.	621	22	16	210,663	107,976	280,656	2,003,600	8,905,621 04
1849.	581	21	12	196,110	100,944	248,492	2,281,100	7,321,160 69
1850.	510	20	13	171,484	92,892	200,608	2,869,200	7,743,880 98
1851.	502	24	27	171,971	99,591	328,483	3,966,500	10,042,536 94
1852.	558	27	35	193,990	78,872	84,211	1,259,900	5,720,455 23
1853.	599	30	32	206,286	103,077	260,114	5,652,300	10,730,637 94
1854.	602	28	38	208,399	73,696	319,837	3,445,200	10,710,748 80
1855.	584	20	34	199,842	72,649	184,015	2,707,500	9,391,182 98
1856.	585	21	29	199,141	80,941	197,890	2,592,700	10,589,844 74
1857.	593	22	40	204,209	78,440	230,941	2,058,900	10,491,597 28
1858.	587	18	49	203,148	81,941	182,223	1,540,600	7,643,997 07
1859.	561	19	45	195,115	91,408	190,411	1,923,850	8,467,393 41
1860.	508	19	42	176,842	73,708	140,005	1,337,650	6,555,700 65
1861.	459	14	41	158,746	68,932	133,737	1,038,450	3,233,393 15
1862.	372	10	41	125,465	55,641	100,478	763,500	5,001,688 49
1863.	301	10	42	103,888	65,055	62,974	488,750	5,936,507 17
1864.	258	6	43	88,754	64,372	71,863	760,450	7,875,662 56
1865.	226	7	43	80,053	33,242	76,238	619,350	6,897,285 15
1866.	199	8	56	71,869	36,663	74,302	920,375	7,037,88♮ 68
1867.	222	10	80	80,383	43,433	89,289	1,001,397	6,294,663 82
1868.	223	17	89	82,304	47,174	65,575	900,850	5,470,256 61
1869.	223	25	88	82,768	47,936	85,011	603,603	6,196,947 54
1870.	218	22	81	80,885	55,183	72,691	708,335	4,497,300 10
1871.	216	18	54	76,712	41,534	75,152	600,655	3,807,071 65
1872.	172	12	34	52,701	44,881	31,395	193,742	2,950,288 80
38	17,685	907	1,351	6,037,551	3,671,772	6,553,014	66,687,580	$272,274,916 27

The average number of vessels employed annually for these years was five hundred and twenty-four, aggregating 158,883 tons, and the amount of oil taken yearly was a fraction over 96,625 barrels of sperm, and 172,448 barrels of whale; The number of Sperm Whales required to produce this amount of sperm oil (allowing them to average twenty-five barrels each) would be 3,865; add to this ten per cent. for whales mortally wounded, lost after capture, etc., brings the number up to 4,253, or thereabouts. The black whales annually destroyed, which includes Right Whales, Bowheads, California Grays, and Humpbacks, allowing them to average sixty barrels each, would make the number 2,875; add to this twenty per cent. for whales lost, increases it to 3,450; so that the number of Sperm and black whales annually destroyed was 7,703. According to this estimate, during the thirty-eight years, there were no less than 292,714 whales captured or destroyed by the American whaler's lance.

The history of many of the old whale-ships is of peculiar commercial interest, large numbers of them having performed scores of voyages in the merchant service, or served as vessels of war, before being transformed into cruisers for oil and bone. Among them was the ship *Maria*. This vessel was built at Pembroke (now called Hanson), Mass., during the year 1782, for a privateer, but was purchased by the celebrated whaling merchant, William Rotch. It was one of the first vessels to display the American flag in the Thames after the War of Independence,[*] being at that period employed as a freighter. The *Maria* concluded her first whaling-voyage September 26th, 1775, and from that time continued in the business for seventy years, during which service she performed twenty-seven voyages. She sailed from New Bedford upon her last whaling-voyage under our flag on the 29th of September, 1859; the oil taken in all these expeditions, including eight hundred barrels on her final voyage, being 24,419 barrels of sperm, and one hundred and thirty-four barrels of whale oil. The vessel was commanded and officered by Nantucket-men while owned by Mr. Rotch; and after his decease, in 1828,[†] she passed into the hands of his descendants. On her last, unfinished voyage mentioned above, she was sold at Talcahuano, Chile, February, 1863, being then eighty-one years old. At this epoch in her history, the venerable craft changed her name and nationality, being christened the *Maria Pacheco*, and, instead

[*] Preble, in his *History of the American Flag* (page 215), states that "The honor of displaying our flag in England for the first time does not, however, rest with any vessel, if a printed representation of it can be considered. In that case, to John Singleton Copley, of Boston, the American painter, and the father of the late Lord Lyndhurst, must be assigned the honor."

[†] *Vide* Sanford's *Letters*.

of the "stars and stripes," the banner of Chile—red, white and blue, with its star, emblems of republican power and prowess—was raised at her peak, when she again resumed the work of a common carrier. But, in 1866, she was fitted for a whaling-voyage; and it is asserted by one authority, that the *Maria Pacheco* foundered at sea in 1870; and another record maintains that she sunk at her anchors, the same year, in the roadstead of Payta, at the advanced age of eighty-eight. This memorable old vessel was one of those models which combined great capacity with fast sailing, for her time: her length being "eighty-six feet; breadth, twenty-three feet and one inch; depth, eleven feet six and a half inches; and measurement, two hundred and two and twenty-eight ninety-fifths tons."

In 1820, a whale-ship was built at Plymouth, Mass., named the *Mayflower*. This vessel made several voyages from that port, after which she was sold to a firm in New Bedford; and in April, 1849, she was among the gold-fleet which sailed for California, making a passage of one hundred and sixty-five days, entering the Golden Gate September 13th, and soon after rested on the mud-flat in front of the then tented city of San Francisco. Here she was dismantled, mutilated, and turned into a store-ship, and her cabin was transformed into convenient quarters for a gentleman and his wife, where they made it a pleasant sub-aquatic residence. The vessel was of that ancient build which presented a swelled stern and drooping bow, with her masts standing plumb or pitching forward; and the question was frequently asked by passing gold-miners, on their way to the "diggings," if she was really the ship that brought over the Pilgrims? It is said, too, by good authority, that pieces of timber were taken from her sides, as *souvenirs*, by several California adventurers, who believed her to be the old Pilgrim ship of 1620. After being battered as a receptacle of merchandise for several years, the capacious port which had been cut in her side was closed up, and she was again refitted for a whaling-cruise; but the expedition proved to be unsuccessful, and she again returned through the Golden Gate, with a broken voyage and in a leaky condition. Soon after, however, she was turned into a lumber-carrier, and literally pumped her way back and forth between Puget Sound and San Francisco; until, becoming so shattered that she could no longer efficiently perform sea voyages, was made to transport lumber across the Strait of Juan de Fuca, to Victoria, in the time of the Frazer River gold fever; and, after a changing career of forty years, returned to San Francisco, where she was dismantled for the last time, and her hull broken up.

The question is frequently asked, What has become of the large number of whale-ships which were but a few years ago engaged in the fishery? In answer, we will state, that the scattered wrecks of many are found in every quarter of the globe ; while others have been sold into the merchant service, or broken up at home. San Francisco Bay and Sacramento River were the last ports many of the old ships made. The Charleston Bar swallowed up the stone fleet, which was chiefly made up of old whalers ; and the cruisers, during the Rebellion, destroyed many valuable vessels while at sea ; and, last of all, the ice of the Arctic made a fell swoop upon the northern fleet, in the fall of 1871.

CHAPTER V.

CALIFORNIA SHORE-WHALING.

Although brief mention has been made in the Natural History department of this work, relative to the shore-whaling along the coasts of Upper and Lower California, yet it may be well to devote a chapter especially to this fishery. California shore-whaling was commenced at Monterey, in the year 1851, by Captain Davenport, formerly a whaling-master of much experience and enterprise. The whales were pursued in boats from the shore, and when captured were towed to the beach and flensed, much in the same manner, doubtless, as it had been done by our New England whalers more than one hundred and fifty years ago. At the point where the enormous carcass was stripped of its fat, arose the "whaling station," where try-pots were set in rude furnaces, formed of rocks and clay, and capacious vats were made of planks, to receive the blubber. Large mincing-tubs, with mincing-horses and mincing-knives, cutting-spades, ladles, bailers, skimmers, pikes, and gaffs, with other whaling implements, surrounded the try-works; and near by, a low structure, covered with brush-wood, constituted the store-house for the oil. A light shanty, with four apartments, served the purpose of wash-room, drying-room, store-room, and cooper's shop; and a sort of capstans, termed "crabs," were used in lieu of the ship's windlass, whereby the falls to the heavy cutting-tackles were hove-in, when fastened to the blanket-piece, which served to roll the massive forms of the captured animals on the beach during the process of flensing.

From this experiment of local whaling sprung up a system of shore or coast whaling, which has been prosecuted for over twenty years, and which now extends from Half Moon Bay (latitude 37° 30′), on the north, to Point Abanda (latitude 32° 20′), in Lower California. At the present time, there are eleven whaling parties scattered along this belt of coast, located at Half Moon Bay, Pigeon Point, Monterey Bay (two), Carmel Bay, San Simeon, San Luis Obispo, Goleta, Portuguese Bend (near San Pedro), San Diego, and Point Abanda. The organization of each party is nearly on the same plan as that of the whale-ship's officers and crew—all being paid a certain share, or "lay," which corresponds to the position or individual services rendered by each member. A "whaling company," as it is termed, consists of one captain, one mate, a cooper, two boat-steerers, and eleven men; from these, two whale-boats are provided with crews of six men each, leaving four hands on shore, who take their turn at the lookout station, to watch for whales, and attend to boiling out the blubber when a whale is caught. The stock of the company consists of boats, whaling implements, and whaling-gear, which is divided into sixteen equal shares, and the "lay" of each member is the same. The captain and mate, however, are paid a bonus of two or three hundred dollars for the term of engagement, which is one year, and they are also exempt from all expenses of the company.

The whaling year begins on the first of April, this being about the time that the California Gray Whales have all passed toward the Arctic Ocean, and the Humpback Whales begin their northern passage. The cruising limits of the local whalers extend from near the shore-line to ten miles at sea. At dawn of day, the boats may be seen, careening under a press of sail, or propelled over the undulating ground-swell by the long, measured strokes of oars, until they reach the usual whaling-ground, where the day is passed plying to and fro, unless the objects of pursuit are met with. Each boat is furnished with Greener's harpoon-gun, mounted at the bow, besides the bomb-gun in general use, which imparts to them more of a military appearance than the usual aspect of a whaling-craft. Generally, whales are first seen from the boats; but occasionally they are discovered by the man on watch at the station, who signals to the boats by means of a flag elevated upon a pole, with which he runs toward the quarter where the whales are seen; or a series of signals are made from a tall flag-staff.

The cetaceous animals frequenting the coast, having been so long and constantly pursued, are exceedingly wild and difficult to approach; and were it not for the utility of Greener's gun, the coast fishery would be abandoned, it being now next to impossible to "strike" with the hand-harpoon. At the present time, if the whale can be approached within thirty yards, it is considered to be in reach of the gun-harpoon. When the gunner fires, if he hits his game, the next effort made is to haul up near enough to shoot a bomb-lance into a vital part, which, if it explodes, completes the capture; but, if the first bomb fails, the second or third one does the fatal work. The prize is then towed to the station; and if it be night, it is secured to one of the buoys placed for the purpose, a little way from the surf, where it remains until daylight, or until such time as it is wanted, to be stripped of its blubber. The whales generally taken by the shore parties are

WHALEBOAT WITH GREENER'S GUN MOUNTED.

Humpbacks, and California Grays; but occasionally a Right Whale, a Finback, or a Sulphurbottom is captured.

The localities of several of the stations are quite picturesque. Some of them are nearly concealed from seaward view, being inside some rocky reef, or behind a jagged point, with its outlying rocks, upon which each successive wave dashes its foam, as if forbidding the approach of ship or boat. The one which most interested us is half-hidden in a little nook, on the southern border of the Bay of Carmel, just south of Point Pinos. Scattered around the foot-hills, which come to the water's edge, are the neatly whitewashed cabins of the whalers, nearly all of whom are Portuguese, from the Azores or Western Islands of the Atlantic. They have their families with them, and keep a pig, sheep, goat, or cow, prowling around the premises; these, with a small garden-patch, yielding principally corn and pumpkins, make up the general picture of the hamlet, which is a paradise to the thrifty clan in comparison with the homes of their childhood. It is a pleasant retreat from the rough voyages experienced on board the whale-ship. The surrounding natural scenery is broken into majestic spurs and peaks, like their own native isles, with the valley of the Rio Carmel a little beyond, expanded into landscape loveliness.

Under a precipitous bluff, close to the water's edge, is the station; where, upon a stone-laid quay, is erected the whole establishment for cutting-in and trying-out the blubber of the whales. Instead of rolling them upon the beach, as is usually done, the cutting-tackles are suspended from an elevated beam, whereby the carcass is rolled over in the water—when undergoing the process of flensing—in a manner similar to that alongside a ship. Near by are the try-works, sending forth volumes of thick, black smoke from the scrap-fire under the steaming cauldrons of boiling oil. A little to one side is the primitive store-house, covered with cypress boughs. Boats are hanging from davits, some resting on the quay, while others, fully equipped, swing at their moorings in the bay. Seaward, on the crest of a cone-shaped hill, stands the signal-pole of the lookout station. Add to this the cutting at the shapeless and half-putrid mass of a mutilated whale, together with the men shouting and heaving on the capstans, the screaming of gulls and other sea-fowl, mingled with the noise of the surf about the shores, and we have a picture of the general life at a California coast-whaling station.

The aggregate amount of oil taken by the several shore parties, since their first establishment, may be estimated at not less than 95,600 barrels; of this amount, 75,600 barrels have been obtained from the California Gray Whales, and

20,000 barrels from the Humpbacks, Finbacks, and Sulphurbottoms. The value of the oil may be placed at about thirteen dollars a barrel, which would give a gross amount of $1,242,800, or an annual product for twenty-two years of $56,490. To obtain this oil, not less than 2,160 California Grays, and eight hundred Humpbacks and other whalebone whales, were robbed of their fatty coverings. If we add to this one-fifth for the number of whales that escaped their pursuers, although mortally wounded, or were lost after being killed either by sinking in deep water or through stress of weather, we shall swell the catalogue to 3,552. To this add one-eighth for unborn young, and the whole number of animals destroyed would be 3,996, or about one hundred and eighty-one annually. This may be regarded as a low estimate; doubtless the number of these creatures destroyed every year by the enterprising California whalemen far exceeds the above estimate. But this peculiar branch of whaling is rapidly dying out, owing to the scarcity of the animals which now visit the coast; and even these have become exceedingly difficult to approach.

CHAPTER VI.

LIFE AND CHARACTERISTICS OF AMERICAN WHALEMEN.

In taking a general view of whaling life, we find it replete with incidents of daring adventure, hardship, and deprivation. The vessels first employed in deep-sea whaling were so contracted, that no degree of comfort could be afforded to their crews, who, by sheer, ambitious hardihood, maintained existence on board during their short voyages. As the pursuit became extended, requiring larger vessels, the barks and brigs of the fishers were much improved, while the absence from their native shores was more prolonged. At this period a system for fitting out vessels for long voyages was inaugurated, as well as the establishment of effective discipline on board, for which well-regulated whale-ships have always been noted; and the whale-fishery steadily advanced under the judicious management of those able and systematic business gentlemen, whose names have long since become as familiar in the remotest parts of the ocean world, as the ships named in their honor. The broad expanse of the Atlantic soon became too limited a field for the vast enterprise, and in consequence of this, the fourth epoch in the fishery was inaugurated, when still larger vessels were sent out to search the nearly unknown waters of the Pacific and Indian Oceans. These vessels doubled Capes Horn and Good Hope, in their wanderings, which were so protracted, under the most favorable auspices, that the "green hands," many of whom never had snuffed the ocean's breezes until afloat on board a whaler, returned to their New England or Western homes, transformed into seamen and whalemen.

The Cape Horn and Indian Ocean voyages were at first of comparatively short duration; but as the pursuit was followed to more distant seas, three years or more passed away before the return of these cruisers.* During this long absence,

---

*The sperm-whaling voyages were the most protracted and tedious. Some forty years ago, an incident transpired on board a sperm whale-ship, while cruising about the equator, in the Pacific, which was amusingly illustrative of the tact and energy of her master in managing affairs, after wearing away nearly a whole season with indifferent success. Near the close of

an occasional vessel would bring them news from home. Really, the only legitimate means of communication, in early times, was by the outward-bound and homeward-bound ships;* and as a natural result, a system of transmitting letters was faithfully carried out. Speaking and visiting between whale-ships was a universal practice; and a custom of signaling and "gamming" was established, to prevent, as far as possible, any detriment to the voyage. A ship desiring to speak with another, out of ordinary signal distance, would haul up her mainsail; and the vessel with the wind free would bear up and run down to the new-comer on the ground, who, being hauled aback, awaited the approach of the visitor. There is, usually, considerable formality observed in these casual communications, especially if between strangers. The captain of the ship making the signal to speak, hails first, and asks whatever questions he may desire; after which, the master of the other vessel does likewise, and mutual invitations are exchanged to visit. If either accept, the rule is for the chief mate of the ship visited by a captain, to return, in the same boat, on a visit to his executive officer. If whales are raised during the time of gamming, the vessels generally "mate," in order that all shall have a motive in working together effectively; and, if there has been no previous agreement to meet the exigency, a flag is hoisted at the peak of the

the cruise, the supply of fresh water had become alarmingly short for the allotted time before returning to port. This was a source of regret, with both officers and men, as it was hoped they could fill the ship before the season terminated; and the captain would not have listened for a moment to the proposition to put the crew on a short allowance, had it been suggested. He, however, ordered a drinking-cup made, so as to be easily secured to, or detached from, the royal-mast head. Having placed it in its exalted position, all hands were mustered, and given to understand that they would have their regular allowance of tea and coffee served night and morning; but when anyone (including himself) desired to quench his thirst during the day, he must go aloft, get the drinking-cup, bring it on deck, obtain and drink the water (without spilling a drop), then take it back and place it at the mast-head again. The narrator of this episode jocosely remarked that,

" It was wonderful to observe what a 'persuader' against too much drinking was the exercise of 'shinning' to the royal truck twice, for a pot of water." And, by this means, the supply held out; and before the end of the cruise, they improved the timely opportunity of filling every empty cask with oil, and trimmed their sails for the homeward passage.

* Post Office Bay, upon the north-western side of Charles Island, took its name from the custom established by the whalers (before it was inhabited), of depositing letters in a box, placed upon a post for the purpose; "and homeward-bound ships," says Findlay, in his *South Pacific Directory*, "examined the directions, taking with them all which they might have the means of forwarding." A similar place of deposit for letters was established on the island of Juan Fernandez. We have heard, too, that a letter-box was at one time posted on the island of New Zealand.

captain's ship, which familiar sign (especially on Sperm Whale ground) is readily understood; and when the boats are lowered for the chase, the visiting captain takes charge of the mate's boat of the ship he is on board, and the executive officer visiting heads the captain's boat. If successful in capturing whales, the oil they obtain is divided. It was rarely, however, that a distant signal was made for the sole purpose of gamming; but the desire for letters from mothers, fathers, wives, children and other relatives, and friends, was sometimes irresistible. During these occasional meetings, not only is there an exchange of news verbally, but also an exchange of books and other reading matter that either ship can supply. It is a spirited sight, on a rough sea (or, as is sometimes said, "when too rugged to whale, but just right for a gam"), to watch these fragments of the commercial world, with swelling sails, surging over the breaking waves, until brought into close communion; and to observe the formal salutes between their commanders, while "speaking ship;" or, if they are old acquaintances, to witness the boisterous and hearty mutual greetings, heralded through trumpets, together with the general desire of everyone to associate, even for an hour, with some person besides his comrades, who are confined with him on his own reeling deck. Next to the joy of being on the return passage, with everything full, is the meeting of the old-time, voyage-worn whaleman, with a ship just out from home. Letters are received, and perhaps books and stores of other reading material, fresh to them, after having been borne half-way round the globe, for the space of six months (perhaps a year), are ravenously devoured; and a hundred and one inquiries are made about "How were things when you left home?" "What was the price of oil and bone?" "Were any new ships fitting out?" "Was there any danger of a war?" etc. A whole day was often spent under such gladsome circumstances; and the officers and men, passing and repassing to each other's vessels, always observed the same rules with regard to changing boats' crews as did their superiors. In these pleasant meetings, no effort was spared on the part of the hosts to entertain their guests most hospitably. The cabin table was spread with the best the ship could afford; many a plump porker of Oceanica, or a choice terrapin from the Galapagos, was sacrificed, and a general feast enjoyed fore and aft.*

In the course of these prolonged voyages, there was hardly a ship's company

---

*It may be noted that some etiquette was observed at the table, peculiar to the whaling service, where all appeared at the board in their shirt-sleeves! This is said to have originated from the nature of the work when taking oil, their outer garments necessarily becoming soiled. Hence, when coming to the table at meal time, the jacket or coat was thrown aside.

which did not experience many changes; men were lost through casualties, died of disease, deserted, or were exchanged, sometimes discharged, and frequently a smart youth would be promoted to an advanced position before his first voyage terminated. Anyone who gave promise of the requisites for a good whaleman had but little difficulty in shipping as a boat-steerer on the second voyage. At first, as has been previously stated, the colonial whaling-craft were manned almost exclusively by the colonists and Indians; but at length the fleet became so numerous, that, in a majority of cases, it was only practicable to obtain Americans for the principal officers, the rest of the ship's company being made up, as one might say, of all nations; and not unfrequently, in the forecastle, would be found runaway American youths of the best blood, ambitious farmers' sons from the interior, who were intent on becoming sea-captains, together with criminals in disguise, and hapless emigrants from the old country—Portuguese from the Azores, and negroes from the Cape de Verdes*—altogether making up a motley crew, which could only be controlled by strict discipline. Much has been written about the duplicity and sharp dealing of the owners of whaling-vessels, and the heartless severity of whaling-captains; but it is found that the authors of these glaring complaints were usually impracticable or discontented characters, who went drifting about the world with no fixed purpose of action, being generally dissatisfied with themselves and everyone with whom they came in contact—more especially if subjected to their control; or they were of that class who imagined they could make a convenience of the vessel to sail around the world—their chief object being to gratify their curiosity in sight-seeing, regardless of the faithful discharge of their duties— or, to say the least, they took no interest in the success of the voyage; hence their view of everything pertaining to whaling presented no pleasing features. Unfeeling and unprincipled men are sometimes found holding the responsible positions of mates and masters of whaling-vessels, as may be found in all other branches of the marine service; but that the majority of whaling-masters are unjust and tyrannical to those under their command, is a libel on their humane characters. It is not surprising that the discontented adventurer regards the practical discipline on shipboard as severe, and the commanding bearing of the officers as unnecessary. On the other hand, the officers, who have learned by their protracted schooling in a hardy and perilous profession that the success of the voyage

*It has been a general custom for outward-bound whalers to call at the Azores, or at the Cape de Verdes, if the season of the year was favorable, for the purpose of obtaining supplies of vegetables and fresh provisions; and at such times they made up their complement of men, if full crews had not been shipped at home ports.

depends upon the prompt performance of all duties, and they hold in utter contempt those malcontents, who, as faithful Jack terms it, "are in everybody's mess and in nobody's watch." It is to the interest of the commander of a whaler, to keep his crew in good heart and spirit; to this end they must be well fed, and otherwise made as comfortable as circumstances will permit. If these sanitary measures are not carried out, sickness and discontent ensue, which defeat the object of the expedition. On an average, the whale-ship's company is not actually on duty more than eight hours out of the twenty-four, and they are provided with an abundance of wholesome and substantial food, and as good quarters as the vessel will afford. If duty permits, during the hours from four to eight o'clock in the evening, all hands, except those immediately engaged in sailing the vessel, are allowed to amuse themselves in any way they please, so long as the ship is not disgraced.

When cruising for whales, the day's work begins and ends as regularly as the sun rises and sets; and a vessel engaged in sperm-whaling may remain on one cruising-ground for months (sometimes nearly half the year) without "breaking black-skin"—a whaler's term for not having an opportunity to harpoon a whale—and with nothing to change the monotony of the surrounding sea and sky view, except a transient sail, or some consort, who may have been more fortunate than herself, sending forth the signal of good luck in wreaths of blackened smoke from the try-works. During these discouraging times, if there is any insubordinate element in human nature, it is very sure to manifest itself in no mild form; and he is no ordinary man, although he may be a good disciplinarian, who can command and maintain implicit obedience. From the moment the captain steps upon the quarter-deck, until the voyage terminates, he leads a life of constant care and anxiety, for the expedition is fraught with uncertainty as to its results; moreover, his compensation for years of watchful toil, as well as of those under his command, depends entirely upon the amount of cargo gathered from the ocean. And, in these times of adversity, the indefatigable qualifications of the American whaling-master are promptly brought out; for, with the co-operation of the owner at home, who has well "fitted" his ship, the finale of the voyage is crowned with success. A landsman can not imagine the disheartening situation of the whalers, after months of watchfulness, from "sun to sun," when not even the shadow of a whale is seen; but when the spout of the long-sought prey is discovered in the distance, and the welcome cry of the men on the lookout is heard, the ship, fore and aft, becomes the scene of hopeful excitement. All hands are called —or they are already on deck without calling; orders are vehemently given and

Plate XXVII

C.M.Scammon. del.

Lith.Britton & Rey,S.F.

IN AZURE STATION AT CARMEL BAY

responded to. The boats are in readiness; they are "hoisted and swung;" and when the time comes for "lowering," they are dropped into the water with every man in his place. Springing to the oars, the boats bound over the waves; and in approaching the whale, the officer of the boat in advance carefully "cons" his little craft, and orders the "harpooniersman" by word or motion, to stand ready, with his weapon poised, as a rattling, rippling sound is heard, and a huge black form breaks the water, with the harsh, ringing noise of its first respiration. Instantly the deadly spear flies from ready hands, and plunges into the mammoth creature. The water is lashed into a pyramid of bloody foam, the boat is "fast," and the whale in vain endeavors to escape by running over the surface of the sea, then diving to the depths below; but its human pursuers still cling to the line attached to the fatal harpoon. The whale rises again to the surface, in some degree exhausted. Another boat approaches, and darts its murderous weapons, and the pursuit is continued with renewed vigor. When, at last, a vital part is pierced, the animal deeply crimsons its pathway with its remaining life-blood, and lashes the sea into clouds of spray in its dying contortions. Then follow wild cheers by the crews in the boats; while the ship bears down under reduced sail, and the whale is secured by the ponderous fluke-chain. The boats are again hoisted, and all hands are on board. Everyone is cheerful, and works with a will; up goes the cutting-gear, and the implements are in readiness for cutting-in the whale. The officers being on the cutting-stage, a few strokes with their spades, and the order is given to "heave away." The men at the windlass heave around cheerily, to the tune of a boisterous song, and the animal is soon stripped of its rich covering; the decks are cleaned up, the try-works are "started," and under the smoke of the torching scrap-fire, amid the din of the cooper's hammer preparing the oil-casks, and the general hum-drum incident to boiling out and stowing down, Jack spins his yarns of past exploits, savoring of good luck and thrilling adventures.

We have said that ill success brings its accompanying evils, which the captain is obliged to contend with; for, sometimes, when the whales are found in plenty, through the selfish maneuvering of some officer with his boat's crew, the chase may be a fruitless one. Good whalemen are full of the sportsman's spirit; and, like the buffalo hunters of the plains, they have no passion to pursue small game; and any marine animals inferior to the whale fail to lure them into the exciting chase. Hence, when in hot pursuit, the impulse to become the captors is so tempting, that many a valuable whale has been "gallied," through the reckless strife of some boat-header, in his efforts to be first to strike the animal. A more unfortunate state of affairs can hardly exist than "opposition whaling" by officers of the same ship; and in some cases it has been found indispensably necessary to keep a willful and refractory officer's boat "on the cranes," in order that the other boats may engage in the chase harmoniously. This measure generally brings the guilty party to his senses, for a more summary punishment could not be administered to a game whaleman than to be kept on board as an idle spectator of the exciting pursuit and capture.

Sperm whaling is chiefly prosecuted within the temperate latitudes, and often in the heated atmosphere of the torrid zone; but the Right and Polar Whales are hunted almost exclusively about the frozen oceans of the world, both north and south. In former years, however, these great animals were found in vast numbers within the temperate zones; but the work of the harpoon and lance, by the combined whaling-fleets of Europe and America, has long ago nearly annihilated those species inhabiting the middle water-belts of the northern and southern oceans, and at the present day the animals are driven to their remotest haunts in ice-bound seas. The principal field of pursuit for the whalebone whales, exclusive of the rorquals, is along the icy barrier of the Arctic Ocean. Here the ships cruise from the time the field-ice opens, until the October snows and gales drive them from that gloomy coast, which is strewn with wrecks and records of disaster. The positions of the officers of an Arctic whale-ship, as well as those of the crew, are no sinecure. "Standing mast-heads" in the biting cold, which is varied by storms of sleet and dismal fogs—constantly on the watch, not only for whales, but for the treacherous movements of the ice-fields or bergs—is a tedious duty, of inordinate exposure; yet, of the whole company, the captain's work is the most arduous, for on him rests the greatest responsibility, and he must be on the alert both night and day, being aloft on the lookout more hours than any of his officers. On leaving the frozen regions, the whaler wends his way southward through adverse gales; if favored with leading winds, he seeks the most desirable port, where the needful supplies of fresh provisions can be obtained, and a few weeks of relaxation and amusement for the crew may be enjoyed on shore. By far the most noted resort for supplies in the northern hemisphere was Honolulu, Sandwich Islands; yet Hilo and Maui, of the same group, were frequently resorted to. Here, the genial climate and fruitful soil, which yielded abundantly the needful "recruits," and the open, easy life of the natives, caused it to become a favorite place for the whalers to congregate. The brief time of "giving liberty" and "recruiting ship" being over, a short winter cruise called the "line season" may be made about the equator, for Sperm Whales; or the vessel may go to the coast of California, to engage in "bay-whaling," or "kelp-whaling." In either case, the ships usually touch again at some port to obtain fresh supplies; and sometimes the season's catch of oil is discharged or reshipped before she returns to the Arctic cruising-grounds. California bay and kelp whaling has been a peculiar feature of the fishery. The whales there pursued are a distinct species of the baleen tribe, whose natural history is given in this work, under the head of "The California Gray Whale." They are the most dangerous of all whales to attack, and, compared with the number of ships which formerly engaged in their capture, more casualties have occurred than in any other branch of whaling, many men having lost their lives, while others have been irrecoverably crippled. But we have never yet learned of any place of resort for whales which can possibly be approached, either by ship or boat, that has not been the scene of slaughter by their human captors. Many whaling-masters—after buffeting the gales and ice of the Arctic regions—have hurriedly fled to this inland whaling-ground on the California coast, and in order to reach the most advantageous localities, far up the shallow estuaries, lightened and careened their vessels, and by means of their heavy ground-tackle forced them across shoals which were nearly bare at low tide. The difficulty and danger connected with this fishery seems to have lured on many a reckless and venturesome spirit to the encounter, which has been appropriately named "devil-fishing," and the successful whaler is christened a good "devil-fisherman." While engaged for six years in whaling, sealing, and Sea Elephant expeditions upon the coast of California and Mexico, we passed the winter seasons in lagoon or bay whaling, and our experience in the capture of the California Grays may serve as an outline picture of whaling-life in those inland waters.

LAGOON - WHALING.

When arrived in the lagoons, a suitable anchorage is selected, and the ship is moored for the season; the heavy sails are unbent, and much of the running rigging unrove, landed and housed under canvas, together with shooks, spare lumber, etc., so as to clear the ship of cumbersome materials not required until the vessel is nearly filled with oil or the season is over. The "tender" is fitted for cutting-in the whales, the cutting-gear of the ship is sent aloft, and with the cutting-stage placed over the side, preparations for the slaughter are completed. When sufficient numbers have assembled at the head-waters of the estuaries, the boats are lowered in pursuit. A cow with a young calf is usually selected, so that the parent animal may be easily struck; yet the race is sometimes so prolonged as to nearly exhaust the boats' crews; and when at last the creature lags, so that her tired offspring may keep near, thereby presenting the opportunity to the "harpooniersman" to thrust effectively with his weapon, the murderous blow often causes the animal to recoil in its anguish, and give a swoop of its ponderous flukes, or a toss of its head, which, coming in contact with the boat, produces a general wreck, and more or less injury to the men. In the winter of 1856, we were whaling about the *esteros* of Magdalena Bay, where, in attacking sixteen whales, two boats were entirely destroyed, while the others were staved fifteen times; and out of eighteen men who officered and manned them, six were badly jarred, one had both legs broken, another three ribs fractured, and still another was so much injured internally that he was unable to perform duty during the rest of the voyage. All these serious casualties happened before a single whale was captured. However, after a few days' rest, while the boats were being repaired and new ones fitted to take the place of those destroyed, the contest with the "Devil-fish" was again renewed, and with successful results. Several whales were taken without accident, and no serious casualty occurred during the rest of the season.

During the spring and summer months of 1857, we were engaged with the brig *Boston* in whaling, sealing, and Sea Elephant hunting, but with ill success. The crew was shipped for eight months only; hence we would have been obliged to return to port with nearly an empty vessel, had not nearly all the men volunteered to engage for the winter season, rather than leave the vessel, penniless. Only three men desired to leave the brig, who were landed at Santa Barbara. Having previously ascertained that a large lagoon branched from the Bay of San Sebastian Viscaino (heretofore unknown to whalers), where the California Grays, in the season, probably resorted, a small schooner as a tender, with men to increase our deficient ship's company, was dispatched from San Francisco, and joined the brig at the appointed place of rendezvous, in the snug harbor of Catalina Island. All being in readiness, both vessels sailed, the last of November, 1857, for the new whaling-ground. Nothing of special interest transpired until we arrived off our first landmark—now known as Lagoon or Safety Head. Under this land both vessels anchored for the night. On the following day, three boats and the tender were dispatched to explore the coast to the southward, and "sound out" the channel into the lagoon. Two days passed, when a messenger returned with the report that the tender had entered the estuary without difficulty, and that there was sufficient depth of water on the bar for the brig to pass over. It was afternoon before we got under way. A brisk breeze was blowing, and would have carried us to a land-locked harbor before evening, had it not failed us when nearly on the shoalest part of the entrance, obliging both vessels to anchor—the tender having previously joined us. Night came on, dark and misty; and as the tedious hours wore away, an increasing heavy swell rolled in, breaking fitfully around both brig and schooner. Nothing could relieve us from our perilous situation but a strong land-breeze, to take the vessels back to the first anchorage or to sea. Not a soul on board slept during that night. A light puff of wind, at long intervals, came through the mouth of the lagoon, each time giving us hope for the desired land-breeze; but it only increased the dismal sound of the angry surf as it beat upon the sandy shores. At daylight, a gentle air came in from seaward, when signal was made for both vessels to get under way; but before the anchors were lifted, it fell calm again, and near noon the wind came from the northward, when we were quickly under all sail, and soon passed through the turbulent passage, and cast anchor behind a sheltered point of the lagoon. It was too early to commence whaling; and being short of wood to last through the season, the time and opportunity were improved to obtain a supply from the wreck of a ship which lay strewn about the contiguous ocean shore. To reach the "wooding" place, it was necessary to land inside the passage and go some distance along the beach, as no boat could approach from the outer coast. One day having been spent in preparing the fuel, another was expected to be ample time to put it on board. All the boats engaged in transporting it were moored near the shore in the lagoon, and left in charge of a boat-keeper, it being impracticable to haul them up at high tide on account of the broad, flat beach exposed at low water. All the wooding party being out of sight when at the wreck, the boat-keeper concluded to refresh himself by a bath, and conceived the idea of converting one of the boats into a bath-tub, by pulling out the plug in the bottom. The boat soon became water-logged, and the fellow, carelessly enjoying his ablutions, got too far to one side of the craft, which instantly capsized, turning him into the lagoon. The current running swiftly, dragged the anchor, and the man, in his fright, swam to the shore, abandoning his boat, to which three others were fast, and all four went drifting out of the passage. The alarm was given to the party on shore, and it was a disheartening sight to behold the four boats drifting through the breakers, for everyone knew that without them our voyage would be fruitless. There were several Kanakas among the crew, who immediately saw the necessity of saving the boats; and selecting pieces of plank, to be used as "surf-boards," put off through the rollers to rescue them. Our carpenter was an expert swimmer; and as soon as he saw the boats drifting along the shore into the breakers, he threw off his clothes, plunged into the surf, and had nearly reached them, when the anchor, which had been dragging all the while, brought up, and the current swept both the carpenter and Kanakas out of reach. They then made for the shore, which all of them regained in an exhausted condition, except the carpenter, who was never seen again. The officers present, with a portion of the crew, were so much discouraged that they gave up all hopes of regaining the boats, and openly avowed that our anticipated successful voyage must be abandoned. Permission was asked to go in search of the tender, which was engaged in sounding out the channel of the lagoon, that those on board might be advised of the disaster and come to our relief, as we could not return to the brig for the want of a boat—the tender having the only one left between the two vessels. Their request was granted, while the rest of the crew remained with me at the site of the ill-fated wreck; they were immediately directed to take stations along the beach, and watch for the carpenter's remains and for the re-appearance of the boats. It was nearly low tide when the catastrophe occurred, and we had a faint hope that the change of the flood would bring some of the boats, even in a wrecked condition, back or near to the passage of the lagoon. It was but a short time after the lookouts were stationed, before a hawk-eyed youngster, who had climbed a sand-hill, reported that a boat was in sight; when the preconcerted signal was given, and in a moment a dozen men, at the risk of their lives, grappled it in the surf, and dragged it far beyond high-water mark. They had hardly accomplished the feat, before another appeared, which, in a few moments, drifted within reach, and was soon placed beside the first one; a third appeared, was seized, and quickly transported beyond the other two, with a spontaneous cheer from the men, for all now knew that our means of rescue, and for pursuing the whales—which had already appeared in large numbers—were restored to us. Toward evening, the party that went in search of the tender returned; but it was late in the night before all the men were embarked, when we returned to the brig, tired and dejected over the day's disasters, involving the loss of a favorite shipmate.

At an early hour on the following day, all hands that could be spared from the vessel were busily employed in transporting the boats along the beach to a place where they could be launched into the lagoon; but it required three days to complete, the transportation of boats and fuel. Meanwhile, a vigilant search was made for the body of the carpenter; but no traces of it could be found. As the last of the wood came alongside, a norther broke upon us in all its fury, and both vessels struck adrift, but were brought up by their anchors. On the third day the gale abated, when the brig and her consort made the best of their way up to the head of the hitherto unexplored waters. Here the whales were found in great numbers. On the next day the boats were sent in pursuit, and two large cows were captured without difficulty, which gave all hands confidence in our ultimate success. Early the next morning, the boats were again in eager pursuit; but before the animal was struck, it gave a dash with its flukes, staving the boat into fragments, and sending the crew in all directions. One man had his leg broken, another had an arm fractured, and three others were more or less injured—the officer of the boat being the only one who escaped unharmed. The relief boat, while rescuing the wounded men, was also staved by a passing whale, leaving only one boat afloat. The tender being near at hand, however, a boat from that vessel rendered assistance, and all returned to the brig. When the first boat arrived with her freight of crippled passengers, it could only be compared to a floating ambulance crowded with men—the uninjured supporting the helpless. As soon as they reached the vessel, those who were maimed were placed on mattresses upon the quarter-deck, while others hobbled to their quarters in the forecastle. The next boat brought with it the remains of the two others, which were complete wrecks. Every attention was given to the wounded men, their broken limbs were set, cuts and bruises were carefully dressed, and all the injured were made as comfortable as our situation would permit; but the vessel, for several days, was a contracted and crowded hospital. During this time no whaling was attempted, as nearly half of the crew were unfit for duty, and a large portion of the rest were demoralized by fright. After several days of rest, however, two boat's crews were selected, and the pursuit was renewed. The men, on leaving the vessel, took to the oars apparently with as much spirit as ever; but on nearing a whale to be harpooned, they all jumped overboard, leaving no one in the boat, except the boat-header and the boat-steerer. On one occasion, a bulky deserter from the U. S. Army, who had boasted of his daring exploits in the Florida War, made a headlong plunge, as he supposed, into the water; but he landed on the flukes of the whale, fortunately receiving no injury, as the animal settled gently under water, thereby ridding itself of the human parasite.

It was useless to attempt whaling with men who were so completely panic-stricken; and the officers and boat-steerers combined could not muster the complement to man two boats. Our situation was both singular and trying. The vessel lay in perfect security in smooth water; and the objects of pursuit, which had been so anxiously sought, were now in countless numbers about us. It was readily to be seen that it was impossible to capture the whales in the usual manner with our present company, and no others could be obtained before the season would be over. Among the officers there were two who had been considered good shots with the bomb-lance gun, one of whom we personally knew to be unequaled as a marksman. There seemed to be but one way to successfully capture these sprightly animals, and that was by using the bomb-lance. The officers were called together, and the matter plainly set before them; the best marksmen were selected, and informed that if they could kill a whale without expending more than three bomb-lances, our supply was ample to insure a "full ship." They were then directed to place their boats on the side of the narrowest channel in the lagoon, near where the whales passed, but in shallow water, so that they could not possibly reach the boat, and there wait until one would come within gunshot. The idea was a novel one, and to old whalemen it seemed impracticable. Three boats were at once dispatched—two prepared for shooting, and the third as a relief boat in case of emergency. They took their positions as ordered, and it was not long before three whales had been "bombed"—the third one was killed instantly and secured. On returning to the vessel, the officers reported their good luck; and on the following day they were again dispatched, but with instructions to first board the tender, and take a look from her mast-head for the whales that had been bombed the day previous, as we confidently expected that either one, or both, would be found dead not far from where they were shot. It was a pleasant surprise to the chief officer, when, on going half-way up the tender's rigging, both whales were seen floating dead near the head of the lagoon; and no time was lost in securing them.

From that time, whaling was prosecuted without serious interruption. Whenever a whale was wanted, one or two boats were sent off, and it was not long before the reports of the guns would be heard, which heralded a capture, without the staving of boats or injury to the men. The try-works were incessantly kept going—with the exception of a day, now and then, when it became necessary to "cool down," in order to stow away the oil and clear the decks—until the last cask was filled. Nor did we stop then; for one side of the after-cabin was turned into a bread-locker, and the empty bread-casks filled with oil; and the mincing-tubs were fitted with heads, and filled, as well as the coolers and deck-pots; and, last of all, the try-pots were cooled, and filled as full of oil as it was thought they could hold without slopping over in a rough sea. Both vessels having been literally crammed with oil, a few days were spent in cleaning and washing ship, and getting ready for sea. Our supply of fresh water was becoming reduced; but as it was only about fifty miles from the lagoon to the watering-place on Cerros Island, and having in former voyages obtained fresh water at Magdalena Bay, by digging wells in the sand-beaches, a few yards from high-water mark, we gave ourselves little anxiety about the needed supply, should we be unavoidably detained in the lagoon.

All being in readiness, we took advantage of a light morning air to work down toward the bar; but the fresh sea-breeze soon after setting in, compelled us to anchor; and a tedious week was passed before we reached the sandy heads of the estuary. The change of the moon brought with it adverse gales from the north-west, and an accompanying heavy sea, which broke "feather-white" seaward, as far as the eye could discern from the mast-head, precluded all attempts, during such weather, to pass the bar and work the vessels across the open bay of San Sebastian Viscaino, to Cerros Island. Day after day we anxiously watched for a favorable change; but two weeks passed away before the wind moderated. Meanwhile, our supply of water had become so reduced, as to compel us to put all hands on an allowance of one pint a day. As soon as the gale had settled into a strong breeze, we at once made every effort to get to sea, even under shortened sail. The brig and tender, having laid at anchor for months, became very foul, and for this reason made their way at a snail's pace through the breakers that still surrounded us, and while the vessels were passing over the shallow water, their keels stirred the sandy bottom, so that their wakes were whitened for a long distance astern. At last we passed the bar, and felt that we were once more at sea, or, at least, clear of the shoals, which presented a forbidding barrier to the ingress or egress of those inland waters; but, as night approached, the wind again increased to a gale, and a heavy, breaking sea continually washed over the vessels, from stem to taffrail. Early the following morning, we were well up to the watering-place at Cerros; but nearly the whole day was spent before we gained the anchorage, and we had barely time to make all snug before the gale burst upon us with increased fury, and continued for two days. As soon as it abated, a boat was dispatched for an immediate supply of water. Here we remained for several days, employed in recleaning ship and in obtaining wood and water, after which we set sail for San Francisco, where we arrived in due time, with the vessel so deeply laden that her scuppers were washed by the rippling tide. Thus ended a voyage which in no small degree was a novel one.

LAGOON-WHALING INCIDENTS.

The following season found us again in the lagoon, with a little squadron of vessels, consisting of one bark and two small schooners. Although this newly discovered whaling-ground was difficult of approach, and but very little known abroad—and especially the channel which led to it—yet, soon after our arrival, a large fleet of ships hovered for weeks off the entrance, or along the adjacent coast, and six of the number succeeded in finding their way in. The whole force pursuing the whales that season numbered nine vessels, which lowered thirty boats. Of this number, at least twenty-five were daily engaged in whaling. The different branches of the lagoon where the whales congregated were known as the "Fish-pond," "Cooper's Lagoon," "Fort Lagoon," and the "Main Lagoon." The chief place of resort, however, was at the head-waters of the Main Lagoon, which may be compared to an *estero*, two or three miles in extent, and nearly surrounded by dunes, or sand-flats, which were exposed at neap tides. Here the objects of pursuit were found in large numbers, and here the scene of slaughter was exceedingly picturesque and unusually exciting, especially on a calm morning, when the mirage would transform not only the boats and their crews into fantastic imagery, but the whales, as they sent forth their towering spouts of aqueous vapor, frequently tinted with blood, would appear greatly distorted. At one time, the upper sections of the boats, with their crews, would be seen gliding over the molten-looking surface of the water, with a portion of the colossal form of the whale appearing for an instant, like a spectre, in the advance; or both boats and whales would assume ever-changing forms, while the report of the bomb-guns would sound like the sudden discharge of musketry; but one can not fully realize, unless he be an eye-witness, the intense and boisterous excitement of the reckless pursuit, by a large fleet of boats from different ships, engaged in a morning's whaling foray. Numbers of them will be fast to whales at the same time, and the stricken animals, in their efforts to escape, can be seen darting in every direction through the water, or breaching headlong clear of its surface, coming down with a splash that sends columns of foam in every direction, and with a rattling report that can be heard beyond the surrounding shores. The men in the boats shout and yell, or converse in vehement strains, using a variety of lingo, from the Portuguese of the Western Islands to the Kanaka of Oceanica. In fact, the whole spectacle is beyond description, for it is one continually changing aquatic battle-scene.

It was no unusual occurrence for the whales, after being struck, to run in different directions, thereby endangering collisions with the boats, or crossing lines; and it was frequently only by the most dexterous management of the crews that serious disasters were avoided. Sometimes a line was cut, or let go, and again recovered, or the whale escaped with the harpoon. Our tenders being anchored at the scene of action, afforded an excellent opportunity to observe, from their mast-heads, all that was transpiring. One dull, quiet morning, with a light fog-cloud above us, the voices of the men in the pursuing flotilla could be distinctly heard for miles distant. At least twenty boats were quickly changing their positions, as the "fast" fish might take them; or perhaps some unlucky craft would suddenly stop, and the next moment, boat, oars, whaling implements, and men, would be seen flying through the air, or scattered upon the water around some Devil-fish, which, in whaling parlance, was "the devil among cedar." The boats of two different ships, which were fast to whales, passed quite near us; and while the officers of each party had no relish for keeping close company, the two whales exhibited no disposition to separate; and as the group swiftly approached, we heard loud voices and saw violent gesticulations. Very soon we distinctly heard a burly fellow, who stood at least six feet in his stockings, bare-headed, with his long locks streaming behind, shouting to his opponent: "That won't do! that won't do! cut your line! I struck my whale first! Cut that line, or you'll be into us! Cut that line, or I'll put a bomb through you!" But the officer of the opposing boat very coolly replied: "Shoot, and be d——d, you old lime-juicer! I won't let go this line till we git 'tother side of Jordan!" Then, turning to his crew, he said: "Haul line, boys! haul ahead! and I'll give old Rip-sack a dose he can't git to the 'pothecary's! Haul ahead, and I'll tap his claret-bottle!" By this time the two whales had separated, and the boats were beyond hearing; but both whales were seen spouting blood, and soon after pyramids of foam showed that they were in their "flurry."

The whale being dead, and floating, the grapnel is brought into requisition, and the animal's head is hooked and hauled up, when holes are cut through the lips, and a short warp is rove through, by which means its mouth is closed, and the tow-rope is made fast; then the prize is taken in tow to the vessel. Usually the whales are killed during the morning hours, or in the fore part of the day; and before noon, trains of boats would be seen towing them, with sails spread to a leading breeze, or they wended their way slowly down the lagoon by the long, steady strokes of oars, and not unfrequently a boat song, with a lively chorus, cheered the men at their laborious work. Sometimes a casualty prevented some whaling-gang from making their capture after a hard chase, or "working upon" some cunning Devil-fish which baffled their skill to destroy; or, if the capture were made, it might be when the day was far advanced, or perhaps the shades of evening would compel them to "cut line," thereby giving up the chase, and returning to the ship with everyone jaded by a long and unsuccessful battle. Notwithstanding the danger in lagoon-whaling, we have known of the California Gray being killed during the darkest hours of night. An instance of this kind came to our notice. When the whale had been bombed repeatedly, lanced, and spouted thin blood, its tenacity of life was truly surprising. Long after dark, the crippled creature, with the pursuing boats clinging to it by the lines and harpoons, was heard coming toward the vessel, and, on closer approach, we could see the "white water," as the animal writhed in its agony. The boat-header, lance in hand, worked with might and main, hoping at every dart to give it a fatal thrust. We could hear the usual orders of "Pull ahead!" "Hold the boat!" "Stern all!" "Lay the boat off!" etc., with now and then the encouraging words to the crew that the whale was "spouting blood as thick as tar." When the party passed their ship, the captain hailed them, and advised the officer in charge to cut his line and give up the whale. He replied: "Aye, aye, sir; I've killed the bloody Greek seven times, but he won't turn up—he's got more lives than a Kilkenny cat; but I'll quiet him in less than five minutes—he can't last much longer." And, a few moments after, the exhausted creature made its last gasping struggle, and "turned up." A wild cheer from the boats' crews told that the fatal work was finished, and all returned to the ship, fatigued by the long combat, but in good spirits, for their prize was secured.

The use of the bomb-lance has greatly diminished the danger of capturing the California Gray; and it has been mentioned, in preceding pages of this work, that this whaling was first prosecuted in the bay and lagoons of Magdalena, in the year 1846. In the winter of 1848, fifty ships anchored there to pass the "between seasons" in bay-whaling, which began with flattering prospects; but it was a new whale-ground, in shallow water, and the animal a strange one to the fishers, whose actions, when pursued, they knew nothing about; hence, there was hardly a ship that did not have one or more of her boats staved whenever they made an attack. Again, although the bay and lagoons were of great extent, and the whales plentiful, the fleet was large, and it was a time when all the ships "broke out and coopered their oil." Every ship's cooper and his gang were busily at work with their heavy hammers, driving the hoops on the casks, and the whole combined produced a deafening noise upon the water, which echoed from cliff to crag along the mountain island of Margarita. This, with the chase and capture of the animals, the staving of boats, and the smoke and blaze from try-works by night, soon drove the whales to the outside shores. The ardent hopes of the most sanguine were sadly dampened. A parley was held by the captains, and the matter was fully discussed, what course to take in order to secure a good season's catch. Rules and regulations were drawn up and agreed to by all that decided to remain and try their luck through the season; but many ships, after the first few days' whaling, left to cruise in the open sea for Sperm Whales, until the northern season should come round again. Disappointed in their new whaling enterprise, they usually left with many maledictions on Margarita Bay (as it was usually called), and on the whales especially, which had already been given a multitude of significant names. After suspending whaling for a few days, and a number of ships leaving meanwhile, the whales again returned to their favorite haunt, and, the whalemen soon learning how to "work around them," the ships that remained generally made a fair season's catch.

The dangers incident to whaling in Magdalena Bay and lagoons gave rise to many a marvelous tale, some of which were literally true, while others, though amusing, partook strongly of that flavor which sailors term "fishy." After the first few years of "gray"-whaling, the pursuit came to be regarded as somewhat impracticable; and the oil obtained being of an inferior quality, without the accompanying yield of bone, as in the Right Whale and Bowhead, this branch of the fishery was for a time nearly abandoned. A few ships, however, passed a portion of the winter months in pursuing the Devil-fish of Magdalena; and one captain in particular made periodical visits to a favorite estuary, where the animals were found in great abundance, and were captured with less than the usual difficulty; but a season never passed without casualties occurring—sometimes serious ones. This indefatigable master (whom we will call Captain L.), in order to play a little game of bluff with his boon companions, would, on his return to the Sandwich Islands to recruit ship for the north, bring with him one of his boats which had been staved beyond repair, that those interested might have convincing proof of the terrors of "ripsack-whaling." Added to this, his spicy yarns when dilating upon the dangerous chase, created in those unacquainted an aversion to engage in so precarious a pursuit. At length, however, the northern whales becoming scattered and difficult to capture, caused some of the most enterprising captains to try their hand with the Grays. At the time we are writing about, a large fleet had concentrated at Honolulu, after the accustomed summer cruise to the north; and at these periodical gatherings, the whalers, from the steerage-boy to the captain, enjoyed a season of relaxation from the restraint of strict discipline, as well as from the duties on board ship, and a good deal of familiarity was tolerated on shore during their brief stay, which at sea would have been promptly suppressed. Everyone seemed to follow his own inclinations in seeking pleasure wherever, or in whatever way, it could be found. And one of Captain L.'s felicitous amusements was in dilating upon the terrors of "devil-fishing" (he familiarly termed it) "over to Margarita." At one time, when in the midst of a romance, one of his brother captains ironically remarked that, as he "told the truth so often, he hardly knew when to believe him." "You don't, eh?" retorted Captain L.; "well, *you* have a heap of good manners, I think, to interrupt a gentleman when he's talking? Now, look here, old Doubtful, I'll tell you what happened to me in my own boat, up in the 'mud-hole,' season afore last. We was chasing a cow and calf, and I charged my boat-steerer to be careful and not touch the young sucker, for if he did, the old whale would knock us into chop-sticks; but no sooner said than done—slam went two irons into the critter, chock to the hitches, and that calf was 'pow-mucky' in less than no time; and the boat-steerer sung out: 'Cap'n, I've killed the calf, and the old cow is after us.' Well, just about this time, I sung out to the men to pull for the shore as they loved their lives; and when that boat struck the beach, we scattered. I'll admit I never stopped to look round; but the boat-steerer yelled out: 'Cap'n, the old whale is after us still,' when I told all hands to climb trees!" This graphic picture of "ripsacking" was received with a shout of laughter by the knot of listeners who had circled about the loquacious captain, and all admitted that he was the king of skippers in Devil-fish lore.

But with all the warnings and direful tales, Magdalena Bay whaling was resumed with ardor about the years 1855 and 1856, and was continued and extended along the whole coast of both Upper and Lower California. Every navigable lagoon of the region was discovered and explored, and the animals were hunted in every winding and intricate estuary which were their resorting or breeding places. In the seasons of 1858 and 1859, not only the bays and lagoons were teeming with all the varied incidents of the fishery, but the outside coast was lined with ships, from San Diego southward to Cape St. Lucas. A few vessels of this fleet cruised near the shore by day, standing a little way off at night; but by far the largest number anchored about the islands, points, and capes, wherever the animals could be most successfully pursued. It was a novel sight to view a single ship, or a small squadron, anchored off some exposed headland or island, rolling and surging at their cables in the ugly ground-swell, and the fleet of boats lying along the line of kelp just without the surf-bound shore, or, with their sails spread to the breeze, skimming over the waves in the various directions the gigantic game led them. At such times, a feature was observed in this fishery which is not often witnessed, namely: the peculiar marks or devices pictured upon the sails of the boats belonging to the different vessels. Some had a large cross covering the mainsail, while others would have the whole sail of blue, with a white jib or gaff-topsail. On another boat's canvas would be figured one, two, or three balls; or stars, or crescents; or a large letter or number designated the ship to which they belonged. The diversity of colors, and the different tastes displayed in painting the boats, added another pleasing feature: some were pure white, others black, still others of a lead color; or fancifully striped with tri-colors, or with the bow red, blue, or green, while the rest of the craft would be of a contrasting shade. Sometimes a huge eye on either side of the stem, or a large circle, would be the designating mark; all these combined making up an extended group of dashing water-craft, especially pertaining to the California coast and fishery.

As the success of a whaling-voyage depends chiefly (when whales are plentiful) upon the officers being good whalemen, there is frequently more or less contention among captains and agents to obtain those of unquestionable skill; so that the "crack" men of the harpoon and lance have often dictated their own terms as to their lay and bonus; and in former years the advance wages and extra pay received by officers of great reputation as right-whalemen and devil-fishermen, might be considered enormous. But it was not always that these "bonus men" proved to be equal to the reputation which they perhaps had obtained either by accident or purely good fortune. Ill luck sometimes robbed a good whaleman of his prestige, and many a game man for a Right Whale of the North-western Coast found himself quite unequal to the task of "turning up" a California Gray. We recollect an instance which occurred on board a New London ship, where the mate returned on board after a hard chase and combat with an old cow and her calf in one of the shallow estuaries. As this officer approached his captain, to give an account of his mishaps, he became greatly excited; but at last he said: "I didn't know, sir, that the whale was within fifty fathoms of me, when up we went—and there ain't enough left of the boat to kindle the cook's fire." On another occasion, a famous New Bedford captain flew into a fit of passion at his "bonus mate," for coming on board with a staved boat, instead of bringing alongside a dead whale. Words ran high with the "old man;" but his chief officer seemed to take things philosophically. He remained silent until his commander had vented his spleen, when he replied as follows: "Look a-here, Cap'n Simmons, I don't ask no odds of any living man that can pull an oar or dart an iron. I can catch as many whales as the next one, ef ye'll give me a fair show. I don't say as I cud do any more; but did'nt I bring as many whales to the ship, down to the Rosemerry Islands, as all the rest of your boat-headers that was counted as bein' great on a Humpback? And what kind uv whales did they git, anyhow?—calves, and old cows that had been sucked down till they was too poor to skin—why, the blubber on 'em wouldn't make coal-tar ef you biled it a week; and the most of the whales I had the luck to captivate was them old white-bellied fellers that had a fin on 'em like a seventy-four's breast-hook, and would turn up sixty barrels apiece, without skimmin'-slicks; and didn't I catch my share of whales on the Nor'-west?" "Yes," replied the captain; "I had no fault to find until we came in here to Devil-fish it." "Yes, well," replied the mate; "I hain't no growlin' to do, only one thing: I shipped to this ship to go a-whalin'; I'd no idea of bein' required to go into a duck-pond to whale after spotted hyenas. Why, Cap'n, these here critters in this bay ain't whales!" "Well, if they ain't whales, what are they?" asked the captain, in a husky voice. "Well," replied the mate, "I don't know rightly what they be; but I hev a strong notion they are a cross 'tween a sea-serpent and an alligator. Why, these Mussel-diggers will turn round in their tracks, Cap'n; and it's no use—you can't git these here Ripsacks without a good deal of boat-staving; but I'll bring my whale, or split the cedar, else my name ain't Cooper."

These incidents are only given as illustrative of whaling life in the lagoons of California; yet, with all the hazard pertaining to the fishery, such extremely daring efforts have been put forth by many whaling-masters to capture the California Gray, that we will, in justice to them, further mention that, where ships were of too heavy draught to pass the bars of several of the lagoons, they anchored near the breakers at the confluence of those inland waters, where they were exposed to the sweep of the wind and waves from seaward, remaining there the whole season, the boats passing and repassing the bars during fine weather, in order to reach the prey in their coverts, or were employed in attacking them around the shoals of the harbor's mouth, when the sea was comparatively smooth; but even there an occasional breaker would roll up its foaming crest, when the "fast" fish would run through it, as if by instinct, to rid itself of its relentless enemies; yet, in many cases, this endeavor to escape proved abortive, as the whalemen would "fleet aft" in their boats, in order to elevate their bows to meet the sea, when with one bound the danger was passed, without shipping much water, or what might be taken in was quickly bailed out, and, being then in the open sea, the work of capture would be renewed effectively.

AGAIN TO THE NORTH, AND HOME.

It is time to leave the coast of California, as the bay-whaling season is over; and the ship having been thoroughly cleaned, and a supply of wood taken on board, with perhaps a recruit of green turtles for a sea-stock of fresh meat, the anchor is weighed, and her prow is turned once more to frozen seas. The temperate latitudes are passed, and she emerges into a region of gloom, where fog, mist, and storm follow in quick succession, varied at long intervals with clear weather, which reveals a nearly ice-fettered ocean on one hand, and a snow-clad mountain coast on the other. A treacherous channel may be open between the shore and the main body of the ice, but it is thickly beset with floes; and among these the whale-ship threads her way along the Kamschatka shore, if bound to the Arctic, through Behring Sea and Strait, unless she is delayed by captures *en route*. At length, about mid-summer, having arrived at the icy barrier of the Arctic Ocean, the vessels cruise "off and on," along its margins, in quest of the Bowhead. Following the belt of open water, in their persistent search, ships sometimes pass far beyond Point Barrow; but it is not long before the autumnal gales drive them from this haunt, when they again return to warmer latitudes, and a port of recruit is sought, where all hands are refreshed; when, if the ship is not full, perhaps a cruise is made in the southern hemisphere, upon the coast of New Zealand, or Australia, and the Indian Ocean, before being fairly on their homeward passage. Many a ship, which would have otherwise returned with a broken voyage, has been filled by taking her last season on the New Zealand, or New Holland (as Australia was formerly called) ground. And, as has been mentioned in that portion of this work devoted to the chronological history of the American whale-fishery, the New London and Sag Harbor whalemen were noted for pursuing their prey in stormy latitudes; and when referring to the former, we have frequently heard the remark made, "O, they are under-water fellows!" Some thirty years ago, an incident transpired which vividly portrays the perseverance with which the fishery was then prosecuted. A New London ship, and another from Sag Harbor, having been unfortunate in their efforts to obtain a full fare of oil and bone upon the North-western Coast, resorted, as a last effort, to the coast of Australia, where the two captains met during a "gam" off Geographe Bay. This place being an open roadstead, exposed to the heaviest prevailing gales of that region, was considered an unsafe anchorage; but the two captains, with their officers, concluded if the ships could possibly ride them out, that during the intervals of moderate weather enough whales could be taken to fill both vessels. They all agreed that they had but little choice between going home with empty ships, and dragging ashore in a gale of wind. Accordingly, by agreement, both vessels anchored in the best positions, and, as a forlorn hope, began the battle—not only with the whales, but with the boisterous elements of the Indian Seas. All the ground-tackle of both vessels was laid down to the best advantage; and when a gale came on, heavy tackles were hooked to the cables, then led aft, and secured to the mainmast, to relieve the strain that would otherwise come on the windlass.   In this way a succession of severe blows were ridden out in safety ; and during the intervals of good weather, whaling was carried on with such vigor, that, before the season was over, both ships departed for home with full cargoes.

Right-whaling in the Indian Ocean, and the taking of Sea Elephants upon the shores of Kerguélen's Land, was a special branch of the oil commerce, which, to a great extent, was prosecuted by the New Londoners, their main dependence being the catch of Sea Elephants ; consequently there was but little attention paid to whaling while making the passage from home, and on their return, the vessels being full, precluded the usual routine of standing mast-heads, and the casual "lowering for whales."   When outward bound, however, a spirited chase, attack, and capture, would sometimes be made upon a shoal of Cachalots, although the boats were in no wise well prepared.   An episode of the kind occurred many years ago with a large ship on her way to Desolation.   When off the island of St. Helena, a school of Sperm Whales was descried ; but none of the boats were properly fitted, and some had not a line coiled.   Among the officers was one (a favorite, both among men and after-guard, as well as the owners at home) who was by his messmates familiarly dubbed "Jube."   Jube was a fine type of a mariner — muscular (or, as Jack expressed it, "well put up"), ready for an adventure of any kind, made the best of everything, could hold on to a Right Whale when running to windward around the Crozets (and the ship under double-reefs), and counted it a laughable joke if all hands in the boats were drenched to the skin "afore he could git the critter mauger."   At this time his boat had no line prepared ; but jumping below, he seized a new coil, tumbled it into his boat, and, with a single harpoon and lance, lowered away with the other boats in quick pursuit.   The whales were down ; but when they came up, his boat had "the chance."   "Pull ahead, my hearties !" he shouted ; "a fool for luck, and a poor man for babies !" and in a moment more they were fast.   The whale sounded ; and away went the line, tearing and smoking through the "chocks," till it became kinked and tangled, when, in his efforts to clear it, he was taken overboard, and disappeared beneath the waves ; but a moment after the harpoon loosened from the whale.   Slowly the crew hauled in the fouled line, bemoaning the loss of their officer ; but as they drew it in, they found him clinging to it, where it wound around his body. He was quickly released, and laid in the boat for dead, when they hastened to the ship, where the captain at once made every effort to restore him to life ; and, to the great joy of all, he was soon resuscitated.   He was well cared for, and, with a little rest, was all right again. On awaking from a refreshing sleep, a chum, in his expressions of joy at his recovery, said: "Well, Jube, how did you like it down there?" "O!" replied he, "it is a lonesome road to travel. There are neither mile-stones nor guide-boards that I could see!" Such was the reckless hardihood and bearing of those men whose lives were passed upon the ocean, or about the forbidding shores of the Antarctic regions.

In former days, when whaling was in its highest state of prosperity, much of the leisure time during those long voyages, and especially while on the homeward passage, was occupied in "scrimshawing," by those of a mechanical turn of mind, who manufactured useful or fancy articles from whalebone, or rare woods obtained from the tropical coasts. Canes, swifts, knitting-needles, stamps, bodkins, etc., were made from the jaws or teeth of the Sperm Whale; and the shells of the cocoa-nut were fashioned into unique drinking-cups. Sometimes a large plate of baleen would be finely polished, and the history of the prominent incidents of the voyage engraved upon it in hieroglyphical figures. A variety of articles were wrought out of wood, ivory, or shell, which were carefully put by for presents to relatives and friends at home. Many of these articles were fine specimens of workmanship. The smaller blocks, and the belaying-pins, of some of the first-class sperm whale-ships, were made of white whalebone; and sometimes the decks were, with infinite pains, inlaid with diamond-shaped pieces of ivory. Many of the junior officers and boat-steerers kept regular journals, similar to the ship's log-book, some of which were examples of good penmanship, giving a brief but clear account of what transpired on board every consecutive day during three or four years; while others were embellished with sketches of ships spoken, headlands and islands seen; and whenever a whale was taken, his full figure was stamped on the margin of the page recording the event; or if a whale was struck, and lost, his head only was represented; while for one that was chased, but not harpooned, the flukes and a portion of the small were figured.

But under the most propitious circumstances, the vast extent of ocean to be traversed rendered the homeward passage tedious; for buffeting the gales off Cape Horn, running down the trades, and contending with the equatorial squalls, with a deluge of rain, made up the general weather record; and when approaching the American coast in the Atlantic, one of those heavy blows which are often experienced would sometimes drive them far off to sea again, after having seen the land they had left years before. At last, however, the welcome cry of "Land ho!" is again heard from aloft; and soon a trim craft, with a number in her sail, and the Union jack flying at the main, gives the cheering and welcome news that the pilot is on the lookout. The ship is hove to, and he is soon alongside. He clambers up the vessel's side, vociferates his orders to trim sail, and assumes full command on board. All now becomes hurry and bustle, and a scene of joyful excitement ensues. If a full ship, the old iron cannon, which has been used as a signal-gun at night and in foggy weather on the whaling-grounds, is brought out to send forth a salute, at intervals, as the ship glides along the inland waters, until anchored in her destined port, and the voyage of years' duration is completed. Then comes the greeting of friends on board, or a restless desire to meet them on shore, there to pass a time of rest and recreation before again launching upon the deep for another expedition involving peril and uncertainty.

APPENDIX.

CATALOGUE

OF THE

CETACEA OF THE NORTH PACIFIC OCEAN

CATALOGUE

OF THE

CETACEA OF THE NORTH PACIFIC OCEAN,

WITH

OSTEOLOGICAL NOTES, AND DESCRIPTIONS OF SOME NEW FORMS;

WITH SPECIAL REFERENCE TO

THE FORMS DESCRIBED AND FIGURED IN THE FOREGOING MONOGRAPH OF PACIFIC
CETACEA, BY CAPTAIN C. M. SCAMMON, U. S. R. M.

By W. H. DALL,

SMITHSONIAN INSTITUTION.

THE object in the following Catalogue—besides bringing together condensed descriptions of the species of Cetaceans reported from the Pacific, and such of unknown habitat as might have come from that ocean, with references to such figures and fuller descriptions as may be readily consulted by the student—has been especially to determine, as exactly as possible, the genera and species described by the author in the preceding pages of this work, in order that his figures and contributions to our knowledge of the habits and natural history of those animals may have their fullest value for the scientific student of the group in question.

I have adopted in full the general groups eliminated by Professor Theodore Gill, of the Smithsonian Institution, in the *Catalogue of the Families of Mammals* published by the Institution ; a course warranted not less by the scientific standing of the author in question, than by the paucity of works of reference on this coast, and the confusion which has hitherto existed among the best naturalists in regard to the classification of the Cetacea. For convenience in reference I have also, for the most part, adopted the minor divisions used by Dr. J. E. Gray in his *Supplementary Catalogue of Seals and Whales in the British Museum*, 1871; though many of them appear to have a more subordinate value than that ascribed to them by that eminent naturalist. In quoting his works, for greater brevity, I have simply referred to them by their dates, namely: the *British Museum Catalogues* of 1850 and 1866; the *Synopsis of Whales and Dolphins*, 1868 (containing, with others, the plates of the *Zoölogy of the Erebus and Terror*, partially published in 1846); and the *Supplementary Catalogue* of 1871.

I have to thank Captain C. M. Scammon for placing all the material and information in his possession at my disposal, for examination; also, Professor S. F. Baird and Doctor Theodore Gill, of the Smithsonian Institution, for assistance. rendered in many ways, without which I should hardly have been able to complete this Catalogue.

I have also incorporated extremely brief notices of the material from which each species has been described, and the museum in which the specimens are preserved; "S. I." referring to the National Museum, in charge of the Smithsonian Institution at Washington. I have also endeavored to refer to all the remains of Cetacea preserved in the collections on the west coast.

Completeness is not claimed for this list; in fact, it can hardly hope to be attained for a considerable period, when the difficulties and expense connected with these researches are appreciated. Still, it is to be hoped that, in bringing together this material, something has been accomplished in rendering the path easier for subsequent students.

The references to plates opposite the specific name adopted, are to the plates and figures in the preceding portion of this volume.

Order **CETE.**

Suborder **Denticete.**

Superfamily DELPHINOIDEA.

Family DELPHINIDÆ.

Subfamily *DELPHINAPTERINÆ.*

Genus **Delphinapterus**, Lac.

Delphinapterus, Lacépède, Lilljeborg, Gill, 95.

Beluga, Gray, 1871, p. 94. Auctorum.

Delphinapterus catodon. Pl. xviii, fig. 1.

Beluga, of Scammon, Proc. Phil. Acad. 1869, p. 57.

Beluga catodon, Gray, 1866, p. 307, fig. 61; 1871, p. 94.

Physeter catodon, Linn., S. N. 107.

Delphinus leucas, Gmelin, S. N. 1232.

Delphinapterus beluga, Lacépède, Cét. 243, 1804.

Arctic Seas, Bering Sea, Ochotsk, Japan?

Pure white. Twelve to sixteen feet long. Skulls in B. M. Three skulls from Norton Sound, Dall, Coll. S. I. Doctor Gray, having examined skulls collected by Captain Kellett, R. N., from Bering Strait, unites the beluga of the western seas with that of the north of Europe. The teeth in specimens (80 or 90 in number) examined by me, in Norton Sound, Bering Sea, varied from $\frac{8}{8}$ to $\frac{11}{11}$; often being unequal in number on opposite sides.

Genus **Monodon**, Linn.

Monodon monoceros.

Monodon monoceros, Linn. Faun. Suec. 2, 16; S. N. i, 105.

Narwhal.

Arctic Seas.

Specimens are sometimes brought overland, across eastern Siberia, by the natives, and sold to traders in the Ochotsk Sea.

Subfamily *DELPHININÆ,* Gill, p. 95.

Genus **Delphinus**, Gray.

Delphinus, Gray, 1871, p. 67.

Delphinus Bairdii. Pl. xix, fig. 1.

D. Bairdii, Dal. Prel. Descr. Proc. Cal. Acad. Sci. v, Jan. 1873.

Back, posterior sides, fins and flukes, black. Anterior sides gray, with two narrow lateral white stripes. A white, lanceolate, belly-patch. Full descriptions of the colors and measurements of two female specimens taken by Captain Scammon, off Point Arguello, California, will be found in his monograph. Length, six feet and seven to nine inches. Dorsal falcate, immediately over the navel. Front of head prominently bulbous or convex beyond the even curve of the back of the head; a slight convexity below, behind the vent. Beak slender, elongated. The following are the dimensions of the cranium, in inches and decimals:

Length of skull in straight line	18 .76
Internal length of brain cavity	4 .40
Length of beak anterior to maxillary notches	11 .90
Length from tip of beak to anterior margin of superior nares	13 .40
Length from tip of beak to posterior notch of palate in the median line	13 .90
Length from tip of beak to posterior tooth	10 .50
Height of skull at vertex	6 .00
Greatest breadth at zygomatic process of squamosals	6 .95
Breadth at supra-orbital ridge	6 .10
Breadth between maxillary notches	3 .40
Breadth at middle of beak	2 .00
Breadth of the two premaxillaries at middle of beak	0 .90
Width of condyles	3 .70
Closest approximation of condyles below the foramen	0 .90
Height of foramen magnum	1 .40
Width of foramen magnum	1 .60
Entire length of ramus of lower jaw	15 .90
Tip to posterior edge of last tooth	9 .80
Length of symphysis	2 .10
Height of ramus at coronoid process	2 .75
Width between outsides of articular surfaces	6 .10
Width between posterior teeth	2 .10
Length from tip to anterior notch of dental foramen	11 .40
Length of largest teeth, sharply conical	0 .56
Greatest diameter of same	0 .13
Length from tip of beak to superior transverse ridge behind the frontals	15 .60

Teeth in the specimen before me, $\frac{43}{44}$ by $\frac{43}{44}$. The anterior six on each side above are barely indicated, and do not project above the gums; the next four on each side, though projecting, are very small. Below, 47 teeth on each side are plainly visible, and there is room for four or five more between the most anterior tooth and the end of the symphysis. The teeth are very sharply conical, rather wider transversely than in the direction of the ramus, and slightly incurved at the tips. The number in the other specimen is reported to have been $\frac{54}{46}$ on each side.

The principal features of the cranium, as compared with the other species of the genus *Delphinus* as restricted by Gray (1871), are the great length of the beak as compared with the brain-case, and the remarkably deep channels in the maxillary bones on each side of the palatal ridge, which actually overlaps on each side to the extent of 0.2 of an inch. Six and a half inches behind the end of the beak, a groove commences in the median line of the palate, which widens anteriorly, exposing the premaxillaries near the end of the beak. Behind the point mentioned, the palate rapidly rises as a narrow ridge (from 0.7 of an inch to one inch in width), evenly rounded on the edges and slightly convex in the middle, contracting a little in width after passing the posterior end of the tooth line; its edges overlapping the lateral channels, and its inferior face extending at its junction with the palatines to the distance of 1.2 inch below the superior arch of the maxillaries. A groove extends posteriorly between the palatines and pterygoids, terminating in a slight notch between the latter, which notch is a little posterior to the posterior termination of the narial septum. The pterygoid and tympanic bones are wanting in this specimen, with the exception of those portions of the former which form the deeply-notched lateral walls of the posterior nares, and which are continuous with the very broad lateral expansions of the basi-occipital. The occipital condyles are nearly an inch apart at their closest approximation below; the foramen magnum is large, rounded below, and angular, rather than notched, above. There is a sharp vertical lamina on the inner side of the supra-occipital, extending forward in the median line, nearly an inch from the inner surface of the supra-occipital, and terminating below about half an inch above the foramen in a small triangular tentorium, from which slight laterally extending ridges indicate the boundary of the cerebellar fossa.

The superior aspect of the cranium presents no very distinctive features. Compared with *Clymenia microps*, Gray, as figured in the *Zoölogy of the Erebus and Terror*, pl. 25 (also, in *Synopsis of Whales and Dolphins*, 4to., Gray, 1868, pl. 25), the following differences are noted : The premaxillæ are narrower, more elevated above the maxillæ; the nasal triangle extends half an inch beyond the posterior end of the tooth line instead of falling about as far behind it, and is much more acute in front in *D. Bairdii*. The posterior angle of the supra-orbital process in *D. Bairdii* is much less prominent, when viewed from above, than in *microps*, and the extension of the maxillaries over the jugals is less elevated, being evenly rounded off at the sides and in front. The supra-occipital is pressed in above the condyles, and the superior portion of it is more roundly convex than in *microps*. The proportion of the beak to the brain-case is greater than in *Clymenia stenorhynchus*, Gray, and the beak is wider, both at the notches and anteriorly. The laterally channeled palate would in any case distinguish it from the species of *Clymenia* and *Steno*, to which it bears a superficial resemblance. In the anterior third of the beak, the premaxillæ evenly slope off toward the maxillæ in the same plane, and are separated by the mesethmoid cartilage. Behind this, however, the premaxillæ are solidly united, and much more elevated above the maxillæ, forming a ridge with nearly parallel and vertical sides, rounded off above, and attaining a maximum height above the maxillæ of 0.43 of an inch. The nasal triangle is evenly excavated, divided by an open suture terminating in a notch above the narial septum. The mesethmoid plate is provided with a submedian ridge, and terminates above in three points. The nasals are knob-like and rounded transverse, forming the vertex of the skull.

CERVICAL VERTEBRÆ. — These are coössified into three groups, as hereafter mentioned; but it is probable that individuals vary in this respect to some extent. The first mass has a total diameter, from point to point of the transverse processes, of 5.35 inches; and from the middle lower anterior edge of the atlas to the bifurcation of the spinous process of 3.65 inches. The neural arch is 1.10 inch high and 1.53 inch wide; the extreme width across the condylar facets is 3.3 inches. The centrum of the third cervical is 1.3 inch wide by 1.0 inch high. The neural arch (incomplete at the top), 0.92 inch high by 1.0 inch wide; the extreme width from point to point of the vertebra is 1.65 inch. The fifth cervical has a total width between the points of the lower transverse processes of 1.57 inch. The height of the centrum is 1.1 inch; of the neural arch, 0.8 inch; the width of the centrum is 1.15 inch; of the neural arch, 0.89 inch. The length of that part of the vertebral column composed of third, fourth, fifth, sixth, and seventh cervicals is 1.2 inch, and that part composed of the atlas and axis, 1.0 inch more. The neural spine of the seventh cervical is 0.8 inch long, and the width from point to point of the transverse processes, 3.65 inches; of the second thoracic, the spine is 1.6 inch, and the width 3.55 inches.

The first mass consists of the atlas and axis solidly coössified both by their spines and bodies, so that the only vestige of separation is an ovate and somewhat oblique opening between the pedicels of the arches. The inferior portion of the atlas is much produced forward, giving an oblique appearance to the whole bone, which is of an approximately triangular shape. Its arch is transversely ovate, with a broad triangular space between the condylar facets. The first spinal nerve enters by a shallow groove over the latter. The transverse processes appertaining to the atlas are rather long and obliquely flattened above and below, with a slight knob, indicating a superior transverse process, just above them. These two processes are separated by a narrow groove from two nodular projections which indicate the corresponding parts in the axis. A slight ridge exists on the inferior surface of the centrum. The neural spine is very broad, stout, and moderately long; it tapers from before backward, and has a stout, blunt, bifid, posterior termination. The anterior face is broadly triangular, the base of the triangle (forming the superior portion of the neural arch) being straight. The spine is concave below and grooved throughout its extent; the triangular portion of it overshadowing the arches of the third and fourth vertebræ. The pedicels of the axis are very slender.

The centra of the third and fourth vertebræ are coössified, but not the arches. The summit of the arch in the third is incomplete in this specimen, and the pedicels in this and the succeeding cervicals are slender and compressed. In the third and fourth, the superior transverse processes are only slightly indicated, and the inferior are absent; the centra are slightly pointed below and flattened above, though generally rotundate.

The fifth and sixth cervicals are ankylosed by their centra and inferior transverse processes, and the sixth by its centrum to the seventh cervical, forming the third mass previously mentioned.

In the fifth and sixth, short inferior transverse processes are developed, though the superior ones are insignificant. The centra are more squarely shaped than in the preceding. There are no spinous processes, but the superior portion of the arches is rather pointed. The planes of the zygapophyses are nearly horizontal, and the arches are not coössified. The pedicels of the seventh cervical are much broader, and long recurved superior transverse and spinous processes are developed, though the inferior transverse processes are barely indicated. Two rounded knobs, which are nearer the summit of the centrum than the processes of the preceding cervicals, serve as points of articulation for the head of the first rib. In the first thoracic, this tubercle appears to be missing, though it re-appears on the second. Both the first and second thoracic have strong, stout, superior transverse processes, with large and prominent facets for the tubercular articulations of the ribs. The vertebræ rapidly increase in size and the spinous processes in length, and the centra assume a more rounded outline.

Two specimens of this species were obtained October 29th, 1872, by Captain C. M. Scammon. The entire skeleton of one specimen, and the skull and cervical vertebræ of the other, above described, were preserved. The former is now in the Mus. S. I. Of the species included under the genus *Delphinus*, as restricted by Gray (*Supl. Cat.* 1871, pp. 68–9), *D. longirostris* is entirely black, of different proportions, with the posterior part of the palate keeled instead of grooved, and the triangle extending only to the tooth line instead of beyond it. (Reported from Japan.) *D. major* has the grooves on each side of the palate, "very wide and rather shallow, scarcely extending behind the hinder half of the beak." (Habitat unknown.) *D. Forsteri* is differently colored and proportioned. (Norfolk Island.) *D. obliquidens*, Gill, belongs to another genus. The remainder are all Atlantic species.

Of other species of unknown or Pacific habitats, which have been described from drawings, or of which the skull is unknown, and to some of which this species might be suspected to belong, *D. Novæ Zelandiæ* is differently colored (though the distribution of the color is somewhat similar), and has a short beak; the pectorals are white and the flukes slate color; *D. obscurus*, Gray, to which Peale's *Phocæna australis* and D'Orbigny's *D. bivittatus* have been referred by Cassin and Gray, belongs to an entirely different group. None of Peale's other species resemble this one at all, and after long and careful consideration, I am forced to the conclusion that the species is undescribed; and it is with great pleasure that I have followed the request of Captain Scammon, and dedicated it to Professor S. F. Baird, of the Smithsonian Institution, to whose never-tiring courtesy and unfailing liberality nearly every American naturalist is more or less indebted.

Delphinus longirostris.

D. longirostris, Gray, 1866, p. 241; 1868, p. 5; 1871, p. 68. Schlegel, F. Jap., pl. 24.

Japan?

Eighty-one inches long. Black, with large high dorsal. Skull, 22 inches; beak, 13¾ inches; teeth, $\frac{55}{54}$. Stuffed specimen, Cape of Good Hope; B. M. Skull, Malabar; Mus. Paris. Drawing, Japan; Schlegel.

Delphinus major.

> *D. major*, Gray, 1866, p. 397; 1868, p. 5; 1871, p. 68.

Habitat?

Skull, 21 inches; beak, 12½ inches; width at notch, 4¼ inches. Teeth, $\frac{44}{47}$, five in an inch. Palate grooves very wide and rather shallow. Skull only, B. M.

Genus **Clymenia**, Gray.

> *Clymenia*, Gray, 1868, p. 6; 1871, p. 69.
>
> *Clymene*, Gray, 1866, p. 249.

Type *D. clymene*, Gray, 1866, p. 249.

Clymenia alope.

> *C. alope*, Gray, 1866, p. 252; 1868, p. 6, pl. 32; 1871, p. 70.

Cape Horn.

Cranium, 16¾ inches; beak, 10¾ inches; width at notch, 3½ inches. Teeth, $\frac{48}{46}$. Skull only, Mus. Warwick.

Clymenia stenorhynchus.

> *Delphinus stenorhynchus*, Gray, 1866, pp. 240, 396.
>
> *C. stenorhynchus*, Gray, 1868, p. 6; 1871, p. 69.

Habitat?

Cranium, 18 inches; beak, 12 inches; width at notch, 3 inches. Teeth, $\frac{53}{53}$. Like *C. microps*, but larger, with proportionally longer beak. Skull only, B. M.

Clymenia dorides.

> *Tursio dorcides*, Gray, 1866, p. 400.
>
> *C. dorides*, Gray, 1868, p. 6; 1871, p. 71.

Habitat?

Skull thick and heavy; beak once and one-third the length of the brain-case; twice and one-third the width at the notch. Palate flat. Teeth, $\frac{43}{43}$, slender, five in an inch. Skull only, B. M.

Clymenia obscura.

> *Delphinus Fitzroyi*, Waterhouse.
>
> *D. bivittatus*, D'Orbigny.
>
> *Phocœna australis*, Peale, Zoöl. U. S. Ex. Exp., pl. 6, fig. 2, 1848.
>
> *Tursio obscurus*, Gray, 1866, pp. 264, 400.
>
> *C. obscura*, Gray, 1868, p. 6, pl. 16; 1871, p. 71, fig. 3.

Cape of Good Hope, South Pacific.

Black, with oblique diverging streaks at the sides; beneath, whitish. Length, 15 feet. Skull, 14 inches. Teeth, $\frac{24}{24}$ to $\frac{31}{31}$. Full material, B. M.

Clymenia æsthenops.

> *Delphinus æsthenops*, Cope, Proc. Phil. Acad. 1865, p. 201.
>
> *C. æsthenops*, Gray, 1871, p. 72.

Habitat?

Cranium, 15 inches; beak, 9 inches; width at notch, 3.3 inches. Teeth, $\frac{36}{36}$? to $\frac{36}{42}$. Skull only, Mus. Peabody Academy of Science, Salem, Mass.

Clymenia crotaphisca.

> *Delphinus crotaphiscus*, Cope, l. c., 1865, p. 203.
> *C. crotaphiscus*, Gray, 1871, p. 72.

Habitat?

Cranium, 16 inches; beak, 10 inches, flat; width at notch, $3\frac{3}{4}$ inches. Teeth, $\frac{4}{43}$. Temporal fossa small; a keel in front of superior nares. Skull only, Mus. Peabody Academy.

Clymenia longidens.

> *Delphinus longidens*, Cope, Proc. Phil. Acad. 1866, p. 295.

Habitat?

Teeth, $\frac{30}{27}$. Skull, 15.25 inches. Beak, to maxillary notches, 8.25 inches. Breadth at notch, 3.55 inches. Skull only, S. I.

Professor Cope, in criticising Doctor Gray's arrangement, suggests that *Steno, Delphinus, Lagenorhynchus*, and *Tursio* can form but one genus if further characters can not be brought forward. While this criticism might be somewhat justified by the confused arrangement of the Catalogue of 1866, yet it would seem as if that of 1871 to some extent remedied the difficulty, and that the groups there indicated are natural ones, and recognizable, though perhaps some of them are of less value than supposed by Doctor Gray. In this new light Professor Cope's view would hardly seem tenable.

Clymenia plagiodon.

> *Delphinus (Tursio) plagiodon*, Cope, l. c., p. 296.

Habitat?

Skull, 17 inches. Beak to notch, 9.8 inches. Width at notch, 3.55 inches. Greatest width of skull, 7.25 inches. Teeth, $\frac{3}{4}$. Triangle advancing a little before the last tooth. Resembles Gray's figure of *C. doris*. Skull only, S. I.

Genus **Tursiops,** Gervais.

> *Tursiops*, Gervais, Mammif., p. 323.
> *Tursio*, Gray, 1866, p. 254.
> Type *D. tursio*, Linn.

Tursiops Gillii. Outline, p. 102.

> *T. Gillii*, Dall, Prel. Descr. Proc. Cal. Acad. v, January, 1873.
> *Cowfish*, Scammon, Proc. Phil. Acad. 1869, p. 45.

Monterey, California.

Dull black, lighter on the belly. Dorsal low, falcate. Teeth, $\frac{23}{22}$ to $\frac{24}{23}$?

A lower jaw of the present species, which is the only portion of the animal yet collected by Captain Scammon, has twenty-two teeth on each side. The rami are solid and strong, especially their anterior halves. The symphysis is short, extending backward as far as the fifth tooth. The gonys is more produced downward than in any of the species figured by Gray, and is evenly rounded upward in front. The ramus has the least height about the middle of the tooth line, which rises before and behind. The anterior six teeth are smaller than the others, and much more incurved. The teeth are solid and conical, with the tips attenuated and sharply pointed, which accounts for the ease with which they may become truncated. The outer margins of the alveoli are remarkably rough, being produced in arborescent points resembling the septa of some ammonites. The gonys is somewhat keeled. The condyles are broad, of a rounded triangular shape, with the inner edges obliquely inclined to the vertical plane of the ramus. The measurements, in inches and decimals, are as follow :

Length from end of beak to condyles.. 16 .80
Length from end of beak to end of coronoid process........................ 15 .80
Length from end of beak to end of tooth line............................... 9 .30
Length from end of beak to inner notch of dental foramen................... 11 .00
Length of symphysis.. 2 .00
Width between outer edges of condyles...................................... 9 .75
Width between inner corners of condyles.................................... 6 .50
Width between two posterior teeth.. 3 .50
Width between teeth at posterior end of symphysis.......................... 1 .40
Width between anterior teeth... 0 .75
Height of ramus at coronoid process.. 4 .40
Height of ramus at posterior tooth... 2 .25
Height of ramus at twelfth pair of teeth................................... 1 .50
Height of ramus at middle of symphysis..................................... 1 .70
Thickness of ramus at twelfth pair of teeth................................ 0 .85
Height of largest tooth above alveolus..................................... 0 .80
Height of smallest tooth above alveolus.................................... 0 .42
Transverse diameter of larger teeth.. 0 .38
Diameter in the plane of the ramus... 0 .33

The angle at which the rami meet behind the symphysis is quite acute. The anterior end of the symphysis from above appears bluntly rounded, and has a narrow median groove.

This species does not appear to have been described, and though the material at hand is unfortunately very slender, I have applied to it the name of *Tursiops Gillii*. The specimen was obtained at Monterey, California, in 1871. The hardly-worn appearance of the teeth suggests that it was a young animal, though the bones are thoroughly solidified. The only other species which may be found in the books, from the Pacific or its vicinity, is the *T. catalania*, Gray, N. W. Australia, and it is described as being lead-colored.

Genus **Cephalorhynchus,** F. Cuvier.

Cephalorhynchus, F. Cuvier, Cétac., p. 158.
Eutropia, Gray, P. Z. S. 1862, p. 145 ; 1866, p. 262 ; 1871, p. 75.

Cephalorhynchus Eutropia.

Delphinus Eutropia, Gray, P. Z. S. 1849, p. 1.
Eutropia Dickiei, Gray, P. Z. S. 1866, p. 215 ; 1868, p. 7, pl. 34 ; 1871, p. 75.
Tursio Eutropia, Gray, 1866, p. 262.

Coast of Chile, South Pacific Ocean.

Skull, 15 inches ; beak, 8 inches ; width at notch, 3.5 inches. Sides of skull bent down behind the notch. Teeth, $\frac{34}{34}$, five or six in an inch. Skull only, Coll. Dickie.

Some one of the species described from drawings, and of which the skull is unknown, may be identical with this.

Genus **Lagenorhynchus**, Gray.
Lagenorhynchus, Gray, Zoöl. E. and T., 1846, p. 34; 1850, p. 97.

Section *Electra*, Gray.
Electra, Gray, 1866, p. 268; 1871, p. 76.

Lagenorhynchus electra.
>   *L. electra,* Gray (1846), 1866, p. 268.
>   *Electra obtusa,* Gray, 1868, p. 7, pl. 13; 1871, p. 76.

Habitat?
Skull, 17.5 inches; beak, 9.75 inches; width at notch, 5.5 inches.   Teeth, $\frac{25}{24}$, four in an inch.
Skull only, B. M.

Lagenorhynchus asia.
>   *L. asia,* Gray, 1866, p. 269.
>   *Electra asia,* Gray, 1868, p. 7, pl. 14; 1871, p. 76.

Habitat?
Skull, 16.75 inches; beak, 9 inches; width at notch, 4.75 inches.   Teeth, $\frac{24}{24}$.   Skull only,
B. M.

Lagenorhynchus clanculus.
>   *L. clanculus,* Gray, 1866, p. 271.
>   *Electra clancula,* Gray, 1868, p. 7, pl. 35; 1871, p. 77.

South Pacific, New Zealand.
Skull, 14.5 inches; beak, 7.25 inches; width at notch, 4.75 inches.   Teeth, $\frac{33}{33}$.   Skeleton and
skulls, B. M.

Lagenorhynchus thicolea.
>   *L. thicolea,* Gray, 1866, p. 271.
>   *Electra thicolea,* Gray, 1868, p. 7, pl. 36; 1871, p. 77.

West coast of North America.
Skull, 14.5 inches; beak, 8.33 inches; width at notch, 3.9 inches.   Teeth, $\frac{40}{40}$?   Skull only,
B. M.
Compare *Clymenia crotaphisca,* Cope.   This is very likely to be one of the species described
from drawings by Peale.

Section *Leucopleurus*, Gray.
Leucopleurus, Gray, P. Z. S. 1866, p. 216; 1868, p. 7; 1871, p. 78.

Lagenorhynchus obliquidens.   Plate xix, fig. 2.
>   *L. obliquidens,* Gill, Proc. Phil. Acad. 1865, p. 177.
>   *Delphinus obliquidens,* Cope, Proc. Phil. Acad. 1869, p. 21; Gray, 1871, p. 69.
>   *Striped* or *Common Porpoise* of Scammon.

California.
Not the "Bottle-nosed Grampus" of Scammon, as supposed by Cope, *loc. cit.*
I have been able to identify this species by means of photographs of Professor Gill's typical
specimen, which were kindly sent me by Professor Baird.   It differs, however, in some particulars,
from those I have examined.   The skull is a little larger and longer, the pterygoids are less
pointed, the temporal fossa smaller, and the edges of the triangle are higher and more extended

laterally, than in the specimens which I have seen. The teeth are more numerous ($\frac{34}{31}$), and the occipital condyles less rounded and prominent, but larger. It is quite possible that this skull may be that of a male. Those which I have examined were both of females. I consider the differences as at most no more than sexual, and probably only individual peculiarities; and I have no doubt whatever of the identity of Captain Scammon's species with that described by Professor Gill.

It is evidently the most abundant species on the coast of California, and varies considerably in size with age. It is very close to *L. leucopleurus* of the Atlantic.

The following are the measurements of two crania, in inches and decimals:

	No. 1.	No. 2.
Length of skull in a straight line	16 .00	15 .50
Internal length of brain cavity	5 .00	5 .00
Length of beak before the maxillary notches	8 .00	8 .20
Tip of beak to anterior margin of superior nares	10 .25	10 .00
Tip of beak to posterior notch of palate	9 .75	?
Tip of beak to posterior tooth	7 .40	7 .75
Height of skull at vertex	6 .75	5 .50
Greatest breadth at zygomatic process of squamosals	8 .20	7 .50
Breadth at supra-orbital ridge	7 .20	6 .30
Breadth between maxillary notches	4 .60	4 .00
Breadth at middle of beak	3 .40	2 .80
Width of condyles	4 .00	3 .25
Closest approximation of condyles below the foramen magnum	0 .12	0 .18
Height of foramen magnum	1 .35	1 .30
Width of foramen magnum	1 .35	1 .50
Entire length of ramus of lower jaw	13 .00	12 .00?
Tip to posterior edge of last tooth in lower jaw	7 .50	6 .75
Length of symphysis	1 .30	1 .00
Height of ramus at coronoid process	3 .00	2 .60
Height of ramus at four inches from tip of anterior end	1 .00	0 .95
Width between outsides of articular surfaces	7 .25	6 .40
Width between posterior teeth	3 .50	3 .50
Length from tip of beak to superior transverse ridge behind frontals	13 .00	12 .00
Length from tip of ramus to anterior notch of inferior dental foramen,	9 .00	7 .75
Greatest width of premaxillaries	3 .75	?
Width of premaxillaries at middle of beak	2 .10	1 .60

The surface of the beak in No. 1 is moderately and quite regularly arched from side to side, no grooves separating the maxillæ and premaxillæ. The nasal triangle is nearly plane, but elevated, and its surface rough; behind, it gradually ascends; before, it is gradually incurved, and is continued as a narrow internal margin to the premaxillæ, to the anterior fourth of the beak; its greatest width is less than half the width of the cranium. The mesethmoid groove is wide, and scarcely contracted in the middle. The supra-occipital projects forward, nearly or quite touching the nasals. The temporal fossæ project far backward.

The teeth are $\frac{29}{29}$ in number, elongated and boldly curved, about four in an inch. The occiput is deeply impressed above the condyles. The mesethmoid plate is sharply pointed above, and divided into three lobes behind the narial openings, by perpendicular sutures, which are evident for an inch and a half vertically. The mesethmoid is evident for nearly an inch between the premaxillæ in front of the superior nares. The pterygoids are obtusely keeled below, but not at the sides, and deeply roundly notched laterally. The palate is flat, constricted slightly at the palatines, and somewhat concave in the anterior half of the jaw. The periotics are wanting. A very peculiar feature of the cranium is the enormous development of the tentorium. The septum above it projects into the brain-case nearly two inches. From the base of this septum, half an inch above the foramen magnum, the broad arch of the tentorium, as long in its axial diameter as the septum, extends on each side a little farther than the upper exterior angles of the condyles, thence giving out a triangular wing on each side, which, attenuating as it descends, reaches the floor of the brain cavity in advance of the opening between the alisphenoid and ex-occipital, and is ankylosed with the former. The cerebellar fossa is thus almost completely inclosed, communicating with the cerebral fossa only by an opening in the front of the arch but little larger than the foramen magnum, and by the narrow openings between the outer edges of the wings of the tentorium, bounded below by the alisphenoid, and laterally by the ex-occipital wall. The septum ceases abruptly in front, below the frontal and supra-occipital suture. A ridge from the front of the tentorial wings is coössified with the orbito-sphenoid, above the sphenoidal fissure; the latter in this species being posterior to and distinct from the foramen rotundum, which opens into the cerebral cavity.

In No. 2, the dimensions were constantly smaller, the skull belonging to a younger, though fully adult individual. The teeth were $\frac{30}{29}$, the tip of the lower jaws being mutilated. The tentorium presented the same features as in No. 1, and the skull offered no special peculiarities not common to the other.

The scapula and cervical vertebræ of a third specimen, of which the entire skeleton was preserved, offered the following peculiarities: The external face of the scapula is flattened, slightly excavated in the middle, and with a slight ridge behind. The prescapular fossa is inconspicuous, but has a width of three-quarters of an inch on the outer face of the scapula, above the acromion. The latter is ∾ shaped, notched above behind, with a projecting process below in front. The upper anterior corner is connected with the anterior angle of the prescapular fossa by a strong ligament; the anterior termination of the acromion is incurved, and externally convex. The coracoid is triangular, with the distal edge thickened, anteriorly excavated, and knobbed at the corners. The external surface is concave. The glenoid cavity is sub-rotundate; the post-scapular edge is evenly rounded in a sigmoid curve. Beyond the upper posterior corner a triangular mass of cartilage extends beyond the bone, an inch in its greatest width. The inner face of the scapula is flattened, with three or four narrow low ridges radiating from the glenoid border. The inner surface of the coracoid is convex, and of the acromion concave. The measurements are as follow, in inches and decimals:

Greatest length of scapula..	9 .50
Greatest length of acromion..	3 .00
Greatest length of coracoid	2 .25
Greatest diameter of glenoid cavity...	1 .30
Glenoid cavity to anterior angle...	6 .25
Glenoid cavity to superior border	6 .00
Glenoid cavity to posterior angle..	6 .00
Glenoid cavity to anterior angle of acromion...................................	4 .50
Glenoid cavity to anterior angle of coracoid...................................	3 .00
Glenoid cavity to posterior angle of coracoid..................................	2 .00

The cervical vertebræ offer some differences from those of *Delphinus Bairdii.* The atlas and axis are solidly coössified by both body and spines; the others are all free, though whether in aged individuals this condition continues, is a matter of doubt. It is probable, from the generally abnormal condition of the cervical vertebræ in the Cetacea, that comparatively wide variations in the amount of ankylosis may obtain in different individuals of the same species, and also in the same individual at different ages. The bones in this individual are larger and stronger than in *D. Bairdii,* but the spinal canal is proportionately smaller. The canal of the first spinal nerve, which in *D. Bairdii* is a shallow groove behind the upper edge of the condylar facets, is here (by a slender process extending upward and backward from that edge, and coalescing with the anterior base of the spinous process) converted into a foramen. The spine is keeled and convex below, instead of excavated, and flat, with a very narrow median keel, above. The spine is broader, and not distinctly bifurcated. The lower transverse processes in the axis, instead of being obsolete, as in *D. Bairdii*, are here produced into sharp points. A median triangular area on the lower surface of the centrum (wanting in *D. Bairdii*) is here very prominent, and continued backward by a strong, deep keel. In the posterior vertebræ, all except the third are provided with a more or less evident spinous process, while in *D. Bairdii* none except the seventh shows any spine. In the present species the cervicals behind the axis are more nearly equal in size than in the former, and the upper and lower transverse processes are more strongly developed. In the third, fourth, and fifth cervicals in the median line, below and in front of the base of the neural spine, projects a small triangular prolongation of the bone, connected with the axis in the third, and with the preceding vertebræ in the fourth and fifth, by a small but unmistakable articular surface or facet. The pedicels of the neural canal are more arched laterally than in *D. Bairdii*, giving the passage a more flattened appearance than in that species. The following measurements will facilitate a comparison:

Coössified atlas and axis, extreme width, 6.0 inches; from the middle of the lower anterior edge to the posterior point of the spine, 4.1 inches. Height of neural arch, 1.0 inch; width, 1.5 inch. Extreme width of condylar facets, 3.6 inches. Third vertebra: width of centrum, 1.58 inch; of neural arch, 1.15 inch; height of centrum, 1.42 inch; of arch, 0.8 inch. Extreme width of vertebra between the points of the transverse processes, 2.25 inches. Length of that part of the vertebral column consisting of the five posterior cervicals, 1.6 inch. Atlas and axis, 1.35 inch more. The neural spine of the seventh cervical is 0.93 inch, and the extreme width between the points of the transverse processes is 3.75 inches. The spinous processes of the fourth, fifth, and sixth cervicals average about 0.3 inch in length. The head of the first rib articulates with the body of the seventh cervical, as in *D. Bairdii*.

The animal is rather thick in proportion to its length; black above, with a strongly falcate dorsal. Below, white, to the edge of the patch passing from the lower lip below the pectorals and terminating a short distance behind the vent. A broad gray smouch on each side above the line of the black color, and interrupted about the middle of the animal on each side; the edges of the gray are ill defined. The posterior edges of the pectorals and dorsal are also grayish. Length of animal, 7 feet and 3 inches; breadth of flukes, 2 feet; tip of snout to anterior edge of dorsal, 3 feet.

Full descriptions of the colors and full measurements are given by Captain Scammon in the preceding monograph. A complete skeleton and the additional skull above described were obtained from two female specimens taken at Monterey, November 20th, 1872; besides which, one other skull is in Captain Scammon's possession, and one in the collection of the California Academy of Sciences.

Lagenorhynchus albirostratus?

Delphinus albirostratus? Peale, U. S. Ex. Exp. 1848; pl. 6, fig. 2.
D. ceruleo-albus (Mayen) Cassin, l. c., p. 31, pl. vi, fig. 2.

Pacific Ocean, latitude 2° south, longitude 174° west. Peale.

Blue gray, with small vermicular white spots. End of snout white; dorsal nearest the head. Six feet and seven inches long; teeth, $\frac{40}{40}$. No specimens; described from drawing (Peale).

This species is referred by Cassin (as I think, erroneously) to *D. ceruleo-albus*, Mayen, a south Atlantic species; and to *D. Chamissonis*, Wiegm., by Gray.

Captain Marston, of the schooner *Maggie Johnstone*, on a voyage from Tahiti to San Francisco, obtained a specimen of a porpoise which is not improbably the species described by Peale. He informed me that the animal was gray, lighter below and darker above; that some of the same "school" had white noses, but in others the snout was light gray. The dorsal is rather small. The specimen was obtained in latitude 13° north. The skull presents intermediate characters between several of Gray's sections, and agrees with none of the skulls described or figured in the works accessible to me. It is in the collection of the California Academy of Sciences.

The following are its dimensions, in inches and decimals:

Length of skull in straight line... 14 .00
Internal length of brain cavity.. 4 .25
Length of beak anterior to maxillary notches .... 8 .00
Length from tip of beak to anterior margin of superior nares................. 6 .30
Length from tip of beak to posterior notch of palate...................... 9 .20
Length from tip of beak to posterior tooth................................ 6 .75
Height of skull at vertex.. 5 .40
Greatest breadth at zygomatic process of squamosals....................... 6 .50
Breadth at supra-orbital ridge.. 5 .50
Breadth between maxillary notches .... 3 .25
Breadth at middle of beak... 1 .75
Width of condyles... 3 .20
Closest approximation of condyles below the foramen magnum................ 0 .22
Height of foramen magnum. .... 1 .40
Width of foramen magnum... 1 .50
Entire length of ramus of lower jaw... 11 .90
Tip to posterior edge of last tooth in lower jaw........................... 7 .00
Length of symphysis... 1 .50
Height of ramus at coronoid process... 2 .20
Height of ramus 3.5 inches from tip of anterior end........................ 0 .60
Width between outsides of articular surfaces............................... 5 .20
Width between posterior teeth... 1 .70
Length from tip of beak to superior transverse ridge behind frontals.......... 11 .25
Length from tip to anterior notch of inferior dental foramen................ 7 .70
Greatest width of premaxillaries.. 2 .50
Width of premaxillaries at middle of beak................................... 0 .90

Teeth, $\frac{38}{38}$, six in an inch, subcylindrical, conical, recurved at tip, sharply pointed. Coronoid process, slender, inconspicuous; jaws thin and light. Anterior three teeth minute. Premaxillæ separated widely by the mesethmoid cartilage, approximating more nearly at the middle of the beak, hard, rather flat in front. Beak rather flat, evenly shelving at the sides. Nasal triangle passing an inch before the hinder tooth, rough anteriorly, subcarinate in the middle behind, on the left side not reaching the nasals. Maxillæ sharply turned up before the notch, evenly rounded off behind it. All the bones of the left side a little shorter behind, and the left nasal smaller and in advance of the right. Brain cavity larger on the left side. Septum and tentorium small and inconspicuous. Lateral keels of the pterygoids flattened. Vomer extended back as far as the posterior edge of the zygomatic process of the squamosals. Posterior ridge of the temporal fossa obsolete. Mesethmoid appearing between the maxillæ for $1\frac{3}{4}$ inch in the middle of the beak, and succeeded by the premaxillæ, to the end of the beak. Palatines separated by a slight groove. Lateral notches of the pterygoids, narrow, small. The portion of the basi-occipital gutter formed by the vomer and pterygoids, narrower than the inferior nares. Palate flattened above, impressed before the palatines, with a tendency toward lateral grooves at the outer edges. Skull evidently of a young animal.

Genus? **Feresa,** Gray.

Feresa, Gray, P. Z. S. 1870, p. 77; 1871, p. 78.

Feresa intermedia.

Feresa intermedia, Gray, 1871, p. 78.

Orca intermedia, Gray, 1866, p. 283; 1868, p. 8, pl. 8.

Habitat?

Skull resembling *Orca*, but only 14 inches long; beak, 7 inches; width at notch, $4\frac{1}{2}$ inches. Teeth, $\frac{11}{11}$. Skull only, B. M.

Species incertæ sedis.

The following species are known only from drawings, or very insufficient materials; most of them (unless we except those of Mr. Peale, whose delineations have proved in at least one case to be remarkably accurate) can hardly hope for identification, and it is very probable that many of them are identical with species described from skulls only. It is of course impossible to determine the genus of any of them; and it would be a relief, if they, together with the species erected on aboriginal pottery and carvings, and drawings of Chinese and Japanese artists (!), could be wiped away from our books altogether.

DELPHINUS ALBIMANUS, Peale, Zoöl. U. S. Ex. Exp., ed. i, p. 33, 1848; Cassin, Mamm. ditto, p. 29, pl. vi, fig. 1.

Coast of Chile.
Head, back, and flukes, black; sides, tawny; belly, white; top of pectorals, white. Length, 6 feet 6 inches. ♀ Snout to eye, 12 inches. Teeth, $\frac{43}{44}$.
No specimens known. Referred to *D. Novæ-Zelandiæ* by Cassin, but not by Gray.

DELPHINUS FORSTERI, Gray, 1868, p. 6, pl. 24.

New Caledonia.
Rust colored above; beneath, white; a small white spot on the disk of the dorsal and pectoral fins. Six feet long. Teeth, $\frac{44}{44}$. No specimens known. Described from Forster's drawing. Perhaps the same as *C. microps*, Gray.

DELPHINUS LATERALIS, Peale, l. c., p. 35, pl. 8, fig. 1, 1848; Cassin, Mamm. ditto, p. 32, pl. vii, fig. 1.

Pacific Ocean, latitude 13° north, longitude 161° west.
Dark above, purplish gray below, with a dark lateral line with light spots above and below it. Fins and snout, black. Length, 90 inches. Teeth, $\frac{44}{44}$. No specimens; described from drawings. Referred to *Lagenorhynchus*, by Cassin.

DELPHINUS PECTORALIS, Peale, l. c.; Cassin, p. 28, pl. v, fig. 2.

Near the Sandwich Islands.
Black above; belly, reddish white; a frontal band of slate color extending behind the eyes; a white spot on each side before the fins. Length, 8 feet 8 inches. Teeth, $\frac{23}{23}$. No specimens.

DELPHINUS CHINENSIS, Desmoul., Gray, 1850, p. 132.

China Seas.
"Shining white;" no specimens; perhaps a beluga.

DELPHINUS LUNATUS, Lesson, Voy. Coq., pl. ix, fig. 4.

Coast of Chile.
"Tunenas" of the Chilenos. No specimens. From sketch of animal swimming!

DELPHINUS NIGER, Lacépède, Mém. Mus. iv, p. 475.

China?
Black, with white edges to lips and fins. No specimens. From Chinese drawing!

DELPHINUS LORIGER, Schreb. Saugeth., pl. 362.

Habitat?
Lead colored; middle of sides, chest, and belly, white. No specimens.

Delphinus styx, Gray, has been referred with doubt to Scammon's "Common Porpoise," and the North Pacific habitat thus indicated has been credited to *D. styx* by Gray in his last supplementary catalogue, but there are no good grounds for considering it a West American species, and the type is known to come from West Africa.

Genus **Leucorhamphus,** Lilljeborg.

Leucorhamphus, Lilljeborg, Gill.
Delphinapterus, Gray (not Lacépède), Zoöl. E. and T., 1846, p. 35; 1871, p. 72.

Leucorhamphus Peronii.
> *Delphinus Peronii,* Lacépède, Cét., p. 517, 1804.
> *D. leucorhamphus,* Brooks, Cat. Mus., p. 39, 1828.
> *Delphinapterus Peronii,* Gray (Lesson), 1866, p. 276; 1868, p. 6, pl. 15; 1871, p. 72.

West coast of South America, latitude 50° south (Pickering).

Black above, white below; the dividing line passing from the middle of the forehead below the eye, above the pectorals, and stopping at the flukes, which are black. Skull, 18.25 inches; beak, 10 inches. Teeth, $\frac{44}{44}$, six in an inch. Skulls, Mus. Paris, and drawings of animal.

Leucorhamphus borealis. Pl. xix, fig. 3.
> *Delphinapterus borealis,* Peale, Zoöl. U. S. Ex. Exp., p. 38, 1848; Gray, 1866, p. 277.
> *Delphinus borealis,* Cassin, Mamm. U. S. Ex. Exp., p. 30, pl. vii, fig. 2.
> *Right Whale Porpoise,* of Scammon.

West coast of North America.

Form elongate; black, with a lanceolate white spot beneath, extended in a narrow line nearly to the tail. Length, 4 to 6 feet. Teeth (?). Skull, Mus. S. I. Notes and measurements from life.

A specimen of this species was obtained by me off Cape Mendocino, October, 1868. Careful notes, a sketch, and measurements were secured, together with the cranium, now in the National Museum. On comparison with Mr. Peale's original drawing, they agreed exactly, except that my specimen was considerably larger, measuring about six feet. Unfortunately, these notes are not now accessible. Cassin and Gray refer to it as being probably the young of a species of beluga; but why they should do so, I can not imagine, as there are no grounds apparent for such a belief. It is unquestionably a dolphin.

Genus **Orca,** Gray.

Orca, Gray, Zoöl. E. and T., 1846, p. 33; 1866, p. 278.
Ophysia, Gray, P. Z. S. 1870, p. 76; 1871, p. 93.

Orca magellanica.
> *O. magellanica,* Burmeister, An. Mag. Nat. Hist., Ser. 3, xviii, p. 101, pl. 9, fig. 5; Annals Mus. Buenos Ayres, i, p. 373, pl. 22.

Patagonia.
Skeleton, Mus. Buenos Ayres.

Orca destructor.
> *O. destructor,* Cope, Proc. Phil. Acad. 1866, p. 293.

Payta, Peru.
Teeth, $\frac{8}{9}$. Skull only, S. I.

Orca rectipinna. Pl. xvii, fig. 1.

    O. rectipinna, Cope, Proc. Phil. Acad. 1869, p. 25; Scammon, l. c., p. 56, fig. 15, 16.

North Pacific, coast of California, Bering Sea.

Black, with high, erect dorsal. Skull? coll. Scammon. Skull, coll. Cal. Acad. Sci. Established on Scammon's figures and descriptions.

    The first skull referred to is supposed to be that of *O. rectipinna,* but this is not absolutely certain. The most notable peculiarities are the turning up and in of the posterior ends of the maxillaries, by the side of the nasals, and to some extent over the posterior ends of the premaxillaries. The transverse frontal ridge is very high and thin, the back of the skull behind it quite flat; in the temporal fossa, in the line of union of the squamosals and parietals, and extending some distance each side of the suture, is a ridge, or blunt carina, nearly as long as the fossa. The measurements of the cranium are as follow, in inches and decimals. The individual was doubtless rather aged:

Length of skull in a straight line	39 .00
Length of brain cavity, internally	11 .00
Length of beak before the maxillary notches	21 .00
Length from tip of beak to anterior margin of superior nares	24 .50
Length from tip of beak to posterior notch of palate	25 .00
Length from tip of beak to posterior edge of last tooth	17 .00
Length from tip of beak to frontal ridge	32 .50
Height of skull at vertex	16 .50
Greatest breadth (at zygomatic process of squamosals)	25 .00
Breadth of supra-orbital ridge	23 .00
Breadth between maxillary notches	11 .50
Breadth at middle of beak	10 .50
Breadth of the two premaxillæ at middle of beak	4 .60
Breadth of the fissure between them	0 .75
Breadth of condyles	7 .50
Closest approximation of condyles beneath the foramen magnum	0 .40
Height of foramen magnum (notched above)	3 .25
Width of foramen magnum	2 .75

Teeth in upper jaw, 12 or 13 (lost.)

Orca ater. Pl. xvii, fig. 2.

    O. ater, Cope, l. c., p. 23; Scammon, l. c., p. 58, fig. 17.

    O. atra, Gray, 1871, p. 92.

Coast of California and Oregon.

Smaller, with a white spot before the pectorals; white below, with a maroon colored, crescentic spot behind the dorsal. Established on Scammon's descriptions and figures.

    A jaw, supposed, with some probability, to belong to this species, is in Captain Scammon's possession. It is of an adult individual, but retains all the teeth, and measures as follows, in inches and decimals:

Length of ramus	28 .00
Tip to posterior edge of last tooth	13 .00
Length of symphysis	6 .25
Height of ramus at coronoid process	8 .50
Width between outsides of articular surfaces	21 .00
Width behind posterior teeth	10 .00
Length from tip to anterior notch of dental foramen	17 .00?
Height of largest teeth above alveoli	1 .30

Greatest diameter of the same (transverse)................................... 1 .00
Antero-posterior diameter of same... 0 .70
Height of jaw at gonys.. 3 .00
Height of jaw at posterior tooth.. 4 .00
Length to coronoid process from tip.. 25 .50
Width at posterior end of symphysis.................................... .... 7 .50
Thickness of ramus at seventh pair of teeth from tip........................, ..., 2 ,50
Number of teeth on each side, 12,

Orca ater, var. **fusca,** Pl. xvii, fig. 3,

A variety (?) of the above, with a lower falcate dorsal, with the belly, spots, and crescent of a yellowish cream color, instead of white and maroon, reported by Scammon from similar localities, may take the above varietal name until more material in regard to it is obtained. An *Orca*, under the name of *Delphinus orca*, is reported by Chamisso from the North Pacific and Kamchatka; very likely one of the above mentioned forms.

Orca pacifica.
> *O. capensis*, Gray, 1868, p. 8, pl. 9,
> *Ophysia pacifica*, Gray, P. Z. S. 1870, p. 76; 1871, p. 93.

Skull only, B. M. Reported by Gray to be probably from the South Pacific or Chile, but originally stated to be from the North Pacific. I can see no grounds for separating this from *Orca*, even subgenerically.

Genus **Phocæna,** Gray.

Phocæna, Gray, 1866, p. 301; 1871, p. 81.

Phocæna vomerina. Pl. xviii, fig. 2–4.
> *P. vomerina*, Gill, Proc. Phil. Acad. 1865, p. 178; Cope, l. c., 1869, p. 24; Scammon,
> l. c., p. 54.
> *Bay Porpoise*, of Scammon.

San Francisco, California.
Full material, skulls and skeleton, Mus. S. I. Figures and photographs from nature, and measurements. Eight blunt spines were noticed by me on the dorsal of a specimen of this species obtained in the harbor of San Francisco, February 8th, 1873. A dark line extended from the corner of the mouth to the pectorals. The belly was white, shading gradually into dark slate color on the back. The teeth in this species vary considerably in their shape, in some specimens being spade shaped, in others nearly tricuspid, and in still others truncated squarely.

Genus **Sagmatias,** Cope.

Sagmatias, Cope, Proc. Phil. Acad. 1866, p. 294.

Sagmatias amblodon.
> *S. amblodon*, Cope, Proc. Phil. Acad. 1866, p. 294.

South Pacific? U. S. Ex. Exp.
No triangle. Teeth "numerous," rounded, obtuse, stout. Skull, 15.25 inches. End of beak to notch, 7.6 inches. Width at notch, 3.79 inches. Allied to *Phocæna*. Skull only, S. I.

Genus **Neomeris,** Gray.

Neomeris, Gray, 1866, p. 306 ; 1871, p. 81.

Neomeris phocænoides.

N. phocænoides, Gray, 1866, p. 306; 1868, p. 6; 1871, p. 82.
Delphinapterus molagan, Owen.

Japan. Reported also from the Indian Ocean.

Black; no dorsal fin. Teeth, $\frac{16}{16}$. Full material, Japan, figured in *Fauna Japonica.* Skull, Mus. Leyden.

Subfamily *GLOBIOCEPHALINÆ,* Gill, p. 96.

Genus **Globiocephalus,** Gray.

Globiocephalus, Gray, 1850, p. 86. (Lesson.)

Globiocephalus Sieboldii.

G. Sieboldii, Gray, 1866, p. 323; 1871, p. 85.
G. sibo? Gray, 1871, p. 85. (From Japanese account!)
G. chinensis? Gray, 1866, p. 323; 1871, p. 85. (From anonymous description in Chinese Repository.)

Japan.

Black, with a paler streak beneath. Figure of animal and skull in *Fauna Japonica.* Skeleton (*ubi?*). The synonyms above quoted appear to have been established on very insufficient evidence, and without specimens.

Globiocephalus Scammoni. Pl. xv, fig. 1–3.

G. Scammoni, Cope, Proc. Phil. Acad. 1869, p. 22; Scammon, l. c., p. 59, fig. 15, 16.
Blackfish, of Scammon.

Lower California.

Entirely black. Teeth, $\frac{10}{8}$ to $\frac{12}{10}$. Fifteen feet long. Skull, etc., in Mus. S. I.

Genus **Grampus,** Gray.

Grampus, Gray, 1868, p. 9 ; 1871, p. 82.

Grampus? sakamata.

G. sakamata, Gray, 1866, p. 301.

Japan.

Genus uncertain. The species, whatever it may be, is said to be black, with white spots on the belly, back, and sides. Described from a Japanese account, and figure published by Schlegel, *Fauna Japonica,* p. 25. No specimens or reliable figures.

Grampus Stearnsii. Outline figure, p. 102.

G. Stearnsii, Dall, Prel. Descr. Proc. Cal. Acad. v, January, 1873.
Whiteheaded or *Mottled Grampus,* of Scammon.

Two lower jaws, evidently belonging to an animal of this genus, are in my hands for examination. As no *Grampus* appears to have been described from the Pacific, I feel warranted, though with some hesitation, in applying a specific name to the animal described by Captain Scammon. The following are the measurements, in inches and decimals:

	No. 1.	No. 2.
From end of beak to condyles	17 .50	17 .50
From end of beak to posterior end of coronoid process	16 .40	16 .20
From end of beak to posterior end of alveoli	9 .00	9 .50
From end of beak to anterior end of dental foramen	9 .75	10 .00
Height at coronoid process of ramus	5 .00	4 .60
Height at inferior dental foramen	3 .50	3 .00
Height at posterior end of symphysis	1 .45	1 .30
Height of gonys	2 .00	1 .90?
Length of symphysis	2 .00	2 .75
Width behind posterior teeth	3 .00	2 .90
Width at inferior dental foramen	7 .00	7 .20
Width at coronoid process	10 .30	10 .00
Width at inner corners of condyles	11 .20	11 .00
Width at outer corners of condyles	14 .00	14 .00?
Thickness of ramus behind posterior tooth	0 .90	1 .00

The ramus is quite thin and light behind; the inferior dental foramen is large; the coronoid process almost evanescent. The alveoli are entirely filled with spongy bone behind the posterior end of the symphysis. The posterior angle formed by the junction of the rami at the symphysis is rather broadly rounded. The end of the beak is moderately pointed. The gonys is very short, and produced in a rather sharp point below. No. 1 has three teeth on each side; No. 2, four. They are inclined forward and outward; most of them are broken off or truncated. The teeth are much the shape of an orange-seed: solid, and without any cavity in their proximal ends. The crown, or portion covered with enamel (which, from the discoloration, seems to be the only portion projecting above the gums), is slightly, but distinctly, differentiated from the rest of the tooth, of which less than one-half is inclosed in the alveolus. The crown is attenuated, slightly recurved, and sharply pointed, which may account for the ease with which it becomes truncated. The remainder of the tooth is irregularly subcylindrical, transversely compressed, and pinched off at the bottom. The dimensions are as follow: Length of crown, 0.52 inch; of whole tooth, 1.43 inch. Diameter at base of crown, 0.37 inch; transverse diameter of root, 0.5 inch; greatest diameter of ditto, 0.6 inch. Length of the tooth line in No. 1, 2.25 inches; in No. 2, 2.5 inches. Animal, 12 to 15 feet. The specimens were obtained at Monterey, California, by Captain Scammon.

Superfamily PHYSETEROIDEA, Gill, p. 96.

Family PHYSETERIDÆ, Gill, p. 96.

Subfamily *PHYSETERINÆ*, Gill, p. 96.

Genus **Physeter,** Linn.

Physeter, Linn., S. N. i, p. 106; Gill, p. 96.
Catodon, Gray, 1866, p. 196; 1871, p. 58.

Physeter macrocephalus. Pl. xiv, xv.

> *P. macrocephalus*, Linn., S. N. i, 107.
> *Catodon macrocephalus*, Gray, 1871, p. 58.
> *Catodon Colneti*, Gray, 1866, p. 209.
> *Sperm Whale*, of authors.

Ubiquitous in the warmer seas.

A lower jaw, probably of a young animal, Mus. Cal. Acad., has 22 teeth on each side, for the most part sharply pointed.

Subfamily *KOGIINÆ*, Gill, p. 96.

Genus **Kogia,** Gray.

Kogia, Gray, Zoöl. E. and T., p. 22, 1846.
Euphysetes, Wall, Hist. New Sperm Whale, pp. 50, 53, 1851.

Kogia Floweri.

> *K. Floweri*, Gill, Am. Nat. iv, p. 738, fig. 167, 172, 1871.

Mazatlan.

Black above, yellowish white below, including the end of the snout. Nine feet long. Teeth long, slender, recurved, $\frac{7}{14}$. Dorsal very low. Snout pointed and projecting beyond and above the mouth. Jaw and drawing from nature in Mus. S. I.

Suborder **Mysticete.**

Family BALÆNOPTERIDÆ, Gill, p. 97.

Subfamily *AGAPHELINÆ*, Gill, p. 97.

Genus **Rhachianectes,** Cope.

Rhachianectes, Cope, Proc. Phil. Acad. 1869, pp. 14, 15.

Rhachianectes glaucus. Pl. ii, fig. 1; pl. iii, fig. 1, 2; pl. v; baleen, p. 55.

> *R. glaucus*, Cope, l. c., p. 17; Scammon, l. c., p. 40, fig. 8.
> *Agaphelus glaucus*, Cope, l. c., 1868, p. 225.
> *California Gray Whale*, of Scammon.

Arctic Seas to Lower California.

This species was originally described from specimens and notes obtained by me at Monterey, California, in January, 1866, and now in the Mus. S. I. A peculiar barnacle, *Cryptolepas rhachianecti*, Dall (pl. x, fig. 6), and the *Cyamus Scammoni*, Dall, (pl. x, fig. 1), appear to be restricted to this species. They are described in the Proc. Cal. Acad. Sci. 1872, vol. iv, pp. 281, 300. A skull collected by me at Monterey, California, is now in the collection of the Cal. Acad. Sci., and another in Mus. S. I.

Subfamily *MEGAPTERINÆ*, Gill, p. 97.

Genus **Megaptera,** Gray.

Megaptera, Gray, An. Mag. N. H. 1864, pp. 207, 350; 1866, p. 117.

Megaptera versabilis. Pl. vii, fig. 1; pl. viii, ix; outline figure, pp. 47, 48; baleen, p. 55.

> *M. versabilis*, Cope, Proc. Phil. Acad. 1869, p. 17; Scammon, do., p. 50, fig. 5, 6; Gray, 1871, p. 51.
>
> *North Pacific Humpback*, of Scammon.

Arctic Seas to Lower California.

Established on Scammon's measurements and descriptions. Vertebræ, ribs, and humerus in Mus. Cal. Academy. Baleen, Mus. S. I. Parasitic on this species are the *Coronula diadema* and *balænaris*, Lam., *Otion Stimpsoni*, Dall, and *Cyamus suffusus*, Dall (pl. x, fig. 3, 5), described in Proc. Cal. Acad. Sci. 1872, vol. iv, pp. 282, 301.

Megaptera kuzira?

> *M. kuzira*, Gray, 1866, p. 130; 1871, p. 50.

Japan.

Ten gular folds. Belly, gray or white; back, black. Described from Japanese accounts and drawings. No specimens. A skull from Java, reported to be of this species, is said to be in the Leyden Museum; but, from the habitat, the identity seems doubtful.

Subfamily BALÆNOPTERINÆ, Gill, 97.

Genus Sibbaldius, Gray.

> *Sibbaldus*, Gray, P. Z. S. 1864, p. 223.
>
> *Sibbaldius*, Flower, P. Z. S. 1864, p. 392; Gray, 1866, p. 169.
>
> *Flowerius*, Lilljeborg, Nov. Act. Upsala, vi, 1867.

Sibbaldius sulfureus. Pl. xii, fig. 1; baleen, p. 55.

> *S. sulfureus*, Cope, Proc. Phil. Acad. 1869, p. 20; Scammon, l. c., p. 51, fig. **11**; Cope, Proc. Am. Phil. Soc. 1870, p. 108.
>
> *Sulphurbottom*, of Scammon.

Coast of California.

Brown above, sulphur yellow beneath. Described from baleen (Mus. S. I.), and Scammon's descriptions and figures.

Sibbaldius tectirostris, Cope, is an Atlantic species, but is erroneously credited to the Pacific by Gray, 1871, p. 56.

Genus Physalus, Gray.

> *Physalus*, Lacépède, Gray, P. Z. S. 1847, p. 88; 1866, p. 139; 1871, p. 52.

Physalus? Tschudii.

> *Balænoptera Tschudi*, Reich, Cet., p. 33.
>
> *P. fasciatus*, Gray, 1850, p. 42; 1866, p. 162.

Coast of Peru.

"Head and back, brown; belly, whitish; tips of fins, and a streak from the eye to the middle of the body, white. Length, 38 feet." Described from the preceding notes of Tschudi! No specimens.

Physalus? Iwasi.

    P. Iwasi, Gray, 1850, p. 42; 1866, p. 163.

    Balænoptera arctica, Schlegel, Faun. Jap. Mamm. 26, pl. 30.

    Japan.

    Black; sides, white spotted; belly, white. Length, 25 feet. Described from Japanese accounts and drawings. No specimens.

    To the above senseless additions to the catalogues may be added the following names, applied to Chinese drawings, Japanese clay models, Aleutian wooden carvings, and similar trash, by authors of scientific reputation:

    Balænoptera punctulata, B. nigra, B. cærulescens, B. maculata, Balæna lunulata, and *B. Japonica,* Lacépède, Mém. du Mus., iv, p. 473; from Chinese drawings.

    Balæna agamachschik (!), *B. kuliomok,* Aleutian Islands, and *B. tschiekagluk,* Kamchatka, Cham. Nov. Act. Curs. 259, Pallas, Zoöl. Ross, Asiat. i, 289. These are from Aleutian models in wood. They should be entirely expunged; but the *B. kuliomok,* or *cullamach,* has obtained to some extent an entrance into scientific literature, *vide Balæna Sieboldii.*

    Balæna australis, Temm. Faun. Jap., pl. 28–29. Japan. Described from clay model. No specimens.

Genus **Balænoptera,** Gray.

Balænoptera, Gray, 1866, pp. 114, 186; 1868, p. 3; 1871, p. 56.

Balænoptera velifera. Pl. ii, fig. 2.

    B. velifera, Cope, Proc. Phil. Acad. 1869, p. 18; Scammon, l. c., p. 53, fig. 9, 10.

    Finback, of Scammon; *Oregon Finner.*

    Oregon and California.

    Brownish black; belly, white. Described from baleen and Scammon's descriptions. Baleen, Mus. S. I.

Balænoptera velifera, var. **borealis.** Outline figure, p. 37.

    Northern Seas and Aleutian Islands.

    The form found in the more northern waters is distinguished, according to Captain Scammon, by a larger and higher dorsal fin. I observed many of them, during the summer of 1872, in the Shumagin Islands. In some individuals the flukes were black; in others, white below; and in a few the white extended above over the external points of the flukes. Those of Oregon appear to have a dorsal intermediate in size between the northern and the small-finned southern forms.

Balænoptera Davidsoni. Pl. vii, fig. 2.

    B. Davidsoni, Scammon, Proc. Cal. Acad. Sci. iv., p. 269. (Printed in advance, October 4th, 1872.)

    Admiralty Inlet and Straits of Fuca.

    Small, closely resembling the *B. rostrata* of the North Atlantic. Described from measurements and drawings taken from the animal by Captain Scammon. Skull in Mus. S. I.

    A skull and jaws of a small *Balænoptera* of unknown locality, presented by Mr. Merrill, are in the Mus. Cal. Acad. It evidently was an adolescent individual, but a number of facts tend to confirm the opinion that it is of this species. The ex-occipitals are wanting, having been removed, probably to clean out the brain cavity. The supra-occipital is quadrate. The two anterior sides measure along the suture ten and a half inches; the posterior sides, six and a half inches; the anterior angle is bluntly rounded. Above, in front, the bone is very slightly impressed; behind, slightly convex; but, on the whole, is flattened. There is no median ridge or groove. The principal feature of the upper aspect of the skull is the wide narial opening; the very narrow premaxillæ are rounded and elevated above the flattened maxillaries, bend boldly out from the nasals, approximating only in the anterior third of the beak, then continuing parallel, become flatter and wider, and extend slightly beyond the maxillæ.

The posterior angles of the maxillæ are spatulate, the vomer is hidden by the mesethmoid cartilage. Below, the vomer appears as a thin flat plate an inch wide, extending to the anterior fourth of the beak. The palatines are broad, with the anterior lateral angles obliquely truncate; they have, on the whole, an abbreviated "dice-box" shape. Their greatest length is 9.5 inches; width at the anterior and posterior ends across the two, 10 inches. Their least width in the middle, 8 inches.

The length from the tip of the beak to the median notch of the inferior nares is thirty-eight inches; from the bottom of the notch to the posterior recurved process of the alisphenoid, four inches; to anterior basi-occipital suture, five inches—the middle of the otic bullæ being in the same transverse line. The anterior ends of the bullæ are an inch from the recurved process of the alisphenoid.

The bullæ are very regularly ovoid, and smooth below; the lateral external edges have two deep grooves separating three bulbous prominences. They were so attached by dried membranes to the cranium that a fuller examination was impracticable. The width of the inferior surface of the maxillæ, in the middle of the beak, is 6.5 inches. The height of the narial septum, behind, is 1.5 inch. Depth of brain cavity, 8 inches; height of orbit, 4.5 inches. The condyles of the lower jaw are large and thick; the rami are stout in proportion to their length. There is no angular process; the coronoid process is sharp and high; the dental foramen large, just before the condyle. The inferior groove between the occipital condyles is almost evanescent.

Dimensions of cranium, in inches and decimals:

Length of skull in a straight line	48 .00
Breadth of condyles	4 .50?
Breadth of ex-occipitals (to outer edge of suture)	17 .00
Breadth of squamosals	27 .00
Height of foramen magnum	2 .00
Length of supra-occipital	13 .00
Length of articular process of squamosal antero-posterior	8 .00
Length of orbital process of frontal, right to left	10 .00
Breadth of orbital from curved border of maxillary to hinder edge of orbital process of frontal	9 .00
Breadth of orbital at upper surface of outer end	6 .50
Nasals, length	4 .50
Nasals, breadth of the two at posterior end	1 .00
Nasals, breadth of the two at anterior end	2 .50
Length from curved border of maxillary to tip of beak	30 .00
Length of maxillary	33 .00
Projection of premaxillary beyond maxillary	1 .50
Breadth of maxillaries at hinder end	6 .00
Breadth of maxillaries across orbital processes	12 .50
Breadth of beak at base*	16 .50
Breadth of beak at one-quarter its length from base	12 .00
Breadth of maxillary at one-quarter its length from base	2 .50
Breadth of premaxillary at same point	1 .00
Breadth of beak at middle	9 .00
Breadth of maxillary at middle	2 .50
Breadth of premaxillary at middle	1 .50

* All measurements across beak include the curve of the superior surface.

Breadth of beak at three-quarters its length from base........................ 6 .00
Breadth of maxillary at three-quarters its length from base.................... 1 .50
Breadth of premaxillary at three-quarters its length from base............ ... 1 .25
Length of lower jaw in a straight line..................................... 47 .00
Height at coronoid process... 6 .00
Length from posterior end of condyle to coronoid process........ .... 7 .50
Height of ramus at middle... 4 .00
Amount of curve... 6 .50
Length of otic bullæ.. 3 .50

The thinner edges being covered with dry membranes, have been somewhat gnawed by vermin.

Family BALÆNIDÆ, Gill, p. 98.

Genus **Balæna,** Gray.
Balæna, Gray, 1866, p. 78.
Eubalæna, Gray, 1866, p. 78.

Balæna Sieboldii. Pl. xii, fig. 1. Baleen, p. 55.
    Eubalæna Sieboldii, var. *Japonica,* Gray, 1866, p. 97; 1871, p. 43.
    Balæna cullamach? Cham., Cope, Proc. Phil. Acad. 1869, p. 15; Scammon, l. c., p. 38,
        fig. 4.
    Pacific Right Whale, of Scammon.

Arctic, Bering, and Ochotsk Seas. Lower California. Japan?
    The *Eubalæna Sieboldii* was founded on a drawing of a Japanese clay model, named *B. australis* in the *Fauna Japonica;* and the supposed variety *Japonica,* from baleen from the North-west Coast. The description properly rests upon this baleen, as the former basis is utterly insufficient for the introduction of a specific name into a scientific system. The figure of the baleen agrees with the baleen of the Right Whale of Scammon, and I have little doubt that they belong to the same species. The name *Japonica* had previously been used by Lacépède, and is, to some extent, a misnomer, so I have preferred to retain the original name of Gray. This species is doubtfully referred to the *B. cullamach* of Chamisso, by Cope; but it does not, as he observes, possess the recurved rictus attributed to that species, which itself rests upon no scientific foundation, and hence I have preferred to use a name for which there is some slight basis in the shape of specimens by which the species may be hereafter satisfactorily identified. It reaches the length of sixty feet, is dark colored above and lighter below. Baleen in B. M. and Mus. S. I.
    Cyamus tentator, Dall, and *C. gracilis,* Dall, are parasitic upon this species.

Balæna mysticetus. * Pl. xi, fig. 1; baleen, p. 55.
    B. mysticetus, Linn., S. N. i, 105; Gray, 1866, p. 81; 1868, p. 1, pl. 1, f. 4 (baleen);
        1871, p. 38; Cope, Proc. Phil. Acad. 1869, p. 15; Scammon, l. c., p. 33.
    Bowhead, of Scammon.

Bering, Ochotsk, and Arctic Seas.
    The *Cyamus mysticeti,* Dall, pl. x, fig. 2, is parasitic on this species.

?Variety **Roysii.** Page 56, outline figure.
    Roys' Bunchback, of Scammon, l. c., p. 35.

Ochotsk Sea.
    No special differences appear to separate the Bowheads of these regions from those of the

       * See illustration of skeleton at the conclusion of this Catalogue.— C. M. S.

North Seas of Europe. The differences which distinguish the variety from the common form, according to Captain Scammon, are as follow: The spout-holes are said to be higher, and a bunch, or hump, rises from the "small" of the back, about six feet forward of the flukes, extending along the back two or three feet, and rising above it about six inches. They are also said to yield a larger proportion of baleen to the oil than the others. They have been frequently taken in the north-east gulf of the Ochotsk Sea. Before the variety can be confirmed, a more thorough knowledge of it is, of course, indispensable. Baleen of the normal form in B. M. and Mus. S. I.

Summary.

Out of forty-four species which appear to be more or less thoroughly characterized, ten are of unknown habitat. Leaving these out (with all species based on insufficient material), we have as the approximate distribution of the known Pacific Cetacea: Japan, five species; northern seas, six species, including two or three which visit California; warm seas and South Pacific, eleven species; coast of western North America, from the Aleutian Islands to Central America, eighteen species, including several visitors from the Arctic Seas. The species are as follow:

JAPAN.

Delphinus longirostris?
Neomeris phocænoides.
Globiocephalus Sieboldii.
Megaptera kuzira.
Balæna Sieboldii?

NORTHERN SEAS.

Delphinapterus catodon.
Orca rectipinna.
Rhachianectes glaucus.
Megaptera versabilis.
Balænoptera velifera?
Balæna mysticetus.

WARM SEAS AND SOUTH PACIFIC.

Clymenia alope.
C. obscura.
Tursiops catalania.
Cephalorhynchus eutropia.
Lagenorhynchus clanculus.
Physeter macrocephalus.

Lagenorhynchus albirostratus.
Leucorhamphus Peronii.
Orca magellanica.
O. destructor.
O. pacifica.

The absence of *Phocæna*, and of well-defined species of the *Mysticeti*, from the warm seas, is very marked, as is the paucity of *Denticeti* in the northern seas, while in the north European seas the latter are well represented.

WEST COAST OF NORTH AMERICA.

Delphinus Bairdii.
Tursiops Gillii.
Lagenorhynchus thicolea.
L. obliquidens.
Leucorhamphus borealis.
Orca rectipinna.
O. ater.
Phocæna vomerina.
Globiocephalus Scammoni.

Grampus Stearnsii.
Kogia Floweri.
Physeter macrocephalus.
Rhachianectes glaucus.
Megaptera versabilis.
Balænoptera velifera.
B. Davidsoni.
Sibbaldius sulfureus.
Balæna Sieboldii.

It is highly probable that to this list may be added two or three species of grampuses and dolphins, of which sufficient material has not yet been obtained for secure identification.

The only fossil remains of whales found up to this time on this coast, are a portion of a ramus of a lower jaw (described by Cope, Proc. Phil. Acad. 1872, as *Eschrichtius Davidsoni*), obtained in digging a well at San Diego, California, and presumed to be of miocene age; a caudal vertebra obtained by me in the miocene sandstones of the Shumagin Islands, Alaska; and some remains of cervical vertebræ and the adjacent portions of the skull, very much injured, obtained from the Tertiary sandstones, near Point Conception, California, by Mr. George Sceva; these, as far as their characters are apparent, resemble *Megaptera*.

The following Cetacea, mentioned by Captain Scammon, are not at the date of this paper represented by material sufficient to indicate their zoölogical position:

Grampus, Panama.	Grampus, San Diego Bay.
Grampus, Puget Sound.	Scrag Right Whale, northern seas.
Grampus, Bottlenosed.	

The other marine mammals mentioned, are the Walrus (*Rosmarus obesus*, Illiger); the Leopard Seal, pl. xxii, fig. 1 (*Phoca Pealii?* Gill); the Banded Seal, pl. xxi, fig. 2 (*Histriophoca equestris*, Gill); the Fur Seal, pl. xxi, fig. 1 (*Callorhinus ursinus*, Gray); the Sea Lion, pl. xx, fig. 2 (*Eumetopias Stelleri*, Gill); the Sea Elephant, pl. xx, fig. 1 (*Macrorhinus angustirostris*, Gill); and the Sea Otter, pl. xxii, fig. 2 (*Enhydra marina*, Fleming). It is, however, quite probable that under the common name of Leopard Seal, several species of similar aspect are included by non-scientific observers.

SAN FRANCISCO, CALIFORNIA, March, 1873.

NOTE.—To Mr. Dall's Catalogue may be added the Squareheaded Grampus and Brownsided Dolphin of Santa Barbara Channel.—C. M. S.

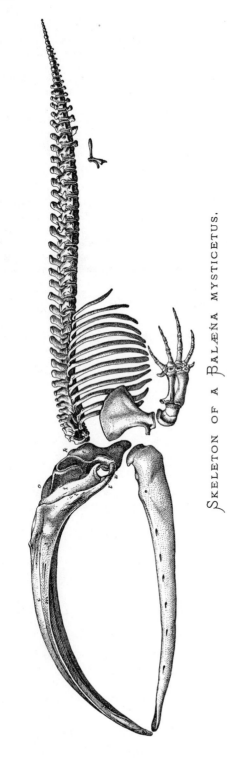

Skeleton of a Balæna Mysticetus.

As the first part of the preceding work is devoted almost exclusively to the natural history of whales, without reference to their osteology, and the Catalogue also, which is embodied in the Appendix, supplying but little information in that department relative to the baleen whales, we have thought it well to add to the Catalogue the representation of the skeleton of a *Balæna mysticetus*, it being a reduced copy of the original excellent figure which embellishes the elaborate work of Professors Eschricht and Reinhardt upon the *Greenland Right Whale*, published by the Ray Society in 1866.

This faithful delineation of the animal's bone-frame gives also a general idea of the relative osteological construction of all the baleen whales.

"In the cranium of this skeleton, the letters have the following significations:

b. The left parietal.
f. The frontal.
i. The intermaxillary.
k. The right condyle of the occipital.
l. The left lachrymal.
m. The superior maxillary.
o. The squamous portion of the occipital.
t. The left temporal.
z. The zygomatic temporal.
a. The pelvic bones.

"The caudal vertebræ have been brought somewhat nearer to one another than in their fresh state by the drying up of the intervertebral cartilages; the tail is, therefore, on the whole somewhat too short."

GLOSSARY

OF

WORDS AND PHRASES USED BY WHALEMEN.

Bailer.—A copper or iron vessel used in dipping up oil. Two of these utensils are used on board of a whaler: one with a short, upright handle, called the hand-bailer; the other, with a staff to it six feet long, used at the try-works for bailing the oil from the pots, is called a long-handled bailer. For illustration, see fig. 4, p. 239.

Becket.—A thing used in ships to confine loose ropes, tackles, or spars.

Black-skin.—The rete-mucosum and the cuticle, the principal seat of color in whales.

Black-whale, or black-whale oil.—Is that produced from all the baleen whales, including the rorquals. All these varieties of whales are sometimes termed black whales, in contradistinction to the Sperm Whale.

Blanket-piece.—A strip or section of blubber cut from a whale in a spiral direction, and raised by means of the cutting-tackle. It varies from two to four feet or more in width, and is in length from ten to twenty-five feet.

Blasted.—A term used to signify that a whale is much swollen, or far advanced in decomposition after death.

Blink, or ice-blink.—A stratum of lucid whiteness which appears in the lower part of the atmosphere over ice and land covered with snow.

Blow.—Blow signifies the action of the whale in making one respiration.

Blubber-fork.—A utensil used in pitching the minced blubber from the tubs into the try-pots. For illustration, see fig. 1, p. 239.

Blubber-hook.—A stout iron hook of seventy-five to a hundred pounds weight, which is used in flensing a whale. See illustration, p. 232.

Boarding-knife.—A sharp two-edged instrument, principally used in cutting the toggle-hole in the blubber of a whale, for the purpose of inserting the strap to the cutting-tackle, so as to hoist up the mass of fat called the blanket-piece. For illustration, see pl. xxv.

Bolting.—Signifies the action of a whale when it leaps out diagonally to the surface of the water.

Bone-spade.—A cutting-spade, with a thin, long shank to it. See cutting-spade, pl. xxv.

Bonnet.—Cheever defines the bonnet of a Right Whale "as being the crest or comb where there burrow legions of barnacles and crabs, like rabbits in a warren, or insects in the shaggy bark of an old tree." [NOTE.—This description applies especially to the southern Right Whales; in the northern Right Whale's bonnet, but very few barnacles are present, and comparatively few parasites of any description.]

Bomb-shot.—The distance a bomb-lance can be fired into a whale effectively, which is about twenty yards.

Breaching.—Signifies the movement of a whale when leaping out of the water, in nearly a perpendicular direction or otherwise.

Breaking black-skin.—The act of darting a harpoon into a whale.

Bring-to.— The act of a whale when it ceases its progressive motion.

Broken voyage.— An unprofitable voyage, or a losing voyage.

Case.— The sack or cavity which lies on the right side and upper portion of the head of a Sperm Whale, and which contains oil and spermaceti. These combined constitute what is called "head-matter."

Cooler.— A copper or iron tank into which the oil from the try-pots is first bailed.

Cutting-spade.— A sharp, flat implement, like a thin chisel, which is fixed to a pole ten or more feet in length, and is used in cutting the blubber from a whale. A "bone-spade" is merely a cutting-spade, with a long, thin shank to it. It is employed in cutting out the throat-bone of a baleen whale. The "head-spade" is thicker and heavier than the ordinary cutting-spade, and is used in cutting the skull-bone, which separates the whale's head from the body. See illustration, pl. xxv.

Darting distance.— The distance the harpoon is usually thrown effectively by hand, which is about eighteen feet.

Deck-pot.— An iron pot of similar shape and size with the try-pots, but having legs to it.

Fast.— A term used when the harpoon penetrates the whale, "as the boat is fast," signifying that the boat is fastened to the whale by means of the harpoon attached to the line.

Fins.— The pectorals or side fins of a whale are called fins, in contradistinction to the flukes, or caudal fin.

Finning.— The action of a whale when lying partly on its side, raising one fin out of the water, and striking it upon the surface, causing a splash.

Fire-pike.— An instrument used in feeding and stirring the fires when trying out oil. See illustration, fig. 5, p. 239.

Flukes.— The posterior extremities, or caudal fin of a whale.

Flukes, to cut flukes out, or the whale cuts its flukes out.— Is a whaler's phrase to describe the action of the animal when it throws its caudal fin sidewise and upward, upon or above the surface of the water, which is an indication that the creature has taken fright, and suddenly endeavors to escape. "He attempted to cut his flukes out," is a slang expression in whaling parlance, when any members of a ship's company become refractory, or attempt in any manner to create disturbance on board.

Gaff, or gaff-hook.— A sharp, strong iron hook attached to a short or long wooden handle, and used in handling blubber. See pl. xxv.

Galley.— Frightened; as, "The whale is gallied," or "The boat-steerer got so gallied he could not strike the whale." The state of being frightened.

Gam.— Signifies two or more ships meeting, and their companies exchanging visits. Gam also signifies a large collection or herd of whale-bone whales.

Gamming.— To visit from one whaling-vessel to another.

Gurry.— Is the term by which the combination of water, oil, and dirt is known when collected upon the ship's deck and below, during the time of cutting in and boiling out a whale.

Head-spade.— A thick, heavy cutting-spade used in cutting the head-bones of a whale. See head-spade, pl. xxv.

Hopper, or scrap-hopper.— A flaring wooden box used as a receptacle for the scraps when taken from the try-pots.

Hose-cock.— A large brass cock attached to the end of the oil-hose.

Hose-scuttle.— A small opening in a whaling-vessel's deck through which the oil from a cask runs into the hose-tub.

Hose-tub.— A large wooden tub, or copper tank, with a strainer in the bottom to which the oil-hose is attached. The tub is lashed close beneath the deck, immediately under the hose-scuttle.

Hump.— A protuberance or elevation upon the top of a whale's body, and generally nearest to the posterior extremity. In some species it appears somewhat like a dorsal fin.

Junk.— A wedge-shaped mass of cellular membranous substance, filled with oil and spermaceti, which lies between the case and the white-horse of a Sperm Whale's head.

Knuckle-joint.— The joint of the fin, or pectorals, which connects with the shoulder-blade of a whale.

Lay on, or lay the boat on.— Is to turn the

head of the boat toward any object by means of the steering-oar.

Lay off, or **lay the boat off.**—Is to turn the head of the boat from any object, by means of the steering-oar.

Leaning blubber.—To cut the flesh, or lean meat, etc., from it.

Leaning-knife.—A large knife used in cutting the flesh, or other tissue destitute of oil, from the blubber, preparatory to trying it out.

Lipper.—A piece of thin blubber cut into an oblong square, and punctured, so as to admit a man's fingers to hold it, when used in wiping up the gurry from the decks, etc.

Lipper off the decks.—Is to wipe the gurry off with lippers.

Lobtailing, or **loptailing.**—The action of a whale when it raises its flukes high out of water, and strikes them down with great force upon the surface. 2d. A whale beating the surface of the water with its caudal fin.

Loose irons.—Harpoons which are darted into a whale with no line attached.

Mate.—This word is used by whalers to signify a partnership between two vessels in pursuing whales.

Mill.—To turn in an opposite direction, or nearly so; as, "The whale was running to windward, but 'milled,' and ran to leeward."

Mincing-knife.—A thin, broad steel implement, sharp on one edge, with a handle on each end, which is used in cutting the blubber into thin slices, preparatory to being boiled or tried out. For illustration, see page 238.

Mux, or **muxing.**—To perform work in an awkward or improper manner; as, "He made a mux of it, and missed the whale," i. e., by improper management a whale was not struck, which otherwise might have been secured.

Noddle-end.—The anterior and upper portion of a Sperm Whale's head.

Nib-end.—The anterior and upper portion of a whalebone whale's head.

Nisket.—The anus of a whale.

Oil-hose.—A stout hose made of grained leather, for the purpose of conducting the oil from a vessel's deck into empty casks in the hold.

Piece.—This word is frequently used for briefness, instead of the word blanket-piece.

Pike.—A pointed iron or steel implement fixed to the end of a pole, and used in pitching or handling the pieces of blubber, etc. For illustration, see plate xxv.

Raising whales.—When first seeing a whale from the mast-head, or other place, it is termed "raising a whale." It is also used to express the fact of seeing any object, as, "We raised the land, sixty miles distant."

Recruits.—Fresh provisions and supplies for a whale-ship. 2d. Various articles put on board the ship to purchase recruits with (at remote islands or coasts), such as clothing, calicoes, tobacco, and a variety of other domestic articles.

Ridge.—The upper portion of a whale's "small."

Ripple.—The agitation of the surface of the water by a whale when swimming near it, but still not visible, as, "I can not see the whale, but can see its ripple."

Rounding, or **rounding out.**—The attitude of a whale when curving its small in order to descend below the surface of the water.

Rugged.—The state of the sea when agitated. A rough sea, accompanied with blowing weather, is termed by whalers "rugged weather."

Sampson-post.—A heavy upright timber, firmly secured in the deck (and extending about two feet above it), to which the fluke-chain, or fluke-rope, is made fast.

Scooping.—This term is applied to the action of whalebone whales when feeding.

Scrap-hopper.—A flaring wooden box which is placed beside the try-works to receive the scraps when skimmed from the try-pots. It has holes in the bottom through which the oil that drips from the scraps runs into a tub called a "strainer-cooler."

Scraps.—The residue of the blubber after the oil is extracted by boiling.

Scrimshawing, or **to scrimshaw,** or **skimshander,** as sometimes termed.—Is to execute any piece of ingenious mechanical work. It is applied particularly to polishing and engraving upon whalebone or whale's teeth, or manufacturing fancy articles from the same materials.

Skimmer.—A broad scoop composed of copper, iron, and wood. The utensil is about seven feet long, and is used in removing scraps from the try-pots. For illustration, see fig. 3, p. 239.

Skimming-slicks.—A phrase used by whalemen when employed in saving any small amount of fat from the entrails or from the exterior of the carcass after the blubber has been stripped off.

Slumgullion.—The offal from the blubber of a whale.

Small.—The posterior portion of a whale, between the vent and caudal fin.

Sounding.—Is the term signifying the descent of the whale after being fastened to.

Stern, or stern all.—Is the invariable order given to the whaleboat's crew, when it becomes necessary to propel the boat stern foremost.

Stirring-pole.—A wooden pole six or seven feet long, used to stir the blubber in the try-pots. See illustration, fig. 2, p. 239.

Stopped.—To confine a rope, or ropes, usually by a smaller line, as, "Stop the line to the 'iron-pole'" (or harpoon staff), *i. e.,* confine the line to the pole by passing one or more turns of twine, or rope-yarn, around both line and pole, and confining the ends by knotting them together.

Suds.—The foam on the surface of the water caused by the violent actions of a whale in the course of its capture, as, "In order to get a good chance to kill the whale, you must keep close to the suds."

Sweeping.—The action of a whale when wielding its flukes from side to side in an offensive or defensive manner, causing a great commotion on the water.

Toggle.—A large wooden pin, about three feet long, and six or eight inches in diameter, with a swell or shoulder near the middle. It has a hole near one end, through which a rope is attached, which is termed the toggle-lanyard. This lanyard is used in handling or confining the toggle. See illustration, p. 234.

Turning flukes.—The last action of a whale upon the surface of the water when making its descent beneath, which is to elevate its caudal fin in the air as the body assumes nearly a perpendicular attitude.

Trying out.—To extract the oil from the blubber by boiling.

White-horse.—An extremely tough and sinewy substance resembling blubber, but destitute of oil, which lies between the upper jaw and junk of a Sperm Whale.

White-water.—The foam or spray caused by the violent actions of a whale.

LIST OF STORES AND OUTFITS

FOR A

FIRST-CLASS WHALE-SHIP, FOR A CAPE HORN VOYAGE,

EXCLUSIVE OF

THE INVENTORY OF A MERCHANT-SHIP, WHICH, ALTHOUGH INCLUDED IN A
WHALE-SHIP'S OUTFIT, IS NOT HERE ENUMERATED.

PROVISIONS, ETC.

350 barrels of bread.
100 barrels of flour.
180 barrels of mess beef.
90 barrels of extra prime pork.
1,000 barrels of fresh water.
1,600 pounds of codfish.
2 barrels of mackerel.
1,200 gallons of molasses.
1,200 pounds of sugar.
2,000 pounds of butter.
6 barrels of Indian meal.
300 pounds of rice.
33 bushels of corn.
20 bushels of beans.
400 pounds of dried apples.
300 pounds of cheese.
2 barrels of cucumber pickles.
15 bushels of onions.
50 pounds of raisins.

200 pounds of tea.
1,200 pounds of coffee.
50 pounds of chocolate.
2 pounds of hops.
6 bottles of essence of spruce.
12 bottles of pepper-sauce.
8 pounds of ginger.
25 pounds of pepper.
6 pounds of allspice.
1 mat of cassia.
6 bottles of ground mustard.
1 quart of mustard-seed.
1 pound of nutmegs.
60 pounds of saleratus.
1 pound of cloves.
½ bushel of fine salt.
6 bottles of lemon syrup.
3 pounds of sage.
3 pounds of summer savory.

12 bushels of coarse salt.
300 gallons of vinegar.
6 dozen 2-℔ cans roast beef.
4 dozen 2-℔ cans roast mutton.
6 dozen 2-℔ cans soup and
    bouillon.
6 dozen 2-℔ cans clams.
4 dozen 1-℔ tins canned lob-
    ster.
4 dozen 2-℔ tins canned oys-
    ters.
4 dozen 2-℔ tins canned tur-
    key.
1,800 pounds soap.
1 barrel oil-soap.
50 pounds sperm candles.
12 gallons whale oil for burn-
    ing.
2 gallons sperm oil for burning.

MEDICAL DEPARTMENT.

1 large medicine chest, full.
5 gallons New England rum.

2 gallons brandy.
2 gallons port wine.

6 dozen pain-killer.
3 dozen rat exterminator.

[313]

BLACKSMITH'S DEPARTMENT.

20 bushels charcoal.
14 bushels Cumberland coal.
100 pounds assorted iron.
 1 bar steel.
 1 soldering iron.
 1 vice.
 2 sledges.
 1 hand hammer.

1 wrench.
1 lot of old bolts.
1 anvil.
$\frac{1}{2}$ pound borax.
$\frac{1}{2}$ pound spelter solder.
2 pounds soft solder.
1 tuer-iron.
1 bellows.

2 pairs tongs.
1 set taps and dies.
1 screw-plate.
1 dozen assorted files.
3 punches.
1 cold-chisel.
1 swedge.

COOPER'S DEPARTMENT.

3,500 barrels of oil-casks.
 $2\frac{1}{2}$ tons hoop iron.
100 pounds 5d. rivets.
100 pounds 4d. rivets.
 5 pounds 3d. rivets.
 5 pounds 2d. rivets.
16 barrels sand.
800 pounds flags.
50 new staves.
300 feet yellow pine heading.
 1 piece red cedar for worm pecks.
50 pounds chalk.
 1 double iron jointer.
 1 large croze.
 1 small croze.
 1 patent croze-iron.

1 pair compasses.
5 vices.
1 bit-stock.
$\frac{1}{2}$ dozen bits.
2 spokeshaves.
1 saw.
1 bilge-plane.
3 marking irons.
2 anvils.
1 inshave.
1 heading saw.
2 bung-borers.
2 tap-borers.
1 axe.
1 adze.
2 chamfering knives.
2 drawing knives.

1 stock howeling knife.
1 leveling plane.
8 cast-steel hammers.
18 cast-steel drivers.
8 cast-steel punches.
8 cast-steel cold-chisels.
2 rivet sets.
2 worm-punches.
3 flagging-dogs.
1 round plane.
1 cooper's horse.
1 harness-cask.
1 water-butt.
1 grindstone-tub.
6 line-tubs.
1 cooper's bellows.
500 bungs, assorted sizes.

CARPENTER'S DEPARTMENT.

700 feet white pine lumber.
12 pine and spruce planks, assorted lengths.
100 feet oak plank.
900 feet cedar boat boards.
24 boat timbers.
12 boat knees.
 2 boat stems.
 1 boat keel.
 1 oak plank for gunwales.
40 white-oak butts.
 3 grindstones with cranks.
 1 calking mallet.
 4 calking irons.
 1 panel-saw.
 1 wood-saw and 1 extra plate.
 2 handsaws.
 1 splitting-saw.
 1 back-saw.

1 compass-saw.
$\frac{1}{2}$ dozen augers, assorted sizes.
1 broad-axe.
2 jointers.
2 fore-planes.
2 smooth-planes.
1 hollow-plane.
3 round-planes.
1 adze.
1 iron square.
1 carpenter's rule.
1 bevel.
2 board gauges.
2 compasses.
1 scarfing chisel.
3 socket chisels.
7 firmer chisels, assorted.
1 try-square.
4 socket gouges, assorted.

6 firmer gouges, assorted.
2 chalk lines.
2 spike gimlets.
2 deck-nail gimlets.
12 nail gimlets.
2 rough gimlets.
3 claw-hammers.
1 boat hammer.
1 pump hammer.
5 whetstones.
2 sandstones.
6 wood files.
1 pair large boat nippers.
1 pair small boat nippers.
4 narrow axes.
6 broad hatchets.
2 deck hatchets.
1 hold hatchet.
2 large half-round wood rasps.

5 flat files, assorted.
3 half-round files.
12 hand-saw files.
4 small saw files.
3 round files.
1 saw-set.
1 screw-driver.
1 bit-stock.
5 gimlet bits.
11 assorted bits.
1 spoke-shave.
1 drawing-knife.

20 pounds clinch nails.
12 pounds timber nails.
5 pounds wood-end nails.
2 pounds lap nails.
4 pounds foot nails.
10 pounds ceiling nails.
6 pounds 6d. wrought nails.
6 pounds 8d. wrought nails.
12 pounds 10d. wrought nails.
15 pounds 8d. cut nails.
25 pounds 10d. cut nails.
10 pounds 12d. cut nails.

5 dozen iron and brass screws, assorted.
50 pounds old lead.
20 pounds sheet lead.
10 pounds coppering nails.
5 pounds sheathing nails.
50 pounds wrought iron spikes.
12 sheets yellow metal.
1 pound clinch copper nails.
2 pairs steelyards.
18 roughs and clinches.

CABIN AND COOKING FURNITURE, ETC.

1 caboose, complete.
2 sets grates for same.
2 sets linings for same.
1 spare tea-kettle for same.
1 spare steamer for same.
1 spare boiler for same.
4 stew-pans.
2 frying-pans.
1 cook's ladle.
1 cook's fork.
1 cook's skimmer.
1 cook's bellows.
1 tinder-box (flint, steel, etc.)
1 chopping-knife.
1 chopping-tray.
1 sieve.
1 coffee-mill.
1 mortar and pestle.
1 table-bell.
1 cabin-bell.
2 stoves and pipes.
2 tables.
2 table-covers.
2 dozen table-cloths.
2 dozen birch brooms.

2 dozen corn brooms.
2 dust-pans.
2 dust-brushes.
2 chairs.
4 stools.
2 looking-glasses.
1 molasses gate.
1 carving knife and fork.
1 set of table knives and forks.
16 spare knives and forks.
1 dozen spoons (table).
1 dozen spoons (tea).
1 britannia soup ladle.
1 table steel.
1 tumbler basket.
1 hand basket.
2 bushel baskets.
1 gross of matches.
2 dozen flints.
2 scrubbing brushes.
½ dozen Bristol brick.
1 tinned iron wash-basin.
2 cook's shovels.
1 corkscrew.
1 pair scissors.

4 large platters.
1 dozen assorted bowls.
4 nappies.
3 bakers.
1½ dozen soup plates.
2 dozen dinner plates.
1 dozen dessert plates.
1½ dozen mugs.
1½ dozen saucers.
2 butter dishes.
2 sugar bowls.
3 pitchers.
1 large stone pitcher.
1 chamber.
2 soup tureens.
1 large covered dish.
1 castor, complete.
3 spare bottles for same.
1 dozen tumblers.
2 salt-cellars.
1 large oval dish.
1 gravy dish.
2 spittoons.
1 cabin clock.

NAUTICAL INSTRUMENTS, STATIONERY, ETC.

1 sextant, provided by the captain.
Quadrants and octants, provided by the officers.
2 chronometers.
1 barometer.
1 thermometer.
1 spy-glass.

2 binocular glasses.
2 fourteen-second glasses.
1 transparent compass.
4 brass boat compasses and 2 wooden ones.
2 brass binnacle compasses.
1 mast-head compass.
1 binnacle lantern.

1 log-book.
2 log-slates.
4 nautical almanacs for successive years.
2 account books.
4 memorandum books.
3 sticks sealing-wax.
½ dozen lead pencils.

1 dozen slate pencils.
6 dozen steel pens.
½ dozen pen-holders.
2 bottles of ink.
2 inkstands.

100 envelopes.
3½ quires letter and note paper.
½ quire bill paper.
4 inward manifests.

1 Gunter's scale and dividers.
1 set charts around the world.
1 set harbor charts (foreign.)
1 parallel rule.

WHALING CRAFT.

4 whaling bomb-guns.
150 bomb-lances.
5 powder-flasks.
5 chargers.

15 two-flued harpoons.
150 toggle harpoons.
35 cast-steel lances.

4 Pierce's harpoon bomb-lance guns.
50 Pierce's bomb-lances.
10 pounds bomb-gun powder.

BLOCKS, CORDAGE, CANVAS, ETC.

1 set cutting blocks.
1 set cutting-guy blocks.
2 3-sheave purchase blocks.
1 4-sheave purchase blocks.
2 2-sheave purchase blocks.
1 set of burton blocks.
1½ dozen spare sheaves.
1½ dozen spare sheave-pins.
1½ dozen spare jib-hanks.
1 dozen spare hoops (stay and gaff).
4 mast-hoops.
1 lot belaying-pins.
2 sets pump gear.
1 pump hook.
6 handspikes.
4 watch-tackle blocks.
2 dozen assorted blocks.
30 coils of whale-line.
1½ coils of 4-inch tarred rope.

2 coils of 15-thread ratline.
2 coils of 12-thread ratline.
1 coil 2-inch tarred rope.
1 coil 2¼-inch tarred rope.
1 coil 2¾-inch tarred rope.
½ coil 3½-inch tarred rope.
½ coil 3¼-inch tarred rope.
504 pounds old tarred rope, assorted.
4 coils 2-inch Manila rope.
3 coils 2½-inch Manila rope.
2 coils 1¾-inch Manila rope.
1 coil 1½-inch Manila rope.
1 coil 5¼-inch Manila rope (for cutting-falls).
2 coils 18-thread ratline.
1 coil 2-yarn spunyarn.
1 coil 3-inch Manila rope.
3 coils 2¼-inch Manila rope.
1 coil 9-thread worm-line.

1 coil 6-thread worm-line.
1 coil seizing stuff.
1 coil 3-yarn spunyarn.
1 coil 3¾-inch Manila rope.
1 coil 3¼-inch Manila rope.
1 coil 2¾-inch Manila rope.
1 coil 4½-inch Manila rope (cutting-guys).
1 spare cutting-fall.
1 spare lance line.
2,000 pounds old junk.
1 ship's ensign.
1 agent's signal.
1 set private signals.
2 spare log-lines.
2 spare hand-lead lines.
2 dozen fish lines.
1 deep-sea lead line.
1 deep-sea lead.
1 hand lead.

PAINTS, OILS, ETC.

400 pounds white lead.
250 pounds black lead.
60 gallons linseed oil.
2 gallons Japan varnish.
2 gallons spirits turpentine.
10 pounds verdigris.
12 papers lampblack.
10 gallons bright varnish.

1 gallon copal varnish.
10 pounds whiting.
50 pounds putty.
50 pounds chrome green.
50 pounds yellow ochre.
10 pounds Venetian red.
3 pounds Prussian blue.
10 pounds red lead.

12 large size paint-brushes.
6 sash tools.
3 seam brushes.
25 panes window glass.
4 pounds chrome yellow.
10 pounds burnt umber.
½ barrel coal tar.

SPARE SPARS AND SAILS.

1 spare lower yard.
1 spare topsail yard.
3 rough spars.

1 spare topmast.
1 spare jibboom.
1 foresail.

1 fore-topsail.
1 main-topsail.
2 topgallant-sails.

1 fore spencer.
1 fore-topmast staysail.
1 jib.
1 flying jib.

1 mainsail.
2 royals.
1 main spencer.
1 mizzen-topsail.

2 mizzen-topgallant-sails.
1 spanker.
15 bolts assorted canvas.

CLOTHING, ETC.

4 dozen pairs of blankets.
4 dozen suspenders.
4 dozen comforters.
6 dozen Scotch caps.
10 dozen woolen drawers.
10 dozen cotton drawers.
8 dozen Guernsey frocks.
6 dozen duck frocks.
6 dozen handkerchiefs.
8 dozen hats.
4 dozen pea-jackets.

2 dozen monkey jackets.
4 dozen short jackets.
6 dozen sheath-knives.
6 dozen jack-knives.
6 dozen mittens.
20 dozen stockings.
10 dozen shoes.
4 dozen red twilled kersey shirts.
4 dozen drab twilled kersey shirts.

7 dozen striped cotton shirts.
20 pieces of calico.
6 dozen sheaths and belts.
6 dozen blue woolen trowsers.
6 dozen drab woolen trowsers.
6 dozen duck trowsers.
25 pounds of thread.
10 pounds linen thread.
1 gross assorted needles.
4 dozen thimbles.
6 gross of pipes.

RECRUITS, OR TRADE.

5 bales bleached cotton cloth.
7 bales brown cotton cloth.
7 bales blue cotton cloth.
40 pieces of prints.
6 dozen of shoes.

10 dozen of pumps.
20 dozen of boots.
50 boxes of soap.
10 boxes of sperm candles
1,000 pounds of tobacco.

3 dozen axes.
3 dozen hatchets.
6 reams writing paper.
6 reams letter paper, etc.

MISCELLANEOUS.

20 cutting-spades.
2 wide spades.
2 throat-spades.
2 head-spades.
8 boat-spades.
3 blubber-hooks.
1 large boat-hook.
8 small boat-hooks.
2 steel blubber-forks.
1 long-handled pike.
6 short-handled pikes.
6 gaffs.
3 boarding-knives.
6 leaning-knives.
1 mincing-machine.
2 mincing-knives.
2 line-hooks.
6 shackles for topsail sheets.
3 sets can-hooks.
1 single can-hook for cooper.
10 marline-spikes.
250 iron poles.

6 boat masts.
40 spruce poles for spare masts, sprits, etc.
24 lance-poles.
40 cords oak wood.
6 cords pine wood.
40 barrels saw-dust.
7 new whale-boats.
1 old whale-boat.
9 sets of oars (45 oars).
9 steering oars.
7 sets rowlocks (35 rowlocks).
1 pair lifters.
1 cradle.
18 scrapers.
3 shovels.
1 hoe.
8 dozen fish-hooks, assorted.
1 copper cooler and cock.
1 hose-cock and joints.
1 scuttle-butt cock.
3 copper hand-pumps.

2 skimmers.
3 long handled bailers.
2 hand bailers.
1 copper vent-pipe (large).
1 copper vent-pipe (small).
1 copper tunnel.
2 copper tunnel noses.
1 branding iron (ship's name).
1 binnacle bell.
1 ship's bell.
1 tin bailer.
1 tin oil-tunnel.
3 tin assorted tunnels.
2 deck scoops.
1 large signal lantern.
1 bowsprit lantern.
1 side lantern.
2 side lights.
1 globe lantern.
1 cabin lantern.
6 boat lanterns.
1 cook's lantern.

1 binnacle lamp.
12 chimneys for ditto.
2 blubber-room lamps.
2 candlesticks.
2 britannia lamps.
6 Japan stand-lamps.
8 jacket lamps.
6 bake-pans for oven.
6 pie plates.
5 large tin pans.
5 small tin pans.
4 dozen sailor pans.
3 coffee-pots.
3 tea-pots.
1 britannia tureen.
1 one-pint measure.
1 one-quart measure.
1 two-quart measure.
1 three-quart measure.
1 gallon measure.
1 molasses cup.
6 tinder boxes, complete.
1 brass speaking-trumpet.
1 tin speaking-trumpet.
1 pepper-box.
1 nutmeg grater.
3 lamp feeders.
2 cullenders.
1 tea canister.
1 coffee canister.
3 pudding-bags.
1 flour-box.
2 flour-scoops.
1 bread-tray.
2 cook's dippers.
3 tin wash-basins.
3 spare frying-pans.
1 match safe.
4 dozen tin pots.
1 crowbar.
1 stowing bar.
12 chain-hooks.
1 set marking irons for craft.
4 grapnels.
3 fluke-chains.

1 fin-chain.
3 head-straps.
1 chain stopper.
1 fish hook.
4 chain punches.
1 pair of grains.
1 rope-jack.
28 hooks and thimbles.
18 thimbles.
4 boat anchors.
1 set chain pendants.
1 fire pike.
½ dozen oil-scoops.
3 shackles.
3 cutting-toggles.
1 masthead waif.
½ dozen large marline needles.
3 dozen small marline needles.
3 dozen roping needles.
5 dozen assorted sail needles.
1½ dozen sewing palms.
4 balls shoe thread.
20 pounds whipping twine.
50 pounds sail twine.
2 pounds lamp-wick.
2 dozen corks.
4 pounds brimstone.
6 Bath brick.
1 side pump leather.
2 sides rigging leather.
50 pounds cannon powder.
25 pounds musket powder.
2,000 percussion caps.
1 signal-gun.
1 dozen muskets.
2 barrels clay.
1 barrel lime.
3 barrels tar.
½ barrel rosin.
3 try-pots (two sets in the try-works).
1 deck-pot and 1 spare deck-pot.
4 tons hard coal.
200 bricks.

1 oil hose and cock.
1 hose-tub.
1 draw-bucket.
2 sets chest hinges.
8 grate bars for try-works.
4 iron knees for try-works.
4 smoke pipes for try-works.
2 iron doors for try-works.
1 caboose stove (large) and apparatus.
1 Horsburgh's East India Directory.
2 trowels.
1 blubber-room steel.
2 rigging screws.
12 pairs handcuffs.
1 screw cutting-plate and dies.
20 boat paddles.
6 boat anchors.
4 boat grapnels.
6 boat kegs.
4 lantern kegs.
4 drags.
6 line-tubs.
4 fog-horns.
1 dozen boat knives.
1 dozen boat hatchets.
4 boat crotches.
4 tub-oar crotches.
4 boat buckets.
1 dozen nippers.
4 dozen chock-pins.
1 case bucket.
1 turning-lathe.
1 set turning gouges.
1 set turning chisels.
3 dozen floats, or coarse files, for working whalebone.
12 brad-awls.
3 saddler's awls.
3 sewing awls.
4,000 copper tacks.
4,000 iron tacks.
1,000 pounds of tobacco.
Books for ship's library.

NOTE.—Many of the articles herein enumerated are made on board ship from materials supplied for the purpose, while there are many others of but trivial importance which are not mentioned. Relative to the quantity of clothing and recruits—the last named being also called "trade"—they vary materially with different owners of ships and the nature of the voyage undertaken. Hence, the lists referred to can only be regarded as approximative. A Cape Horn voyage, as termed, ordinarily involves the time of three years or more. A ship that takes three seasons north, after arriving in the Pacific, generally prolongs her absence from home to three years and a half. Sperm whalers are not so much confined to the regular annual seasons for pursuing their prey as are the Right or Polar whalemen, as they change from one ground to another through the year, and their voyages are frequently extended from three and a half to four years. Vessels fitted out for the North Pacific, Arctic Ocean, Okhotsk Sea, or Japan Sea, generally sail from home in the fall of the year, in order to make the passage of Cape Horn or Cape of Good Hope during the summer season of that region; and all whalers, as far as practicable, return to the home coast in the spring months; yet we may say they are continually coming and going. But the old routine of whaling-voyages is now much changed, especially with the larger class of vessels which ply their vocation in the Pacific and contiguous waters. Many of the ships are now ordered by their owners to San Francisco, California, at the termination of each northern season, where an agent meets the vessels, and transacts the business of transshipping oil and bone, refitting ship, and changing officers and crews, which now often occurs.

INDEX.